AMYRAUT & O\

Amyraut & Owen Tested

And Found Wanting

David H.J.Gay

Set up signposts, make landmarks (Jer. 31:21)

BRACHUS

BRACHUS 2015
davidhjgay@googlemail.com

All books
by David H.J.Gay
are available on
Amazon Books and Kindle

Articles are available in 'Edocs' at
David H J Gay Ministry (sermonaudio.com)
and at
David H J Gay (christmycovenant.com)

Free Mobi and Epub downloads
are available in 'Links' at
David H J Gay Ministry (sermonaudio.com)

Free audio books of the author reading his books
are available at
David H J Gay Ministry (sermonaudio.com)

Free pdf downloads
are available on
archive.org and openlibrary.org

Video clips
are available at
David H J Gay Ministry (youtube.com)

Contents

Note to the Reader 7
Foreword to Particular Redemption 9
Introduction 11
Preamble 16
For Whom Did Christ Die? and Why? 19
The Two Forms of the Mistaken Formula 25
The Wrong Form: Amyraut's Position 27
The Meaningless Form: Owen's Position 42
The Objection: Particular Redemption Rules Out the Free Offer .. 47
The Objection Answered: General Principles 49
General Principles Applied to the Three Forms of the Objection .. 71
Pulling It All Together 91
A Warning and a Challenge 93
Preaching Particular Redemption and the Free Offer 96
Appendix 106
Source List 134

Note to the Reader

The first edition of *Particular Redemption and The Free Offer* represented my first attempt at publishing on-line, and I am afraid it showed. In the second edition, I brought the extended notes into the main body of the work by means of an 'Excursus' at appropriate points. I clearly indicated this so that the reader could, if desired, skip the excursus and carry straight on with the main text, hoping the text in that second edition would prove less tortuous. 'Less' is the operative word. When I came to read the book for my audio-book series, I immediately realised I still had not got it clear enough. However, being encouraged to carry on, I published the audio book of the second edition, all the while knowing that I was going to have to re-set the work. Here is the result – if you like, the third edition of the original book – but I have renamed it 'Amyraut & Owen Tested' with the subtitle: 'And Found Wanting'. I hope this new version will make my work more accessible.

But with the best typesetting in the world, the subject itself would still demand hard thought. As I said in the first edition, the question I have tried to answer in these pages calls for detailed argument and fine distinctions; inevitably, therefore, the result is no easy read. Even so, I offer the finished work to the public because of the importance of the subject. As for my extracts from other authors, where necessary I have changed spelling and grammar without altering the sense.

Foreword to Particular Redemption

In the past fifty years there has been a striking God-given recovery throughout the English-speaking world of those truths associated with what historically have been called the doctrines of grace. During the first half of the twentieth century these glorious truths found few supporters. But at the beginning of the twenty-first century, how different the situation is. Publishing houses and authors, conferences and seminaries have arisen that proclaim these truths loudly and clearly. And for these mercies God is to be praised and thanked.

But as has happened in the past, this recovery has been accompanied by the emergence of a position that claims to exalt the sovereignty of God, but does so at the expense of the free, unfettered preaching of the gospel to all and sundry. Various eighteenth-century authors such as the Baptists Alvery Jackson and Caleb Evans, Andrew Fuller and John Ryland Jr had to fight a hyper-Calvinism that cut the nerve of evangelism. And their writings can be of great service today in responding to those who would argue that the free offer of the gospel is unbiblical and cannot be squared with such biblical truths as particular redemption. But how good it is to also have contemporary authors who have studied the relevant Scripture texts and thought through the theological principles involved and can provide a new response to this old error.

Such a work is this present study by David Gay. Impressive in its discussion of theological perspectives and fully competent in its handling of Scripture, here is an excellent resource for thinking through the nature of biblical evangelism and how it relates to the scriptural theme of the sovereignty of God in salvation, especially as the latter relates to the death of Christ. May those who are tempted to cool their passion for the salvation of sinners in light of convictions about Christ's redeeming work read this book and have that passion re-ignited by the fiery light of God's truth.

Michael A.G.Haykin
Dundas, Ontario, January 10, 2007.

Introduction

The Bible teaches particular redemption *and* the free offer. But this raises a question: How can the two be reconciled? After all, they seem like a contradiction in terms. Let me spell it out. Take these as working definitions:

Particular redemption: Christ died to redeem the elect only

The free offer: God has revealed that the gospel preacher must invite and command all sinners to trust Christ, telling them it is their duty, and promising them salvation if they do

The seeming contradiction is self-evident, is it not?

Neither the Arminian nor the hyper-Calvinist, however, sees a problem; the former denies particular redemption; the latter, the free offer. Both the Arminian and the hyper-Calvinist are logical from a human point of view. But both are wrong.

Many Calvinists take another tack. While not denying either particular redemption or the free offer, they use the formula: 'Christ's death, sufficient for all men, but effective only for the elect', and this, they think, solves the problem. They are wrong. Even though many have adopted this idea, it is a mistake – fundamentally, the same as that of the Arminian and the hyper-Calvinist; namely, the use of human logic to try to rationalise a paradox in God's word.

My underlying thesis in this book is the same as in my book *The Gospel Offer* **is** *Free*; that is, the seeming contradiction[1] can't be reconciled (by us – God, of course, has no need, since there is no contradiction). But not only can we not reconcile its two parts, we have no right to go beyond Scripture and draw on human logic to try. This is the root issue in all this debate. What is more, we have no *need* to explain the seeming contradiction. What we are required to do is to accept what God says in his word, admit the paradox, and preach it as it stands. Indeed, we should go further; we should glory in the paradox, and preach both sides fully and freely.[2]

Some will object to my use of the word 'offer'. This, of course, is not a term found in Scripture. But neither is 'trinity', 'sensible sinner', 'elect sinner', 'non-elect', 'total depravity', 'unconditional election', 'particular redemption', 'limited atonement', 'definite atonement', 'effectual calling' or 'irresistible grace'. But is the *concept* there? That is the question! I say it is. Even so, reader, if you still find the word objectionable, when thinking about addressing sinners with the gospel would 'invite', 'exhort', 'command', 'try to persuade',[3] 'reason with', 'plead', 'beseech', 'beg', 'implore', 'make overture to', 'tender', 'proffer', do instead?[4]

Speaking for myself, however, I still prefer 'offer' – *because for me it embraces all the other terms which are used in Scripture*, and thus admirably sets out what is involved in preaching the gospel. For it is not enough just to 'declare', 'publish' or 'present' the gospel to sinners, to 'set it before' them. A preacher is not a mere stater of facts; he is a pleader with men for God. He does not stand merely to describe the glories of the gospel; he is to offer Christ to sinners, and do all he can to get them to receive him.[5]

I acknowledge the obvious fact that not all the writers I quote in support of what I say would agree with me in every detail. In particular, not all of them have used the word 'offer'. I am not trying to mislead you, reader, but it would be irritating and confusing to find me constantly chopping and changing to the terms favoured by each individual I mention. The fact is, I believe, at least at the point where I quote them, they all held to the *principle* of what I understand by the free offer, whether or not they used the term itself. And, after all, I am not contending for a *word*, but *what it stands for*.

* * *

And to any who might be saying, with a weary sigh: 'What! Not yet another book on this same old topic!', J.C.Philpot might have an answer:

> The Scriptures are full of general exhortations to men to perform what certainly appear, at first sight, spiritual actions [Philpot cited Ezek. 18:30-31; Matt. 3:2; Mark 1:15; Acts 8:22]. These and similar passages undoubtedly call upon natural men to repent, believe and pray, all which are spiritual acts, and as such can only be performed by spiritual persons, and by them only when and as

> God works in them to will and to do of his good pleasure. Now these passages are as much a part of God's word as those which set forth the glorious doctrines of grace... There they are, whether we like them or not; and we believe that many Calvinists have as much wished them out of the word as Arminians have wished the ninth chapter of... Romans blotted out of the Bible... But there the passages are still... There they are... there they still are.

In these two sets of scriptures, clearly, we have a seeming contradiction, from which we cannot run away. Rather, as Philpot said:

> Any help, then, in this deeply important matter, any sound and scriptural contribution to remove these difficulties, any real approach to disentangle this perplexing question, we desire to receive thankfully... We do not... consider this a dry doctrinal discussion, a dispute of words, a barren, useless controversy, but one full of interest to those who have been painfully perplexed, and that in proportion to the tenderness of their conscience towards God's word. Were it a dry controversy, we would stand by while the sturdy rams and great he-goats battered in each other's heads. We would take no part in the contest, but would let the bulls of Bashan fight it out, while we were seeking to lie down in the green pastures, and drink of the still waters. The great interest, then, of the subject must be our apology, if we seem to draw out our observations to any unreasonable length.[6]

* * *

Finally, I acknowledge the force of John Davenant's words:

> It is truly a matter of grief and exceedingly to be deplored... that those mysteries of our religion, which were promulgated for the peace and comfort of mankind, should be turned into materials for nothing but contention and dispute. Who could ever have thought that the death of Christ, which was destined to secure peace and destroy enmity, as the apostle speaks (Eph. 2:14,17; Col. 1:20-21), could have been so fruitful in the production of strife?[7]

I hope my book will not contribute to this strife. I recognise that the believers I write against take the Scriptures as seriously as I do, and just as sincerely hold their beliefs as I hold mine. Although I criticise their views on the extent of the atonement and its connection with the free offer, I imply no slur on their trust in the Saviour, their faith in his precious blood to cleanse them from their sin by the grace of God, and their desire to see sinners saved. Even so, I think their views on this subject are mistaken. Not that everything they say about it is wrong, of course – indeed, much of it is stimulating, edifying and challenging. Nevertheless, on the central point – the link between the extent of the atonement and the free offer – they are mistaken. Or so I contend. And, since I am convinced the issue is of the utmost importance, I have to write.

Why? Why have I written this polemical work? For two reasons. *First*, to try to clear away some of the misunderstanding which surrounds and complicates this subject. *Secondly*, having, I hoped, succeeded in that, I want to stimulate the preaching of the free offer of Christ to sinners, having set it on its right and proper basis.[8]

I am, however, conscious of the danger Davenant spoke of in writing (and reading) a polemical work on the atonement. Deploring strife over the death of Christ, he went on to suggest a reason for it:

> This seems to arise from the innate curiosity of men, who are more anxious to scrutinise the secret councils of God, than to embrace the benefits openly offered to them. Hence it comes to pass that from too much altercation on the points: *For whom did Christ die, and for whom did he not die?* little is thought by mankind individually of applying to ourselves the death of Christ, by a true and lively faith, for the salvation of our own souls.[9]

Davenant was right. Arguing about the extent of the atonement and the free offer is one thing, but it counts for less-than-nothing compared to a felt-sense of a personal application of the work of Christ to the soul. I sincerely hope my book does not obscure Christ and his glorious redemption. Rather, believer, I hope you will find your 'true and lively faith' in 'the death of Christ' to 'the salvation of your soul' is strengthened, your concept of Christ's redemption enlarged. I hope, also, you will be encouraged to offer him and his salvation more freely to sinners. What is more, if you, reader, should start my book without this 'lively faith' in 'the death of Christ', nothing would please me more than to know that by reading my words you have come to saving faith in the Redeemer; that you, from your heart, should be able to say of the Lord Jesus

Christ: 'The Son of God, who loved *me* and gave himself for *me*' (Gal. 2:20).

In all this, I want to exalt Christ and his atonement. True it is, men think too little of the death of Christ. My conviction is, we cannot think too much!

* * *

Before I begin, I want to thank Michael Haykin for his very generous Foreword – which he kindly offered to write after reading the manuscript. I hope, reader, you find the book half as good as he said it is!

I record my debt to David Woodruff of the Strict Baptist Historical Library, Dunstable, for a photocopy of J.C.Philpot's review of James Wells' *Moral Government*, and the use of Abraham Booth's out-of-print *Works*.

As always, I must thank Nigel Pibworth for all his help – not least in the provision of resource material and stimulating conversation.

I am grateful to those who have read the manuscript and made valuable comments – especially Jon Bevan, Simon Gay, Michael Haykin and Nigel Pibworth. Furthermore, I have greatly appreciated the correspondence I have received from others – some of which will make an appearance in the book. Especially, in this regard, I thank Alan Clifford for his correspondence which, as I will explain, moved me to write in the first place.

Mona, my wife, has been invaluable in helping me to proof-read the extracts and prepare the index. Only those who have tried it, know what this involves! I thank her.

The responsibility for what follows is, of course, all my own.

Preamble

Following the publication of my book *The Gospel Offer* **is** *Free* – my reply to George M.Ella's *The Free Offer & The Call of the Gospel* – I received some friendly correspondence from Alan Clifford, including a copy of his *Amyraut Affirmed*. The point at issue was this: How could I believe in both a free offer and particular redemption? And why, in my book, had I not dealt with those biblical texts which (seem to)[10] speak of universal redemption?[11] My reply was twofold. *First*, since Ella had not raised the issue with me, I had not delved into the matter. *Secondly*, I do not think the extent of the atonement has any bearing on the free offer, and I had said as much in my book.

But on reflection, I see I was remiss. There was more than enough in Ella's book for me to have tackled the issue, and I should have done so. I now put the matter right. One benefit of the delay, however, is that I am now able to engage with Clifford's work.[12]

And this is important. My view of the free offer is criticised by Calvinists[13] on two fronts; hyper-Calvinists – Ella, for instance – and 'four-pointers' – Clifford, for instance.[14] Those who preach a free offer must hold to universal atonement, they say, since it is not possible to hold particular redemption *and* make the free offer.[15] There is, however, a world of difference in their criticisms. Ella utterly disagrees with the free offer, and is scathing of my position, convinced I undermine the doctrines of grace.[16] Clifford, on the other hand, wholeheartedly agrees with the free offer, but thinks I would make my case complete by adopting universal atonement.[17] Both are mistaken.

Before I get to grips with this, let me spell out what is not at stake. Total depravity is not in question; all men are sinners and have no power to repent and believe. Unconditional election is not in question; God the Father has freely determined those whom he will save, his choice being without any foreseen merit in the sinner. Irresistible grace or effectual calling is not in question;[18] God the Holy Spirit works in the elect sinner, irresistibly calling him to Christ through faith and repentance.[19] The perseverance of the redeemed and believing elect is not in question; God works in them, keeping them throughout their earthly pilgrimage, to present them faultless in glory at the last day. None of this is at issue here. Let me say it again: *None of this is at issue here.*

So what is? Just this: What, exactly, is offered to sinners in the free offer?[20] If the redemption Christ wrought is particular in its scope – that is, limited in its extent – how can the offer be free and sincere to every sinner? Putting it the other way: If Christ has not died for every sinner, how can every sinner be offered salvation? There are two questions here. *First*, what is the extent of the atonement? *Secondly*, if this is limited, how does it impinge on the free offer?

Before I set out my answers to these questions, let me explain my purpose. There is a theological issue, yes, and it is vital to be as accurate and as clear as we can when forming our doctrines and practices. But I am not writing this book merely to engage in an academic debate. As I said in my *Offer*:

> The free offer is an important principle or doctrine, yes, but it is not so much a controversy over doctrine which is at stake; *it is the practical consequences of that controversy*. I want to let believers know how far we have fallen away from real gospel preaching. Above all, I pray that preachers who read my book – and I include myself – may be moved to fulfil the task God has laid upon them.[21]

The same applies to this book. I am convinced we need to preach the free offer without fear or embarrassment. Some, who would like to do this, feel that particular redemption militates against it.[22] Wanting to be true to Scripture, they think limited atonement stops them making invitations to all. They are mistaken.

But my aim is not merely to prove a point. Yes, I want to do what I can to remove, in a biblical way, hindrances from the path of those who would like to be free with sinners – to rebut, especially, the mistaken view that particular redemption rules it out.[23] Indeed, I hope to show that the opposite is the case; without a particular, definite and absolute redemption for all the elect, there would be no free offer to sinners.

Yes, I want to do all that. But I want to go further. I pray that my book will encourage all who are seeking to address sinners with the free offer – to encourage them to go on with it, and to be even more bold, to have even more love for sinners, to reach full biblical freeness in the glorious work. Indeed, above all, I hope my book will contribute to the dawning of a better day than many of us know at present – a day in which God raises up men who will not only biblically address sinners with the full and free offer of Christ, *but do so with success.*[24]

So let us begin.

For Whom Did Christ Die? and Why?

These are fundamental questions. They demand clear and unequivocal answers. Here are mine: Christ did not die to make redemption a possibility, to provide[25] redemption, to make sinners redeemable. Christ died as a substitute for sinners to accomplish eternal redemption, a guaranteed redemption, and he did it for all the elect, and only for the elect. There are many passages of Scripture which make this very clear (Matt. 1:21; John 10:11,15; Acts 20:28; Rom. 8:31-39; 1 Cor. 15:3; Eph. 5:25; 1 Thess. 5:9-10; Tit. 2:14; 1 John 3:5,16; 4:10; Rev. 5:9 *etc*.) From this, plainly, I hold to a limited atonement, a particular redemption, a definite accomplished redemption.[26] But what of those passages which seem to speak of a general redemption, a universal atonement? There are several, often involving the word 'all' or 'world' (Isa. 53:6; John 1:29; 3:16-17; 6:32-33,51; 12:47; Rom. 5:18; 2 Cor. 5:14-15,19; 1 Tim. 2:4-6; Heb. 2:9; 1 John 2:2 *etc*.) These, I am convinced, do not teach universal redemption, although, at first glance, it might appear so. Ella, I am sure, is at one with me on this, whereas Clifford takes such passages in a universal sense.[27] I will not, however, exegete these passages now[28] – this has been exhaustively done by excellent authors, and there is no need to repeat their arguments here.[29] After all, I am not at this time setting out to establish that Christ's redemption was limited – this I take for granted.[30] The issue is: How to square this with the free offer? If these passages could be shown to teach universal redemption, the 'problem' would vanish.[31] My point is, they teach particular redemption. The 'problem', therefore, remains.

As for the extent of the atonement,[32] the question lies, not in the number, but the nature;[33] not in the arithmetic, but the quality.[34]

It is not merely for whom Christ died; but what did God design by his death, and what did he accomplish by it? So, for example, when we read that 'the LORD has laid on him the iniquity of us all' (Isa. 53:6), that God 'did not spare his own Son, but delivered him up for us all' (Rom. 8:32), that 'Christ died for our sins' (1 Cor. 15:3), that 'God did not appoint us to wrath, but to obtain salvation through our Lord Jesus Christ, who died for us' (1 Thess. 5:9-10), that 'Christ Jesus... gave himself a ransom for all' (1 Tim. 2:5-6), that he is 'the Lamb of God who takes away the sin of the world' (John 1:29), and that 'he himself is the propitiation for our sins, and not for ours only but also for the whole world' (1 John 2:2), then Christ *has* carried the sins of *all* for whom he stood, and *all* for whom he paid the ransom *are* redeemed, and for *all* of them God *is* propitiated. There are five main ways[35] of interpreting this:

1. Christ has redeemed all without exception, with no limit on the redemption or the 'all' for whom it was accomplished. This is the view of the Universalist. All men without exception are redeemed; all men without exception will be saved.

2. Christ has redeemed all without exception, but the redemption is conditional. If a man believes, the redemption is effectual; if he does not, it is ineffectual. In other words, the 'all' is without limit, but the redemption is emasculated. This is the Arminian view.

3. Christ has redeemed all without exception, sufficiently but conditional on faith; but for some, the elect, it is an effective redemption. In other words, while there is no limit on the 'all', the redemption is qualified; it is a twofold redemption. For all, God designed and Christ accomplished a provisional redemption, sufficient to redeem them, but conditional on their believing; for the elect, Christ's redemption is effective or efficient. A minority[36] of Calvinists take this view. It was the view of Moïse Amyraut.[37]

4. Christ has redeemed the elect, but his death is sufficient for all. This is the view of perhaps a majority of Calvinists. John Owen was a typical exponent.

5. Christ has redeemed all the elect without exception, and no others. The maxim, 'efficient for the elect, sufficient for all', is not used. This, along with some others,[38] is my position.[39]

As can be seen, apart from the first, all impose some sort of limit on the statement. Either the redemption is in some way or another limited, or the 'all' is; that is, the atonement is limited either in its nature or its extent. Universalist and Arminian views do not concern us here; it is the last three which do.

But, reader, before I move on, I want to clear up a possible misunderstanding about my use of 'limited atonement' and my disavowal of 'sufficiency'.

A nice distinction

As for 'limited atonement', I agree with Andrew Fuller: 'All the limitation I maintain in the death of Christ arises from pure *sovereignty*; it is a limitation of *design*'.[40] I will return to this.[41] And as for the 'sufficiency',[42] I want to make a nice, but important distinction.[43] Let me spell it out. There is a big difference between saying Christ is a perfect, complete, all-sufficient Saviour, and saying Christ's redemption is sufficient for all. And, though this anticipates the climax of my book, there is a big difference between saying Christ as an all-sufficient Saviour is offered to sinners in the gospel, and saying a redemption sufficient-for-all is the basis of the free offer. To tell sinners: 'Come to Christ, as God commands you in his word, and you will find him an all-sufficient Saviour', is one thing; to tell sinners: 'Christ has provided a redemption sufficient for all, sufficient for you, and this is the basis upon which you are to come', is quite another.[44]

As to Christ being an all-sufficient Redeemer for all the elect, take Owen:

> The first thing that we shall lay down is concerning the dignity, worth, preciousness and infinite value of the blood and death of Jesus Christ... The Scripture... is exceeding full and frequent in setting forth the excellency and dignity of his death and sacrifice... Christ [is]... an all-sufficient Saviour, with whom is plenteous redemption, and who is able to save to the utmost them that come to God by him, and to bear the burden of all weary labouring souls that come by faith to him... [There is] the superabundant sufficiency of the oblation of Christ in itself, for whomsoever (fewer or more) it be intended.[45]

John Bunyan:

> Would Jesus Christ have mercy offered in the first place to the biggest sinners...? Then, by this... you must learn to judge of the sufficiency of the merits of Christ; not that the merits of Christ can be comprehended, for that they are beyond the conceptions of the whole world; being called the unsearchable riches of Christ... Consider what offers... he

makes of his grace to sinners; for to be sure, he will not offer beyond the virtue of his merits; because... his merits are the basis and bounds upon and by which his grace stands good and is let out to sinners... There is a sufficiency in his blood to save the biggest sinners... If he had not been able to have reconciled the biggest sinners to his Father by his blood, he would not have sent to them... the doctrine of remission of sins; for remission of sins is through faith in his blood... Upon the... worthiness of the blood of Christ, grace acts, and offers forgiveness of sin to men... The blood of Christ is of infinite value, for that he offers mercy to the biggest of sinners... Now, the biggest sinners cannot be saved but by an abundance of grace... He has unsearchable riches of grace and worth in himself... He is still as full as ever. He is not a jot the poorer for all the forgivenesses that he has given away to great sinners... Since his grace is extended according to the worth of his merits... there is the same virtue in his merits to save now as there was at the very beginning.
[Again:] The grace that is offered to sinners as sinners... is a sufficiency of righteousness, pardoning grace, and life, laid up in the person of Christ, held forth in the exhortation and word of the gospel, and promised to be theirs that receive it; indeed, I say, in so universal a tender, that not one is by it excluded or checked in the least.[46]

John Gill, too, spoke of the all-sufficiency of Christ for all the elect:

There is a fullness of fitness and abilities in Christ to discharge his work and office as mediator, which greatly lies in his being both God and man, or in the union of the two natures, divine and human, in one person. Hereby he becomes abundantly qualified to be... the mediator... Being God as well as man, there is a sufficient virtue in all his actions and sufferings to answer what they were designed for; in his blood to cleanse from all sin, in his righteousness to justify from it, and in his sacrifice to expiate and atone for it. Being the mighty God, he could travel in the greatness of his strength, draw nigh to God for us, offer up himself to God, bear our sins, and all the punishment due unto them, without failing or being discouraged; his own arm alone was capable of bringing salvation to himself and us; there is nothing wanting in him, to make him a complete Saviour of the body, and head of the church... This fullness is inexhaustible... The grace of our Lord has been abundant, superabundant; it has flowed, and overflowed; there has been a pleonasm,[47] a redundancy of it in the case of a single believer. O what must the aboundings of it have been to all the saints in all ages, times and places, since the foundation of the world! And still there is enough for the family [of God] on earth yet behind... His grace is still sufficient for them; it is like the author of it, who has treasured it up in Christ, it changes not, and, like the subject in whom it dwells, it is the same today, yesterday, and for ever.[48]

But, I repeat, to say that Christ is an all-sufficient Saviour for all the elect is not the same as saying he has provided a redemption sufficient for all without exception, and that this universal sufficiency is the basis upon which sinners are invited to Christ. Not the same at all. Booth was clear on the issue. While he had no doubts about the all-sufficiency of the Saviour and his sacrifice for the elect,[49] he did not adopt the 'sufficient for all' formula:

We cannot perceive any solid reason to conclude that [Christ's] propitiatory sufferings are sufficient for the expiation of sins which he did not bear, or for the redemption of sinners whom he did not represent as a sponsor when he expired on the cross. For the substitution of Christ, and the imputation of sin to him, are essential to the scriptural doctrine of redemption by our adorable Jesus. We may, therefore, safely conclude that our Lord's voluntary substitution, and redemption by his vicarious death, are both of them limited to those for whom he was made sin – for whom he was made a curse – and for whose deliverance from final ruin, he actually paid the price of his own blood. Consequently, that redemption is particular, and peculiar to the chosen of God.[50]

Fuller: 'The death of Christ... [is] a sacrifice of infinite value... his sufferings were of infinite value'.[51] In another place, he spoke of 'the all-sufficient redemption of Jesus Christ'.[52]

John Brown:

When we think that those for whom [Christ] died are 'an innumerable company, out of every kindred, and people and tongue', and when we reflect on the number, and variety and duration of the blessings which he has secured for every one of these, we cannot help perceiving that if [since] the dignity of his person stamped an infinite value on his sacrifice, the efficacy of that sacrifice reflects a glorious light on the dignity of his person.[53]

So, reader, I hope I have made myself clear. While I hold to a limited atonement, and do not say that Christ's redemption is sufficient for all, the limit is simply that which God intended. I do not imply the slightest deficiency in the work of Christ. Certainly not! Perish the thought!

Let me put it positively, in biblical terms. The worth of Christ's person and work? They are 'indescribable' (2 Cor. 9:15), of 'unspeakable' (AV) perfection and fullness, over which 'words fail'. We are speaking of 'the unsearchable [unfathomable, NASB] riches of Christ' (Eph. 3:8) which 'cannot be traced out... cannot be comprehended'.[54]

Thus I concur with Clifford when he said that the 'intrinsically infinite value' of 'Christ's sacrifice' 'derived from his person', is 'a view shared by all parties'.[55]

And I agree with Dort:

Those who possess Jesus Christ through faith, have complete salvation in him. Therefore, for any to assert that Christ is not sufficient, but that something more is required besides him, would be too gross a blasphemy... All his benefits, which, when become ours, are more than sufficient to acquit us of our sins... Relying and resting upon the obedience of Christ crucified alone, which becomes ours when we believe in him... is sufficient to cover all our iniquities, and to give us confidence in approaching to God; freeing the conscience of fear, terror and dread.[56]

The worth of Christ's sacrifice? Let the Scriptures sum it up:

'Our Lord Jesus Christ... gave *himself*' (Gal. 1:3-4), 'gave *himself*' (Gal. 2:20), 'has... given *himself*' (Eph. 5:2), 'gave *himself*' (Eph. 5:25), 'gave *himself*' (1 Tim. 2:6), 'gave *himself*' (Tit. 2:14). He came to 'give' *his 'flesh*' (John 6:51), 'to give *his life*' (Matt. 20:28), '*his soul*' (NASB margin), 'gives [lays down] *his life*' (John 10:11,15,17-18). God 'did not spare *his own Son*' (Rom. 8:32), who 'purchased' 'the church of God... with *his own blood*' (Acts 20:28), 'with *his own blood* he entered the Most Holy Place' (Heb. 9:12), 'and washed us from our sins in *his own blood*' (Rev. 1:5).

Reader, God gave his own Son, who gave *himself*, his flesh, his life, his soul, his own blood. What more could he give (John 15:13; Rom. 5:8)? He gave ***himself*** – HIMSELF!

Now to go on.

The Two Forms of the Mistaken Formula

In passing, I have mentioned the 'sufficiency formula'. It is time to look at it more closely. Putting it simply, it states:

Christ died for all. He died efficiently or effectively for the elect only, but sufficiently for the whole world.

This form of words was invented by the Schoolmen,[57] Peter Lombard and Thomas Aquinas. It was a mistake. Even so, it was adapted and adopted by Reformed writers,[58] and many Calvinists have continued to use it.

D.Martyn Lloyd-Jones: Christ 'died for the church; he died for nobody else. His death, as Calvin and other expositors remind us, because it was eternal and because he is the Son of God, is sufficient for the whole world; but it is efficient only for the church'.[59] Thomas Boston: 'Christ did not die a sacrifice for every man and woman in the world. It is true, there was virtue and efficacy enough in his oblation to satisfy offended justice for the sins of the whole world, yes, and of millions of worlds more;[60] for his blood has infinite value, because of the infinite dignity and excellency of his person. And in this sense some [Calvinists]... understand those places of Scripture where he is called the Saviour of the whole world. Yet the efficacy and saving virtue of his sacrifice extends not unto all... To affirm that Christ offered up himself a sacrifice with a design and intention to save all mankind, great absurdities would follow... Christ died for the elect, and for all the elect, and none else. God designed to save [only] some of the lost posterity of Adam... From [various scriptures] we may be fully convinced that Christ died only for the elect'.[61] John Murray: 'Unless we believe in the final restoration of all men we cannot have an unlimited atonement. If we universalise the extent we limit the efficacy... The doctrine of "limited atonement" which we maintain is the doctrine which limits the atonement to those who are heirs of eternal life, the elect. That limitation ensures its efficacy and conserves its essential character as efficient and effective redemption'. On the other hand, 'there must be... a certain universalism belonging to the redemptive events that lays the basis for and warrants the universal proclamation... Many benefits accrue to the non-elect, from the redemptive work of Christ... In this sense, therefore, we may say that Christ died for non-elect persons'.[62] And so say many others.[63] The atonement, they assert, is 'sufficient for all, but efficient only for the elect'.

Advocates of this formula take one of two approaches.[64] Some say God intended the atonement to be general in that he designed it to be efficient for the elect but sufficient for the world, provisional for every sinner, sufficient to save them all – on condition that they believe. This is what God intended by Christ's redemption. I will call this the Amyraldian position. Others say, first of all, there is nothing potential or conditional about Christ's redemption; it is absolute. Then, they say, the atonement, though efficient only for the elect, and not provisional for all, is sufficient for all because of the worth of Christ's person.[65] For simplicity, I will call this the Owenite position, not that it originated with Owen – but taking him as, perhaps, its most thorough exponent.[66]

As I will show, both schemes are wrong. The first, the Amyraldian, is contrary to Scripture; the second, the Owenite, goes beyond Scripture into the realm of speculation, and is, in addition, meaningless.

Take the first.

The Wrong Form: Amyraut's Position

Let me remind you, reader, of Amyraut's position: God the Father intended and designed the atonement to be universal in that he decreed Christ should redeem the whole world, sufficiently for all on condition that they believe, but effectively only for the elect. God, therefore, had a twofold will, purpose or intention in redemption; consequently, Christ wrought this twofold redemption. Amyraut: 'Jesus Christ died for all men sufficiently, but for the elect only effectually... His intention was to die for all men in respect of the sufficiency of his satisfaction, but for the elect only in respect of its quickening and saving virtue and efficacy... This was the most free counsel and gracious purpose both of God the Father, in giving his Son for the salvation of mankind, and of the Lord Jesus Christ in suffering the pains of death, that the efficacy thereof should particularly belong unto all the elect, and to them only'.[67] Thus, as Clifford said: 'Correlating with the twofold will of God, Amyraut's view of the atonement's design involved a twofold intention... [which led to] a potential universal provision'. 'Notwithstanding the limited efficacy of the atonement, the divinely-intended provision is universal according to... Amyraut'.[68] 'The Amyraldian position [is]: Christ died (with dual intent) for all "provisionally" but for the elect "receptively". We believe in a "particular efficacious redemption" as well as a "general sufficient redemption"'.[69]

This is wrong. God did not design the atonement to be efficient only for the elect, but sufficient for all on condition of faith. Such a statement cannot be found in Scripture, nor can the doctrine be inferred from Scripture. Indeed, it runs counter to Scripture. For six reasons.

1. God does not have a twofold decree in Christ's redemption

There is a twofold aspect to the one will of God, the secret and the revealed, yes; God's secret decree to save his elect, and his revealed desire to save all.[70] This is written large in Scripture.[71] But to say that God, in his secret will, his decree, intended Christ's redemption to be effective for the elect, but sufficient for all on condition of faith, means that God's decree in Christ's death is twofold; it means that the Father has decreed, and Christ has wrought, two very different redemptions; one effective, the other conditional.[72] This is wrong. As James Durham put it: 'The Scripture makes not two considerations of Christ's death'.[73] God had a single will of intention or decree in the death of Christ.[74] 'I have come to do your *will*' (Heb. 10:5-10), Christ said; not: 'I have come to do your *wills*'.[75] '*It* is finished' (John 19:30), he cried; not: '*They* are finished'. Paul could speak of 'the eternal *purpose*'; not 'the eternal *purposes*', but 'the eternal *purpose* which [God] accomplished in Christ Jesus' (Eph. 3:11; see 1:11). 'Our Lord Jesus Christ... gave himself for our sins, that he might deliver us from this present evil age, according to the *will* of our God and Father' (Gal. 1:3-4). Christ came to do his Father's will; the Father willed that Christ should come and save all whom he had given him, the elect; Christ redeemed them all; all of them will come to Christ (John 4:34; 5:30; 6:37-40; 17:1-26). Thus the believing elect can say: 'By that *will* we have been sanctified through the offering of the body of Jesus Christ once for all' (Heb. 10:10), that is, once for all time, by 'one sacrifice for sins for ever' (Heb. 9:12,26; 10:12,14). One will in one sacrifice; not two wills in one sacrifice.

This can be pressed a little further. According to the Amyraldian, Christ died for all – effectively for the elect, but only sufficiently for the non-elect. If so, when he died, he must have been united to the elect (and they to him), but not united to the non-elect (nor they to him),[76] both at the same time in the one sacrifice. In other words, in addition to dying for, and in union with, those whom he knew his Father had elected, in whom he knew the Spirit would work effectually, and for whom he himself would intercede, Christ must have died for, but not in union with, those whom he knew his Father had not elected, in whom he knew the Spirit would never work effectually, and for whom he himself would never intercede, and all according to the ordination of God in the one sacrifice.[77] If this does not represent two distinct 'redemptions', or two wills in one redemption, what does?[78]

This, of course, means that the Amyraldian is wrong. God does not have a twofold decree in the redemption accomplished by Christ – one, absolute; the other, conditional.[79]

And this leads to the next point.

2. God's decree is not conditional

Not only does God not have a twofold decree – one absolute; the other, conditional – but how, in any case, could God's *decree* be conditional?[80] It is absolute (Ps. 33:11; Isa. 14:24-27; 46:11; Rom. 9:18-19; Eph. 1:11; Rev. 4:11 *etc.*) It must be absolute. It can be nothing else but absolute.[81] When God decreed the death of his Son, for whom he intended it, and what he intended by it, that decree was totally free of conditions, absolutely certain of fulfilment. There can be no question of any conditional decree in God.

Nowhere is this more true than in the death of Christ. Booth: 'Both reason and revelation concur to forbid our supposing that the Son of the blessed [God] should engage as mediator, and act as substitute, for he did not know whom; or that the counsels of heaven should terminate in mere peradventures'.[82]

Just so! God cannot have a conditional decree; in particular, he does not have a conditional decree in Christ's redemption. This is the second reason why the Amyraldian form of the sufficiency formula is wrong.

3. Christ earned the gift of faith for the elect

Christ did not die for believers.[83] Nor did he die for any on condition that they believe.[84] He died for sinners; sinners as unbelievers. But saving faith is essential, yes, and all the elect will be brought to it. Why? This is a crucial question. Why will all the elect come to faith? Because God decreed it; in choosing them to salvation, he decreed that they should come to faith in Christ.[85] Yes. But this is not the whole story; the elect do not come to faith 'merely' because God elected them, as Amyraldians say.[86] A sinner comes to faith because God elected him *and Christ died for him and purchased*[87] *the gift of faith for him* in fulfilment of God's decree in election.[88] This is no splitting of hairs. I have just said it is a *crucial* question. I go further; it is the ***cardinal*** question.

Why? Why is it the cardinal question? For this reason: If Christ, in his death, earned the gift of faith for sinners, he could not have done so provisionally or conditionally. To say that Christ purchased *the gift of faith* for sinners, *on condition that they believe*, would be utterly ludicrous; the two emphasised parts of the statement are patently self-contradictory, mutually exclusive. No! If Christ purchased the gift of faith for sinners by his death, he did so absolutely. Consequently, if, in his death, Christ purchased the gift of faith, he could have died only for the elect, because only the elect come to faith.[89]

The cardinal question is, therefore: Did Christ earn the gift of faith? I say: Yes. Although, I admit, no verse simply states that Christ purchased the gift of faith, this is far from conclusive; it can be properly inferred from Scripture.[90]

Of course, I am not saying there is a 'cause-and-effect relationship between the atonement and the bestowal of faith'[91] – the cause of the whole system of salvation – including the gift of faith – is the will of God, his loving decree to elect those he would save; that is, to redeem, call, keep and glorify them. Nevertheless, this can only mean that at the very least there is a direct connection between God's decree, Christ's redemption, and the gift of faith to the elect. But it is stronger than that; much stronger. In his decree – which can only be a unity entirely consistent from start to finish[92] – God designed Christ's redemption in which he merited and earned the entirety of salvation for the elect, including 'the bestowal of faith' by the Spirit (Eph. 2:8).[93] Indeed, in Christ,[94] God blesses his elect with 'every spiritual blessing' (Eph. 1:3).[95] Saving faith is a spiritual blessing, is it not?[96] Thus God blesses his elect by giving them saving faith. And he gives it to them, with all the other blessings, *in Christ*; that is, he gives them faith, and every other blessing, by Christ's work, because of the redemption which he designed and accomplished in Christ.[97] 'God was *in Christ*' accomplishing reconciliation (2 Cor. 5:19).

The elect are saved by grace through faith – and that not of themselves, 'it is the gift of God' (Eph. 2:8),[98] the 'grant' of God (Phil. 1:29),[99] 'the faith which comes through [Christ]' (Acts 3:16), which 'they have obtained [or received]... by the righteousness of our God and Saviour Jesus Christ' (2 Pet. 1:1);[100] that is, by the Father's promise to Christ for the completion of his will in redemption.[101] Christ, having been given 'all authority', 'being exalted to the right hand of God, and having received from the Father [the fulfilment of] the promise of the Holy Spirit,[102] he poured out' all the blessings of Pentecost (and since) – including faith and repentance to those who had been 'appointed to eternal life' (Matt. 28:18; Acts 2:33; 13:48). As I have already noted, it matters not whether Paul was speaking of the faith or the grace (in Eph. 2:8); the grace encompasses the faith. God in Christ gives faith as he gives repentance: 'Him [Christ] God has exalted to his right hand to be Prince and Saviour, to give repentance' (Acts 5:31; see also Acts 11:18). Why has Christ been given this authority? Because he earned it; he, by his death, earned the gifts of faith and repentance for his elect,[103] earned the right to bestow these gifts upon them – in accordance with the promise of the Father in consequence of his obedience. Thus, all the means of salvation – regeneration, conviction, conversion, repentance, faith and so on – all are the gift of God to his elect, earned and deserved for them by Christ.[104] 'Christ... suffered once for sins, the just for the unjust, that he might bring us to God' (1 Pet. 3:18). He died for sinners that he might – in order to[105] – bring them to God.[106] In other words, he did not merely *provide* salvation for the sinners for whom he died; he died to earn all that was necessary to bring them to God, including faith. Indeed, he died to *bring* them to God! 'In Christ Jesus you who once were far off have been brought near by the blood of Christ' (Eph. 2:13).[107] Christ did not make it *possible* for the elect to come to God, to draw near to him, to *be brought* to him; he died to *bring* them to God. Hence his dogmatic assertion: 'All that the Father gives me will come to me' (John 6:37); he earned and guaranteed their coming by his death. All was accomplished and announced with his last triumphant cry: 'It is finished' (John 19:30). So now we must say: 'What do [we] have that [we] have not received?' (1 Cor. 4:7); 'the excellence of the power [is] of God and not of us' (2 Cor. 4:7); 'we are [God's] workmanship, created in Christ Jesus' (Eph. 2:10); 'his divine power has given to us all things that pertain to life and godliness, through the knowledge of him' (2 Pet. 1:3). *All* things!

If not, we end up with the absurdity that Christ died to procure the end of redemption, but not its means (faith and repentance). Durham rightly called it 'a strange assertion, that [Christ] has bought life, and not the condition [of that life]; the end, and not the [means]'.[108] No! Christ died to obtain both eternal redemption and the application of it, *and he did it for the same people*. There is nothing conditional about it.[109] Christ 'bore the sin of many', being 'wounded for' their 'transgressions' (that is, he wrought certain redemption for them), so that the same 'many' are healed or justified (that is, he obtained the certain application of it to them) (Isa. 53:5,11-12). Those for whom God did not spare his own Son, but for whom he delivered him up (that is, to die for them to earn their redemption), to them he freely gives all things (Rom. 8:32).[110] Using this verse, James Haldane drew attention to the mistake of assuming 'that there is a possibility of the gifts of God being separated'. As he observed:

> Christ is God's unspeakable gift. Now, the supposition that this gift was bestowed on all, while the secondary, and consequently inferior gifts of faith, repentance, pardon and salvation, are withheld, is utterly unscriptural. This is decided by the question: 'He that spared not his own Son, but delivered him up for us all, how shall he not with him also freely give us all things?'[111]

And this includes faith – and whatever else is required to bring the elect to everlasting salvation.[112] As a consequence, it is absolutely certain (I use the words advisedly) that Christ 'shall see his seed... he shall see the labour of his soul, and be satisfied' (Isa. 53:10-11).

4. The ultimate condition of redemption is Christ's death, not faith

If Christ's redemption is provisional for any, conditional on faith, then their redemption is to be assigned, ultimately, to man and not God,[113] turning faith into a work and thus leading to salvation by works, something utterly ruled out by Scripture (Rom. 11:5-6; Eph. 2:8-9; 2 Tim. 1:9; Tit. 3:5).[114] The question for the Amyraldian is: 'Who makes the (supposedly) provisional redemption effective?'

Durham: To 'say that though he has not bought all men absolutely, nor died to procure life absolutely to them, yet that he did so conditionally, and upon supposition that they should afterward believe on him', is wrong, because 'there can be no conditional satisfaction intended' in Christ's death, since a conditional redemption leaves the effect of that redemption 'suspended... on man's will'.[115] Again, if any sinner is saved on this basis, then instead of *ascribing to the death of Christ* his freedom from all accusation – which is Paul's doctrine (Rom. 8:33-34) – he will be able to ascribe it to his faith; an unbiblical, dreadful suggestion.[116]

It is *Christ's* righteousness, his obedience – *not their faith* – which is imputed to believers for justification (Rom. 5:14-19).[117] It is true that Christ, the believer's righteousness, 'the LORD our righteousness' (Jer. 23:6), 'the righteousness of God', has to be received by faith (Rom. 1:17), but Christ had to die – and *this* was *the* condition which had to be fulfilled for the elect to be saved.[118] Christ met the condition.

Booth:

This pardon, far from being suspended on conditions to be performed by us, flows from sovereign grace, is according to the infinite riches of grace, and is intended by Jehovah to aggrandise his grace in the view of all the redeemed, and before the angels of light, both here and hereafter... When the blessed Jesus died, he did not do something to assist our weak but willing endeavours to save ourselves; he did not lay in a provision of grace, or purchase the Spirit for us, by which... we... [might be] rendered capable of performing the condition of our justification. But... when he bowed his head and expired, he, by himself alone, perfectly finished that righteousness which is the proper condition and the grand requisite of our justification. That the [gift of the] Spirit of grace and truth... is a precious fruit of the death, resurrection and glorification of Christ, is freely acknowledged; but that Jesus died to purchase the Spirit to work in us any part of that righteousness, on account of which we are accepted of God, must be denied.[119]

Quite! Christ accomplished redemption for the elect. He did not provide a redemption sufficient for all on condition that they believe. And this is the fourth reason why the Amyraldian form of the sufficiency formula is wrong.

5. *No good purpose is served by any supposed redemption for the non-elect*

If God decreed that Christ should die to atone provisionally and sufficiently for the non-elect, will any of the non-elect be saved? Clifford: 'No, by definition the question makes no sense... That said, I believe the gospel provision is made conditionally and sufficiently for all, not to [for?] elect or non-elect but to [for?] sinners in general, all being "potentially" recoverable. Empowered by special grace, only the elect "actually" fulfil the conditions of faith and repentance. Then the all-sufficient atonement becomes particularly efficacious in their salvation. Thus those who are saved are still saved on the basis of a redemption made conditionally available for all'.[120]

If this is so – Christ died for the non-elect, but they will not be saved – why, I ask, did God decree to provide redemption for them? why did Christ die for them?[121] Is it: 1. To try to justify God's offer of salvation to the non-elect, even though he knew they would refuse it and perish? Clifford: 'God decreed to provide redemption for them to express the generosity of his grace even when he permits the non-elect to perish in their ingratitude. Thus Christ still offered himself to those whom he knew would reject him (see John 6:32)'.[122] Or is it: 2. To give himself a reason for justly condemning the non-elect, on the ground that they refused a redemption that was made for them? Clifford: 'Unbelievers are... rejecting redemption provided'.[123]

Both suggestions are wrong – and worse. As for the first, the basis of the offer is not some supposed universal atonement – I will return to this.[124] What is more, talk of God *permitting* the non-elect to perish is a smoke screen which masks the reality of the Amyraldian position: God does not *permit* the non-elect not to believe and perish; nor is he a mere *observer* of the scene. The fact is, God has not *decreed* to give them faith because he has not *elected* them.[125] Even so, according to the Amyraldian, he decreed to redeem them. That is, as I have already noted, the Amyraldian says God decreed to give his Son for the redemption of the non-elect, even though he decreed not to give them the necessary faith to benefit by that redemption; and this, to express his 'generosity'!

It is hard to accept that Christ should die for such an end. So much for the first possible 'explanation' of why Christ should die for all.

As for the second, as John Leland put it, to think 'that many will gain nothing by the atonement but an aggravated curse, the heart sickens to think that God would be at so much expense to get a pretence to condemn men'.[126] Owen: 'To what purpose serves the general ransom, but only to assert that Almighty God would have the precious blood of his dear Son poured out for innumerable souls whom he will not have [that is, whom he has not decreed][127] to share in any drop thereof, and so, in respect of them, to be spilt in vain, or else to be shed for them only that they might be the deeper damned?'[128] The fact is, as Gill said: 'God might have required repentance of men, and have justly condemned them for final impenitence, supposing Christ had never died at all, or for any at all'.[129]

In short, no good purpose is served by any supposed redemption for the non-elect. And this is the fifth reason why the Amyraldian form of the sufficiency formula is wrong.

6. The Amyraldian scheme fatally weakens the atonement

It bears repeating: The Amyraldian scheme fatally weakens the atonement.[130] I have already noted how vital the *nature* of the atonement is;[131] imputation and substitution,[132] union with Christ,[133] vicarious sacrifice, propitiation, reconciliation and redemption are at its heart. To think that any of this might be conditional on the sinner's response, is breath-taking. Fuller's reply to Dan Taylor (though an Arminian and not an Amyraldian)[134] is excellent. Did Christ have 'any absolute determination in his death to save any of the human race?' asked Fuller. If so, 'the limited extent of that purpose must follow of course. The reason is plain', he said:

> An absolute purpose must be effectual. If it extended to all mankind, all mankind would certainly be saved. Unless, therefore, we will maintain the final salvation of all mankind, we must either suppose a limitation to the absolute determination of Christ to save, or deny any such determination to exist... [Taylor's] scheme, instead of making redemption universal, supposes that Christ's death did not properly redeem any man, nor render the salvation of any man a matter of

certainty. It only [in its advocates' view] procured an offer of redemption and reconciliation to mankind in general.[135] We apprehend this is diminishing the efficacy of Christ's death, without answering any valuable end. Nor is this all; such an hypothesis appears to be utterly inconsistent with all those scriptures where God the Father is represented as promising his Son a reward for his sufferings in the salvation of poor sinners... If [since] the doctrine of eternal, personal and unconditional election be a truth, that of a special design in the death of Christ must necessarily follow.[136]

A provisional atonement? Certainly not! Christ's death procured an absolute propitiation, an absolute reconciliation and an absolute redemption for all the elect. 'It is finished', he said (John 19:30); not 90% finished. 'Christ Jesus came into the world to save sinners' (1 Tim. 1:15).

This is the sixth reason why the Amyraldian use of the sufficiency formula is wrong.

* * *

For these six reasons,[137] to speak of a redemption which God decreed to be universal, sufficient for all, but conditional on faith, is contrary to Scripture. Amyraut was wrong.[138] God sent his Son to accomplish an unconditional redemption for the elect – that is, a redemption which included the certainty of their believing. He did not send his Son to provide a redemption for all on condition that they believe.[139]

Booth[140] tackled this (Amyraldian) 'hypothesis respecting the limitation of our Lord's atonement'. He traced where it came from, and why:

Extremely adverse and irreconcilable as the necessary consequences of maintaining, on the one part, that Christ, by his death, made an atonement for all mankind,[141] and, on the other, that he made an atonement for the elect only, are usually thought [to be], a reconciling expedient or compromise between them has been invented. This expedient, if I mistake not, may be justly represented in the following position: The particularity of the atonement consists in the sovereign pleasure of God, *with regard to its application*. By viewing the subject in this light, it is imagined that provision is made for the satisfaction of all reasonable demands on each side of the question.

In other words, on this (Amyraldian) hypothesis, Christ wrought a redemption for all; the particularity consists only in its application; that is, in limiting the bestowal of this general redemption to those to whom God has decreed to give it – the elect. Before dealing with the 'invention' itself, Booth spelled out what is involved in 'the application of redemption'. What are we talking about when we use such a phrase? As he said, it is impossible to divorce God's intention[142] in the application of redemption from his intention in its accomplishment:

It is necessary to be observed, before we enter into the merits of this position, that the application of the atonement is here to be understood as including not only what the New Testament denominates, *receiving* the atonement – the sprinkling of the blood of Jesus Christ – and, faith in his blood (Rom. 3:25; 5:11; 1 Pet. 1:2), but also the *absolute intention* of Christ in his death to save all those who shall be finally happy.

That is, the application of redemption involves not only the sinner's reception of it, but God's intention in accomplishing it. Booth, rightly stressing 'intention', argued that Christ *intended* to make reconciliation by his death, knowing full-well those for whom he intended that atonement, and that this intention covered not only the *benefit earned* by his death, *but also its application*:

That our Lord had a completely wise and most serious intention, in laying down his life to make an atonement for sinners, neither the perfection of his character, nor the nature of the case, will suffer us to doubt. But this very consideration forbids our supposing that he made an atonement with his own blood for any whom he did not intend it should be applied; or that he died as a sponsor for any of those whom he did not intend should live through him... But is it not strange and unnatural, to connect the idea of peculiarity with an *application* of the atonement, while implicitly [explicitly?] denying that any such limitation attaches to the *work* of [the] atonement? As it is natural to suppose that our Lord's atonement, whatever limits may attend its *application*,[143] should virtually prescribe those limits, it seems unreasonable to imagine that its *application* should impose limits which would not otherwise have existed... Whatever peculiarity there is in the latter, must be included in the former; or else the atonement by blood, and the *application*[144] of it by power, must wear different aspects, and be at variance.[145]

On the (Amyraldian) 'hypothesis' Booth was criticising, however, 'the one' – the *accomplishment* of the atonement – is said to be 'general and unconfined', that is, to all men, while 'the other' – the *application* of the atonement – is said to be 'particular, and, it should seem, peculiar to God's elect'. Booth observed that this system 'has very much the appearance of the... Arminian [scheme of] redemption', though he admitted it is not.[146] But on this (Amyraldian) 'hypothesis', Booth declared:

> There is nothing in the [Amyraldian concept of the] atonement of Christ that infallibly ascertains its application to all those for whom it was made... Millions of those for whom our Lord, by the sacrifice of himself, made expiation, for want of the necessary application [of it], must finally perish under the curse... On this principle, therefore, myriads and millions, for whom divine benevolence provided an atonement, must everlastingly perish for want of that atonement being applied. Must we then consider Jesus Christ as intending to make, and as actually making, a real atonement for mankind in general? But how, or in what way, was atonement made for those who, in consequence of not having it applied to them, sink into perdition? Was it by the death of Jesus? If so, he must have died for them; which, in the estimation of Paul, was perfectly good security against final condemnation (Rom. 8:34)... On the [Amyraldian] principle [Booth was opposing]... Jesus Christ is to be considered as making atonement for all mankind; by shedding the same blood, by undergoing the same sufferings, and precisely at the same time, equally for [all – both the ultimately lost and saved.[147] But, according to Rom. 4:25,] the atonement for sin depended on the death of our substitute, so that the justification of our persons depended on the discharge of our substitute, in his resurrection from the dead, by the divine Father; which two grand blessings, perfect atonement and complete justification, have been usually considered... inseparable. But according to the [Amyraldian] sentiment here opposed, there is no certain connection between atonement for sin by the death of Jesus, and justification before God. For, with regard to the atonement... [on this system] Peter and Judas were on a perfect level, the whole of the important difference in favour of Peter arising from the application [of the atonement, but not the atonement itself].

This is wrong: 'As, therefore, the only atonement for sin, the only redemption for sinners, and the only satisfaction made for our crimes, have the same Jesus for their author – suffering under the same character – effecting the whole by shedding the same blood –

and precisely at the same time, we may safely conclude that, in the design of our divinely merciful substitute, they are commensurate with regard to their application; that the application of them all is made at the same instant; and that their efficacy and consequences must be commensurate'.[148]

Haldane put his finger on it. When Amyraldians insist that 'the peculiarity of redemption consists in its *application*, according to the sovereign pleasure of God', an inevitable conclusion follows; not only an inevitable conclusion, but a conclusion obviously false: 'Whence it inevitably follows that men are not saved by the atonement [*per se*], *but by its application*; and, consequently, that the Holy Spirit, and not Christ, is the Saviour'.[149] The Amyraldian view of the atonement, therefore, inevitably leading as it does to this false conclusion, is clearly wrong.

As a consequence, I am at one with Gill when he said:

> The distinctions of Christ dying sufficiently for all, but intentionally only for the elect, and for all if they will believe and repent... for my own part, I [cannot][150] admit... I firmly believe that Christ died for all the elect of God, and them only; that, by his death, he has procured for them actual pardon, reconciliation and salvation; and, that in consequence... faith and repentance are bestowed upon and wrought in these persons... in which way they are brought to the full enjoyment of that salvation Christ has obtained for them.[151]

As Gill observed: Anxious sinners can find no comfort in a universal or provisional atonement which 'leaves the salvation of every man very precarious and uncertain... when it depends on conditions to be performed by themselves'. What comfort is it to tell a sinner that Christ died for him 'and yet he may be damned [even so] for all this...?' None at all! 'Whereas the doctrine of particular redemption ascertains the salvation of some, and all that believe in Christ have reason to conclude their interest in it, and take comfort from it, [rightly] believing that they shall have, in consequence of it, every blessing of grace here, and eternal life hereafter'.[152]

Haldane again:

> When we consider the dignity of the Redeemer's person, it may be asked: Was his atonement of infinite value? and if so: Why might not all mankind have been saved by it? We answer: Such was not the will

of God; he had a special [specific] end in view, and this shall be fully accomplished. But does it, in the smallest degree, derogate from the glory of the Redeemer that his atonement extended no farther than the commission which he received when he became the Father's servant, and undertook to redeem all the children given him from death and to ransom them from the power of the grave?[153]

Certainly not! The upshot? This:

Admitting that it was not God's *intention* to save all by the atonement, [as Amyraldians do, then the sufficiency formula as used by them] gets rid of no difficulty.[154]

Just so.

* * *

I close this long chapter by raising once again 'the cardinal question': Did Christ earn the gift of faith in his redemption? He did or he did not. If the latter, then the elect come to faith simply by God's decree. And this makes faith unique in the spectrum of salvation – since all the other gifts, graces and ends of salvation are purchased for the elect 'in Christ', by him in his death, and conveyed to them by the Holy Spirit poured out by the exalted Christ. Faith, apparently, is the exception!

This cannot be! As I have shown, Christ earned the gift of faith for his elect in his death. This, Amyraldians deny. They are wrong.[155]

What is more, this fact – that Christ earned the gift of faith for his elect – explodes their case. Whatever their assertions in terms of the sufficiency formula, on their scheme Christ did not die effectively for any. He died sufficiently for all, yes, but effectively for none. He died as much for the non-elect as the elect. In particular, he did not obtain the gift of faith for any. That essential gift – essential because without it there is no salvation – is given to the elect simply through God's decree, independent (whatever the Amyraldian's protestations)[156] of the death of Christ.

As I have shown, this is contrary to Scripture. Why is any sinner saved? Because God the Father, from eternity, elected him to salvation in his Son, so that Christ should redeem him, and thereby merit the gift of the Spirit to bestow *all* the means and ends of salvation upon him, and bring him to everlasting glory. Nothing is left out. All is included. None of it is merely sufficient or provisional. All is absolute.

So much for the first expression of the formula. What about the second?

The Meaningless Form: Owen's Position

Let me remind you, reader, of Owen's position: The atonement, though efficient only for the elect, and not provisional for all, is sufficient for all because of the worth of Christ's person. I repeat the extracts I quoted earlier: Christ's 'death, as Calvin and other expositors remind us, because it was eternal and because he is the Son of God, is sufficient for the whole world'. 'There was virtue and efficacy enough in [Christ's] oblation to satisfy offended justice for the sins of the whole world, yes, and of millions of worlds more; for his blood has infinite value, because of the infinite dignity and excellency of his person'.[157]

These are not Amyraldians speaking. So what do their words mean? Let Owen be their spokesman; let him set out his stall. As so often with Owen, however, his reasoning takes some following; this time, more so. Indeed, I think he contradicts himself – or gets very close to it. And, when all the logical twists and turns of his argument have been negotiated, the result is, as I have already said, meaningless. Nevertheless, let me spell out his line of reasoning as clearly as I can.

Owen began by speaking of Christ's 'sacrifice of infinite worth, value and dignity', of such value that it was 'sufficient in itself for the redeeming of all and every man'. Indeed, that 'it was... the purpose and intention of God that his Son should offer a sacrifice of infinite worth, value and dignity, sufficient in itself for the redeeming of all and every man'. But then Owen added a qualifying clause: 'If it had pleased the Lord to employ it to [for] that purpose':

It was... the purpose and intention of God that his Son should offer a sacrifice of infinite worth, value and dignity, sufficient in itself for the redeeming of all and every man, *if it had pleased the Lord to employ it to [for] that purpose*... Sufficient... was the sacrifice of Christ for the redemption of the whole world, and for the expiation of all the sins of all and every man in the world... It was in itself of infinite value and sufficiency to have been made a price to have bought and purchased all and every man in the world... The value and fitness of it to be made a price arises from its own internal sufficiency.[158]

According to Owen, therefore, the death of Christ was, by God's design and intention, a sufficient price to redeem all men, and that because of its own innate sufficiency; Christ being of infinite worth, and his pain in suffering being so great, therefore his work was sufficient to redeem all.[159] But although God intended that Christ's death, because of its infinite value, should be sufficient for the redemption of all, God never intended that it should actually be a redemption for all; in itself it was, but God never designed it for that purpose.[160] Consequently, said Owen, the sufficiency-efficiency formula, 'that old distinction of the Schoolmen...[161] is most true... for [Christ's blood] being a price for all or some does not arise [merely?][162] from its own sufficiency, worth or dignity, but from the intention of God and Christ using it to that purpose'. God intended that Christ's blood would be sufficient for the redemption of all; and it was. Moreover, it would have been a redemption for all – *if God had intended it to be* – but he did not:

Therefore, it is denied that the blood of Christ was a sufficient price and ransom for all and everyone, not because it was not sufficient, but because it was not [intended to be] a ransom [for all]. And so it easily appears what is to be owned in the distinction [that is, the formula]... If it intend no more but that the blood of our Saviour was of sufficient value for the redemption of all and everyone, and that Christ intended to lay down a price which should be sufficient for their redemption, [then the formula] is acknowledged as most true. But... that... 'to die for them', holds out the intention of our Saviour, in the laying down of the price, to have been their redemption... we deny.[163]

Christ did not die for all! Certainly not! His work was by God's design in itself sufficient to have redeemed all, and it could have redeemed all – if God had intended to redeem all; but he did not. Consequently, Christ died only for the elect.

What, according to Owen, made the infinitely sufficient work of Christ an effective redemption for the elect? The will, the intention of God *in the redemption itself.* If God had intended it to redeem all, it would have been a redemption for all; but since he intended it for the elect only, it was a redemption for them only, not for all. Nevertheless, according to Owen, as God intended, it was sufficient for all, and would have redeemed all, if God had intended it as a redemption for all:

That it should be applied unto any, made a price for them, and become beneficial to them, according to the worth that is in it, is external to it, does not arise from it, but merely depends upon the intention and will of God... That it did formally become a price for any is solely to be ascribed to the purpose of God, intending their purchase and redemption by it. The intention of the offerer and accepter... is that which gives the formality of a price unto it; this is external... Its being a price for all or some does not arise from its own sufficiency, worth or dignity, but from the intention of God and Christ using it to that purpose.[164]

Again:

The value of any satisfaction in this business arises not from the innate worth of the things whereby it is made, but purely from God's free constitution of them to such an end... All their value arises merely from that appointment; they have so much as he ascribes to them, and no more.[165]

This approach is radically different to Amyraut's.[166] God intended, Amyraut argued, not only that Christ's sacrifice should be sufficient for all, but that it should be a redemption for all conditional on their believing; Owen agreed that God intended Christ's sacrifice should be sufficient for all, but denied that God intended it to be a redemption for all. Amyraut argued that the effectiveness or otherwise of Christ's sacrifice to redeem arose as a result of God's electing decree in the application of the blood of Christ; Owen argued that the distinction arose in God's decree and intention in the sacrifice itself.[167]

But the formula left both men free to talk about the sufficiency of Christ's redemption – even though they meant very different things by it! For Owen, God decreed to redeem his elect by the death of his Son. This is the only redemption – and that, efficacious[168] for the elect. For the non-elect, God in Christ has purchased no redemption. But although God has given Christ to redeem and pay the ransom for the elect only, even so, the infinite worth of Christ's person makes the value of his work infinite, and therefore sufficient for all, even though he has not died to save them all. It is sufficient for all, and would have redeemed all, if

God had decreed to redeem all. But he has not. 'That the atonement... has enough in it, we deny... not because the atonement has not enough in it for them, but because the atonement was not made for them'.[169]

Although, in some senses better (though less logical)[170] than Amyraut's position, this approach is also mistaken. We have no biblical warrant to argue in this way. It is pure speculation; it cannot be found in Scripture, in name or concept.[171] And whereas Amyraut's position is consistent, but wrong, the Owenite position – a scholastic device which takes us outside Scripture – adds nothing to the debate. Rather, it clouds it.

And worse.

Worse? Yes. As above, I ask again: What do these words mean? The answer is patent: *Nothing. They are meaningless.*[172] As Clifford pointed out: 'Owen paid lip-service to the sufficiency-efficiency distinction', but his logic 'led him to deprive the universal sufficiency of all its value. For Owen', whatever his protestations, 'the atonement is only sufficient for those for whom it is efficient'.[173] Clifford was right! For all Owen's attempt to make a logically water-tight case, he ended up with fine-sounding words which, though they might dazzle, really amount to nothing. God, according to Owen, designed or decreed that Christ should offer a sacrifice sufficient for all men, if he wanted to use it to that end, but he did not design or decree to use it to that end or purpose. I say it again: This is meaningless.[174]

What is more, the idea detracts from the biblical doctrine of the atonement. Christ's atonement was designed for the elect, and he accomplished a perfect redemption for them and no others. As for what Christ accomplished for the non-elect, as I have argued, Scripture is silent.[175] Of course, as I have noted, the work of Christ is of infinite worth, and of course he is an all-sufficient Saviour – a perfect Redeemer for all the elect, for all their sins, for ever. But this does not mean we can – or should – speculate about its 'sufficiency for all'. In fact, I repeat, however fine it sounds, the concept is, in the end, illogical and meaningless.[176]

In closing this look at Owen's use of the sufficiency formula, I return to some words I have already used from Haldane:

> When we consider the dignity of the Redeemer's person, it may be asked: Was his atonement of infinite value? and if so: Why might not all mankind have been saved by it? We answer: Such was not the will of God; he had a special [specific] end in view, and this shall be fully accomplished. But does it, in the smallest degree, derogate from the glory of the Redeemer that his atonement extended no farther than the commission which he received when he became the Father's servant, and undertook to redeem all the children given him from death and to ransom them from the power of the grave?[177]

The upshot? This:

> Admitting that it was not God's *intention* to save all by the atonement, [as Owenites do, the sufficiency formula as used by them] gets rid of no difficulty.[178]

So why do so many Calvinists who, while rejecting the idea that God designed and provided a universal atonement conditional on faith, thus avoiding the errors of Amyraldianism, nevertheless still hold to the formula, 'efficient for the elect, sufficient for all', as 'elucidated' by Owen? I suggest three reasons: *First*, it seems to provide an explanation of those texts which appear to speak of a universal atonement. *Secondly*, it is an attempt to justify God against the charge of 'insincerity' for offering salvation to all when he knows the atonement is only for some.[179] *Thirdly*, it appears to provide a logical basis upon which to make the free offer.

For my purpose in this book, the first reason is of no consequence. As I have said, those texts which appear to teach universal redemption, in my opinion do not. What is more, as I noted earlier, the 'sufficiency' argument weakens the atonement spoken of in those passages, and leaves bigger problems than it is thought to solve.[180]

As for the second reason, this is a well-meant mistake,[181] but a mistake all the same. And a serious one. I will return to it.

And the third reason – that the sufficiency formula seems to provide the biblical basis for the free offer[182] – is wrong. It does not do the job.[183] Indeed, far from strengthening the free offer, it weakens it. And this, of course, is the crux of my book. It is time to get to grips with it.

The Objection: Particular Redemption Rules Out the Free Offer

Particular redemption means there can be no free offer; since Christ died only for the elect, salvation cannot be offered to all; Christ can be offered to all only if he died for all; since he died only for the elect, there is nothing to offer the non-elect. Or so it is said.

Take hyper-Calvinists: 'The universal offer cannot be supported without supposing universal redemption; which those who are fond of, and yet profess particular redemption, would do well to consider'.[184] The free offer denies 'the doctrine of special redemption'.[185] 'Another Arminian footprint of the well-meant offer is the teaching of universal atonement'.[186] 'Those that preach a well-meaning offer of God to all men, must and will ultimately embrace the doctrine of universal atonement also... God's well-meaning offer of salvation cannot possibly be wider in scope than the objective satisfaction and justification of the cross of Christ'.[187] In 'the "free offer"... the saving work on the cross is seen as a universal action on the part of Christ who so loved every man that he atoned for all their sins. This atonement is thus there for all men everywhere... Christ died to save everyone... Christ has died for all'.[188] 'All free-offer preachers... generally ignore anything to do with... the purposely limited extent of the atonement'.[189]

Amyraldians, in their turn, say the free offer requires a universal provision: 'If you define "particular redemption" as "Christ died for the elect alone", then how can the "offer" be wider? You have nothing to offer to the world in general. If "Christ and salvation" are "on offer", then he died (with intent) for those to whom he made it available. Therefore, why not simply accept the Amyraldian position... Can't you accept this...?'[190]

And Owenites say the free offer requires – or, at least, is based upon – a universal sufficiency: 'So great was the dignity and worth of [Christ's] death and blood-shedding, of so precious a value, of such an infinite fullness and sufficiency was this oblation of himself, that it was [in] every way able and perfectly sufficient to redeem, justify, and reconcile and save all the sinners in the world, and to satisfy the justice of God for all the sins of all mankind, and to bring them every one to everlasting glory. Now, this fullness and sufficiency of the merit of the death of Christ is a foundation unto... the general publishing of the gospel... If there were a thousand worlds, the gospel of Christ might, upon this ground, be preached to them all... This... is a sufficient basis and ground for all those general precepts of preaching the gospel unto all men, even that sufficiency which we have described... This sufficiency is the chief ground of the proposing it unto them... The sufficiency of the death of Christ for the saving of everyone, without exception that comes unto him, is enough to fill all the invitations and entreaties of the gospel unto sinners, to induce them to believe'.[191]

These, then, are the three basic ways in which the free offer is denied on the basis of particular redemption (as defined with no reference to universal sufficiency) – by the hyper-Calvinist, the Amyraldian and the Owenite, respectively.[192]

All are wrong. I will make my case by first setting out the general principles, then applying them, in turn, to each of these three particular forms of the objection.

The Objection Answered: General Principles

What are these general principles? First, I will set out what is *not* offered, and then what *is*. Then I will delineate to whom this offer is to be made. After which I will spell out the warrant for making the offer, showing that we have no need – or business – to try to reconcile the free offer with particular redemption. I hope in this way to show that particular redemption, far from clashing with the free offer, or stifling it, does the very reverse.[193]

1. What is **not** *offered in the free offer?*

In the gospel offer, sinners are not told: 'Christ died for you'.[194] No! John Kennedy: 'There can be no warrant for saying to all who hear the gospel that... Christ is their... Redeemer'.[195] Such a thing ought not to be preached to sinners, nor are they called upon to believe it.[196] Even if it were possible for the unconverted to believe it, such faith would not be saving,[197] but, as I have pointed out, before conversion, they have no way of knowing it.[198] None but a believer can say: 'The Son of God... loved me and gave himself for me' (Gal. 2:20; see also Gal. 1:3-4; Eph. 1:7; 1 Thess. 5:10; 1 Pet. 1:17-19; Rev. 1:5-6 *etc.*); and when he says it, he is using the language of assurance.[199] Only when a sinner has been brought to saving faith, can he know he has been redeemed, can he justly reason that he is elect, and is thus assured.[200] But all this has nothing whatsoever to do with the free offer. The free offer is to do with the conversion of an unbelieving sinner, and for that a sinner needs to repent and trust Christ.[201] To be speaking of the extent of the atonement, is to be dealing with a saint, his edification and assurance; in preaching to bring a sinner to Christ, the extent of the atonement is irrelevant.[202]

Preachers who confuse the two, mistake chalk for cheese, with dire consequences. Nothing could be more ludicrous than for a preacher to try to call unbelievers – unbelievers! – to Christ by engaging them in a discussion of the extent of election and the atonement.[203] Such questions are not for unbelievers, and it is no part of the gospel call to arouse their curiosity about them.[204] They need to be called to Christ. I am not saying that we should not preach the decrees when unbelievers are present, but such preaching must be with care and discretion, showing the right spirit.[205] There is a very real danger of preaching the decrees as barriers to faith;[206] we must do the reverse, especially showing sinners that no one, *before he trusted Christ*, ever knew he was one of the elect and that Christ died for him.[207] In short, there is no need, nor is it right, to debate with unbelievers about limited atonement, unconditional election or irresistible grace. Unbelievers, I repeat, need to be called to Christ.[208]

John Murray:

> This way of stating the case is parallel to what is true of election. Sinners do not come to Christ because they first believe [or know, or are told] that they have been elected. They come to Christ, and only then may they believe that they were chosen in Christ before the foundation of the world.[209] The same is true in the matter of the atonement. It cannot be declared to men indiscriminately that... Christ died for them. The belief of this proposition is not the primary act of faith. Only in commitment to Christ as freely offered may we come to know that he died for our sins unto our redemption... Christ is offered and faith is first of all commitment to him. It is receiving and resting upon him alone for salvation.[210]

I repeat the point: 'It cannot be declared to men indiscriminately that... Christ died for them. The belief of this proposition is not the primary act of faith'. So much for the negative, that which is *not* offered to sinners.

2. *What* is *offered in the free offer?*

Christ and full salvation in him are offered to sinners – who are to be commanded to repent and believe, and promised that if they do they will enjoy him and all the benefits he obtained for sinners (Ps. 2:12; Isa. 45:22; 55:1-7; Matt. 11:28; Acts 16:31; 17:30; Rom. 10:4,13; Rev. 22:17 *etc.*) That is what is offered to them all.[211]

John Murray again:

> What is freely offered in the gospel?... It is Christ who is offered... It is not the opportunity of salvation that is offered; it is salvation. And it is salvation because Christ is offered and Christ does not invite us to mere opportunity, but to himself.
> [Again]: It is not the mere possibility of salvation, nor simply provision for salvation, that is offered freely in the gospel. It is rather salvation full, perfect and free. For it is Christ in all the glory of his person as Saviour and Redeemer, and in all the perfection of his finished work, who is offered to sinners in the gospel... It is salvation with such completeness and perfection that is presented to lost men in the full, free and unfettered call of the gospel.[212]

I underline this important point. Christ and full salvation are offered to sinners; not merely the *opportunity* to be saved, the *possibility* of salvation, or the *provision* of salvation.

Booth:

> Preaching the gospel... is proclaiming glad tidings to guilty, depraved and ruined creatures – tidings of pardon, of peace, and of salvation through Jesus Christ. Preaching the gospel is preaching Christ himself; or bearing a public testimony to his gracious character and perfect work. Preaching the gospel, therefore, is proclaiming salvation by sovereign grace – is exhibiting Jesus, not as willing to supply the deficiencies in upright characters; nor, merely, as granting assistance to persons already in the way to heaven; but as the only, the all-sufficient, the absolutely free Saviour of the condemned – the worthless – the lost.[213]

Sinners, in Scripture, are never called upon to understand the ins-and-outs of – nor accept – a provisional or sufficient redemption. They are not offered such! They are offered Christ! 'Trust Christ! This is your business! The extent of the atonement (or who is elected) is irrelevant to *you*; Christ and salvation are offered to *you*; it is *your* duty to repent and believe; if *you* come to Christ, *you* will be saved (Acts 16:31; 17:30)'. We must not stray from this simplicity and directness. The debate about particular redemption and the free offer is all well and good among Reformed theologians – but we are talking about dealing with sinners – and seeing them saved.

The point I am making – that it is Christ and full salvation which is offered to sinners in the gospel – is confirmed by looking at it the other way round. Why are sinners condemned? We know it is not because they were not elected, or because Christ did not die for them; no, 'the wrath of God is revealed from heaven against all ungodliness and unrighteousness of men, who suppress the truth in unrighteousness'. God holds them accountable 'because, although they knew God' from his works of creation, they 'did not glorify him as God, nor were thankful, but became futile in their thoughts, and their foolish hearts were darkened... and... they did not like to retain God in their knowledge', with all the attendant corruption this entails (Rom. 1:18-32). Principally, sinners are condemned for not trusting Christ (John 3:18-19,36; 8:24; 16:8-9; 2 Thess. 2:10-12), for rejecting the free offer, for snubbing the Christ who is offered to them, for refusing to repent and believe.[214] Gill hit the nail on the head:

> That [Christ] died for them, is what they are not obliged to believe, that being no part of the revelation made to them; nor will they be condemned for not believing that he died for them, but for their neglect, contempt and unbelief of him and his gospel... [Sinners are not] obliged to believe... that Jesus... died for them, or that he is their Saviour... God might have... justly condemned them for final impenitence, supposing Christ had never died at all, or for any at all... [None] are... condemned for not believing that Christ died for them, but for... the disbelief or contempt of his gospel.[215]

To sum up this point: Christ, with full salvation in him, is offered to sinners in the gospel.

3. To whom is the offer made?

The gospel has to be preached to sinners, obviously! But what kind of sinners? To all sinners, none excepted. And to all of them merely as sinners; *not* as elect sinners, repentant sinners, sensible sinners, redeemed sinners,[216] prepared sinners, or any other kind of sinners; just sinners: 'Go into all the world and preach the gospel to every creature' (Mark 16:15). And to preach the gospel is to freely offer Christ and salvation to sinners, all sinners as sinners,[217] and to call, invite, command and exhort them to come to him.

Election and particular redemption do not come into it.[218] Of course, only elect sinners, sinners for whom Christ died, will come,[219] and they will come only because of the inward working of

God's Spirit (John 3:3,5-8; 6:37,44), but which unregenerate sinners are in that number is beyond our knowledge, hidden in God's secret will, and, as concerning the inviting of sinners, nothing to do with us. What we are considering – all we can and should consider when dealing with unbelievers in the call of the gospel – is his revealed will. And this is plain enough: We have to invite and command all sinners as sinners to trust the Saviour.[220]

Kennedy:

> If we ever come [to Christ] it must be *as sinners*... It would be well if preachers of the gospel were more impressed with [this] great [fact]... how impossible would they then find it to hesitate about requiring faith from all who hear the gospel! No difficulty arising from the sovereignty of God's love, and from the restricted reference of Christ's atonement, could hamper their minds or straiten their feelings in preaching Christ *to sinners*. All the more free and urgent would they be, as they realised a love, whose purposes must take effect, and a death, that shall not be in vain. And how the light of [this] great [fact] would clear men's views of faith, if only they would admit it into their minds![221]

Bunyan:

> God... would have *all men whatever* invited by the gospel to lay hold of life by Christ, whether elect or reprobate; for though it is true, that there is such a thing as election and reprobation, yet God, by the tenders of the gospel... looks upon men under another consideration; to wit, *as sinners*; and *as sinners* invites them to believe, lay hold of, and embrace the same. He does not say to his ministers: 'Go preach to the elect, because they are elect...' but: 'Go preach the gospel *to sinners as sinners*...'... The gospel must be preached *to sinners as they are sinners*, without distinction of elect or reprobate; because neither the one nor yet the other, as considered under these [two] simple acts [of God], are fit subjects to embrace the gospel... but the gospel is to be tendered to men *as they are sinners*... Thus you see the gospel is to be tendered *to all in general... to sinners as sinners*; and so [in this way] are they to receive it, and to close with the tenders thereof.[222]

Fuller: 'He that believes in Jesus Christ must believe in him as he is revealed in the gospel, and that is as the Saviour of *sinners*. It is only *as a sinner*, exposed to the righteous displeasure of God, that he must approach him'.[223] Owen: 'Christ died... only for the elect... Some then tell us we cannot invite all men promiscuously to believe. But why so? We invite... all men *as sinners*; and we know that Christ died for *sinners*'.[224]

4. What is the warrant for the free offer?

Why should we offer Christ and salvation to all? What right do we have? Precisely the same reason and right as doing anything and everything else in the Christian religion. What is the warrant for faith, preaching, baptism, the Lord's supper, and so on? It is not election;[225] it is not the extent of the atonement, certainly not its 'sufficiency'; it is not a knowledge of God's secret will (Deut. 29:29a).[226] So what is it? The warrant for faith and all the rest – in particular, the warrant for making the free offer – is the plain command of Scripture, the revealed will of God (Deut. 29:29b); 'the warrant lies in Scripture alone',[227] 'the simple command and warrant of the word' of God.[228] Let me make my meaning clear: We must obey God in whatever his word commands us to do – whether or not we can fully explain or reconcile the various parts of any particular command. And in trying to understand any principle or practice which God calls us to adopt, we must restrain ourselves to that which Scripture reveals, and not resort to logical contrivances. Let us not 'think beyond what is written' (1 Cor. 4:6). This is what I mean by saying the warrant for the free offer, its ground or basis, is the command and practice of Scripture.[229] I agree with Owen. We know there is:

> The infallible connection, according to God's purpose and will, [between] faith and salvation, which is frequently the thing intended in gospel proposals... The Lord has in his counsel established it, and revealed in his word, that there is an indissoluble bond between these two things, so that 'he that believes shall be saved' (Mark 16:16)... Now, this connection of the means and the end, faith and life, is the only thing which is signified and held out to innumerable [sinners] to whom the gospel is preached; all the commands, proffers and promises that are made unto them intimating no more than this will of God, that believers shall certainly be saved; which is an unquestionable divine verity and a sufficient object for supernatural [that is, saving] faith to rest upon, and which not being closed with is a sufficient cause of damnation: John 8:24, 'If you believe not that I am he' (that is, 'the way, the truth and the life'), 'you shall die in your sins'.

It is a vain imagination of some [that is, Amyraldians], that when the command and promise of believing are made out to any man, though he is of the number of them that shall certainly perish, yet the Lord has a conditional will of his salvation, and intends that he shall be saved, on condition that he will believe; when the condition does not lie at all in the will of God...
The gospel requires a resting upon... Christ, so [revealed] and believed on to be the promised Redeemer, as an all-sufficient Saviour, with whom is plenteous redemption, and who is able to save to the uttermost them that come to God by him, and to bear the burden of all weary labouring souls that come by faith to him.[230]

Booth, commenting on gospel invitations as recorded in Scripture:

Here we have, not only the apostles of Christ, but Christ himself; and, in his ambassadors, even the divine Father, inviting, persuading, entreating the polluted, impoverished, perishing wretches, to regard the vicarious work of Christ, as the only ground of their justification; and the plentiful provisions of divine grace, as containing all that is wanted for their complete happiness. These invitations, therefore, may be justly considered as a direct and perfect *warrant* for sinners of every nation, and of every character, that are indulged with the joyful news, to believe in Jesus... If the gospel is not a complete *warrant* for the most ungodly to believe in Jesus, it must be either because the grace revealed in it is not equal to their wants; or because they are tacitly forbidden, while destitute of holiness, to treat him as the Saviour.[231] Not the former; for the grace revealed is rich, abundant, exceedingly abundant and all-sufficient. Not the latter; for the ungodly... so far from being prohibited, are invited to Christ, and earnestly entreated, by a consideration of his vicarious death, to be reconciled to God (Is. 45:22; 55:1; Matt. 11:28; 2 Cor. 5:20)... Does anyone ask: 'What is my WARRANT [emphasis Booth's] for believing in Jesus Christ?' The answer is... not anything done by you, not anything wrought in you; but the word of grace, or the testimony of God concerning Jesus. Well, reader, what do you think of Christ, and of this gracious *warrant* for the ungodly to believe in him?[232]

William Cunningham:

The sole *ground* or *warrant* for men's act, in offering pardon and salvation to their fellow-men, is the authority and command of God in his word. We have no other *warrant* than this; we need no other; and we should seek or desire none; but on this *ground* alone should consider ourselves not only *warranted*, but bound, to proclaim to our fellow-men, whatever be their... condition, the good news of the kingdom, and to call upon them to come to Christ that they may be saved, the Bible affording us sufficient, indeed, abundant materials for convincing them that, in right reason, they ought to do this, and for assuring them that all who do, shall obtain eternal life. But this has manifestly nothing to do with the question, as to the *ground* or *warrant* of God's act in making unlimited offers, and in *authorising* us to make them.[233]

The warrant, as Cunningham said, 'is the authority and command of God in his word'.

Durham:

Christ's death for you is not the formal *ground* nor *warrant* of your faith, nor yet of the offer of the gospel, but [that ground is] the Lord's will *warranting* you to believe, and calling for it from you, and his commanding you to rest upon Christ for the attaining of righteousness, as he is offered to us in the gospel. We are invited by his command and promise, and we are not first called to believe that Christ died for us, but we are called first to believe in him that is offered to us in the gospel; that is our duty. And folks are not condemned because Christ died not for them, but because when he offered the benefit of his death and sufferings to them, they slighted and rejected it. We are to look first to what Christ calls to, and not to meddle with the other; that is, whom Christ [intended] in his death, till we have done the first. The word bids all believe that they may be saved; and such as neglect this command will be found disobedient... Though Christ has not died for all, yet all that flee unto him by faith, shall be partakers of his death; and from this you should reason, and not from his intention in [that is, the extent of the atonement he accomplished in his] dying.[234]

As Haldane said: 'The good shepherd laid down his life for the sheep, and for them alone, and at the same time commanded the gospel to be preached to every creature'.[235] What does this mean? Just this:

The invitations of the gospel rest upon the Lord's express commandment [Mark 16:15]... This precept is illustrated by the practice of the apostles... Wherever they went, they addressed men indiscriminately... In like manner, the sinner's warrant to trust in Christ for salvation, is not his own [or the preacher's] speculations about the sufficiency of the atonement, but the positive assurance that whosoever will may come and take of the water of life freely. The word of God alone is the warrant of our faith; his purpose to save few or many is not the rule of our obedience. The invitations of the gospel are [as] free as the air we breathe, as the light of heaven; and are to be addressed to all who come under the joyful sound. No qualification is required to entitle us to embrace them; they are clogged with no condition. Not only is the greatest rebel encouraged to come to Christ that he may have life, but he is urged to join in the invitation to his fellow-sinners [Rev. 22:17]... If we believe in Christ – if on the ground of the warrant of the word of God we trust in him for salvation – we have the assurance of being partakers of eternal life, as much as if we saw our names enrolled among God's elect...

The ground of faith, then, is not the extent of the atonement; it is the promise of pardon and eternal life through Jesus to all who believe, without distinction and without exception. Those for whom Christ did not lay down his life, if they come under the sound of the gospel, have the same warrant to believe as those whose sins were expiated on Calvary, whose names were written in the Lamb's book of life, and to whom, in the person of their great head and representative, God, who cannot lie, promised eternal life before the world began... The objection that there can be no *bona fide* invitation to sinners to receive pardon through faith in Christ unless atonement has been made for all, is founded on a variety of errors in regard to the gospel. In the first place, it proceeds on the erroneous supposition that God commands sinners to believe that an atonement has been made for their sins. Now, we have seen that the gospel merely invites[236] sinners to trust in Christ, with the assurance that in doing so they shall be saved. Men are never called in the first instance to believe that they are saved, or that they are of the number of the elect, or that an atonement has been made for their sins. The gospel merely [that is, simply] reveals the sacrifice offered upon the cross, with the assurance that reliance upon it is inseparably connected with salvation. This is a truth entirely independent of the extent of the atonement.[237]

R.Elliot, in his funeral sermon for Whitfield:

The scripture doctrine of election and predestination as we believe and preach it, is no discouragement to sinners, no bar to anyone's conversion; for our *warrant* to come to Christ is not God's secret decree and purpose concerning us, but his inviting, calling and commanding us in his word to repent and believe on Christ. No one indeed can prove or know his election, but by his conversion to God, and obeying the gospel. They that believe aright do not believe in Christ from consideration of their being elected, but from the consideration of their being lost sinners, [that is, the sort] whom Christ came to seek and to save. Neither do they who disobey the gospel, reject Christ and his salvation, from the consideration of their being reprobated, but because they love darkness rather than light, and voluntarily... choose the way that leads unto death. Nor will anyone be condemned at the last day, because God, in righteousness, sovereignly passed him by, and did not elect him in Christ, but because he would not obey God and come to Christ that he might have life... All true believers are God's elect; and... their believing is the fruit and effect of it. On the other hand, they that willingly continue in sin and unbelief to the last, do thereby prove themselves not to be of the number of God's elect, but of them whom he has justly reprobated. Let none of you therefore, through ignorance, stumble at this doctrine, but be persuaded to come to Christ, and you shall be saved.[238]

The warrant for making the free offer, I repeat, has nothing to do with the extent of Christ's atonement. Nothing at all.[239] Certainly, it is not that Christ died for all or that his redemption is sufficient for all.[240] As Owen said: 'Ministers of the gospel... being acquainted only with revealed things... are bound to... warn all men... giving the same commands, proposing the same promises, making tenders of Jesus Christ in the same manner, to all... From the general proposition of Christ in the promises, nothing can be concluded concerning his death for all to whom it is proposed'.[241] John Murray: 'The warrant a sinner has and must have is that which is undiscriminating – the invitation, command, demand, overture and promise of the gospel. The warrant is not any assurance that Christ has saved him'.[242]

5. Particular redemption, the free offer, and human logic

Here we come to the root problem in this discussion. How can we reconcile the free offer and particular redemption? The short answer is: We can't! God has not told us how.[243] But this is no reason to disobey God, and not freely offer Christ and salvation to sinners.[244] The fact is, as I have noted, our inability to explain the seeming contradiction over the free offer does not stop at particular redemption; total depravity,[245] unconditional election[246] and irresistible grace, too, it is argued, contradict the free offer, or must be ignored.[247] But there can be no contradiction between any of the five doctrines of grace and the free offer, nor dare we ignore any, since God has revealed all of them. There can be nothing in the free offer which compromises the decrees, nor *vice-versa*;[248] that is, nothing biblically. And though men raise rational arguments to play one against the other, we have to argue biblically, not on the basis of human reason. The fact is, God, in his word, has not explained how we are to reconcile the offer and the decrees; *nor has he required us to try.* While we are warranted in going as far as Scripture in explaining their connection,[249] we must renounce every attempt to explain away any aspect of these respective truths.[250] That a helpless sinner, a non-elect sinner, a sinner for whom Christ has not died, in whom the Spirit will not work effectually, is to be commanded and expected to obey the gospel, and be sincerely offered salvation, seems contradictory to human logic.[251] But so what? Is human reason to be the great arbiter of what we believe and do?[252] Human logic has to fall before Scripture, and the seeming inconsistency left with God.[253] The biblical response to the objection to the free offer – whether it be made on the grounds of total depravity, unconditional election, particular redemption or irresistible grace – is that all five doctrines of grace are part of God's revealed will, and although sinners are dead in sin, and only the elect will be saved, and Christ died only for the elect, and without the distinguishing irresistible work of the Spirit none will come, nevertheless the Bible teaches that all sinners must be offered salvation.[254] The right and proper answer, therefore, to any who would still cavil that the free offer and the other four cannot be reconciled by man, is: 'O man, who are you to reply against God?' (Rom. 9:20).[255]

To be specific and deal with the question in hand, since God has revealed that Christ accomplished a particular redemption, and that a free offer should be made to all sinners – that all sinners should be commanded to repent and believe – so be it. Since God does not give us an explanation of this, but simply states both, and leaves us with a paradox, that should be the end of the matter.[256]

But still the objector insists that the free offer compromises particular redemption. Why does he say it? Because his logic tells him it must be so. It tells him that a sincere free-offer – which is to all – needs an atonement which is likewise for all, an atonement which is equally effective – or at least sufficient – for all; otherwise, it is said, the offer cannot be sincere.[257] The objector, apparently, will not accept any doctrine, or do anything in obedience to God, unless his poor feeble mind can reconcile the various parts of God's teaching or command, and until his human logic can sort it all out and understand it all. I dealt very fully with this arrogant spirit in my *Offer*, so I will not repeat my arguments here. But that is what it is; it is sheer arrogance to say something cannot be right unless the human mind can grasp it.[258] Man has no right to demand an explanation where God has not provided one. What is more, once we take that path there will be no end of it. Thomas J.Nettles: 'The absolute particularity of the atonement needs no more apology [that is, justification or defence] than does... unconditional election... If the theologian must become enamoured with demonstrating how God's activity releases him from any likelihood of impugnation... election... [will] have to be defended in the same way'.[259] And so will irresistible grace.

If the objector is an *anxious* sinner who is on the point of coming to Christ, but is held back because he wonders if Christ died for him, then such a sinner needs kindly to be told some home truths. 'What if Christ has not died for me?',[260] must be met with: 'This is none of your business. Do not let Satan torment your mind, diverting your attention over it. No unbeliever has to know that Christ died for him, before he trusts him. Never was there an unbeliever who knew such a thing. The fact is, no unbeliever can know it. And such knowledge would not be saving, in any case'.[261] What is the sinner's business? 'You are in desperate need. Infinite mercy in Christ is being extended to you. You are invited to come to Christ and be saved. You are not saved by knowledge or understanding, or having all things sorted out in your mind. You need to trust Christ, now! Trust Christ, and you will know he has died for you! Come to him – he will cast out none that come (John 6:37)'. No sinner is saved because he knows he is elect, knows that Christ died for him, and knows that God will work irresistibly in him.[262] And it is no part of the free offer to try to get sinners to know it; such things are not knowable before faith in Christ. The sinner's sole responsibility is to repent and believe. 'The sinner's warrant to believe... is not the persuasion that Christ died for him'.[263] The sinner's warrant to believe is God's commanding of him to believe.[264]

If the objector is a *defiant* sinner, one who demands to know how the offer squares with particular redemption before he will believe (and, I pause to ask, is this a real case?),[265] such a sinner needs firmly to be told some home truths: 'You must come to God as a beggar, not as an equal demanding satisfaction of your every question before you deign to believe. If you are to be saved, it will be on God's terms, in God's way, and only in God's way. We dare not pander to your demand (indeed, if it really exists) to have every detail of the gospel reconciled to your satisfaction before you will believe. You must submit to Christ in the gospel, not sit in judgement upon God, demanding a justification for what he offers you, and how he offers it.[266] We command you to come to Christ. We warn you of your peril if you will not'. All such talk as: 'I would believe if I knew I was elect, I would believe if I knew God will effectively call me, I would believe if I knew Christ died for me', is nothing other than sheer arrogance. Though it sounds spiritual, it is anything but. No unbelieving sinner has ever been told God the Father elected him in particular, God the Son died for him in particular, God the Spirit will work in him in particular, and therefore he in particular must come. For a sinner to insist on such an assurance before he will believe, is an impertinence of the highest order.[267] He has no right to make such a demand, and no warrant or promise to expect God to satisfy it. Indeed, it is directly ruled out by Deuteronomy 29:29.[268]

Not only must we not pander to sinners by trying to answer questions they have no right to ask, and try to justify God – of which God has no need – or offer an apology for him – which is a blasphemy even to suggest – we must not give them such questions to ask. We have no business to light such a fire, and then feed it. And to try to justify God in this matter, to indulge the sinner, and boost his pride, at the very time he needs to be humbled and submit himself to Christ in the gospel, is catastrophic.[269] The sinner must not impose terms on God, as to how and what he can offer him, and on what basis. Nor must he be allowed to, or encouraged to.[270] The preacher should not be playing the defiant sinner's game here, fuelling his arrogance. The sinner must submit to God in his word, and bow the knee to him in Christ. If he will not do it now in the gospel unto salvation, as it offered to him, he will do so in the day of judgement (Isa. 45:23; Rom. 14:11; Phil. 2:9-11) to his condemnation, and he must be told as much.[271] This, too, is a part of the free offer. Those who will not submit to God in this, not only show a proud spirit; they hurt their own souls.[272]

And preachers who do delve into the decrees with sinners, and refuse to offer Christ to them, seem happy to pluck a harp with only one string: 'The elect have obtained it, and the rest were blinded' (Rom. 11:7). While this is a truth, it is not the whole truth; and Paul did not preach it, as far as I know, to sinners. I do not say we should not preach it to them, but I do say it is not the sum of gospel preaching to sinners. After all, God, who inspired Paul's statement (in Rom. 11:7), also declared, in the same context: 'All day long I have stretched out my hands to a disobedient and contrary people' (Rom. 10:21).[273]

In short, to fail to preach the free offer because we cannot reconcile it with total depravity, unconditional election, particular redemption or distinguishing grace – or, if the offer is preached, to think these cardinal doctrines will be compromised – is tragically wrong. Such objections are either misguided (though often well-intentioned), or else a gross misuse of the decrees to stifle the offer. When we are told: 'Sinners have no ability to believe, we do not know who the elect are, we do not know for whom Christ died, we do not know in whom the Spirit will work, therefore we cannot offer Christ to all', there is but one reply: It is a *non-sequiter*. Of course we do not know any of the afore-mentioned. No preacher knows the secret will of God – in particular whom God has elected and for whom Christ has died – but this is not of the slightest consequence in his addresses to sinners, because such knowledge is no part of preaching the gospel offer.[274] The extent of election and the atonement is hidden in the secret will of God, and does not belong to us (Deut. 29:29), but we do know we have to offer Christ to all. How the sovereign God will work it all out, is none of our business. On the day of judgement, we will not be held accountable for our inability to explain all the mysteries of God – but we will be held accountable if we have not obeyed our Master, and preached his gospel as we should (Ezek. 33:1-9; Acts 20:20-27; 1 Cor. 9:16).[275]

As I have noted, the demand for a logical resolution of the biblical paradox is the fundamental issue in this debate about the free offer. What is more, reader, this demand has tentacles which reach so far, and so effectively strangle the preaching of the gospel, that, in hope of saying something to encourage the hesitant to break its choking grip, I must trespass a little more on your time. Sadly, some preachers who would like to be able to reconcile particular redemption and the free offer, wishing to be free in their addresses to sinners, are still unsure and nervous: 'Unless the redemption is universal, how can the offer be?' Reader, if you are one such, listen to J.L.Dagg: 'If the difficulty... should perplex us, we may obtain relief, as we are compelled to do... by receiving the whole of God's truth on his authority, even though the harmony of its parts is not apparent to our weak understandings. In this way, theological difficulties furnish an opportunity for the exercise of confidence in the divine veracity; and our state of mind is never better or safer than when, in simple faith, we take God at his word'.[276] Just so. We need the humility, *and the faith*, to submit our poor reason to God's sovereign declarations. Nor must we be afraid to tell sinners we cannot reconcile these things. We must let them know that we, like them, have to bow to God in his word, and obey the gospel. And this we gladly do. It matters not that we cannot reconcile it all. We have to accept what God says, and obey him, trusting him through every paradox which this leads us into. This is not only the right course; it is the best; indeed, it is the *biblical* course. God's command and promise is the warrant and basis of the free offer – the warrant for us to offer Christ to sinners, and the warrant for them to receive him.[277]

Dagg again:

If [since] God's word teaches the doctrine of election, and if [since] it contains commands or invitations to all men to seek salvation through Christ, it is highly presumptuous in us to charge God with insincerity, because we cannot reconcile the two things with each other. We ought to remember that we are worms of the dust, and that it is criminal arrogance in us to judge and condemn [or prescribe to] the infinite God. But, in truth, there is no ground whatever for this charge of insincerity. God requires all men to believe in Christ; and this is their duty, however unwilling they may be to perform it. The fact that they are unwilling, and that God knows they will remain unwilling, unless he changes their hearts, abates nothing from the sincerity of the requirement. God proves his sincerity, by holding them to the obligation, and condemning their unbelief. He promises salvation to all who believe in Christ; and he proves his sincerity by fulfilling his promise in every instance. The bestowment of special grace, changing the hearts of men, and bringing them to believe in Christ, is, in no respect, inconsistent with any requirement or promise that God has made... When [men] regard [the call of the gospel] as a solemn requirement of duty, for which God will certainly hold them accountable, they will find no occasion for calling his sincerity in question.

Not only does this apply to total depravity, election and irresistible grace; the same goes for particular redemption:

Some have maintained that, if the atonement of Christ is not general, no sinner can be under obligation to believe in Christ, until he is assured that he is one of the elect. This implies that no sinner is bound to believe what God says, unless he knows that God designs to save him. [Yet] God declares that there is no salvation, except through Christ; and every sinner is bound [obliged] to believe this truth. If it was revealed from heaven, that but one sinner, of all our fallen race, shall be saved by Christ, the obligation [duty] to believe that there is no salvation out of Christ [and this is Christ's and the apostles' teaching (John 14:6; Acts 4:12)], would remain the same. Every sinner... would be bound [obliged as his duty] to look to Christ as his only possible hope, and commit himself to that sovereign mercy by which some one of the justly condemned race would be saved [*cf.* Esther 4:16]. [Now] the abundant mercy of our God will not be confined to the salvation of a single sinner, but it will bring many sons to glory through the sufferings of Jesus, the Captain of our salvation. Yet every sinner, who trusts in Christ for salvation, is bound [obliged as his duty] to commit himself, unreservedly, to the sovereign mercy of God. *If he requires some previous assurance that he is in the number of the elect, he does not surrender himself to God, as a guilty sinner ought.* The gospel brings every sinner prostrate at the feet of the great sovereign, hoping for mercy at his will, and in his way; and the gospel is perverted when any terms short of this are offered to the offender. With this universal call to absolute and unconditional surrender to God's sovereignty, the doctrine of particular redemption exactly harmonises.[278]

I repeat Dagg's excellent response to the demand for reconciliation of the paradox since some charge God with insincerity in the offer: 'There is no ground whatever for this charge of insincerity'. And far from trying to justify God, Dagg baldly set out the true biblical warrant for the free offer: 'God requires all men to believe in Christ; and this is their duty, however unwilling they may be to perform it'. Above all, as I am trying to show at this time, he spelled out the grievous consequences of applying human logic to the offer: Whereas 'the gospel brings every sinner prostrate at the feet of the great sovereign, hoping for mercy at his will, and in his way... *the gospel is perverted when any terms short of this are offered to the offender*'. In short: 'With this universal call to absolute and unconditional surrender to God's sovereignty, the doctrine of particular redemption exactly harmonises'. All talk of not being able to reconcile the offer with the decrees, and to think this means we cannot make a free offer, is wide of the mark. It is tragic.

There is another factor to be borne in mind; an important factor, at that. To admit that we cannot reconcile these things, is not to say the same about God. Indeed, he has no need to reconcile them. There is no contradiction at all. As I said in my *Offer*, and have re-stated in this work: 'To God, there is no conflict whatsoever; the conflict is... entirely and only... as it seems to us'.[279] *There is no contradiction at all*, I say again.

In short, as Robert M'Cheyne Edgar concluded, there are only two positions. The first is to say this is an impossibility; if the atonement is limited, (and if man is totally depraved, and God has unconditionally elected those who are to be saved), the offer cannot be general and sincere. But there is a second position:

> We may believe it possible for the Almighty to reconcile a limited atonement with a general offer, and that he will do so in his own good time, while our duty meanwhile is to proclaim the gospel fully and freely upon the ground of this assurance... It is the attitude of trust. It is the resolve to walk by faith, and not by sight, in this high mystery. The advocates of a universal atonement [whether or not a provisional or sufficient atonement], on the other hand, refuse to give God credit for the ability to make reconciliation between the defined and limited atonement and the general offer of his gospel. They seem to think that the skein becomes too tangled for the divine fingers, that the... [attributes] of God are insufficient as a guarantee against a collision between the electing decree [and/or total depravity, particular

redemption and irresistible grace] and the general offer of the gospel.[280]

It is not only 'the advocates of a universal atonement' who 'refuse to give God credit for the ability to make reconciliation between the defined and limited atonement and the general offer of his gospel'! Edgar's comments apply just as much to those staunch advocates of particular redemption who, though right on that truth, nevertheless misapply it to rule out a free offer. And this leads to the final point.

6. Particular redemption does not rule out the free offer – quite the reverse

Above all, to think that free offer is ruled out by particular redemption (or any other of the five points of Calvinism), is to do more than make a tragic mistake; it is to turn the truth on its head,[281] for it is only within the Calvinistic framework that the free offer can be made.[282] These self-same doctrines, far from hindering the free offer, are its very backbone.[283]

Not least, I say, particular redemption. John Murray:

It is frequently objected that [particular redemption] is inconsistent with the full and free offer of Christ in the gospel. This is a grave misunderstanding and misrepresentation. The truth really is that *it is only on the basis of [particular redemption] that we can have a free and full offer of Christ to lost men.* What is offered to men in the gospel? It is not the possibility of salvation, not simply the opportunity of salvation. What is offered is salvation. To be more specific, it is Christ himself in all the glory of his person, and in all the perfection of his finished work who is offered. And he is offered as the one who made expiation for sin and wrought redemption. But he could not be offered in this capacity or character if he had not secured salvation and accomplished redemption... *It is the very doctrine that Christ procured and secured redemption that invests the free offer of the gospel with richness and power... It is because Christ procured and secured redemption that he is an all-sufficient and suitable Saviour.* It is *as such* he is offered.[284]

As Murray said elsewhere: 'The doctrines of particular election, differentiating love [and] limited atonement do not erect any fence around the offer in the gospel'. Murray referred to the time when Christ, speaking of God's sovereignty in hiding the gospel from some and revealing it to others, immediately called the weary and heavy laden to come to him (Matt. 11:25-30). 'The lesson is that it is not merely [the] conjunction of [the] differentiating and sovereign will with [the] free overture, but that *the free overture comes out from the differentiating sovereignty* of both Father and Son. It is on the crest of the wave of divine sovereignty that the unrestricted summons comes to the labouring and heavy laden'.[285] And, reader, make no mistake, the invitation (or command) in the passage is unrestricted.[286] Thus the freeness of the offer not only goes hand-in-hand with God's sovereignty; it flows out of it. Christ confirmed it, speaking of both in the same breath.

John Calvin on the passage (Matt. 11:25-30):

> That all do not obey the gospel arises from no want of power on the part of God, who could easily have brought all the creatures into subjection to his government... That some arrive at faith, while others remain hardened and obstinate, is accomplished by his free election; for, drawing some, and passing by others, he alone makes a distinction among men, whose condition by nature is alike.

How do many react to such teaching? As Calvin said, like this:

> Many persons, as soon as they learn that none are heirs of eternal life but those whom God 'chose before the foundation of the world' (Eph. 1:4), begin to enquire anxiously how they may be assured of God's secret purpose, and thus plunge into a labyrinth, from which they will find no escape.

And what does Christ say to such? 'Christ enjoins them to come direct to himself, in order to obtain the certainty of salvation'. In short, the proper deduction from all this, said Calvin, 'the meaning therefore is':

> That life is exhibited to us in Christ himself, and that no man will partake of it who does not enter by the gate of faith. We now see that [Christ] connects faith with the eternal predestination of God – two things which men foolishly and wickedly hold to be inconsistent with each other. Though our salvation was always hidden with God, yet Christ is the channel through which it flows to us, and we receive it by faith.[287]

And what of Gill? While not for a moment suggesting that he believed in the free offer(!), nevertheless it is clear that in Matthew

11:25-30 Gill saw God's sovereignty and invitations to sinners running in tandem:[288]

[Christ speaks of] the sovereignty of his Father in the conversion of men... He... leaves [some] men to their own darkness and blindness; so that they cannot see, perceive and understand the beauty, glory, excellency and suitableness of the doctrines of [the gospel]. Now when Christ confesses this, or gives thanks to God for it, it is a declaration that God has done so, and denotes his acquiescence in it... To [others] God reveals... Christ, and all the blessings of grace in him, the mysteries of the gospel, and the unseen glories of another world. The veil of darkness and ignorance is removed from them; spiritual sight is given them... their desires are raised after them; their affections are set on them; their hearts are impressed with them; and they are helped to view their interest in them... Here the word designs [denotes] the sovereign counsel and purpose of God, to which, and to which only, our Lord refers the different dispensations of God towards the sons of men... All the elect of God are delivered to [Christ], to be kept and saved by him; all... to whom it was the Father's will to reveal the mysteries of grace, were his care and charge... and all the glory and happiness of his people, are put into his hands... all that he was to do and suffer for his people, all that he... should communicate to and bestow upon them... Christ having signified that the knowledge of God, and the mysteries of grace, are only to be come at through him, and that he has all things relating to the peace, comfort, happiness and salvation of men in his hands, kindly invites and encourages souls to come unto him for the same.[289]

This is it: 'Christ *having signified* that the knowledge of God, and the mysteries of grace, are only to be come at through him, and that he has all things relating to the peace, comfort, happiness and salvation of men in his hands, *kindly invites and encourages souls to come unto him* for the same'. That is, Christ, having frankly declared the sovereignty of God in grace, freely invites sinners to himself, showing that the sovereignty of God in election and particular redemption, far from contradicting the free offer, is its very life and power.

Edward Griffin captured the note. The sovereignty of God hinders the free offer? Far from it! Having spelled out the distinguishing grace of God which led to the glorious finished work of Christ, and the gift of the Spirit to bring... Reader, I pause; 'to bring'... 'to bring' *what*, do you think? Christ redeemed the elect only; he sent out the Holy Spirit. To do *what*? Griffin went on:

> Christ... sent out the Holy Spirit to bring invitations to a universal world, and to subdue as many as the Father had given him... It was God and not man who undertook to provide that the gospel should be preached to every nation under heaven.

Pulling no punches over the sovereignty of God – 'God has taken into his own hands the salvation of every individual of his elect. It belongs to him to awaken the conscience... to convince of sin... to subdue the resistance which the heart is sure to make to the calls of the Spirit' – even so – no! – because of this! – Griffin freely called to sinners. Using the doctrines of grace, not as a barrier, but as a stimulus, he cried:

> Here also is the only hope of unrenewed sinners. Come hither you mixed multitude of impenitent men, and contemplate the only chance [opportunity][290] which remains for your salvation. Unless that God whom you have made your enemy by wicked works, undertakes for you, all heaven and earth cannot save you. Unless that God whom you daily disobey... to whom you refuse to cry for relief – unless he in mercy to your poor perishing souls, begins and carries on and completes your salvation, you are undone for eternity. Will you any longer treat your only helper with so much neglect and abuse? Remember that you are in his hands. One frown from him and you are plunged into eternal woe; one smile from him and you live for ever. O realise your condition. Hasten to cast yourselves at his feet. 'Seek the Lord while he may be found; call upon him while he is near. Let the wicked forsake his way, and the unrighteous man his thoughts; and let him return to the Lord, and he will have mercy upon him, and to our God, for he will abundantly pardon'. Amen.[291]

* * *

These, then, are the general principles which make up the answer to the objection to the free offer based on the fact that Christ did not die for all men. As I have shown, it is no part of the free offer to tell men that Christ died for them in particular – nor do they have to believe it. No! In the free offer, sinners are to be told that if they repent and trust Christ – he who died for sinners – they will receive full salvation in him. They are to be invited and commanded to come, being warned that if they do not, but refuse the invitation and disobey the command, they will perish. What is more, it is sinners as sinners who are to be given the free offer, invitation and command; not as sinners elect or redeemed. In addition, the warrant for the free offer does not lie in God's decrees, but in the plain word of God; not in God's secret purposes, but in his revealed commands. True, the free offer appears to run counter to human logic in light of particular redemption, but this is nothing out of the ordinary; as always, human logic has to fall before Scripture. Finally, particular redemption – far from ruling out the free offer – is its backbone.

These are the general principles. Now to apply them to the three specific forms of the objection to the free offer.

The General Principles Applied to the Three Forms of the Objection

Having set out the general principles in answer to the objection that particular redemption rules out the free offer, I now want to apply these principles briefly to the three groups of Calvinists who make it: 1. The hyper-Calvinist who says the free offer depends on universal redemption. 2. The Amyraldian who says it depends on a universally sufficient but conditional redemption planned by God. 3. The Owenite who says it depends on a universally sufficient redemption arising from Christ's intrinsic worth.[292]

1. The general principles applied to the hyper-Calvinist's objection: The free offer requires, or leads to, a universal redemption

Of course, if the free offer *does* demand a universal atonement, or leads to it, then the free offer must be wrong. Since the Bible knows only a definite, particular redemption, anything which undermines it must be ruled out.

But I categorically deny that the basis of the free offer is universal redemption. And I challenge all who think it is to produce one biblical example of a gospel invitation or command based upon universal redemption. Where in Scripture are we told, that since Christ died for all, we must preach the gospel to all? May we be given the scriptures where, on the basis that Christ has died for all, sinners are exhorted to trust him? and preachers, on that basis, are warranted to call them to faith and repentance? It cannot be done, *for it is no part of the gospel offer to tell sinners that Christ died for all men.* As their recorded discourses in Acts make clear, Peter did not do it (Acts 2:14-41; 3:12-26; 4:8-12; 5:29-32,42; 8:22; 10:34-43), nor Stephen (Acts 7:2-53), nor Philip (Acts 8:5,35), nor Paul (Acts 13:16-41; 14:15-17; 16:31; 17:22-31; 20:18-35; 22:1-21; 24:10-21,25; 26:2-29; 28:23-28). But we know they preached

Christ, salvation through the grace and gift of Christ, the uniqueness of Christ, and – above all, the resurrection of Christ[293] – commanding sinners universally to repent and believe, assuring their hearers that all who did turn to Christ and trust him would be saved, and so on (Acts 2:36,38; 4:12; 5:31,42; 10:43; 13:38-39; 14:21; 16:31; 17:18,30; 18:5,28; 20:20-21; 26:20), that by the grace of Christ, both Jew and Gentile would be saved (Acts 15:11),[294] and they saw thousands converted. That is, they preached the free offer, and with success, *but they never told any congregation that Christ died for all men*; certainly they never said to any unbelievers[295] that Christ died for all men, including *them*. Indeed, when addressing unbelievers, they never even broached the extent of the atonement.[296]

I realise (like me), of course, hyper-Calvinists do not believe in universal redemption. I also know (unlike me) they object to the free offer. They do so because, they say, it inevitably leads to universal redemption; a free offer must be based upon a universal atonement. But this argument, arising from the desire to be logically consistent at all costs, is false. I repeat what I said earlier: The only ground for making the free offer is the plain command of the word of God; this is its warrant. It has nothing to do with the extent of the atonement; it certainly does not require a universal atonement. It is wrong to tell sinners: 'Christ desires and wants you so much that he has died for you'; it was wrong of Ella to attribute such a sentiment to the free-offer preacher.[297]

Haldane:

It is said the free and unlimited proclamation of the gospel to sinners of mankind is founded on the universality of the atonement; but such is not the case... The notion that the universal proclamation of pardon can only be made on the supposition that Christ died for all, precedes from a false view of what we are commanded to believe [and preach]. The Scripture does not tell us that Christ died for any particular individual; therefore no man is required, in the first instance [that is, before coming to Christ], to believe that Christ died for him. [Indeed, as I have explained, he cannot]... The truth which we are commanded to believe [and preach], cannot be affected by the reception which it experiences. The gospel announces that Christ came into the world to save sinners; it says to all and to each individual who hears it: 'Believe in the Lord Jesus Christ, and you shall be saved'. It proclaims a free pardon to all who will receive it through faith in the blood of Christ... Men are constantly prone to err on the right hand or on the left. While one class who profess the truth have, in order to simplify the gospel, represented the atonement as having being offered [by Christ on the cross] for those that are [ultimately] lost, as well as for the saved,[298] another class [that is, hyper-Calvinists] – who possess much acquaintance with the truth, and who know that the good shepherd laid down his life only for his sheep [and do not speculate about its sufficiency] – object to address[ing] the gospel to all men indiscriminately. They justly hold that the atonement was made exclusively for the church, and from this they infer that there is no ground for preaching salvation indiscriminately, and beseeching men to be reconciled to God. The error on both sides springs from the same source, *viz.* resting the proclamation of salvation upon our speculations as to the sufficiency of the atonement, and not being satisfied with the positive commandment to preach the gospel to every creature, [as] illustrated by the example of the first ministers of the word.[299]

I agree with John Bonar who had no sympathy with 'those who think that... universal offers imply universal atonement as the ground of these offers... [who] think... that the salvation of Christ cannot be consistently offered to all unless the atonement was made alike for all – alike for those that perish and for those that shall be saved; in a word, that... God's offering [Christ to all] supposes redemption wrought... for all'. Bonar was rightly adamant:

No!... We dare neither [limit] what God has left general [that is, the invitation of the gospel], nor make universal what God has made definite [that is, redemption] – we dare not say that Christ died as much for Judas and those who perish, as he did for Paul and those who in heaven are recording for ever his grace in loving them and giving himself for them – but we dare [to] say that Christ is offered to all – freely, truly, fully, and, to all the ends of salvation, offered to all.[300] We dare [to] say that God [was] in Christ reconciling the world to himself, and not imputing to men their trespasses; and, as ambassadors of Christ, yes, as if God did beseech men by us, as in Christ's stead we do beseech men to be reconciled to God... Our views of the nature of the atonement, and the foreordination of God, does [*sic*] not in the least affect our free and full offer of the gospel to all, because we do what God has commanded us to do, knowing that he has commanded, and that he will do as he has said, and that whosoever believes shall be saved... It is the command of God to offer Christ... It is the command of God to receive him... It is the invitation of God to come to him; and it is the promise of God that whosoever comes shall in no wise be cast out.[301]

William Gouge: 'Though Christ is, by the outward dispensation of God's ordinances, offered to all, yet may it not thence be inferred that Christ actually died for all. The offer is made to all, without exception of any that, among those all, they for whom Christ was indeed given might believe'.[302]

Owen rightly rejected the notion that the free offer implies a universal redemption: 'Their objection... is vain, who affirm that God has given Christ for all to whom he offers Christ in the preaching of the gospel; for his offer in the preaching of the gospel' is not an indication of God's purpose but of the sinner's duty. Owen was quite clear about it: Though 'the Lord has given his Son only to [and for] his elect', ministers, not knowing God's secret purpose, or who the elect are, yet desiring good for all men, 'may make a proffer of Jesus Christ, with life and salvation in him'. Indeed, it is their calling and duty to make a free offer of Christ to all sinners, even though the atonement is not universal: 'They command and invite all to repent and believe... they make proffers and tenders in the name of God to all'. 'This offer is neither vain nor fruitless, being declarative of their duty'.[303]

Cunningham tackled what I am denying; namely, 'the alleged necessity of a universal atonement, or of Christ having died for all men, as the only consistent ground or basis on which the offers and invitations of the gospel can be addressed indiscriminately to all men'. He began by conceding some undoubted facts:

> We fully admit the general fact upon which the argument is based – namely, that in Scripture, men, without distinction and exception, have salvation, and all that leads to it, offered or tendered to them – that they are invited to come to Christ and to receive pardon – and assured that all who accept the offer, and comply with the invitation, shall receive everything necessary for their eternal welfare. We fully admit that God in the Bible does all this, and authorises and requires us to do the same in dealing with our fellow-men.

Just so. But, as he said, regarding 'the consistency of a limited atonement with unlimited offers and invitations of gospel mercy, or of the alleged necessity of a universal atonement as the only ground or basis on which such offers and invitations can rest', there are two questions which have to be answered. He spelled them out:

First, is an unlimited atonement necessary in order to warrant ministers of the gospel, or any who may be seeking to lead others to the saving knowledge of the truth, to offer to men, without exception, pardon and acceptance, and to invite them to come to Christ? And, *secondly*, is an unlimited atonement necessary in order to warrant God in addressing, and authorising and requiring us to address, such universal offers and invitations to our fellow-men?... It is the first question with which we have... to do, as it affects a duty which we are called upon to discharge; while the second is evidently, from its very nature, one of those secret things which belong unto the Lord.

Take the first question – do *we* require a universal atonement to warrant *us* making the free offer? Certainly not:

It is very evident that our conduct, in preaching the gospel, and in addressing our fellow-men with a view to their salvation, should not be regulated by any inferences of our own[304] about the nature, extent and sufficiency of the provision actually made for saving them, but solely by the directions and instructions which God has given us, by precept or example, to guide us in the matter... God has commanded the gospel to be preached to every creature; he has required us to proclaim [it] to our fellow-men, of whatever character and in all varieties of circumstances... to hold out to them, in his name, pardon and acceptance through the blood of atonement – to invite them to come to Christ, and to receive him – and to accompany all this with the assurance that 'whosoever comes to him, he will in no wise cast out'. God's revealed will is the only rule, and ought to be held to be the sufficient warrant for all that we do in this matter, in deciding what is our duty, in making known to our fellow-men what are their privileges and obligations, and in setting before them reasons and motives for improving the one and discharging the other. And though this revelation does not warrant us in telling them that Christ died for all and each of the human race – a mode of preaching the gospel never adopted by our Lord and his apostles – yet it does authorise and enable us to lay before men views and considerations, facts and arguments, which, in right reason, should warrant and persuade all to whom they are addressed, to lay hold of the hope set before them, to turn into the stronghold as prisoners of hope.

And then the second question – does the free offer require a universal atonement so that *God* can be cleared of the accusation of insincerity? Cunningham first spelled out the charge:

The second question, as to the conduct of God in this matter, leads into much greater difficulties – but difficulties which we are not bound, as we have no ground to expect to be able, to solve. The position of our opponents is... that it [is] not possible for God, because [it is] not consistent with integrity and uprightness, to address such offers and invitations to men indiscriminately, unless an atonement... [has] been presented and accepted on behalf of all men, of each individual of the human race.

To this assertion, Cunningham replied:

God does not, in offering pardon and acceptance to men indiscriminately, act inconsistently or deceptively, though it is not true that the atonement was universal... And although difficulties will still remain in the matter, which cannot be fully solved, it is easy to show that they just resolve into the one grand difficulty of all religion and of every system of theology – that, namely, of reconciling, or rather of developing, the consistency between the supremacy and sovereignty of God, and the free agency and responsibility of man.[305]

And this 'difficulty', as I have said time and again, is a difficulty for us, but not for God, and it is one to which we have to submit ourselves in humble trust and obedience to his revealed word until the great day.[306] In other words, we preach the free offer and hold to particular redemption, and leave the reconciliation of the two to God.

It can be done, it has been done, and it must be done. Brownlow North, for instance, was one who rightly 'did not preach universal redemption, but regarded Christ as dying as the representative of his covenant people'; yet this 'did not in the least fetter him in making the fullest and freest offer of the great sacrifice to every sinner'.[307]

Of course not! Particular redemption is not the least hindrance to preaching the free offer to sinners. Quite the reverse! As Thomas Shepard declared:

There is a universal offer to all people where the gospel comes. Enemies are entreated to be reconciled; for though [Christ] has not died for all, yet now being king, such is his excellency, that he is worthy of

> [being received by] all. Hence [he] commands all to receive him; and if [since] [it] is a condemning sin to reject him, it is then a command [which] lies upon you to receive him... *Neither does this universal offer infer [*sic*, imply] a universal redemption*, for the gospel, in the offer of it, does not speak absolutely that Christ has died for all, and therefore for you, as the Arminians maintain, but it speaks conditionally.[308] It is for you, if ever the Lord gives you a heart to receive that grace there... *Objection.* But I am not elected, nor redeemed; if I knew that, I [would] dare [to] receive the Lord and his love. *Answer*. What have you to do with God's secret decree of election?... It may be you are redeemed... Receive this love, and it is certain it is for you.[309]

In short, I agree with Ernest Kevan: 'A universal offer does not imply a universal redemption'.[310]

2. The general principles applied to the Amyraldian's objection: The free offer requires a universal redemption, provisional for all, but conditional on faith

I have given my reasons for denying that the redemption Christ wrought is a universally-sufficient redemption, conditional or provisional on faith. If these arguments stand, clearly such a redemption cannot be the basis of the free offer. I challenge all who think it is to produce one biblical example of a gospel invitation or command based upon it. Where in Scripture are we told that since Christ died provisionally for all, we must preach the gospel to all?[311] May we be given the scriptures where, on the basis of Christ dying conditionally for all, sinners are exhorted to come to Christ? It cannot be done, for *it is no part of the gospel offer to tell sinners that Christ died conditionally for all men.* As before, the only ground for making the free offer is God's command. It has nothing to do with the extent of the atonement; it certainly does not require a conditional atonement for all.

But still the objector insists it does. Who says? The Amyraldian.[312] Why does the Amyraldian say it? Because his logic tells him it must be so. It tells him that a sincere free offer – which is to all – needs an atonement which is likewise for all, a conditional atonement, sufficient for all; otherwise, it is said, the offer cannot be sincere.[313] As the hyper-Calvinist, so the Amyraldian demands a reconciliation of the free offer and the extent of atonement. I repeat what I said earlier: 'O man, who are you to reply against God?' (Rom. 9:20). Particular redemption and the universal offer *are* biblical doctrines, and it matters not that we cannot reconcile the two. We have to accept what God says, and obey him in his word. This is the warrant and basis of the free offer.

Haldane:

Those who hold [to] universal atonement, and at the same time admit the doctrine of election [that is, Amyraldians]... tell us Christ died for all, and therefore the gospel is to be preached to all; but they acknowledge that it is only given to a certain number to believe in the Saviour. They admit that, while God beseeches men to be reconciled, he at the same time gives the Spirit – which is as necessary to salvation as the work of Christ – only to those whom he has fore-ordained to eternal life. How, then, can they charge inconsistency on those [like me – JH, DG and others] who maintain that Christ purchased the church – and the church alone – with his own blood? Both acknowledge that the invitations of the gospel are addressed to all in the most unlimited degree; both hold that it is not the purpose of God that all should be saved. The one side maintains that only those for whom the Redeemer stood as surety will listen to the voice of mercy; while the other asserts that although the redemption of all has been purchased, and the sins of all expiated, divine sovereignty restricts salvation to [the elect]. Thus we see that universal atonement removes no difficulty; it still leaves the objection unanswered – [as to] why the gospel is commanded to be preached to the whole world, while divine sovereignty restricts the benefit to a limited number; [God] bestowing only upon some [the necessary] grace to believe, although the Son of God [is said to have borne] the sins of all [mankind] in his own body upon the tree, notwithstanding which, the [non-elect] neither become dead to sin, nor live unto righteousness.[314]

The same goes for effectual calling:

Since it is admitted that the work of the Spirit is as necessary as the work of Christ – that those only whom the Father draws will come to Christ – where is the difficulty of reconciling the universality of the invitations with the veracity of God? It is granted that only a certain number have been elected to eternal life, and that they alone shall be saved. If the doctrine of election does not interfere with the universal proclamation of pardon through faith in Jesus, why should we feel any difficulty in admitting that, while Christ has atoned only for the sins of his chosen people, the gospel should be preached to all mankind to whom we have access? If we knew for whom the atonement was made, or who are the elect, it would be idle to preach to any others; but this is a secret thing which belongs to God. He has told us that faith comes by hearing, and commanded us in the morning to sow our seed, and in the evening not to withhold our hand, for we know not which shall prosper, whether this or that, or whether they may not be both alike profitable. To give the increase is his exclusive prerogative.[315]

In short:

The matter in dispute between the advocates of universal[316] and limited atonement is not as to the number of the saved; both admit that the elect, and the elect alone, shall inherit eternal life; both admit that the gospel is to be addressed to every creature, and that it is only by the almighty power of the Holy Spirit that the alienation of the human heart is so far overcome as to lead us to receive Christ, and salvation in him. The point in dispute is, whether the atonement was made for all, or whether it was made only for the elect; whether it is effectual for all in whose behalf it was offered [by Christ], or whether [many] of those for whom Christ died... perish in their sins... [Now] salvation is the effect of divine sovereignty; both parties admit that God alone makes one to differ from another...
Pardon is proclaimed to all through faith in Christ, and the proclamation is made effectual by the Holy Spirit, for the salvation of all for whom the atonement was made... Thus men's reception of the gospel shows for whom the atonement was made. Election [that is, those who are elect] is a secret thing which belongs to God, but [the fact of] the salvation of all who believe, without exception, is revealed to us.[317]

Thus far, my reply is fundamentally the same as for the first objection. But in addition, as I have already explained, far from being the basis of a universal offer, the notion of a conditional universal redemption, in fact, does untold damage both to the gospel and to sinners. For a start, it boosts the sinner's pride. As he is coming to faith, he is inevitably encouraged to think of himself as meeting the condition to be redeemed, that he is fulfilling something which Christ has left undone. Christ established but a provisional atonement, and the sinner, by his faith, has to ratify it; so he is told. Thus his pride is encouraged. Yet, in addressing sinners, the preacher's task is to do the very opposite; he has to mortify the sinner's pride, and stop him looking to himself, boasting and bragging about what he can do; the need – and the difficulty – is to bring him to look to Christ alone for everything.[318] Thus, far from a conditional, universal and sufficient redemption being the basis of the free offer, it is a source of immense harm to the sinner at the very point where he is most exposed to pride in looking at his own abilities. 'Nothing in my hand I bring', has to be changed to: 'My faith I bring'.[319] And this must lead to the notion of salvation by works, in that the believing sinner is told he has fulfilled the condition which Christ's redemption left undone. And if that is not a ruination of the gospel, what is?

Furthermore, those who believe in a double redemption, have to divide their congregation, do they not? Or, at least, they do divide it. Now as I have made clear, a preacher should be a dividing preacher,[320] but on the right basis – believers and unbelievers. *But not on the basis of those who have been redeemed absolutely and those who have been redeemed conditionally*. When it comes down to it, how do Amyraldian preachers actually address their hearers? Do they speak *of* those who are elect, and thus redeemed effectively – and those who are not elect, but redeemed sufficiently and conditionally? or do they speak *to* them in these ways?[321] If so, what use is it to tell sinners that redemption is provided for all, but God has decreed to give only some – not all – the faith to trust the Redeemer? How does this leave the sinner in any better position than a particular, absolute and unconditional redemption for all the elect?[322] Indeed, he is in a far worse position. When he hears of this conditional redemption, he has to reason thus: 'The offer, after all, is empty. Christ's death, sufficient for me it may be, but am I one of those left to meet the condition and thus make the redemption effective? or am I one of the elect?' Reader, I cannot see how this can do anything but destroy the gospel, and be an immense hindrance to sinners going at once to the Saviour, and trusting him for all. It really takes the sinner into the hyper-Calvinistic camp – making him wonder whether or not he is elected, *before* he trusts the Saviour.[323]

It is worse. James Macgregor defined what he called 'the more malignant aspects of Amyraldianism'. I have already quoted the first; namely, the suggestion that God has a saving purpose which does not infallibly save. The second is its tendency 'to undermine the believer's assurance of hope' since 'many of those for whom

Christ gave his life shall nevertheless fall into death eternal'. The third is – and this will sound the most surprising – is 'to prevent unbelievers from coming to God in "full assurance of faith". It is at this third point that the Amyraldians deem themselves strongest... [but] it is at this point – their strongest [as they think] – that I find them weakest'. Why? Macleod explained:

[Amyraldianism] meant a new approach to the case of the anxious sinner when he was told that our Lord had died for him, and that he must right off receive this as the good news of salvation. This method of approach to him *hid* from the enquirer that when it said that the Saviour had died for him it might prove that he had died either in vain, or with no intention to effect his salvation. For the universal redemption which it taught was – on its own showing – a redemption that did not secure life. In this respect the method of treating the anxious played with the use of *deceitful* terms, and did not compare well with the method that had been formerly in use. This older method told the sinner of a Saviour who had died to save his chosen and called ones, and who was now calling and inviting him to make proof of his saving power by taking himself as the Lord his Righteousness, and so sheltering under the covert of his sacrifice and the shield of his intercession. The older Calvinism did not seek to assure the sinner that Christ had died his death [that is, that Christ had died for him in particular, as his substitute, dying the death he deserved] until he had first, in the obedience of faith, closed with him as a Saviour in his office as mediator.[324]

George Gillespie tackled Amyraldians – those he described as neither Arminian nor orthodox Calvinists, but who 'have found out a middle and singular way of their own, that Christ died for all men conditionally, *viz*., if they shall believe in him, that he has redeemed all on condition of faith'. 'One of their arguments is', he said, 'because otherwise we cannot encourage sinners to believe'. He put his finger on the spot:

When they give... encouragement to sinners upon this ground, that Christ has died for all upon condition of faith, it is to be remembered that... the generality of men can draw no result [conclusion] from the death of Christ (as it is set forth by their doctrine) but [other than] that... whosoever believes on him shall be saved, or that all men shall be saved, if all men believe... So what solid comfort can the soul have from that conditional proposition (which is all the encouragement they do or dare give from the death of Christ [for] all men) – all men shall be saved by Christ if they believe on him. Is it not as true and as certain (may a sinner [not] think within himself) that no man on earth shall be saved, if no man on earth believe; and, for my part, if I believe not, I shall be damned? If all this hang upon the condition of my believing... why, then, has Christ not merited [for] me, and will... not give me, the grace of believing? That new doctrine [Amyraldianism] answers, that Christ has merited faith,[325] and gives the grace of believing, not to all, but to the elect only; that God has, in his eternal decree, intended to pass by... part of mankind,[326] and to keep back from them that grace without which... they cannot believe on Jesus Christ; that though Christ meant that all men should have some sort of call to believe on him, and should be saved upon condition of their believing, yet he has no thought or intention, by his death, to procure unto all men [any man, in fact – see above] that grace without which they cannot believe. This doctrine of theirs, while it undertakes to comfort all men, and to encourage all to believe, it tells them... that all cannot be saved because all cannot believe, that God will not give faith, and so not salvation either, unto millions of sinners. What comfort is it, then, to know that all shall be saved if all believe, when men are told... that all shall not, cannot believe, and so shall not be saved?... Therefore their universal comfort taken from [their supposing of] Christ's dying for all men upon condition of faith, amounts to as much as nothing.[327]

Kennedy was another to speak of those 'Calvinists... [who] teach the doctrine of a double reference of the atonement; representing the atonement as offered in one sense for the elect, and in another sense for all. These maintain that there was a special atonement securing a certainty of salvation to some, and a universal atonement securing a possibility of salvation to all'. He argued against this 'double-reference' system, saying:

It endangers the whole doctrine of the atonement... [and] it is quite unavailing for the purpose to which it is applied. It doubtless sprang out of a desire to find a basis for the offer of Christ to all. To search for it, in a universal reference of the atonement, [indicates] a suspicion that the Calvinistic system [does] not afford it. What helpless ignorance such a suspicion indicates!... They [the Amyraldians] hesitate not to say that without the universal reference they could not preach the gospel at all – in other words, that this is the only basis they find for the call of the gospel. And what do they find there on which to base the offer? A reference [a mere conditional sufficiency for all] that avails for no definite end; that secures no redemption; and that leaves those whom it connects with the death of Christ to perish in their sins. This and no more they find: and on this they base the offer of the gospel! Really! if men cannot preach the gospel without this, it is difficult to see how this can help them.[328]

Haldane:

What difficulty, we ask, is got rid of, by asserting that the 'atonement included all, and the sins of all', when that Almighty power, which is as necessary to salvation as the atonement [itself], is withheld? Without atonement, there can be no salvation; the work of the Spirit, which is bestowed only upon the elect, is equally necessary, and therefore if the one is a palpable contradiction [of the universal invitation], what shall we say of the other?...
If the work of the Spirit is as essential to salvation as the work of Christ, an atonement having been made for all, brings no one nearer to the kingdom of God, for without the sovereign efficacious work of the Spirit, there is an absolute impossibility of a sinner's salvation; so that [the Amyraldian's professed] opening a door of hope for all, is only [like physically][329] uncovering a grave that the dead may come forth; it is [like physically] lighting a candle that the blind may see; it is [like physically] opening a door for a man without legs to walk out of prison.

In other words, it does not do the job. As Haldane went on to explain:

It is not for a moment supposed that either system[330] is free of difficulty... Both schemes agree in maintaining that the elect, and the elect alone, shall be saved; but while the adherents of the one [that is, Amyraldians] maintain that the atonement was made for *all*, they hold that it does not remove the guilt of *any* [of the non-elect], but merely lays a foundation for the general invitations of the gospel, which, they allege, could not have been made had not a universal atonement been offered [by Christ]. To this it is replied [by me – JH, DG and others], that an atonement which does not cancel guilt, is no atonement – it is a contradiction in terms; that, in order to preach peace to sinners through Jesus Christ, there is no necessity for a universal atonement, since, by the gospel, sinners are merely [simply] invited and commanded to trust in the blood of Jesus for pardon and eternal life – and thus the elect are separated from the reprobate by the gospel, which is to the one the power of God unto salvation, and to the other a stumbling-block and foolishness... It is evident that if the general invitations of the gospel are inconsistent with limited atonement, they must be equally so with personal election. It is admitted on both sides that none ever did or will

receive the love of the truth, excepting the elect; to what purpose, then, preach the gospel to all? The answer is: God has been pleased to appoint that by the gospel the elect should receive repentance unto life. Is there any greater difficulty in holding that those for whom the atonement was offered [by Christ on the cross] are made manifest precisely in the same manner?...
I am not careful [concerned] to vindicate the consistency of the exhortations and threatenings addressed to mankind [in the gospel], and I have very little anxiety about justifying the propriety of all being invited to receive salvation, while the atonement was made only for a part of mankind... Although I could give no explanation of the consistency of the two, I would hold both upon God's authority... While the Scripture declares that the death of Christ will be found amply sufficient for all who come to him, we never read of an indefinite sufficiency, which is so much insisted on by the advocates of universal atonement... All who come under the sound of the gospel are freely invited, warned and encouraged to flee from the wrath to come. None who come to Christ shall be rejected; but none do come except the Father draws them. All others reject the counsel of God against themselves... As to the question of the consistency of God's sovereignty and man's responsibility, I am fully satisfied with knowing that both are true, but I am not called [by God] to reconcile them.[331]

Reader, in all this, have I been straining out a gnat? Certainly not! Indeed, nothing could be further from the truth. As Haldane put it:

The difference between those who hold [to] particular redemption, and the advocates of the [Amyraldian] system, is highly important. So far from being a strife about words, it involves the very essence of the gospel. A universal atonement, by which all are not saved, is no atonement... If atonement were made for all, and yet many perish, none are saved by the atonement [*per se*] – they owe their salvation to something else... If Christ made atonement for sin, and if this atonement is universal, either all are justified, or the atonement has proved insufficient.[332]

In short, a universally sufficient but conditional redemption is not the basis of the free offer.

3. The general principles applied to the Owenite's objection: The free offer is based on a redemption which is sufficient for all because of its infinite worth

My reply starts as for the previous two objections. That is, I categorically deny that the basis of the free offer is the intrinsic sufficiency of Christ's redemption. And I challenge all who think it is to produce one biblical example of a gospel invitation or command based upon it. Where in Scripture are we told that, since Christ's death – because of the worth of his person – is sufficient for all, we must preach the gospel to all? May we be given the scriptures where, on that basis, sinners are exhorted to come to Christ? It cannot be done, for *it is no part of the gospel offer to tell sinners that Christ's death is sufficient for all men, and that on that basis they are to trust Christ*. The only ground for making the free offer is God's command. It has nothing to do with the extent of the atonement; it certainly is not based on a universally-sufficient atonement.[333]

But still the objector insists it is; or, at the very least, insists that it is strengthened by such an atonement. Who says? The Owenite. Why does he say it? Because his logic tells him it must be so. It tells him that a sincere free offer – which is to all – needs an atonement which, because of the infinite worth of Christ's person, is sufficient for all; otherwise, it is said, the offer is without foundation; the free offer is grounded on this supposed sufficient redemption. In effect, as with the hyper-Calvinist and the Amyraldian, the Owenite demands – or, at least, seeks – reconciliation of the free offer with the extent of the atonement. I repeat what I said earlier: 'O man, who are you to reply against God?' (Rom. 9:20). Particular redemption and the universal offer *are* biblical doctrines, and it matters not that we cannot reconcile the two. We have to accept what God says, and obey him in his word. This, and this alone, is the warrant for and basis of the free offer. Its 'sufficiency' does not come into it.[334] Those who would try to rationalise what the Bible reveals, but does not explain, must of necessity go outside Scripture. It ought not to be done; it must not be done. And to treat this rationalisation as the warrant for faith, and to preach it as such, is to introduce a dreadful distraction at the most sensitive point in the process of a sinner coming to Christ. Cunningham:

Some [the Owenites]... are accustomed to say that the ground or warrant for the universal or unlimited offers of pardon, and commands to believe, is the infinite intrinsic sufficiency of Christ's atonement, which they generally hold, though denying its universal intended destination or efficiency; while others profess to rest the universal offers and commands upon the simple authority of God in his word [my position precisely] – [he, God] making them himself, and requiring us [in our turn] to proclaim them to others.[335]

Having set out these two views, Cunningham exposed the flaw in the Owenite position:

In regard to the allegation often made... that this act of God is warranted by, and is based upon, the infinite intrinsic sufficiency of Christ's atonement, we would only remark... that we are not aware of any scripture evidence that these two things – namely, the universal intrinsic sufficiency and the unlimited offers – are connected in this way – that we have never been able to see how the assertion of this connection removed or solved the difficulty, or threw any additional light on this subject.

Just so. Cunningham drew the right conclusion:

Therefore, we think it best... to be contented with believing... that God in this, as in everything else, has chosen the best and wisest means of accomplishing all that he really intended to effect; and to be satisfied... with showing that it cannot be proved that there is any inconsistency or insincerity, that there is any injustice or deception on God's part in anything which he says or does in this matter, even though the intended destination of the atonement was to effect and secure the forgiveness and salvation of the elect only – even though he did not design or purpose, by sending his Son into the world, to save any but those who are saved.[336]

Cunningham was right;[337] the device does not resolve the paradox. It is as I have said; however fine it sounds, the concept of a redemption sufficient for all is, in the end, meaningless. It adds nothing to the gospel offer.[338] In fact, it detracts from it, because it detracts from the nature of the atonement. All this is grievous, and has serious consequences for the preaching of the gospel. What do I mean?

William Rushton:

> Whenever the Scriptures speak of the sufficiency of redemption [do they speak of it in the terms of this debate?], they always place it in the certain efficacy of redemption. The atonement of Christ is sufficient because it is absolutely efficacious, and because it carries salvation to all for whom it was made. It is sufficient, not because it affords men the possibility of salvation, but because, with invincible power, it accomplishes their salvation. Hence the word of God never represents the sufficiency of the atonement as more extensive than the design of the atonement, which Mr Fuller [and many another] has done. The Scriptures know nothing of a sufficient redemption, which leaves the captive to perish in slavery, nor a sufficient atonement which never delivers the guilty; but they [always] speak of a redemption every way sufficient and efficacious... which triumphantly accomplishes the salvation of all its objects.[339]

This is right. Nothing must detract from the *effective* nature of the atonement, from the redemption it *accomplishes*. After all, we are talking about the salvation of sinners; the atonement which accomplishes this is effective – or it is nothing.

Furthermore, the Owenite 'sufficiency' argument actually has a nasty aspect to it, totally unintended, of course, by those who use it. When addressing sinners, we have, apparently, to tell them of a redemption which is sufficient for all of them, pleading with them on the basis of this sufficiency, but, in so doing, make it clear that this redemption is quite out of reach – unless they are among the elect. This is tantamount to taunting the sinner. The conditional sufficiency of the Amyraldian at least provides a salvation sufficient for every hearer, *and within reach on condition that he believes* – it is a theoretical possibility in Amyraldian terms – but the Owenite theory of intrinsic sufficiency is a mere academic contrivance – with a gaping hole in it! It does not work for the preacher, since he knows – as much as he tells sinners of the sufficiency of redemption – it is not effective for all. And it certainly does not work for any sinner who is concerned about the particularity of redemption; he might be persuaded of the intrinsic sufficiency of Christ's redemption, but his problem remains: 'Sufficient, Christ's redemption is, but is it *effective* for me? was it *designed* for me?'[340] How will this help an anxious soul? 'If I am not elect, the atonement, though sufficient for me, is totally out of reach. It was never intended for me'. It has introduced an unscriptural notion, and gained nothing. It has, in fact, weakened the atonement and introduced problems which ought not to be brought into the conversion process.

Not least, in the misguided search for a logical justification of the free offer, the Owenite use of the sufficiency formula may even have encouraged those who hold to universal atonement – whether the Arminian or Amyraldian – to persist in their view.[341] It certainly has done nothing to make them think again. Haldane put it this way:

There is, perhaps, no argument upon which the advocates of universal atonement more confidently rely, than the inconsistency of the unlimited invitations of the gospel with [particular redemption]. The opinion that Christ died for the whole human race, has... been... received by not a few, from the mistaken idea that a limited atonement is incompatible with the unlimited proclamation of pardon through faith in Jesus. This has, perhaps, been partly owing to some who, holding scriptural views respecting the extent of the atonement, have founded the general invitations to those who come under the sound of the gospel upon the [supposed] sufficiency of the atonement for all [that is, Owenites]... This [the supposed sufficiency of the atonement for all mankind] is a subject, however, on which the Scripture is silent. It represents the atonement as being amply sufficient for all who come to the Saviour, however aggravated their guilt, but it never speaks of an indefinite sufficiency in the atonement as an inducement to sinners to rest on it for salvation.[342] God is uniformly represented as having a *specific* purpose in the gift of his Son... It is remarkable that so much stress should be laid upon the indefinite sufficiency of the atonement – a question upon which the Scriptures never enter. We have already seen that the word of God furnishes us with a simple ground for preaching the gospel to every creature; namely, his own commandment, illustrated by the example of the inspired apostles. With such a warrant, it is surely altogether superfluous [and arrogant] to dispute upon what principle the commandment rests. We are taught to walk by faith; 'the commandment is a lamp, and the law is [a] light'.[343]

Let me say a little more on my use of 'meaningless'. When a preacher uses Owen's device, he knows it doesn't actually accomplish anything. And the thinking sinner also sees through it – he knows he still has to have been elected, and Christ has to have died for him. In fact, it makes things worse – it can only tend to make some sinners feel they are left out of the invitation. As has been said: 'How does the sufficiency of Christ's death afford ample ground for general invitations, if the design was confined to the elect people? If the benefits of his death were never intended for the non-elect, is it not just as inconsistent to invite them to partake of them as if there were a want of sufficiency? This explanation seems to be no other than shifting the difficulty'.[344] Quite! In the free offer, sinners are to be told that Christ died and earned salvation, and all are invited. Yes, the redemption is particular, but since no one but God knows or can know who the elect are, all are equally invited. It is the classic 'double-blind'; neither the preacher nor the hearer knows who the elect are. Above all, it is the way which is set out in God's word. Thus the preacher can be free in offering Christ, *and so can the sinner in coming to Christ*. And there is nothing merely sufficient about the redemption Christ accomplished, and which is offered to the sinner. The sinner should not concern himself as to whether or not he is elected, or Christ has died for him in particular. He must come to Christ as he is – as he, the sinner, is, and as Christ himself is. And if he comes he will be saved.

Although the warrant for the sinner's coming is not a redemption sufficient for all, he should, of course, be passionately told of Christ's 'all-sufficiency'.[345] Yes indeed! In coming to Christ, the sinner must be persuaded that Christ can and will save him – save him completely and forever – if he comes![346] Thus he is encouraged to come; 'encouraged', I emphasise.

As Gillespie said:

The true and safe grounds of encouragement to faith in Christ are these: First, Christ's all-sufficiency. If he will, he can [*cf.* Mark 1:40]. He is able to save to the uttermost (Heb. 7:25). Are you a sinner to the uttermost? His plaster is broad enough to cover the broadest sore. As God's mercy, so Christ's merit is infinite...[347] This is a good strong foundation of comfort, if a soul, convinced of its own sinful state, and of the vanity of creature comforts, so far settles its thought upon Christ, that as he is the only Saviour, so an all-sufficient Saviour. Then is the sinner so far encouraged... as to resolve: There is virtue enough in the blood of Christ to cleanse my crimson sins, even mine. There is no help for me out of Christ, but in him there is help for all that come unto God by him. It is a great part of true faith to believe that Christ is able and all-sufficient. Therefore he himself said to the blind men (Matt. 9:28-29): 'Do you believe that I am able to do this?' They said unto him: 'Yes, Lord'. Then touched he their eyes, saying: 'According to your faith be it unto you'... So every poor sinner that comes unto Christ as sufficient and believing that Christ, and Christ only, can purge [cleanse] him from all sin, and save his soul, has a true... faith... The soul believes the all-sufficiency of Christ, and that he only is the Saviour... [and] his faith... is a true faith, which Christ will not despise... It is [also] an encouragement to believing that we are commanded to believe (1 John 3:23).[348]

Encouraging! Yes indeed. The fact that Christ's redemption is 'all-sufficient', is most *encouraging* to the coming sinner, yes – and so is God's command. But, I say again, it is God's command which is the sinner's *warrant* for coming.

Above all, stressing the 'nice point' yet again, the warrant for inviting and commanding sinners to come to Christ – the free offer – and the warrant every sinner has for responding to that free offer, and coming to Christ in repentant faith, is not any supposed universal sufficiency – 'sufficient for all' – of Christ's redemption; rather, it is the plain word of God. God's command to sinners to repent and believe – this is all the warrant which is needed and given.

Pulling It All Together

Although I have suggested that the objection to the free offer, supposedly raised by unbelievers on the grounds of particular redemption, may not be as real for them as is often made out, nevertheless it is a genuine question which looms large in the minds of many believers, and has to be faced. As John Murray said: One question 'which the free and unrestricted overture of grace makes unavoidable [is] the extent of the atonement'.[349] In particular, how does particular redemption affect the free offer? Does it mean its abolition? My answer is: Certainly not! And having set out my reasons at length, I conclude with a summary of the main points:

What is offered in the free offer? Full salvation in Christ. *Not that Christ died for you.*

To whom is it offered? To sinners, as sinners, all of them. *Not to sinners as elect sinners, sensible sinners, repentant sinners, awakened sinners, convicted sinners, redeemed sinners, conditionally-redeemed sinners, applicably-redeemed sinners, sufficiently-redeemed sinners, or any other sort of sinners. Just sinners.*

What is the warrant for the offer? God's command. *Not that Christ died for all, whether absolutely, provisionally, conditionally, applicably or sufficiently.*

Who will welcome the offer, and come to Christ? Only the elect. *And no others.*

How will they come? Having been unconditionally elected by the Father, particularly redeemed by the Son, being effectually awakened by the Spirit, and brought in repentant faith to Christ. *And in no other way.*

Does this not seem contradictory? It certainly does.

Can we explain this? No.

Does this matter? No.

Why not? Because God in his word has not required us to explain it, and, consequently, not told us how to do it. Therefore we have no warrant or need to try. As a result, any explanation must be pure speculation, taking us beyond what is written, in an effort to be consistent according to mere human logic.

The conclusion? In our preaching to sinners, let us keep to the simplicity of the gospel: 'Jesus... will save his people from their sins' (Matt. 1:21). There is no call for adverbs to qualify the 'save' – adverbs such as 'sufficiently', 'conditionally', 'applicably' or 'provisionally'. Christ died for his people to save them from their sins. And that is that! But when sinners have come to the Saviour, *then* they can say: 'Christ... suffered once for sins, the just for the unjust, that he might bring *us* to God' (1 Pet. 3:18); *then* they can rejoice individually in 'the Son of God who loved *me* and gave himself for *me*' (Gal. 2:20); *then* they can feel assured of their interest in the one 'who gave himself for *our* sins, that he might deliver *us* from this present evil age, according to the will of *our* God and Father' (Gal. 1:4); and *then* they can rest themselves in the one who 'is faithful and just to forgive *us our* sins and to cleanse *us* from all unrighteousness' (1 John 1:9). Yet, when preaching to unbelievers, what better terms can we use than: 'Christ Jesus came into the world to save sinners' (1 Tim. 1:15)? There is no need for adjectives to qualify the 'sinners'. What the sinner needs to hear is: 'For God so loved the world that he gave his only begotten Son, that whoever believes in him should not perish but have everlasting life' (John 3:16). Consequently, 'God... commands all men everywhere to repent' (Acts 17:30); therefore, 'believe on the Lord Jesus Christ, and you will be saved' (Acts 16:31); for, 'unless you repent you will all... perish' (Luke 13:3,5); and so on.[350]

In other words, particular redemption does not hinder the free offer in any way whatsoever. Quite the opposite. In the free offer, all sinners are offered a definite, full redemption.

A Warning and a Challenge

As I draw to a close, I want to return to a very important point I made in my *Offer*, and to which I referred earlier. That is, many who in theory are persuaded of the rightness of the free offer – and therefore consider themselves staunchly opposed to hyper-Calvinism – are, nevertheless, hypers; albeit, unwitting, *de facto*, or incipient hyper-Calvinists. Hypers? Yes! And yet, although they are failing to preach as they know they ought to sinners, some convince themselves that they are. Others are afraid or too embarrassed to do what they know to be right. Whatever the reason, incipient hyper-Calvinism is the result.[351]

Fuller's comment on Booth is apposite. As I have explained, although the two men disagreed about various aspects of redemption and the basis for the free offer, both were persuaded of the warrant for sinners as sinners to believe.[352] But Fuller had noticed something about Booth:

> I have never been able to learn... from his writings, preaching or conversation, after all that has been said about sinners as sinners being warranted to believe, that he even exhorts them to it; or avows it to be the command of God that they should repent and believe, in such a manner as is connected with salvation.

Fuller attributed this to Booth's holding of:

> The substitution of Christ in a way that does not admit of 'the command to repent and believe being promiscuously addressed to all'... Now what is it, but [other than] his ideas of imputation and substitution that can be the cause of this hesitation? I call it hesitation, because I never heard or saw anything in him that amounted to a denial of it. Yet he does not avow it, though he well knows it was avowed by Calvin, and all Calvinists for more than a century after the Reformation. They held the doctrines of imputation and substitution so as to feel at liberty to exhort sinners, without distinction, to repent and believe in Christ. Mr Booth does not.[353]

I record this episode, not only with some sadness, but with the positive purpose of trying to enforce my complaint that although we can – in theory – be persuaded of the freeness of the offer, we can – in practice – fail to preach it when we address sinners. Whether Fuller was right about the reasons for Booth's 'hesitancy', I cannot say, but as I have tried to show, a belief in particular redemption, including the biblical doctrines of imputation, substitution and union with Christ, is no hindrance whatsoever to the free offer. The point I now want to press, however, is Fuller's claim that Booth, for all his agreement with the free warrant for sinners to trust Christ, when it came to it, did not actually address sinners with those biblical commands and invitations as he ought – my very complaint about incipient hyper-Calvinism. And I have to record that, as far as I have read Booth, neither have I come across what I would call the free offer preached to sinners as sinners.[354] And, if Fuller was right, this was because of Booth's view of particular redemption – the very issue I am tackling.

But! 'Physician, heal yourself!' (Luke 4:23). What about Fuller himself? As far as I have discovered from Fuller's sermons, I have not found *him* pleading with sinners as freely as he ought![355]

All this is more than disappointing, because, although I consider Booth's approach to the atonement and the basis of the offer to be more biblical than Fuller's, both men had much which was excellent to say on the free offer. As I say, I record it as a warning to those of us who reject hyper-Calvinism but who – when it comes to it – are virtual hypers in practice.

But I must not leave it there. For all I have said by way of criticism of Fuller, how apt are his words in the spiritual climate in which we live today. And how necessary! I pay tribute to the man who preached and wrote them:

> The gospel is a message in which... we ought to be firm, and fearless of consequences. Speak boldly... You must not calculate consequences as they respect this life. If you would preach the gospel as you ought to preach it, the approbation of *God* must be your main object. What if you were to lose your friends and diminish your income; indeed, what if you lose your liberty, or even your life – what would this all be, compared with the loss of the favour and friendship of *God*? Woe unto us, if we shun to declare any part of the counsel of God! He that is afraid or ashamed to preach the whole of the gospel, in all its implications and bearings, let him stand aside; he is utterly unworthy of being a soldier of Jesus Christ. Sometimes, if you would speak the whole truth, you may be reproached as unsound and heterodox. But

you must not yield to popular clamour... Stand firm against all opposition... The gospel is a message full of importance, and therefore you must be in earnest. If your message respected the health of your hearers, or their temporal interest, or their reputation, it would be thought important. But what are these compared with the salvation of their souls! Salvation by Jesus Christ is God's last [and only] remedy – his ultimatum with a lost world (Mark 16:16; Acts 4:12). There remains no other sacrifice for sins. Then do not trifle on such subjects as these, lest you lose your own soul. What can be thought of you if you employ your time in making pretty speeches, and turning elegant sentences and phrases, instead of endeavouring to 'save yourself and them that hear you'! What if, instead of beseeching sinners to be reconciled to God, you should crack jokes before them, to excite a laugh![356]

Reader, I do not know about you – but I feel the force of Fuller's words!

Two Examples of Preaching Particular Redemption and the Free Offer

I have made the point that we should not enter into detailed explorations of God's decrees in our preaching to sinners – not, I hasten to add (and now repeat), that we should never mention such when addressing sinners. But as I have explained, this must be done in the right spirit. And what is that right spirit? To illustrate what I have in mind, I reproduce extracts from two preachers who, having set out the glories of the redemption which Christ accomplished, addressed sinners with the free offer. I have chosen George Whitefield's sermon on 'The Lord our righteousness' (Jer. 23:6), and Jonathan Edwards' *History of Redemption*.[357]

Take the Englishman first.

Whitefield, grieving that 'the doctrines of grace, especially the personal all-sufficient righteousness of Jesus, is [*sic*] but too seldom, too slightly mentioned', spelled out what he was talking about: 'Being God and man in one person, [Christ] wrought out a full, perfect and sufficient righteousness for all to whom it was to be imputed'; in other words, particular redemption. Having introduced the subject what did Whitefield do with it? Having indicated at the start of his sermon that his business was to give 'an exhortation to all to come to Christ by faith, that they may be enabled to say... "the Lord our righteousness"', he issued a challenge to his hearers: 'Why then will you not believe on the Lord Jesus Christ, that so he may become the Lord *your* righteousness?' He came to the biting point:

It is time for me to come a little closer to your consciences. Brethren though some may be offended at this doctrine, and may account it foolishness, yet, to many of you, I doubt not but it is precious... But give me leave to ask you one question: Can you say, the Lord our righteousness? I say, the Lord *our* righteousness. For welcoming this doctrine in your heads, without receiving the Lord Jesus Christ savingly by a lively faith into your hearts, will but increase your damnation. As I have often told you, so I tell you again – an unapplied Christ, is no Christ at all. Can you then, with believing Thomas, cry out: 'My Lord, and my God'?

Whitefield probed his hearers as to their sanctification as well as justification, showing, by a series of questions, the need of conviction and longing after Christ – and calling for it:

Were you ever made to abhor yourselves for your actual and original sins, and to loathe your own righteousness, for, as the prophet beautifully expresses it, 'your righteousness is as filthy rags'? Were you ever made to see and admire the all-sufficiency of Christ's righteousness, and excited by the Spirit of God to hunger and thirst after it? Could you ever say: My soul is athirst for Christ, indeed, even for the righteousness of Christ? O when shall I come to appear before the presence of my God in the righteousness of Christ! nothing but Christ! nothing but Christ! Give me Christ, O God, and I am satisfied! My soul shall praise you for ever.
Was this ever the language of your hearts?... Were you ever enabled to reach out the arm of faith, and embrace the blessed Jesus in your souls, so that you could say: 'My beloved is mine, and I am his'? If so, fear not, whoever you are. Hail, all hail, you happy souls! The Lord, the Lord Christ, the everlasting God, is your righteousness. Christ has justified you, who is he that condemns you? Christ has died for you, more, rather, is risen again, and ever lives to make intercession for you. Being now justified by his grace, you have peace with God, and shall, before long, be with Jesus in glory, reaping everlasting and unspeakable fruits both in body and soul... O think of the love of Christ in dying for you!... Think of the greatness of the gift, as well as of the giver!... O think of his dying love!... 'Why me, Lord? why me?'... why is the Lord my righteousness?

Before turning to sinners, Whitefield concluded his address to believers, confessing: 'My friends, I trust I feel somewhat of a sense of God's distinguishing love upon my heart; therefore I must divert a little from rejoicing with you, to invite poor Christless sinners to come to him, and accept his righteousness, that they may have life'. And this is how he did it:

Alas, my heart almost bleeds! What a multitude of precious souls are now before me! How shortly must all be ushered into eternity! And yet, O cutting thought! were God now to require all your souls, how few, comparatively speaking, could really say, the Lord *our* righteousness.

And do you think, O sinners, that you will be able to stand in the day of judgement, if Christ be not your righteousness! No, that alone is the wedding garment in which you must appear. O Christless sinners, I am distressed for you! The desires of my soul are enlarged. O that this may be an accepted time! that the Lord may be your righteousness! For whither would you flee, if death should find you naked? Indeed, there is no hiding yourselves from his presence. The pitiful fig-leaves of your own righteousness will not cover your nakedness, when God shall call you to stand before him. Adam found them ineffectual, and so will you. O think of death! O think of judgement! Yet a little while, and time shall be no more; and then what will become of you, if the Lord be not your righteousness? Do you think that Christ will spare you? No, he that formed you, will have no mercy on you. If you are not of Christ, if Christ is not your righteousness, Christ himself shall pronounce you damned. And can you bear to think of being damned by Christ? Can you bear to hear the Lord Jesus say to you: 'Depart from me, you cursed, into everlasting fire, prepared for the devil, and his angels'? Can you live, do you think, in everlasting burnings?... Can you bear to depart from Christ? O that heart-piecing thought!... What must it be to be banished from him to all eternity?

But thus it must be, if Christ be not your righteousness; for God's justice must be satisfied; and, unless Christ's righteousness is imputed and applied to you here, you must hereafter be satisfying the divine justice in hell torments eternally; indeed, Christ himself shall condemn you to that place of torment. And how cutting is that thought! I think I see poor, trembling, Christless wretches, standing before the bar of God, crying out... but all in vain. Christ himself shall pronounce the irrevocable sentence. Knowing therefore the terrors of the Lord, let me persuade you to close with Christ, and never rest till you can say, 'the Lord our righteousness'. Who knows but that the Lord may have mercy on, indeed, abundantly pardon you?... If the Lord gives you [faith], you will by it receive Christ, with his righteousness, and his all... For are you sinners? So am I. Are you the chief of sinners? So am I... And yet the Lord (for ever adored be his rich, free, and sovereign grace!) the Lord is my righteousness. Come, then, O young men, who (as I acted once myself) are playing the prodigal... come home, come home, and leave your swine's trough. Feed no longer on the husks of sensual delights; for Christ's sake arise, and come home! [The][358] heavenly Father now calls you. See yonder the best robe, even the righteousness of his dear Son, awaits you. See it, view it again and again. Consider at how dear a rate it was purchased, even by the blood of [Christ]. Consider what great need you have of it. You are lost, undone, damned for ever, without it. Come then, poor, guilty prodigals, come home... O that God would now bow the heavens and come down! Descend, O Son of God, descend; and as you have shown in me such mercy, O let your blessed Spirit apply your righteousness to some young prodigals now before you, and clothe their naked souls with your best robe!

But I must speak a word to you, young maidens, as well as young men... Which of you can say, the Lord is my righteousness? Which of you was ever concerned to be dressed in this robe of invaluable price, and without which you are no better than whited sepulchres in the sight of God? Let not then so many of you, young maidens, any longer forget your chief and only ornament. O seek for the Lord to be your righteousness, or otherwise burning will soon be upon you, instead of beauty!

And what shall I say to you of a middle age... who, with all your gettings, have not yet received the Lord to be your righteousness?... Seek for the Lord to be your righteousness, a righteousness that will entitle you to life everlasting. I see, also, many hoary heads here, and perhaps the most of them cannot say, the Lord is my righteousness. O grey-headed sinners, I could weep over you!... You do not know that the Lord is your righteousness; O haste then, haste you aged sinners, and seek an interest in redeeming love! Alas, you have one foot already in the grave, your glass[359] is just [about] run out, your sun is just [about] going down, and it will set and leave you in an eternal darkness, unless the Lord be your righteousness! Flee then, O flee for your lives! Be not afraid. All things are possible with God. If you come, though it be at the eleventh hour, Christ Jesus will never cast you out. Seek then for the Lord to be your righteousness... But I must not forget the lambs of the flock... I know [my Lord] will be angry with me, if I do not tell them, that the Lord may be their righteousness... Do not think that you are too young to be converted. Perhaps many of you may be nine or ten years old, and yet cannot say, the Lord is our righteousness; which many have said, though younger than you. Come, then, while you are young. Perhaps you may not live to be old. Do not wait for other people. If your fathers and mothers will not come to Christ, you come without them. Let children lead them, and show them how the Lord may be their righteousness. Our Lord Jesus loved little children... I pray God will make you willing in good time to take the Lord for your righteousness.

Here, then, I could conclude; but I must not forget the poor [slaves]; no, I must not. Jesus Christ has died for them, as well as for others...[360] O that you would seek the Lord to be your righteousness! Who knows but he may be found of you? For in Jesus Christ there is neither male nor female, bond nor free; even you may be the children of God, if you believe in Jesus... The eunuch belonging to the queen of Candace... believed. The Lord was his righteousness. He was baptised... You also believe, and you shall be saved. Christ Jesus is the same now as he was yesterday, and he will wash you in his own blood. Go home then,[361] turn the words of the text into a prayer, and entreat the Lord to be your righteousness. Even so, come Lord Jesus, come quickly, into all our souls! Amen, Lord Jesus, amen and amen![362]

So much for the Englishman.

Now for the New Englander. Edwards, having set out what he was writing about – namely, 'the preparation and purpose, the application and success of Christ's redemption' – spoke of 'the effect' of this redemption 'wrought on the souls of the redeemed'. By 'this effect', he meant 'the application of redemption with respect to the souls of particular persons, in converting, justifying, sanctifying and glorifying them. By these things, they are actually redeemed, and receive the benefit of the work in its effects... as God carries on the work of converting the souls of fallen men... "Whom he did predestinate, them he also called; and whom he called, them he also justified; and whom he justified, them he also glorified" (Rom. 8:30)'. That is, one of the ends 'of this great work', 'another great design of God in the work of redemption, was to gather together in one all things in Christ, in heaven and in earth; *i.e.*, all elect creatures; to bring all elect creatures... to a union one to another in one body, under one head, and to unite all together in one body to God the Father... God designed by this work to perfect and complete the glory of all the elect by Christ'.

Edwards, having dwelt at large upon what was involved in the preparation for – and accomplishment of – Christ's redemption, came to what he called the 'improvement' or application and use of the truth. 'I begin', he said, 'with... reproof'. He made his meaning clear. He had three sorts of sinners in mind. He was going to give 'a reproof of unbelief, of self-righteousness, and of a careless neglect of the salvation of Christ'. First, unbelief:

How greatly do these things reprove those who do not believe in, but reject, the Lord Jesus Christ! *i.e.*, all those who do not heartily receive him... Let me now call upon such to consider how great their sin in thus rejecting Jesus Christ. You slight the glorious person... You have been guilty of slighting that great Saviour, who, after such preparation, actually accomplished the purchase of redemption... This is the person you reject and despise. You make light of all the glory of his person, and of all the glorious love of God the Father in sending him into the world, and all his wonderful love appearing in the whole of this affair... Sinners sometimes are ready to wonder why unbelief should be looked upon as a great sin; but if you consider what you have heard, how can you wonder? If this Saviour is so great, and this work so great, and such great things have been done in order to it, truly there is no cause of wonder that the rejection of this Saviour is so provoking to God. It brings greater guilt than the sins of the worst of heathens, who never heard of those things, nor have had this Saviour offered to them.

Edwards then moved to those 'who, instead of believing in Christ, trust in themselves for salvation'. He exposed the madness of such a course, the insult it is to God. To think! You are sinners, 'poor, worthless, vile and polluted, yet you arrogantly take upon you that very work for which the only-begotten Son of God became man'. Edwards, having painted the background, having shown what preparations God made for the coming of the Saviour, and what works Christ undertook to accomplish redemption, demanded:

How must such arrogance appear in the sight of Christ, whom it cost so much. It was not to be obtained even by him, so great and glorious a person, at a cheaper rate than his going through a sea of blood, and passing through the midst of the furnace of God's wrath. And how vain must your arrogance appear in the sight of God, when he sees you imagining yourself sufficient, and your worthless, polluted performance excellent enough, for the accomplishing of that work of his own Son.

Edwards showed that such a course is not only defiant, but foolish: 'Alas! how blind are natural men! and especially how vain are the thoughts which they have of themselves! How ignorant of their own littleness and pollution! What great things do they assume to themselves!' He exposed the utter folly of it: 'In attempting to work out redemption for yourself, you attempt a greater thing than', as he had put it a moment earlier, 'the greatest thing that ever God himself did'. In short: 'You take upon you to do the very greatest and most difficult part of this work, *viz.*, to purchase redemption'. Edwards was scathing of such presumption:

If all the angels in heaven had been sufficient for this work, would God have set himself to effect such things as he did in order to [accomplish] it? and would he ever have sent his own Son, the Creator of the angels, into the world, to have done and suffered such things?
What self-righteous persons take to themselves, is the same work that Christ was engaged in when he was in his agony and bloody sweat, when he died on the cross, which was the greatest thing that ever the eyes of angels beheld. Great as it is, [the self-righteous] imagine they can do the same that Christ accomplished by it. Their self-righteousness does in effect charge Christ's offering up himself in these sufferings, as the greatest instance of folly that ever men or angels saw, instead of being the most glorious display of the divine wisdom and grace...
Is it any wonder, then, that a self-righteous spirit is so represented in Scripture, and spoken of, as that which is most fatal to the souls of men?

Edwards then turned to those who 'neglect the salvation of Christ. These live a senseless kind of life, neglect the business of religion and their own souls, not taking any course to get an interest in Christ, or what he has done and suffered, or any part in that glorious salvation he has purchased. They have their minds taken up about the gains of the world, or the vanities and pleasures of youth, and make light of what they hear of Christ's salvation... that they do not... so much as seek after it'.

Edwards contrasted this attitude with that of many in the Old Testament:

Prophets, and kings, and righteous men [who had] their minds so much taken up with the prospect, that the purchase of salvation was to be wrought out in ages long after their death; and will you neglect it when it is actually accomplished?... Indeed, your sin is extremely aggravated in the sight of God... He has put you under a more glorious dispensation, has given you a more clear revelation of Christ and his salvation, and yet you neglect all these advantages, and go on a careless course of life, as though nothing had been done, no such proposals and offers had been made to you.

Noting how even 'the angels', even though they gain no saving benefit for it, have 'been so engaged about this salvation', Edwards drew the lesson:

Now, shall these take so much notice of this redemption, and of the purchaser, who need it not for themselves, and have no immediate concern or interest in it, or offer of it; and will you, to whom it is offered, and who are in such extreme necessity of it, neglect and take no notice of it?
Did Christ labour so hard, and suffer so much to procure this salvation, and it is not worth the while for you to be at some labour in seeking it? Did our salvation[363] lie with such weight upon the mind of Christ, as to induce him to become man, to suffer even death itself, in order to procure it? And is it not worth the while for you, who need this salvation, and must perish eternally without it, to take earnest pains to obtain an interest in it after it is procured, and all things are ready?
Shall the great God be so concerned about this salvation... and when all is said and done, is it not worth your seeking after? What great, what wonderful things has he done... to make way for the procuring of this salvation! And when... the great Saviour [at the right time] comes, passing through a long series of reproach and suffering, and then suffering all the waves and billows of God's wrath for men's sins, inasmuch as they overwhelmed his soul; after all these things [were] done to procure salvation for sinners, is it not worthy of your being so much concerned about it, but that it should be thrown aside, and made nothing of, compared with worldly gain, gay clothing, or youthful diversions, and other such trifling things?
O! that you who live negligent of this salvation, would consider what you do!... Heb. 2:3... Acts 13:41... God looks on you as great enemies of the cross of Christ, as adversaries and despisers of all the glory of this great work. And if God has made such account of the glory of salvation... in order to prepare the way for the glory of his Son in this affair, how little account will he make of the lives and souls of ten thousand such opposers and despisers as you, who continue impenitent, when your welfare stands in the way of that glory! Why surely you shall be dashed to pieces as a potter's vessel, and trodden down as the mire of the streets. God may, through wonderful patience, bear with hardened careless sinners for a while; but he will not long bear with such despisers of his dear Son, and his great salvation, the glory of which he has had so much at heart, before he will utterly consume without remedy or mercy.

Edwards finally turned to offer 'encouragement to burdened souls to put their trust in Christ for salvation':

To all such as are not careless and negligent, but make seeking an interest in Christ their main business, being sensible in some measure of their necessity, and afraid of the wrath to come; to such, what has been said on this subject [the history of redemption] holds forth great matter of encouragement, to venture their souls on the Lord Jesus Christ. And as motives proper to excite you so to do, let me lead you to consider two things in particular.

1. The completeness of the purchase which has been made. You have heard that this work of purchasing salvation was wholly finished during the time of Christ's humiliation. When Christ rose from the dead, and was exalted from that abasement to which he submitted for our[364] salvation, the purchase of eternal life was completely made, so that there was no need of anything more to be done in order to it... 'Behold, I have prepared my dinner; my oxen and my fatlings are killed, and all things are ready; come unto the marriage' (Matt. 22:4). Therefore, are your sins many and great? Here is enough done by Christ to procure their pardon. There is no need of any righteousness of yours to obtain your pardon and justification. No! You may come freely, without money and without price. Since therefore there is such a free and gracious invitation given you, come, come naked as you are; come as a poor condemned criminal; come and cast yourself down at Christ's feet, as one justly condemned, and utterly helpless. Here is a complete salvation wrought out by Christ, and through him offered to you. Come, therefore, accept it, and be saved.

2. For Christ to reject one that thus comes to him, would be to frustrate all those great things which God brought to pass from the fall of man to the incarnation of Christ. It would also frustrate all that Christ did and suffered while on earth; indeed, it would frustrate the incarnation itself. All the great things done were for that end, that those might be saved who should come to Christ. Therefore you may be sure Christ will not be backward in saving those who come to him, and trust in him; for he has no desire to frustrate himself in his own work. Neither will God the Father refuse you; for he has no desire to frustrate himself in all that he did for so many hundreds and thousands of years, to prepare the way for the salvation of sinners by Christ. Come, therefore, hearken to the sweet and earnest calls of Christ to your soul. Do as he invites and as he commands you: 'Come unto me, all you that labour, and are heavy laden, and I will give you rest. Take my yoke upon you, and learn of me; and you shall find rest unto your souls. For my yoke is easy, and my burden is light' (Matt. 11:28-30).[365]

* * *

I can only say, reader, after writing this – and I hope you can echo the same after reading it – let there be no more foolish talk to the effect that those who hold to particular redemption cannot preach the free offer to sinners. More, I appeal to all who hold – or are held by – the doctrines of grace: Let us make sure we address sinners as they ought to be addressed.

Ashbel Green summarised it thus:

> Gospel preaching... that is, the all-sufficiency of the Lord Jesus Christ to save even the chief of sinners, and his readiness to receive them, when they come to him in the exercise of faith and a contrite spirit – his readiness to cleanse them in his atoning blood, to clothe them with his perfect righteousness, to justify them freely, to sanctify them by his Spirit, to adopt them into his family, and to crown them with eternal glory, should be set forth in the most clear and persuasive manner. The true nature of regeneration, of evangelical faith, genuine repentance, and new obedience should be carefully explained and illustrated. The danger of grieving away the Spirit of grace, by those with whom he is striving, and the danger of all delay in accepting the gospel offer, should be often brought into view. The peril to the unawakened and the careless... should often be pressed home on those who remain at ease in their sins.[366]

And may God bless all such preaching!

Appendix

Since, in the body of the book, I did not set out to establish the doctrine of particular redemption, I did not expound those biblical texts which might seem to speak against it – although I did remark on some of them in passing (and, in addition to what I say here, I refer you, reader, to those places). I must, however, comment on Clifford's chapter: 'The Verdict of Scripture'.[367]

A few general remarks

In addition to the heading he gave it, Clifford spelled out his purpose in writing the chapter in question: 'The scriptural evidence will be examined with a view to reaching an authoritative verdict' in 'the debate over the extent of the atonement'.[368] Very well. But with respect, I do not think this is what we get. Since Clifford's chapter is to do with the verdict of Scripture – that is, of course, his understanding of Scripture – it would have been better, I think, if he had given his own explanation of the passages he selected. The chapter as it stands seems more like Clifford using Calvin, Baxter and Wesley to give his (adverse) verdict on Owen's explanation of those passages. While I am not advocating Owen's view on every occasion, and far be it from me to think that such a theological giant[369] needs my defence, Clifford displayed – shall we say – a certain lack of sympathy with Owen. But while he nearly always came out against him, it is not always clear whether or not he agreed with Baxter and Wesley when he quoted them. Even so, his sympathies are not hard to discover! I agree, of course, Owen does gloss;[370] at times he does show prejudice in approaching Scripture with his system in mind; now and then he is guilty of special pleading; on occasion he does use questionable exegesis; and he is prepared to explain one passage by importing another.[371] But all this could be said of Calvin, Baxter and Wesley! Indeed, at times, no doubt, of Clifford and Gay!

As for Clifford glossing, how can we know, for instance, when we should read a verse as *effective* atonement or *sufficient* atonement? What is the rule? And arguing from what the Scriptures *do not* say, while legitimate,[372] is not without risk. Clifford adopted this approach at times; on Romans 8:32, for instance, where, as I have noted, Clifford observed that it does not say that Christ died 'for us *alone*', and thus, wrongly, he felt able to maintain universal provisional atonement in face of the verse;[373] or when quoting Wesley with approval for pointing out that no scripture expressly asserts that Christ did not die for all.[374] In any case, arguing from silence cuts both ways. Papists are prepared to use the technique to try to deny the biblical doctrine of justification, because no verse actually states that we are justified by faith *alone*.[375] So, using Clifford's argument, can we reject his thesis simply because no scripture asserts that Christ died for all *provisionally*? and no scripture asserts that this is the basis of the offer?

Then again, nothing is gained by positing a clash between limited atonement and God's general love and free offer to all; as I have made clear, there is no such clash. From God's expressed desire to see all men saved, nothing can be deduced about the extent of the atonement – just as, from God's expressed desire to see all men saved, nothing can be deduced about the extent of election or reprobation or effectual calling. God's desire belongs to his revealed will; the extent of election, reprobation, redemption and effectual calling, all belong to God's secret will. These two wills are not always the same.[376] God desires to see all sinners saved, but he has decreed to save only his elect by the death of his Son.

* * *

Moving on from these general remarks, I now turn to those passages, selected by Clifford, which call for more detailed comment. They may be broadly classified, *first*, as passages which teach particular redemption; *secondly*, passages which, Clifford claims, teach general redemption; and, *thirdly*, passages which seem to imply that those for whom Christ died can be lost.

Passages which teach particular redemption

The passages in question are John 10 and Ephesians 5:25.

On **John 10**, Clifford was ingenious but weak.[377] Having already looked at the passage, I now simply repeat that the thrust of John 10:26 – 'you do not believe because you are not my sheep' – must not be dismissed as an 'indirect reference to election'.[378] What is more, the passage teaches far more than 'the degree of Christ's commitment' in that 'he would totally care for the sheep'. It teaches definite particular redemption by Christ's death for his elect: 'I am the good shepherd. The good shepherd gives his life for the sheep... I lay down my life for the sheep' (John 10:11,15).[379]

On **Ephesians 5:25**, Clifford was weak.[380] Yes, the passage does teach a man how to love his wife, but it also teaches definite particular redemption. True, the godly husband must be utterly committed to his wife, especially in light of prevalent immorality (Eph. 5:3-5), and Christ is his standard (Eph. 5:25,28-33). Yes. But the fact is: 'Christ... loved the church and gave himself for her, that he might sanctify and cleanse her with the washing of water by the word, that he might present her to himself a glorious church, not having spot or wrinkle or any such thing, but that she should be holy and without blemish' (Eph. 5:25-27). If this does not teach particular definite and efficacious redemption for the elect, words have lost all meaning.

Passages which, Clifford claims, teach general redemption

The passages in question are Luke 23:34, Romans 5:18, 2 Corinthians 5:14-15, John 3:16 and 1 John 2:2.

On **Luke 23:34**, I agree with Clifford;[381] in my opinion, Owen was guilty of special pleading. But the verse makes no contribution whatsoever to the debate about the extent of the atonement.

On **Romans 5:18**, Clifford was wrong.[382] Paul says 'the free gift *came* to all men', not '*is made available* to all men', or '*is offered* to all men'. I am not arguing this from the word 'came', which is supplied,[383] but from the context; namely, all in Adam were constituted sinners; all in Christ are constituted righteous (Rom. 5:12-21, especially verse 19).[384] There is no evading the parallel. Just as there is nothing provisional about the judgement which came through Adam to all, so there is nothing provisional about the justification which came through Christ to all. In Adam, all *are* condemned; in Christ, all *are* justified; the one as absolute as the other.[385] This is what the passage teaches. And, I stress, *all* are condemned in the one man, *all* are justified in the other.[386]

But it is the 'all', and the context of the 'all', which matters. If the 'all' in the second half of Romans 5:18 means 'all men without exception', then all men without exception are constituted righteous in Christ, all men without exception are justified; and this, not provisionally, but absolutely. What is more, not only are all men without exception justified, but all men without exception are predestined, called and glorified: 'Whom he predestined, these he also called; whom he called, them he also justified; and whom he justified, these he also glorified' (Rom. 8:30). That is, all who are included in one of these are included in them all. The man who is called, *is* justified; the man who is called and justified, *is* so because he *was* predestined; and the man who has been predestined, called and justified, *is* glorified. Consequently, if Paul in Romans 5:18 teaches that all men without exception are justified, then it undoubtedly follows that all men without exception are predestined, called and glorified.[387] Similarly in verse 19, where the apostle, continuing and confirming his argument, now speaks of 'the many'.[388] Once again, nobody questions that the first 'many' means 'all mankind'. But if it is claimed that the second 'many' also means 'all mankind', then as Haldane said: 'These verses afford a much stronger argument for universal *salvation* than any passage which can be adduced for universal *atonement*; but the doctrine of universal salvation is... repugnant to the whole tenor of Scripture'.[389]

Of course, Romans 5:18-19 does not mean that at all. Rather, all *who were in Adam* were constituted sinners in *him*, and all *who are in Christ* are constituted righteous in *him*. It is all a question of union – union with Adam, union with Christ.[390] All men are either in Adam or in Christ. All in Adam are constituted sinners; all in Christ are constituted righteous. The one is as certain and absolute as the other.[391]

Consider the parallel passage: 'For as in Adam all die, even so in Christ all shall be made alive' (1 Cor. 15:22).[392] It is, once again, a question of union. The context of 1 Corinthians 15 proves it. Paul is speaking about those who are *in Christ*, and he is speaking about *all of them*. In particular, he is speaking about 'those who have fallen asleep in Christ'; that is, believers who have died. What comfort can he give bereaved believers concerning *them*? This: 'If in this life only we have hope in Christ, we are of all men the most pitiable. But now Christ is risen from the dead, and has become the firstfruits of those who have fallen asleep... For as in Adam all die, even so in Christ all shall be made alive. But each one in his own order; Christ the firstfruits, afterward those who are Christ's at his coming' (1 Cor. 15:18-23). *This* is the comfort Paul gives bereaved believers concerning those who, while alive, had hope in Christ, but now have died. And, of course, it applies to the living believers themselves. It still does. Speaking of believers, it is true of *us ourselves*, since *we* will have to face death one day – unless Christ has returned.[393] This is *our* comfort – not only for *our* deceased believing-friends, but for *us ourselves*. Although *we* (along with all men) died in Adam, *we* have been made alive in Christ, Christ has been raised as *our* firstfruits, and, even though *we* will die physically (unless Christ has returned), all of *us* will be resurrected when he comes again:

If in this life only we [who are in Christ] have hope in Christ, we [who are in Christ] are of all men [without exception] the most pitiable. But now Christ is risen from the dead, and has become the firstfruits of those [in Christ] who have fallen asleep... For as in Adam all [without exception, including the elect] die, even so in Christ all [who are in Christ] shall be made alive. But each one in his own order; Christ the firstfruits, afterward those who are Christ's at his coming.

Haldane:

1 Corinthians 15:22... does not treat of the resurrection of the just and the unjust; for... nothing is said in this chapter of the resurrection of the wicked... the wicked are never said to be 'made alive'...[394] and... the expression is explained in the succeeding verse. 'But every man in his own order: Christ the firstfruits; afterward they that are Christ's at his coming'. Here the expression 'all' [who] shall be made alive is explained by 'those that are Christ's'.[395]

But what of Paul's statement in the preceding verse: 'For since by man came death, by man also came the resurrection of the dead' (1

Cor. 15:21)? At first glance, it might appear that Paul was saying the resurrection of Christ brought about the resurrection of all men. And this, if it *is* what Paul was saying, might be extended to argue against what I have alleged both here and in the body of the book – namely, that Christ's death, burial, resurrection, ascension and intercession are all particular for the elect, not general for all men. Specifically, it might, I suppose, be used to try to counter my assertion that no Scripture teaches that all men benefit in some way by the death of Christ, which, as I have said, might well be right, but I have not met it in Scripture.

But could 1 Corinthians 15:21 be used to justify the claim? Does Paul mean that the resurrection of all men without exception came by the resurrection of Christ? I do not think so. From the context, which, as I have explained, is spiritual union – all are either in Adam or in Christ – from the context, I say, it is patent that the apostle is concerned with those 'in Christ', and only them. True, by Adam, death came upon all men without exception. Yes, the death *even of the elect* came by Adam, but – and this is Paul's point – all the elect, on coming to regeneration and saving faith, are made alive in Christ, made alive *now*, and, after death, will be resurrected at the last day. Paul, I repeat, is speaking only of those 'in Christ'. Consequently, 'since by man came death, by man also came the resurrection of the dead' is to be read and understood as: 'Since by man came death [for all men, not excluding the elect], by man also came the resurrection of the dead *who are in Christ*'.

Charles Hodge:

The connection between this verse and the preceding is obvious. The resurrection of Christ secures the resurrection *of his people*, for as there was a causal relation between the death of Adam and the death of his descendants, so there is a causal relation between the resurrection of Christ and that *of his people*.[396]

And it is more than physical resurrection Paul is concerned with. As I have said, in Christ, the believing elect have life *now*. Yes, they will be raised physically at Christ's return, but this is because they are 'in Christ' *now*, and have life *now*; they must live because they have life. When Jesus comforted Martha at the death of Lazarus by telling her: 'Your brother will rise again', she blunted his words by talking of the general resurrection, as though she was repeating her catechism. No, said Jesus, in effect; it is far more than that: 'I am the resurrection and the life. He who believes in me, though he may die, he shall live. And who ever lives and believes in me shall never die. Do you believe *this*?' (John 11:23-26). As he said to his disciples: 'Because I live, you will live also' (John 14:19).

Gill:

Christ is the meritorious and procuring cause of the resurrection *of his people*... By rising from the dead [he] has opened the graves *of the saints*, and procured *their* resurrection *for them*, obtained *for them* a right to it, and made way for it... He also will be the efficient cause of the resurrection; all the dead will be raised by his power, and at the hearing of his voice – though *the saints only* will be raised by him in virtue of their union to him and interest in him, being members of his body, of his flesh and of his bones.[397]

Fee opened his judicious comments on 1 Corinthians 15:21-22 by laying down the governing principle: 'It must be noted at the outset that the general resurrection of the dead is not Paul's concern, neither here nor elsewhere in the argument'. He explained:

There can be *no* question that [the apostle's] concern is with the resurrection of believers; this is clearly stated in the words 'then those who are his' [verse 23]; had he shown a similar interest in all the dead, one might expect that also to be explicit, not something we must find by means of several circuitous exercises in what one deems to be 'logical' for Paul. The difficulties with this view [that is, the view that Paul is speaking of the resurrection of all men] are several and insuperable. It requires (a) that Christ is the firstfruits even of the perishing; (b) that 'those who have fallen asleep in Christ' (verse 18) includes the perishing, since that is the point picked up in verse 20; (c) that the verb 'shall be made alive' is a synonym for resurrection rather than having to do with 'life' itself; (d) that the Adam-Christ analogy has nothing to do with the creation of a new humanity, but has to do strictly with death and resurrection. Furthermore, it runs aground on the parallel in verses 50-57, where the swallowing up of death in victory is limited strictly to the resurrection/transformation of believers.

Fee rightly continued to emphasise the point:

Both the context and Paul's theology as a whole make it clear that in saying 'in Christ all will be made alive', he means 'in Christ, all *who*

> *are in Christ* will be made alive'...[398] He expected it to be read in the context of his argument... not as a piece of abstract theology... [Starting with verse 17, it is] certain that [Paul] was [here] concerned only with the resurrection of believers... Christ's resurrection makes inevitable the resurrection of those who have fallen asleep *in Christ*... Paul's point is that death is inevitable because of our sharing in the humanity and sinfulness of the one man, Adam. But believers' sharing in the resurrection from the dead through the second man, Christ... is equally inevitable... In saying that 'in Christ all will be made alive', Paul means... those who are 'in Christ'... will just as certainly 'be made alive'... The problem [which the apostle has to solve] is that despite Christ's resurrection (= triumph over death), believers still die. Hence [his solution; namely, the argument that] they *must* be raised, (a) because they are 'in Christ', who is already raised, and (b) only so will death, the last enemy, finally be subdued, so that through the work of Christ, God will finally be 'all in all'. The argument in the rest of this paragraph makes it clear that this is Paul's real concern.

Drawing attention to 'the similar expression' – 'the dead in Christ shall rise first' (1 Thess. 4:16) – Fee observed:

> This does not mean that Christians who have died will be raised before all others,[399] but that *the dead* who are Christians will rise as the first item on the eschatological agenda, after which *the living* who are Christians will be caught up with them. There is simply no interest of any kind in these passages in a general resurrection of the dead, or in a final raising to life in Christ of those who are not his. Prior theological commitments [that is, pre-conceived ideas] in this case have created some strange bedfellows; *e.g.*, dispensationalists and Universalists, who for radically different reasons want Christ's resurrection to be the firstfruits of all human beings.

Fee also noted Paul's use of *zōopoiēthēsontai* (1 Cor. 15:22,36,45) (to cause to live, make alive, give life)[400] instead of *egeirō* (to arouse from the sleep of death, to recall the dead to life) in order to make 'the proper contrast with *apothnēskō* [natural, spiritual, moral and eternal death]; it is difficult', he added, 'to escape the conclusion that the nuance "to give life to" means more than simply the resuscitation of a corpse. They rise to "life" because they already have been given "life" in Christ'. Furthermore, as Fee pointed out, 'the "order" of resurrections is only two; Christ the firstfruits; the full harvest of those who are his at his parousia. Paul shows no interest here in anything beyond these'. But, as he was quick to add, 'this is not to say that Paul *denied* a resurrection of the unjust (Acts 24:15 suggests[401] otherwise), but that it simply lies outside his concern in *this* passage'.[402]

I reinforce the point by underlining something I have already mentioned. Although it is true that all men without exception have died in Adam, Paul's concern is with the elect. The truth is, *even the elect died in Adam*. But *they*, the believing elect, have been made alive in Christ, and, even though they will one day die physically (unless Christ has returned), *they* will be raised physically when he comes again. This is the apostle's concern in 1 Corinthians 15:18-23 – not with all men, but with the believing elect; that is, with those who are 'in Christ'. Even when he is speaking of 'all in Adam', he has the elect particularly in mind. Nor is this nuance missing in Romans 5:18-19. While it is true that all men without exception are condemned in Adam, the elect not excluded, it is particularly true of *them*. Above all, the apostle makes the point most forcibly in Ephesians 2:1-10. As he says, all men are 'dead in trespasses and sins... by nature children of wrath', and so on. And this, of course, is true *even* of the elect, indeed, it is *especially* (for Paul's purpose) true of *them*; the elect, by nature, were 'just as the others'. I cannot stress this too much; 'just as the others', 'even as others' (AV). 'But...', he thunders, 'but...'. Listen to him punching home the truth:

And *you* he made alive... *you* once walked... among whom also *we* all once... were by nature children of wrath, just as the others. But God... because of his great love with which he loved *us*, even when *we* were dead in trespasses, made *us* alive together with Christ... and raised *us* up together, and made *us* sit together in the heavenly places in Christ Jesus... in his kindness towards *us* in Christ Jesus. For by grace *you* have been saved... for *we* are his workmanship, created in Christ Jesus for good works, which God prepared beforehand that *we* should walk in them.

It is difficult to see how Paul could have more compellingly put his case: The elect are by nature dead and condemned in Adam *'just as the others'*, but only they – they only – are savingly loved by God, given life in Christ, raised and seated with him, and have eternal hope in him. *This* is Paul's point.[403]

Nothing could be more plain. In all these passages, Paul was concerned with the believing elect, those 'in Christ'. Consequently, to take what is said of those who are 'in Christ' in Romans 5:18-19 and 1 Corinthians 15:18-23 – especially for my purpose in answering Clifford, Romans 5:18-19 – and apply it to all men without exception, is to miss the target by a mile; indeed, it is to destroy the apostle's argument. His statements concerning Christ dying for all, and being raised and made alive for all, of all being justified in him, being accounted righteous in him, and so on, it must be remembered – as Fee rightly stressed – are not isolated abstracts of theology. They must not be read as such. They appear in a context. They must be read with this in mind.[404] And that context, as I have said, is union. Union! Union with Adam or union with Christ. All men without exception are in Adam, in union with him, and die in him;[405] all the elect are in Christ, in union with him, and died with him, were buried with him, rose with him, and will be glorified in him. There is not an atom of mere sufficiency about it in either case.[406] In fact, the notion is utterly unthinkable in such a context. It is all absolute.[407] The notion of a *sufficient, provisional, hypothetical* or *conditional* union with Christ is, as I have said, risible.[408]

Let Haldane sum this up, starting with the fundamental point; namely the division of the human race into two families under two heads:

The gospel is founded on the fact that Adam and Christ are the... heads and representatives of their respective families. Hence they are termed the first and second man, as if there had been none other but themselves, for the children of each were entirely dependent on their head. In Adam all die; in Christ all are made alive. The first 'all' includes every individual of mankind; the last 'all' is explained by the apostle to mean 'they that are Christ's'... All mankind are, by nature, the children of wrath,[409] and consequently under the bondage of sin. Such is our connection, our union with Adam, that his sin is ours in all its aggravations, as well as in its consequences. All inherit from their first father a corrupt nature,[410] and the seed of every sinful propensity, which grows with their growth, and strengthens with their strength; and, *in exact correspondence with this*, all whom Christ represented, whose substitute and surety he became, are justified and made partakers of [the] divine nature, and of all the blessings which flow from his vicarious obedience and sufferings, such as faith, repentance, love, joy, peace and all the other fruits of the Spirit. It would destroy the beautiful harmony between Adam and Christ, so much insisted on in the word of God, if all whom Adam represented, without exception, were involved in his guilt and condemnation, while [many] of those, whose substitute Christ became, did not partake of his righteousness, justification and life. In this case, there would be no analogy between the head of the natural and [the head] of the spiritual creation...

The Scriptures teach us that by uniting himself with his people, by becoming their brother and near kinsman, Christ had the right of redemption; and that he came to do his Father's will in ransoming from destruction one of the two great families into which mankind had been divided on the first intimation of the coming of the Saviour. By enduring the curse which they had incurred, he obtained for them the blessing of eternal salvation... In consequence of the union between Adam and his posterity, a union as real as that as between the head and the members of the body, all [mankind] were involved in his guilt and condemnation; [likewise], in consequence of the union of the elect with the Son of God, who was made of a woman, made under the law, his obedience and death procured for them [the elect] pardon and eternal life, while justice received full satisfaction; and the truth of God, who had denounced [pronounced?] death to be the wages of sin, was fully vindicated by the redeemed enduring the penalty in the person of their glorious head, representative and surety, and thus becoming dead unto sin, and alive unto God by Jesus Christ...

We were all one with Adam in virtue of the constitution which it pleased God to give to the human race. Hence we existed in [Adam], and were responsible [with him; that is, guilty with him] for his disobedience. So Christ's righteousness belongs to his people on account of his voluntary union with them, and consequent substitution in their place. God imputes to us Adam's guilt, because we were [are] really guilty in Adam; and it is because Christ's people are righteous in him [Christ], that God justifies them, and treats them as righteous; else there would be unrighteousness with God. In both cases, union is the ground of imputation...

In the first Adam, all his posterity were made [constituted] sinners, and, consequently, condemned. The children of the second [last] Adam are all made [constituted] righteous, and, consequently, justified. All sinned in Adam's sin; the [elect] are all justified in Christ's righteousness...

According to the word of God, [Adam and Christ], and their respective families, are so closely united, or rather, *identified*, that the guilt of Adam, and the righteousness of Christ, are the guilt and righteousness of their respective children. Hence all the children of Adam are by nature children of wrath, shapen in iniquity, and conceived in sin; and all Christ's children can challenge the universe to lay anything to their charge.[411]

Romans 5:18 does not teach universal atonement.

On **2 Corinthians 5:14-15**, Clifford was wrong.[412] As he recognised, the 'died' is in the aorist (as is the 'reconciled' in verse 18).[413] Therefore the passage is the same as Romans 6:2-11; 7:4-6 (contrary to Clifford). (See also Gal. 2:19-20; Eph. 2:1,4-6; Col. 2:11-15,20; 3:1,3; 2 Tim. 2:11; 1 Pet. 2:24). We are back in the context of union once again. Clifford was right in saying the two deaths are simultaneous; *as* Christ died, *so* those in him (the elect) died. The same goes for the burial, resurrection and ascension, as I have pointed out. But Clifford confused *decreed* justification, *accomplished* justification, and *applied* or *actual* justification. The elect died with Christ in eternity past (decreed justification), at the cross (accomplished justification), and in their experience (applied justification at regeneration and faith; that is, conversion).[414] This is what being 'in Christ' means. It is simply out of the question to say Romans 6 is one of the three, and 2 Corinthians 5:14-15 is another. The deaths were simultaneous – those in Christ died with him, in union with him, in all three aspects. The two passages are conclusive; they prove definite particular redemption, in decree, accomplishment and experience. The 'all' are the 'all in Christ'. To say, as Clifford did, that 2 Corinthians 5:14-15 'is simply affirming Christ's identification with the human race in his death', is tragically weak, a pitiful conclusion.

Notice also, as Clifford observed, the AV rendering, 'then were all dead', is poor; it should read, 'therefore all died'.[415] 'If one died for all, *therefore* all died'; that is, 'since one died for all, *therefore* all died'. Proper weight must be given to the 'therefore'.[416] As a consequence of Christ's death, as an inevitable consequence of Christ's death, all died. It was because Christ died for all, that all died – they all died as a consequence of his death. As I have said, Clifford rightly emphasised the simultaneous nature of the two deaths, but failed to comment on the second death *as an inevitable consequence* of the first. True, those who died, died 'as and when the "one" died'; but they died also as a result of, *as a consequence of*, the death of the 'one'. The notion of sufficiency just does not fit this. The death of Christ, and the consequent death of all, cannot be provisional. Christ died; that is a definite accomplished fact; he died. *As a consequence*, all died; another definite accomplished fact. What is more, they died at that time; they all died with Christ, in Christ, as Clifford said, 'simultaneously'. They died. It will not do to say they died provisionally at that time,[417] but died effectively when they came to faith.[418] They died with and in Christ as he died. And they died because he died. The upshot? If the 'all' means 'all men without exception', then all without exception died.

Haldane:

> In Christ's death, all the members of his mystical body died... In him who died for all, *all died* (2 Cor. 5:14)... 'If one died for all, then all died'... Does [the Amyraldian] hold that all mankind died in Christ? This must inevitably follow if he died for all.[419]

But this is nonsense; it is *not* what Paul said. As I have shown in the body of the book, the context is 'all in Christ'. 'All in Christ', all the elect, died in and with Christ.

Furthermore, as Paul goes on: 'He died for all, *that* those who live should live no longer for themselves, but for him who died for them and rose again'. Who are those who live? The regenerate, the believing elect, of course.[420] What does the 'that' mean?[421] Christ died for all *so that* all who died and were made alive in him should live for him. On Clifford's reading this must mean that 'since Christ died for all [sufficiently, without exception], therefore all [without exception] died [provisionally]; and he died for all [sufficiently, without exception], that those who live [the elect, when they come to faith] should live no longer for themselves, but for him who died for them and rose again'. But if this is right, what part does the 'that' play? Why should the provisional death of Christ for all without exception mean that the believing elect should live for Christ? I fail to see the connection. However, it makes perfect sense, to me at least, to say that because Christ died for all his elect ('all in him'), all his elect ('all in him') – when they come to faith – should live for him who died for them. And not only *should*. As I have argued, Christ died for all his elect to make it

inevitable – certain – that all his elect *will* live for him. All his elect died in him; all his elect will live for him. Thus the right reading of the passage is obtained by taking the 'all' as 'all in Christ'.[422]
Let me stress once again the 'that'. Christ dying for his elect is not merely the motive for their living for him; his death makes it inevitable; Christ died *so that* they *would* live for him. See 2 Corinthians 5:17. It is because Christ died for his elect that they will live for him. A death which is merely provisional would fail to ensure this inevitability. But his death *does* ensure it. Christ's death is the *cause* of the believing elect living for him. The death of Christ, therefore, is an effectual death for all his elect, ensuring that they live for him.

In short, the elect died in and with Christ; they died because he died for them; consequently all his elect will live for him. This is what the passage teaches.[423]

As for Romans 6:2-11; 7:4-6, note the 'simultaneous' applies to the death, burial, resurrection and marriage in question; the man in Christ died to sin and the law, lives in and with Christ, and is united with him in marriage. Certainly, all this takes place in the believer's experience at conversion by spiritual baptism.[424] But not only there. It happened on the cross and at the resurrection. Not only that; it was all decreed by God in eternity. Above all, this union will be the eternal glory of all the elect. The notion that any of this could be provisional, or merely sufficient, is preposterous. Take but one. Is Christ provisionally or sufficiently married to all the human race? Put it the other way round: Is every member of the human race provisionally married to Christ?[425] What is this *provisional* or *sufficient* marriage?

2 Corinthians 5:14-15 does not teach universal atonement. It teaches particular, effective and absolute redemption for all the elect.

Now for those verses which speak of 'the world', which, according to Clifford,[426] are 'best represented' by **John 3:16**. Few would disagree. While Clifford found some of Owen's explanation of the verse 'rather obvious', overall, to put it mildly, he found it unacceptable, and was much happier with Wesley and Baxter. As for Calvin, however, Clifford had to work hard to salvage as much as he could from his comments, but he was clutching at straws. Calvin saw, quite rightly, that the verse teaches:

Christ came to us, and... was offered to be our Saviour... because the heavenly Father loves the human race, and wishes that they [*sic*] should not perish... Deliverance is offered to us by the faith of Christ... And he has employed the universal term 'whosoever', both to invite all indiscriminately to partake of life, and to cut off every excuse from unbelievers... He shows himself to be reconciled to the whole world, when he invites all men without exception to the faith of Christ.[427]

But the universal offer does not mean that all will be saved, nor that sinners by their own power can turn and believe:

Let us remember, on the other hand, that while life is promised universally to all who believe in Christ, still faith is not common to all. For Christ is made known and held out to the view of all, but the elect alone are they whose eyes God opens, that they may seek him by faith.

John 3:17 immediately follows on. As Calvin noted, Christ 'came not to destroy... [but] that all who believe may obtain salvation by him... The word "world" is again repeated, that no man may think himself wholly excluded'.[428] Obviously, he meant, no man can think himself excluded *from the offer* – the invitation to come to Christ and the duty to believe. But not a whisper here of a universal atonement. A universal offer, yes; God's desire for the salvation of the human race, yes; but a universal atonement, no. Not here at least. Not here, in that verse which 'best represents' those passages which speak of 'the world'.

Now for **1 John 2:2**. This verse is far more apposite to the question in hand than John 3:16; the latter being about the free offer, whereas 1 John 2:2 is concerned with the atonement – 'the propitiation... for the whole world'. Once again, Clifford seemed uncomfortable.[429] Although, it goes without saying, he did not like Owen's view, neither was he at home with Calvin, and yet, as before, had to try to salvage as much as he could from his comments, some of which make far from happy reading for Amyraldians.
Calvin:

Here a question may be raised: How have the sins of the whole world been expiated? I pass by the dotages of the fanatics, who under this pretence extend salvation to all the reprobate, and therefore to Satan himself. Such a monstrous thing deserves no refutation.

Very well. That's dealt with those who want to get universalism out of the text. In addition to calling it 'the dotages of the fanatics' and 'monstrous', Calvin rightly dismissed this as an 'absurdity'. But what of those who use the sufficiency formula?

Calvin again:

They who seek to avoid this absurdity [universal salvation], have said that Christ suffered sufficiently for the whole world, but efficiently only for the elect. This solution has commonly prevailed in the Schools. Though then I allow that what has been said is true, yet I deny that it is suitable to this passage; for the design of John was no other than to make this benefit common to the whole church. Then under the word 'all' or whole, he does not include the reprobate, but designates those who [in the years to come] should believe as well as those [believers] who were then scattered through various parts of the world. For then [when the elect come to faith] is really made evident, as it is meet, the grace of Christ, when it is declared to be the only true salvation of the world.[430]

Reader, I have made my position clear. I think the Schoolmen's formula is either wrong or meaningless, and there I disagree with Calvin. But whatever view is taken of that, even as Calvin said, mere 'sufficiency' will not do as an explanation of 1 John 2:2. The fact is, Christ *is* the propitiation for all referred to in the verse. 'He himself is the propitiation for our sins, and not for ours only but also for the whole world'. Glossing the 'propitiation' or the 'for' is disastrous. Christ *is* the propitiation for 'our sins'. There is nothing provisional about it. He *is* our propitiation. God *is* appeased.[431] And, as John says, he is the propitiation for the sins of 'the whole world'. This does not mean that while Christ is the effective propitiation for our sins, he is the sufficient propitiation for the sins of all the rest. Certainly not! *Just as* he is 'the propitiation for *our* sins', *so* he is the propitiation for the sins of 'the whole world' – 'not for ours only *but also* for the whole world'.[432] Since glossing 'propitiation' is out of the question, therefore, we must explore the meaning of 'ours' and 'the whole world'.

Wait a minute, says an objector; why all this 'glossing'? what is all the fuss about? 'the whole world' means 'just what it says' – 'every human being'; it's obvious! Oh? This – 'just what it says' – is the biggest gloss of the lot! And it gets us nowhere. It is not at all 'obvious' that this is what John means. Begging the question is no solution. What *is* the phrase saying? *That* is the issue. There is nothing forced or unworthy in reading an implied and obvious qualification in 'the whole world'; indeed, it is essential; we must always interpret (gloss) the phrase in terms of the context in which it is situated. And we know that John was quite willing to use it in a sense other than 'every human being'; when, for instance, he said: 'We know that we are of God, and the whole world lies under the sway of the wicked one' (1 John 5:19). Since John distinguished 'we [who] are of God' from 'the whole world', clearly 'the whole world' here cannot mean 'every human being without exception'. It doesn't include believers! Again, although the word 'whole' is absent (but see NIV) in John 12:19, the sentiment, expressed by the Pharisees concerning Christ, is the same: 'The world has gone after him'. Nobody imagines they meant 'every individual throughout the world'.[433]

But in 1 John 2:2, 'the whole world' does include the 'ours'; the 'not for ours only but also for the whole world' proves it. The apostle is clear: Christ is the propitiation for *our* sins – and not only for *ours*, but also for the sins of the whole world, *including ours*. Whatever view is taken of 'ours' and 'the whole world' in this verse, therefore, 'the whole world' must include the 'ours'.

The possibilities for the 'ours' and 'the whole world' can be set out thus:

1. **The elect** (ours), and **the elect and the non-elect** (the whole world)
2. **The elect who were believing in John's day** (ours), and **all the elect of all ages** (the whole world)
3. **Elect Jews** (ours), and **elect Jews and Gentiles** (the whole world)

As for the first possibility, as it stands it is universalism; by suitable glossing of the propitiation, however, it is either Arminianism (provisional for all, effective for none) or Amyraldianism

(provisional for all, effective for some). For the reasons I have set out, however, we cannot gloss 'propitiation'. Whichever of these two alternatives is chosen, therefore, the first possibility is wrong. This leaves the second and third possibilities. Both sustain the doctrine of Scripture; namely that Christ was the propitiation for the sins of the elect, the elect of whatever age or nation.[434]
Above all, consider the context,[435] which, as always, holds the key. John was setting out both a stimulus and a comfort to believers – a stimulus as to their sanctification, and a comfort as to their assurance. How would a provisional propitiation for the non-elect fulfil these roles?[436] If it could be shown that Christ has died for all men, some of whom will not be saved, how would this encourage believers to cease from sin? how would it assure them of God's forgiveness when they did sin? The biblical comfort in such circumstances is: 'It is Christ who died, and furthermore is also risen, who is even at the right hand of God, who also makes intercession for us' (Rom. 8:34). It is not: 'It is Christ who died provisionally or sufficiently for all but effectively for the elect, and furthermore is also risen provisionally or sufficiently for all but effectively for the elect, who is even at the right hand of God, who also makes intercession provisionally or sufficiently for all but effectively for the elect'.

In short, 1 John 2:2 does not teach a provisional atonement for all men. Rather, as I have argued, it tells us that Christ absolutely propitiated the wrath of God for the sins of all the elect of all ages and nations.

Passages which seem to imply that those for whom Christ died can be lost

The passages in question are Romans 14:15 and 1 Corinthians 8:11, and 2 Peter 2:1.

Romans 14:15 and 1 Corinthians 8:11. The weak brother is a *brother*, a genuine brother, one of the elect. This weak brother, one of the elect, one 'for whom Christ died', can be 'destroyed'. Clifford argued that this destruction means 'irretrievable harm';[437] the man perishes in eternal destruction. Clifford, naturally, wanted to limit this to the non-elect, allowing that one for whom Christ died (sufficiently) might perish, but not one of the elect (one for whom Christ died efficaciously). But this is wrong. The man who is destroyed is a brother, one of the elect, one for whom Christ died. As Clifford said, we are talking about 'a fellow believer', one of whom it can be said: 'Christ has died for him... The apostle can only mean that the weak brother must be viewed as a true believer'. But I would put it more strongly. Even on Clifford's terms, he must be one of the elect – one for whom Christ died efficaciously.[438] The man *is* a brother; he *is* a true brother; he *is* a believer; he *is*, therefore, one of the elect; Christ *has* died for him, and died for him *efficaciously*. If not, Paul's point is lost, as I will show. He says that a true believer, one of the elect, one for whom Christ has died, can perish or be 'destroyed'.

A true believer, one of the elect, perish, be destroyed? Impossible, surely? Not at all! It all depends on what is meant by 'destroyed'.

The solution certainly does not lie in glossing the 'for' or the 'died', the one '*for* whom Christ *died*'. The verses do not talk about two brothers – one strong and the other weak – in the sense that Christ *died for* the one brother **efficaciously** and *for* the other brother **provisionally**. Nor do they teach that although the brother *for* whom Christ *died* **efficaciously** cannot be 'destroyed', the brother *for* whom Christ *died* **provisionally** can be. A good job too! In the day-to-day outworking of Paul's teaching, how would we be supposed to know for certain which 'brother' is which? And, from a personal and pastoral point of view, it is important to know, is it not?[439] In any case, what scriptural support is there for saying that the *strong* brother is *elect* and the *weak* brother is *not*? that Christ effectively died for the strong brother, but only sufficiently for the weak brother? What scriptural support is there, I ask, for this sort of interpretation of 'strong' and 'weak'? None! There is no solution to the conundrum in this approach.

The solution lies, as I said, in the word 'destroy'. Clifford argued that this is eternal destruction, which is 'the very basis of the apostle's concern... There can be no doubt that the apostle intends to convey the danger[440] of eternal destruction'. Is this right? Is this what Paul here means by 'destroy'? I agree the warning passages (as in Hebrews) are real. And, yes, the word used here, *apollumi*, can mean eternal destruction (Matt. 10:28; John 3:16; Jas. 4:12), and this is by far its commonest use in the New Testament. But does it always mean that? Does it mean that here? After all, it can mean 'to throw away and decompose' (Matt. 5:29; John 6:12,27), 'to mar or ruin something, making it no longer fit for purpose' (Matt. 9:17; Mark 2:22; Luke 5:37), 'to lose a straying sheep' (Luke 15:4), 'to wander after losing one's way' (Matt. 10:6; 15:24; see Isa. 53:6; 1 Pet. 2:25), 'to be lost, the opposite of being found' (Matt. 18:11; Luke 19:10).[441]

As always, the context is king. And the context of Romans 14 – 15 and 1 Corinthians 8 is clear; the apostle speaks of a stumbling block, an obstacle, an offence, a wounded conscience, a man condemning himself, stumbling, falling into sin, being distressed, hurt, grieved, offended and weakened, giving cause for others (possibly outsiders) to criticise believers, all through the eating of meat, or doing anything else about which a brother has doubts. Could the 'destroy' not speak of the weak brother's own grief and hurt, within his own mind and heart? Because of his scruples, he has been shown contempt, looked down upon, despised and judged – dismissed – by a fellow (stronger) believer, when all the time he has to answer only to God – as does the stronger brother! 'If your brother is grieved because of your food, you are no longer walking in love. Do not destroy with your food the one for whom Christ died... It is good neither to eat meat nor drink wine nor do anything by which your brother stumbles or is offended or is made weak' (Rom. 14:15,21). This is what Paul is speaking about.[442] And this is not 'eternal destruction'.[443]

Again, the weak brother, embarrassed by the mocking he receives, or emboldened by the unwise example of his stronger brother, might eat when it hurts his conscience so to do, and this brings him to condemn himself: 'Happy is he who does not condemn himself in what he approves. But he who doubts is condemned if he eats, because he does not eat from faith; for whatever is not of faith is sin' (Rom. 14:22-23).[444] Are we to understand that a believer can eternally damn himself – damn *himself*, I stress[445] – and do so by a questionable decision he makes over food? Of course not! The stronger brother can hurt the weaker brother, however, and he should take care not to: 'Beware lest somehow this liberty of yours becomes a stumbling block to those who are weak. For if anyone sees you who have knowledge eating in an idol's temple, will not the conscience of him who is weak be emboldened to eat those things offered to idols? And because of your knowledge shall the weak brother perish, for whom Christ died?' (1 Cor. 8:9-11).

The 'shall' must not be misunderstood. Paul proposes a case: If you in some way encourage the weak brother to go against his conscience, he will be ruined. But the apostle was not thinking of any supposed ruin in eternity. No! He will be ruined; he *is* ruined, *now*, said Paul; indeed, he is being ruined, even as we speak.[446] And, as Gill commented: 'The perishing of this weak brother is said to be understood of his peace and comfort, and is explained by defiling his conscience (verse 7) by wounding it (verse 12)'.[447] This is not 'eternal destruction'.

How does Paul describe the opposite? It is to bring peace, to edify, to please, build up and accept each other and not magnify differences and goad each other in these matters, not to produce quarrels, pride and grief. 'We then who are strong ought to bear with the scruples of the weak, and not to please ourselves. Let each of us please his neighbour for his good, leading to edification' (Rom. 15:1-2). The opposite of edification is not 'eternal destruction'.

We get the same concern in another passage to do with the eating of meat offered to idols, where Paul commands: 'Whatever you do, do all to the glory of God. Give no offence, either to the Jews or to the Greeks or to the church of God' (1 Cor. 10:31-32).[448] To 'give no offence' is, literally, 'having nothing for one to strike against; not causing to stumble', and thus 'not leading others into sin by one's mode of life'.[449] Paul is concerned that believers should not 'alienate someone who is already a brother or sister'.[450] And the apostle concludes in much the same way as in the other passages: 'Give no offence... to the church of God', but, rather, follow my example 'just as I also please all men in all things, not seeking my own profit' (1 Cor. 10:32-33). To 'please', to 'profit', here means to edify,[451] the opposite of which is not 'destroy eternally'.

Other passages, too, confirm that we are not talking about eternal damnation. Consider: 'If anyone defiles the temple of God, God will destroy him' (1 Cor. 3:17). 'Defile' is commonly translated as 'destroy' (NASB, NKJV footnote, NIV, AV margin): 'If anyone destroys the temple of God, God will destroy him'. Paul, having used the same word for both 'defile' and 'destroy', unless there is good reason to think otherwise, it should carry the same meaning – the two appearances not only being in the same verse but immediately adjacent in the Greek: 'If anyone the temple of God *phtheipei*, *phthepei* him'. So far so good; the one Greek word should be translated by the same English word.[452] 'Destroy', however, despite the versions which opt for it, is not a good translation here; it conveys quite the wrong impression of what the apostle said – especially if it carries the overtone of eternal destruction. In that case, it would not make sense. How can any man eternally destroy God's temple?[453] Paul was not talking about eternal destruction. While *phtheirō* can mean 'to destroy', it can also mean 'to corrupt' or 'to mar'. And so it does in this verse: 'If anyone mars the temple of God, God will mar him'. The context substantiates it. Take verse 15, where a believer is said to 'suffer loss', *zēmioō* here meaning 'to suffer loss, injury or damage'. Linking this with verse 17, Fee observed: 'The "destruction" in verse 17 seems to imply the church's failure to function any longer as a viable alternative to [pagan] Corinth'. So, when a believer is said to suffer loss (verse 15), Paul does not mean that he will be destroyed in the sense of eternally damned. There is no suggestion whatsoever in any of this that any man for whom Christ died can be lost. Indeed, in the circumstances envisaged, Paul expressly states that he *cannot* be eternally damned: Though 'he will suffer loss... he himself will be saved'. 'Suffer loss', he may, but be lost eternally? Never! Verse 17, therefore, should be understood, as Hodge put it: 'If any man injure the temple of God, him will God injure'.[454]

Again, in 1 Corinthians 11:29-34, Paul speaks of 'judgement'; of believers being 'judged... chastened' but 'not condemned with the world'. Fee: 'The "judgment" of course, as verse 32 makes clear, does not have to do with their eternal salvation, but with the temporal judgement of sickness and death. Beyond that one may only speculate'.[455] Note particularly Paul's categorical statement – the believer, in the circumstances envisaged, cannot be 'condemned with the world'. Clearly, the believer's judgement he is speaking of is not eternal condemnation.

In short, in Romans 14:15 and 1 Corinthians 8:11, Paul commands believers not to hurt in any way a brother, one of the elect, one for whom Christ died. He was certainly not thinking of eternal perdition. If he was, then how few believers will escape! Who can say he has never done anything about which he has some scruple or nagging doubt? Who can say he might not have encouraged (if not wilfully, then by neglect) some other brother to do something against his conscience which leads him to grief? If 'condemn' here means 'everlasting damnation', who can stand in the light of Romans 14:23? Who can say he has never done anything to hurt or offend another brother? Who is clear in this matter? John 8:7 springs to mind. Surely Clifford's interpretation proves too much. And when Paul commands believers not to 'destroy the work of God for the sake of food' (Rom. 14:20), are we to understand that he is saying that God's work will be utterly and irretrievably – eternally – destroyed through this kind of behaviour? Certainly it can be badly damaged, but does 'utterly and completely destroy in everlasting damnation' really fit this? I think not. 'Do not tear down the work of God for the sake of food' (Rom. 14:20 NASB). The context speaks not of consequences in eternity, but of consequences in time, in present experience, both for the individual and the church. As the apostle said to the Philippians: 'Let nothing be done through selfish ambition or conceit, but in lowliness of mind let each esteem others better than himself. Let each of you look out not only for his own interests, but also for the interests of others. Let this mind be in you which was also in Christ Jesus' (Phil. 2:3-5). And we know that 'Christ did not please himself' (Rom. 15:3). Paul does not want a believer to hurt any fellow believer – one for whom Christ died. What a contrast! Here is a strong believer insisting on his right to eat what he likes, when he likes, showing no concern for his weaker brother. Yet Christ died for that weaker brother, as he did for the stronger!

And this takes us back to the crux of the discussion – the death of Christ. If Paul was teaching that a weak brother (one for whom

Christ died provisionally) is destroyed because of the bad behaviour of a strong brother (one for whom Christ died effectively) – if, I say – then he failed to show how the death of Christ aggravates the offence. In the context, it is Christ's death *for the brother who is destroyed* which does that. Christ's death, therefore, for this weak brother, must have been effectual; a provisional death would fail to make Paul's point. Paul's thrust lies in the fact that Christ died effectually for the weak brother who is being hurt – *that is, he died for him as much as for the offending brother*. It is this which aggravates the strong believer's offence; it puts it into perspective.[456] On Clifford's argument, Paul's emphasis has fallen in the wrong place.

What is more, on Clifford's argument, there is no emphasis here at all. Christ, apparently, has died for *all* men provisionally, all of whom (apart from the elect) will be eternally destroyed, professing believers or not. According to Clifford, the behaviour of the true believer *causes* the eternal death of the professing believer (but, in reality, one who is an unbeliever). But this is manifestly not the case. Of course, a believer can be a bad influence on an unbeliever, but the unbeliever's eternal destruction arises out of his own unbelief – his own despising of the death of Christ. This is the emphasis made in Scripture.[457]

Romans 14:15 and 1 Corinthians 8:11 do not teach that one for whom Christ died can be eternally lost.

2 Peter 2:1. 'There will be false teachers among you... even denying the Lord who bought them, and bring on themselves swift destruction'. There are two questions. *First*, what is this 'swift destruction'? Although the word 'destruction', *apōleia*, can be used in a lesser sense – the 'waste' of ointment (Mark 14:4), for instance – it here means 'utter destruction, a perishing, ruin, destruction, the destruction which consists in the loss of eternal life, eternal misery, perdition, the lot of those excluded from the kingdom of God'.[458] *Secondly*, who – rather, what – are these 'false teachers'? They are either regenerate or not. If they are regenerate, they are elect, and Christ bought them efficaciously. This cannot be. *They* cannot perish. So they must be unregenerate, deceived and deceivers. But, evidently, they do not appear to be such. If they did, they would not be accepted as teachers in the church. As a result, Peter describes them as they appear. They *are* teachers; therefore they had been accepted ('among you') as believers and regarded as such, as elect and bought by Christ. But though this is how they appear, in every particular the opposite is the reality. They are not true believers; they are not elect; they were not bought by Christ.

If, however, Clifford was right,[459] and these teachers perish although Christ died for them, it could only be – in his terms – that Christ died for them to provide a sufficient (but not an effectual) atonement. But how can we know that the 'bought' in 2 Peter 2:1 is sufficient, yet efficacious in 1 Corinthians 6:20; 7:23?[460] What is more, allowing Clifford's 'sufficiency' view to stand, the thrust of Peter's case is lost. It all seems a bit unnecessary – over the top – indeed, a truism – since on Clifford's argument Christ has bought everybody provisionally – so why does Peter mention it here? What does it add to his case? All pagans, outsiders, atheists and all the rest – let alone 'false teachers' – apparently, are denying the Christ who bought them. Today, we could include Jehovah Witnesses, Muslims, the lot! So why say it here?

It must be because they were *claiming* that Christ had died for them, and that the people believed them. These were false teachers *in the church*; everybody thought they were believers. Yet, in truth, their doctrine went right against Christ and his atonement. They were saying they were redeemed, they were preaching and promising redemption, but their teaching and lives were denying they had actually received it.

And this is not an isolated instance. Indeed, we find similar complaints throughout the New Testament. Writing to several churches, the apostles could speak of false teachers who had infiltrated themselves among the saints – false teachers, deceived and deceiving – but who did not always appear such:

> Those who cause divisions and offences, contrary to the doctrine which you learned... who... do not serve our Lord Jesus Christ, but their own belly, and by smooth words and flattering speech deceive the hearts of the simple (Rom. 16:17-20)
>
> False apostles, deceitful workers, transforming themselves into [seeming] apostles of Christ. And no wonder! For Satan himself transforms himself into an angel of light. Therefore it is no great thing if his ministers also transform themselves into ministers of

righteousness, whose end will be according to their works (2 Cor. 11:13-15)
There are some who trouble you and want to pervert the gospel of Christ (Gal. 1:6-10)
False brethren secretly brought in (who came in by stealth...)... those who seemed to be something – whatever they were (Gal. 2:4-6)
Men... having a form of godliness but denying its power (2 Tim. 3:1-9)
They profess to know God, but in works they deny him (Tit. 1:9-16)
Many antichrists have come... They went out from us, but they were not of us; for if they had been of us, they would have continued with us; but they went out that they might be made manifest, that none of them were of us... Who is a liar but he who denies that Jesus is the Christ? He is antichrist who denies the Father and the Son (1 John 2:18-19,22-23)
Many false prophets have gone out into the world... They are of the world. Therefore they speak as of the world, and the world hears them... If someone says: 'I love God', and hates his brother, he is a liar (1 John 4:1-6,20)
Many deceivers have gone out into the world... This is a deceiver and an antichrist... Whoever... does not abide in the doctrine of Christ does not have God (2 John 7,9-10)
Certain men have crept in unnoticed... ungodly men, who turn the grace of our God into lewdness and deny the only Lord God and our Lord Jesus Christ... These dreamers... speak evil of whatever they do not know... These are spots in your love feasts, while they feast with you without fear, serving only themselves. They are clouds without water... they mouth great swelling words... sensual persons, who cause divisions, not having the Spirit (Jude 4,8,10,12,16,19)[461]
Those who say they are apostles and are not [but are] liars (Rev. 2:2)[462]

Diotrophes might well have been such a one (3 John 9-10). In short: 'Beware of false prophets, who come to you in sheep's clothing, but inwardly they are ravenous wolves' (Matt. 7:15).[463] The parallel with 2 Peter 2 is unmissable.

Above all, note how Peter goes on in 2 Peter 2:12-22. These false teachers, whom Peter calls 'children' – that is, he describes them once more as they appear – are 'wells without water'; that is, they look like wells but they are not; 'they promise... liberty', but 'they themselves are slaves of corruption'. Peter is describing men who get very close to Christ, look like believers, are accepted as teachers, teach things which sound right (about the atonement), but in reality are living lives which deny it. The truth is, they are destroying the very doctrine (Christ's redemption) they pretend[464] to preach, and profess to have experienced. The people accept their claims – they think these teachers have been redeemed ('the Lord... bought them') – but their works prove they are not (they are 'denying the Lord who bought them'); that is, their works are denying their profession, denying what their hearers believe about them. Such hypocrites do indeed 'bring on themselves swift destruction' (2 Pet. 2:1).[465]

Moreover, Peter uses *miasma*, 'pollution', in his description of these people: 'They have escaped the pollutions of the world' (2 Pet. 2:20). The word means 'defilement, foul, filthy, sullied, soiled'; these people have got rid of... what? Surface defilement, mud stains. As the apostle says, they are like a sow which has been washed from the mire (2 Pet. 2:22). In the context, Peter is speaking of them going back to their old ways, to their foul life-style, returning to the mire from which they had been washed, and wallowing in it (2 Pet. 2:10,22), but the truth is they were a dirty sow to start with, became a clean sow, and then went back to being a dirty sow all over again. Throughout, however, they were and remained a sow; a sow, outwardly clean or outwardly dirty, but a sow all the same; and never anything but a sow. In fact, all the time they were 'corrupt' (2 Pet. 2:12). Whether or not they had escaped *miasma*, they were, underneath, 'corrupt'; that is, they were fundamentally – essentially – in a state of *phthora*. Now this second word is altogether stronger than the first. *miasma* is of the surface; not only is *phthora* deep-seated, it speaks of something far more abominable than the former. These people will 'utterly perish in their own corruption' (2 Pet. 2:12). The word is used of the decay, the rotting, which occurs in nature (Rom. 8:21); of the body in the ground after burial (1 Cor. 15:42); of complete decomposition – like food passing through the digestive system (Col. 2:22; the idea, though not the word, is in Matt. 15:17; 1 Cor. 6:13). The people Peter speaks of have not escaped the spiritual or moral equivalent of this. They have been outwardly washed, yes, but inwardly remain utterly corrupt and unregenerate. Regenerate, true believers, on the other hand, *have* escaped the *phthora* that is the world (2 Pet. 1:4).[466]

In other words, the people in question were never truly washed in the Redeemer's blood. And their profession of Christ throughout was simply that; a mere outward profession, and nothing more. They said Christ had cleansed them, but he had not; they were hypocritical liars.

This, of course, means that the passage does not teach that Christ died for all men, and that some of those for whom he died shall eternally perish.[467]

* * *

In this Appendix, I have looked at the passages cited by Clifford in his attempt to set out his 'verdict of Scripture' on the atonement; namely, that Christ wrought a redemption, general for all, and particular for the elect. In my opinion, none of the passages he cited teach that Christ died efficaciously for some, yet provisionally for all.

Source List

Alford, Henry: *The New Testament for English Readers...*, Vol.2 Part 1, Rivingtons, London, 1865.

Arndt, William F. and Gingrich, F.Wilbur: *A Greek-English Lexicon of the New Testament and Other Early Christian Literature*, The University of Chicago Press, Chicago... and The Syndics of the Cambridge University Press, London, 1957.

Articles of Faith of the Gospel Standard Aid and Poor Relief Societies, The Gospel Standard Societies, Harpenden.

Baird, Allen: 'Amyrauldianism: Historical and Contemporary' in the *British Reformed Journal*, Lutterworth, issue 9.

Baird, Allen: 'The Westminster Standards and the Gospel Offer' in the *British Reformed Journal*, Lutterworth, issue 10.

Baird, Allen: 'Calvin and the Free Offer' in the *British Reformed Journal*, Lutterworth, issue 12.

Beaton, Donald: *Some Foundation Truths of The Reformed Faith*, Sovereign Grace Union, London, 1938.

Bellamy, Terry: A letter in *New Focus*, Apr./May. 2005, Vol.9 no.6.

Bennet, Tyler, and Bonar, Andrew A.: *Nettleton and His Labours*, The Banner of Truth Trust, Edinburgh, 1975.

Berkhof, L.: *Systematic Theology*, The Banner of Truth Trust, London, 1959.

Berridge, John: *The Christian World Unmasked: Pray Come and Peep* in *The Works of... John Berridge...*, Vol.1, edited by... Richard Whittingham, Old Paths Gospel Press, Choteau.

Bonar, Andrew, see Bennet, Tyler.

Bonar, John: 'The Universal Calls and Invitations of the Gospel Consistent with the Total Depravity of Man, and Particular Redemption', first published in *The Free Church Pulpit* in 1844, republished in *The Banner of Truth*, London, 14th issue, Feb. 1959.

Booth, Abraham: *Glad Tidings to Perishing Sinners: The Genuine Gospel a Complete Warrant for the Ungodly to Believe in Jesus* in *The Works of Abraham Booth...*, Vol.2, W.Button & Son, London, 1813.

Booth, Abraham: *Divine Justice Essential to the Divine Character* in *The Works of Abraham Booth...*, Vol.3, W.Button & Son, London, 1813.

Booth, Abraham: *The Reign of Grace...*, Old Paths Gospel Press, Choteau.

Boston, Thomas, notes in Edward Fisher: *The Marrow of Modern Divinity...*, Still Waters Revival Books, Edmonton, reprint edition 1991.

Boston, Thomas: *The Beauties of Thomas Boston...*, edited by Samuel M'Millan, Christian Focus Publications, Inverness, 1979.

Brown, John: *An Exposition of Hebrews*, The Banner of Truth Trust, 1961.

Brown, John: *Expository Discourses on 1 Peter*, Vol.2, The Banner of Truth Trust, Edinburgh, 1975.

Bunyan, John: *The Jerusalem Sinner Saved; or, Good News for the Vilest of Men...* in *The Works of John Bunyan*, Vol.2, edited by Henry Stebbing, John Hirst, London, 1862.

Bunyan, John: *Reprobation Asserted...* in *The Works of John Bunyan*, Vol.3, edited by Henry Stebbing, John Hirst, London, 1862.

Burrows, D: A letter in *New Focus*, Apr./May. 2005, Vol.9 no.6.

Calvin, John: *Institutes of the Christian Religion*, A new translation by Henry Beveridge, James Clarke & Co., Limited, London, 1957.

Calvin, John: *Sermons on The Epistle to the Ephesians*, The Banner of Truth Trust, Edinburgh, 1975.

Calvin, John: *Calvin's Commentaries*, Baker Book House, Grand Rapids, 1979.

Cheeseman, John, and Gardner, Philip, and Sadgrove, Michael, and Wright, Tom: *The Grace of God in the Gospel*, The Banner of Truth Trust, London, 1972.

Clarkson, David: *Of Faith* in *The Works of David Clarkson*, Vol.1, The Banner of Truth Trust, Edinburgh, 1988.

Clifford, Alan C.: *Atonement and Justification: English Evangelical Theology 1640-1790. An Evaluation*, Clarendon Press, Oxford, 1990.

Clifford, Alan C.: *Amyraut Affirmed*, Charenton Reformed Publishing, Norwich, 2004.

Clifford, Alan C.: 'Evangelicalisms: The Case for Amyraldianism', being a computer print-out of a paper given at the third meeting of the Amyraldian Association, Attleborough, 1st April 2005.

Clifford, Alan C.: 'Introduction' to Davenant, John: *Dissertation on the Death of Christ*, Quinta Press, Weston Rhyn, 2006.

Clifford, Alan C.: *Calvinus. Authentic Calvinism: A Clarification*, new edition, Charenton Reformed Publishing, Norwich, 2007.

Clifford, Alan C.: *Jonathan Edwards – Amyraldian?*, Charenton Reformed Publishing, Norwich, 2008.

Crisp, Tobias: *Christ Alone Exalted...*, edited by John Gill, Old Paths Gospel Press, Choteau.

Cunningham, William: *Historical Theology...*, Vol.2, The Banner of Truth Trust, Edinburgh, 1994.

Dabney, Robert L.: 'God's Indiscriminate Proposals of Mercy, As Related to His Power, Wisdom, and Sincerity' in *Discussions: Evangelical and Theological*, Vol.1, The Banner of Truth Trust, Edinburgh, 1967.

Dabney, Robert L.: *Systematic Theology*, The Banner of Truth Trust, Edinburgh, 1985.

Dagg, J.L.: *A Manual of Theology*, Gano Books, Harrisonburg, 1990.

Davenant, John: *Dissertation on the Death of Christ*, Quinta Press, Weston Rhyn, 2006.

Dix, Kenneth: *Strict and Particular: English Strict and Particular Baptists in the Nineteenth Century*, The Baptist Historical Society for The Strict Baptist Historical Society, Didcot, 2001.

Donnelly, Edward: 'Does a Limited Atonement Preclude a Sincere Offer of the Gospel to all Sinners?' in *The Banner of Truth*, Edinburgh, March 2004.

Douty, Norman F.: *The Death of Christ...*, Reiner Publications, Swengel, 1972.

Durham, James: *Christ Crucified: or, The Marrow of the Gospel...*, Edinburgh, 1726.

Dwight, Serenio E.: *Memoirs of Jonathan Edwards* in *The Works of Jonathan Edwards, Revised and Corrected by Edward Hickman*, Vol.1, The Banner of Truth Trust, Edinburgh, 1974.

Edwards, Jonathan: *...Freedom of Will...* in *The Works of Jonathan Edwards... Revised and Corrected by Edward Hickman*, Vol.1, The Banner of Truth Trust, Edinburgh, 1974.

Edwards, Jonathan: *A History of the Work of Redemption...* in *The Works of Jonathan Edwards... Revised and Corrected by Edward Hickman*, Vol.1, The Banner of Truth Trust, Edinburgh, 1974.

Edwards, Jonathan: *Unbelievers Contemn the Glory and Excellency of Christ* in *The Works of Jonathan Edwards... Revised and Corrected by Edward Hickman*, Vol.2, The Banner of Truth Trust, Edinburgh, 1974.

Edwards, Jonathan: *Great Guilt No Obstacle to the Pardon of the Returning Sinner* in *The Works of Jonathan Edwards... Revised and Corrected by Edward Hickman*, Vol.2, The Banner of Truth Trust, Edinburgh, 1974.

Edwards, Jonathan: *The Wisdom of God Displayed in the Way of Salvation* in *The Works of Jonathan Edwards... Revised and Corrected by Edward Hickman*, Vol.2, The Banner of Truth Trust, Edinburgh, 1974.

Edwards, Jonathan: *Christ Exalted... in the Work of Redemption* in *The Works of Jonathan Edwards... Revised and Corrected by Edward Hickman*, Vol.2, The Banner of Truth Trust, Edinburgh, 1974.

Edwards, Jonathan: *The Life and Diary of... David Brainerd...* in *The Works of Jonathan Edwards... Revised and Corrected by Edward Hickman*, Vol.2, The Banner of Truth Trust, Edinburgh, 1974.

Edwards, Jonathan: *Seventeen Occasional Sermons* in *The Works of Jonathan Edwards... Revised and Corrected by Edward Hickman*, Vol.2, The Banner of Truth Trust, Edinburgh, 1974.

Ella, George M.: *John Gill and the Cause of God and Truth*, Go Publications, Eggleston, 1995.

Ella, George M.: *The Free Offer and The Call of the Gospel*, Go Publications, Eggleston, 2001.

Ella, George M.: 'A Brief Response' in *New Focus*, Eggleston, Feb./Mar. 2005, Vol.9 no.5.

Elliot, R.: *A Summary of Gospel Doctrine taught by Mr Whitefield...* in *Select Sermons of George Whitefield...*, The Banner of Truth Trust, London, 1959.

Engelsma, David J.: *Hyper-Calvinism & The Call of the Gospel: An Examination of the 'Well-Meant Offer' of the Gospel*, Revised Edition, Reformed Free Publishing Association, Grand Rapids, 1994.

Erskine, Ralph, see M'Millan.

Fee, Gordon D.: *The First Epistle to the Corinthians* in *The New International Commentary on the New Testament*, William B.Eerdmans Publishing Company, Grand Rapids, reprinted 1991.

Foreman, John: *Remarks on Duty Faith*, Vol.1, Christian Bookshop, Ossett, 1995.

Fuller, Andrew: *The Gospel Its Own Witness...* in *The Complete Works of... Andrew Fuller...*, Henry G.Bohn, London, 1866.

Fuller, Andrew: *The Gospel Worthy of All Acceptation, or the Duty of Sinners to Believe in Jesus Christ...* in *The Complete Works of... Andrew Fuller...*, Henry G.Bohn, London, 1866.

Fuller, Andrew: *Appendix* to *The Gospel Worthy of All Acceptation, or the Duty of Sinners to Believe in Jesus Christ...* in *The Complete Works of... Andrew Fuller...*, Henry G.Bohn, London, 1866.

Fuller, Andrew: *A Reply to Mr Button's Remarks* in *The Complete Works of... Andrew Fuller...*, Henry G.Bohn, London, 1866.

Fuller, Andrew: *Reply to the Observations of Philanthropos* in *The Complete Works of... Andrew Fuller...*, Henry G.Bohn, London, 1866.

Fuller, Andrew: *The Reality and Efficacy of Divine Grace...* in *The Complete Works of... Andrew Fuller...*, Henry G.Bohn, London, 1866.

Fuller, Andrew: *Strictures on Sandemanianism...* in *The Complete Works of... Andrew Fuller...*, Henry G.Bohn, London, 1866.

Fuller, Andrew: *Three Conversations on Imputation, Substitution, and Particular Redemption* in *The Complete Works of... Andrew Fuller...*, Henry G.Bohn, London, 1866.

Fuller, Andrew: *Six Letters to Dr Ryland respecting The Controversy with... A.Booth* in *The Complete Works of... Andrew Fuller...*, Henry G.Bohn, London, 1866.

Fuller, Andrew: *Antinomianism Contrasted...* in *The Complete Works of... Andrew Fuller...*, Henry G.Bohn, London, 1866.

Fuller, Andrew: *Exposition of the Sermon on the Mount* in *The Complete Works of... Andrew Fuller...*, Henry G.Bohn, London, 1866.

Fuller, Andrew: *Sermons and Sketches of Sermons* in *The Complete Works of... Andrew Fuller...*, Henry G.Bohn, London, 1866.

Fuller, Andrew: *The Great Question Answered* in *Miscellaneous Tracts...* in *The Complete Works of... Andrew Fuller...*, Henry G.Bohn, London, 1866.

Fuller, Andrew: *The Awakened Sinner* in *Miscellaneous Tracts...* in *The Complete Works of... Andrew Fuller...*, Henry G.Bohn, London, 1866.

Fuller, Andrew: *Reviews* in *The Complete Works of... Andrew Fuller...*, Henry G.Bohn, London, 1866.

Fuller, Andrew: *On the Satisfaction of Christ* in *Fugitive Pieces* in *The Complete Works of... Andrew Fuller...*, Henry G.Bohn, London, 1866.

Gay, David: *Battle For The Church*, Brachus, Lowestoft, 1997.

Gay, David H.J.: *The Gospel Offer* **is** *Free*, Brachus, Biggleswade, 2004.

Gill, John: *Gill's Commentary*, Baker Book House, Grand Rapids, 1980.

Gill, John: *The Cause of God and Truth*, W.H.Collingridge, London, 1855.

Gill, John: *Sermons and Tracts*, Old Paths Gospel Press, Choteau, 1997.

Gill, John: *A Complete Body of Doctrinal and Practical Divinity; or, A System of Evangelical Truths, Deduced from the Sacred Scriptures*, W.Winterbotham, London, 1796.

Gillespie, George: *A Treatise of Miscellany Questions...* in *The Works of George Gillespie...*, Vol.2, Still Waters Revival Books, Edmonton.

Goold, William H., see Owen, John: *The Death of Death in the Death of Christ...* in *The Works of John Owen*, Vol.10, edited by William H.Goold, The Banner of Truth Trust, London, 1967.

Gospel Hymns, The Strict and Particular Baptist Society, Robert Stockwell, Ltd., London, 1915.

Gospel Standard.

Gouge, William: *Commentary on Hebrews*, Kregel Publications, Grand Rapids, 1980.

Griffin, Edward D.: *The Life and Sermons of Edward D.Griffin*, The Banner of Truth Trust, Edinburgh, 1987.

Haldane, J.A.: *The Doctrine Of The Atonement...*, Old Paths Gospel Press, Choteau.

Hanko, Ron: 'The Well-Meant Offer and Reprobation' in the *British Reformed Journal*, Lutterworth, issue 12.

Haykin, Michael A.G.: 'Particular Redemption in the Writings of Andrew Fuller (1754-1815)' in Bebbington, D.W. (ed): *The Gospel in the World*, Paternoster Press, Carlisle, 2002.

Helm, Paul: *Calvin and the Calvinists*, The Banner of Truth Trust, Edinburgh, 1982.

Hendriksen, William: *1 and 2 Thessalonians*, The Banner of Truth Trust, Edinburgh, 1976.

Henry, Matthew: *An Exposition of the Old and New Testament*, James Nisbet & Co., Limited, London.

Hodge, Charles: *A Commentary on Romans*, The Banner of Truth Trust, London, 1972.

Hodge, Charles: *A Commentary on the First Epistle to the Corinthians*, The Banner of Truth Trust, London, 1958.

Hodge, Charles: *A Commentary on the Second Epistle to the Corinthians*, The Banner of Truth Trust, London, 1963.

Hughes, Irfon: 'The Satisfied Saviour' in *The Banner of Truth*, Edinburgh, March 2004.

James, John Angell: *An Earnest Ministry The Want of The Times*, Hamilton, Adams & Co., London, 1848.

Jenkins, David Llewellyn: 'Amyraut On Other Religions...', being a paper read at the fourth annual conference of Amyraldian Association, 2006.

Kelly, Douglas F.: *Preachers With Power...*, The Banner of Truth Trust, Edinburgh, 1992.

Kennedy, John: *Man's Relations to God...*, The James Begg Society, 1995.

Kevan, Ernest: *Salvation*, Evangelical Press, London, 1973.

Kruse, Colin: *The Second Epistle of Paul to the Corinthians...*, Inter-Varsity Press, Leicester, 1987.

Lillie, John: *Lectures on... First and Second... Peter*, Klock & Klock Christian Publishers, Minneapolis, reprinted 1978.

Lloyd-Jones, D.M.: *Romans: An Exposition of Chapter 5. Assurance*, The Banner of Truth Trust, Edinburgh, 1971.

Lloyd-Jones, D.M.: *Romans: An Exposition of Chapter 6. The New Man*, The Banner of Truth Trust, Edinburgh, 1972.

Lloyd-Jones, D.M.: *Romans: An Exposition of Chapter 8:17-39. The Final Perseverance of the Saints*, The Banner of Truth Trust, Edinburgh, 1975.

Lloyd-Jones, D.Martyn: *Preaching and Preachers*, Hodder and Stoughton, London, 1971.

Lloyd-Jones, D.M.: *God's Ultimate Purpose... Ephesians 1:1-23*, The Banner of Truth Trust, Edinburgh, 1978.

Lloyd-Jones, D.Martyn: *God's Way of Reconciliation: Studies in Ephesians 2*, Evangelical Press, London, 1972.

Lloyd-Jones, D.M.: *The Unsearchable Riches of Christ... Ephesians 3:1-21*, The Banner of Truth Trust, Edinburgh, 1979.

Lloyd-Jones, D.M.: *Life in the Spirit... Ephesians 5:18 to 6:9*, The Banner of Truth Trust, Edinburgh, 1974.

Lumpkin, William L.: *Baptist Confessions of Faith*, Judson Press, Valley Forge, 1989.

Macleod, John: *Scottish Theology in Relation to Church History since the Reformation*, The Banner of Truth Trust, Edinburgh, 1974.

Manton, Thomas: *Sermons Upon John XVII*, Sovereign Grace Publishers, Wilmington, 1972.

M'Cheyne, Robert Murray: *A Basket of Fragments*, Christian Focus Publications, Inverness, 1975.

M'Millan, Samuel: *Beauties of... Ralph Erskine...*, Vol.1, Khull, Blackie & Co., Glasgow, 1821.

Moody-Stuart, K.: *Brownlow North: His Life and Work*, The Banner of Truth Trust, London, 1961.

Morden, Peter J.: *Offering Christ to the World...*, Paternoster Press, Carlisle, 2003.

Murray, Iain H.: *Jonathan Edwards*, The Banner of Truth Trust, Edinburgh, 1987.

Murray, Iain H.: *Spurgeon* v. *Hyper-Calvinism: The Battle for Gospel Preaching*, The Banner of Truth Trust, Edinburgh, 1995.

Murray, John: *Redemption Accomplished and Applied*, The Banner of Truth Trust, London, 1961.

Murray, John: *The Epistle to the Romans...*, Two Volumes in One, Marshall, Morgan & Scott, London, 1974.

Murray, John: *Collected Writings...*, The Banner of Truth Trust, Edinburgh, 1976,77,82.

Naylor, Peter: *Picking up a Pin for the Lord: English Particular Baptists from 1688 to the Early Nineteenth Century*, Grace Publications, London, 1992.

Ness, Christopher: *An Antidote Against Arminianism...*, Sovereign Grace Union, London, 1920.

Nettles, Thomas J.: *By His Grace and for His Glory...*, Baker Book House, Grand Rapids, 1990.

Nicole, Roger: *Standing Forth: Collected Writings...*, Mentor, Fearn, 2002.

Oliver, Robert W.: 'Andrew Fuller and Abraham Booth' in Haykin, Michael A.G. (ed): *'At the Pure Fountain of Thy Word'...*, Paternoster Press, Carlisle, 2004.

Owen, John: *An Exposition of Hebrews*, 7 Volumes in 4, Sovereign Grace Publishers, Evansville, 1960.

Owen, John: *Meditations and Discourses Concerning the Glory of Christ; Applied unto Unconverted Sinners...* in *The Works of John Owen*, Vol.1, edited by William H.Goold, The Banner of Truth Trust, London, 1965.

Owen, John: *The Doctrine of Justification by Faith...* in *The Works of John Owen*, Vol.5, edited by William H.Goold, The Banner of Truth Trust, London, 1967.

Owen, John: *Gospel Grounds and Evidences of The Faith of God's Elect...* in *The Works of John Owen*, Vol.5, edited by William H.Goold, The Banner of Truth Trust, London, 1967.

Owen, John: *An Exposition upon Psalm 130* in *The Works of John Owen*, Vol.6, edited by William H.Goold, The Banner of Truth Trust, London, 1966.

Owen, John: *A Display of Arminianism...* in *The Works of John Owen*, Vol.10, edited by William H.Goold, The Banner of Truth Trust, London, 1967.

Owen, John: *The Death of Death in the Death of Christ...* in *The Works of John Owen*, Vol.10, edited by William H.Goold, The Banner of Truth Trust, London, 1967. [I have indicated this as Owen: *Death* in *Works* Vol.10].

Owen, John: *Of the Death of Christ, the Price He Paid, and the Purchase He Made; or, The Satisfaction and Merit of the Death of Christ Cleared...* in *The Works of John Owen*, Vol.10, edited by William H.Goold, The Banner of Truth Trust, London, 1967.

[I have treated this as Appendix to Owen: *Death* in *Works* Vol.10].

Owen, John: *A Vindication...* in *The Works of John Owen*, Vol.14, edited by William H.Goold, The Banner of Truth Trust, London, 1967.

Packer, J.I.: *Introductory Essay to John Owen's The Death of Death...*, Dallas.

Philpot, J.C.: 'Editor's Review' of James Wells: *The Moral Government of God...* in the *Gospel Standard*, March/April 1841.

Philpot, J.C.: *Meditations on Matters of Christian Faith and Experience*, First Series, J.Gadsby, London, 1875(?).

Philpot, J.C.: *Answers to Inquiries... (1850-1866)*, Farncombe & Son, London, 1905.

Philpot, J.C.: *Selected Sermons*, Vol.1, C.J.Farncombe & Sons Ltd., London, 1935.

Philpot, J.C.: *The True, Proper and Eternal Sonship of the Lord Jesus Christ...*, The Gospel Standard Publications, London, 1962.

Pink, Arthur W.: *Exposition of the Gospel of John: Three Volumes... in One*, Zondervan Publishing House, Grand Rapids, 1978.

Poole, Matthew: *A Commentary on the Holy Bible*, Vol.3, The Banner of Truth Trust, Edinburgh, reprinted 1975.

Popham, J.K.: *Stand Fast, being some of The Polemical Works of J.K.Popham...*, with an Introduction by J.R.Broome, Gospel Standard Trust Publications, Harpenden, 2006.

Pratt, John H. (ed): *The Thoughts of the Evangelical Leaders...*, The Banner of Truth Trust, Edinburgh, 1978.

Rainsford, M.: *Lectures on... John 17*, John Hoby, London.

Ramsbottom, B.A.: Review of Gay, David H.J.: *The Gospel Offer* is *Free* in the *Gospel Standard*, Luton, March 2005.

Randalls, Andrew G.: *Today's Gospel and Apostolic Exhortations: A Study in the Presentation of the Gospel*, The Huntingtonian Press, Windmill Hill, 1997.

Rushton, William: *A Defence of Particular Redemption...*, Hamilton, Adams, and Co., London, 1831.

Scott, John L.: *A Manual of the Doctrines of Grace*, Birmingham, 1890.

Sheehan, Clint: 'Great and Sovereign Grace; Fuller's Defence of the Gospel Against Arminianism' in Haykin, Michael A.G. (ed): *'At the Pure Fountain of Thy Word'...*, Paternoster Press, Carlisle, 2004.

Shepard, Thomas: *The Ten Virgins*, Tyndale Bible Society, Florida.

Sower.

Sprague, William B.: *Appendix* to *Lectures on Revival of Religion*, The Banner of Truth Trust, London, 1959.

Spurgeon, C.H.: *Around the Wicket Gate...*, Passmore & Alabaster, London, 1896.

Spurgeon, C.H.: *The New Park Street Pulpit... 1858*, Vol.4, The Banner of Truth Trust, London, 1964.

Spurgeon, C.H.: *The Metropolitan Tabernacle Pulpit... 1865*, Vol.11, Passmore and Alabaster, London, 1866.

Spurgeon, C.H.: *The Metropolitan Tabernacle Pulpit... 1884*, Vol.30, The Banner of Truth Trust, London, 1971.

Spurgeon, C.H.: *The Metropolitan Tabernacle Pulpit... 1888*, Vol.34, Passmore and Alabaster, London, 1889.

Thayer, Joseph Henry: *A Greek-English Lexicon of the New Testament*, Baker Book House, Grand Rapids, Ninth Printing 1991.

The Banner of Truth, Edinburgh, March 2004.

The Concise Oxford Dictionary of Current English, Eighth Edition, BCA, London, 1991.

The Shorter Oxford English Dictionary on Historical Principles, Third Edition, Guild Publishing, London, Reprinted 1988.

The Three Forms of Unity..., Protestant Reformed Churches of America, 1991.

Trench, Richard Chenevix: *Synonyms of the New Testament*, Macmillan and Co., London, ninth edition, improved, 1880.

Underwood, A.C.: *A History of the English Baptists*, The Carey Kingsgate Press Limited, London, 1947.

Van Til, Cornelius: *Common Grace*, The Presbyterian and Reformed Publishing Company, Philadelphia, 1954.

Vincent, M.R.: *Word Studies in the New Testament*, Macdonald Publishing Company, Florida.

Watts, J.A. and Buss, G.D.: *A Goodly Heritage or An Insight into The Gospel Standard Articles of Faith*, Gospel Standard Trust Publications, Harpenden, 2006.

Wells, James: *The Surrey Tabernacle Pulpit... 1868*, G.J.Stevenson, London, 1868.

Wells, Tom: *A Price for a People: The Meaning of Christ's Death*, The Banner of Truth Trust, Edinburgh, 1992.

Whitefield, George: *Sermons on Important Subjects by... George Whitefield*, Thomas Tegg, & Son, London, 1838.

Whitefield, George: *Select Sermons of George Whitefield...*, The Banner of Truth Trust, London, 1959.

Whitefield, George: 'A Letter to... John Wesley...' in *George Whitefield's Journals*, The Banner of Truth Trust, London, 1960.

Whitefield, George: *Letters of George Whitefield for the period 1734-1742*, The Banner of Truth Trust, Edinburgh, 1976.

Williams, Hugh L.: 'Preaching the True Gospel Properly' in *British Reformed Journal*, issue 9, Jan-March 1995.

Young, Edward J.: *The Book of Isaiah*, Vol.3, William B.Eerdmans Publishing Company, Grand Rapids, 1972.

Zanchius, Jerom: *The Doctrine of Absolute Predestination Stated and Asserted...*, translated by Augustus Montague Toplady, The Sovereign Grace Union, London, 1930.

[1] I emphasise the 'seeming'; I am talking about a *seeming* contradiction. I completely agree with B.A.Ramsbottom: 'There are many paradoxes in the Bible, and many things that we do not understand, but we cannot see that there can be any utter contradictions' (Ramsbottom p95). Neither can I. There are no *utter* contradictions in the Bible. But there are many *seeming* contradictions. Cornelius Van Til: 'Our position is naturally charged with being self-contradictory. It might seem at first glance as though we were willing, with the dialectical theologians, to accept the really contradictory. Yet such is not the case. In fact we hold that our position is the only position that saves one from the necessity of ultimately accepting the really contradictory... While we shun as poison the idea of the really contradictory, we embrace with passion the idea of the *apparently* contradictory. It is through the latter alone that we can reject the former... [For instance,] the relation between human responsibility and the counsel of God is... *apparently* contradictory. That all things in history are determined by God must always *seem* [emphasis mine], at first sight, to contradict the genuineness of my choice. That the elect are certainly saved for eternity must always *seem* to make the threat of eternal punishment unreal with respect to them. That the reprobate are certainly to be lost must always seem to make the presentation of eternal life unreal with respect to them' (Van Til pp9-10, emphasis his, except where stated). But only 'seem', I repeat! John Berridge: 'Every fundamental doctrine meets with something which seems directly to oppose it... these seeming contradictions...' (Berridge pp287-288). J.C.Philpot did not mind using the phrase – see the thirty-two 'Characteristics of a Believing Christian, in Paradoxes and Seeming Contradictions' (*Gospel Standard* 1857 pp299-302). Again: 'In reading such passages [Acts 13:34,37]... there seems to be an apparent contradiction... [a] seeming contradiction' (Philpot: *Answers* pp158-159). Again: 'Do you mean to receive nothing as divine truth which involves apparent contradictions? We say apparent, for we cannot allow them to be real. If you answer: "I can receive nothing which I cannot understand and reconcile to my reasoning mind", then you had better be a Socinian at once, for that is just his very position. He says: "I cannot receive the doctrine of the trinity, for it contradicts the unity of God, which I receive as a fundamental truth; and to assert that three are one and one is three, is to contradict all my fundamental notions of number". And thus he stumbles... You and the Socinian really stand on the same ground – the ground of natural reason and carnal argument... Neither he nor you submit your minds to the Scriptures. You both really stand upon infidel ground, for both of you prefer your own reasonings, and your

preconceived notions to the truth as revealed in the word of God... Is it not more consistent with the obedience of faith to believe the Lord's own testimony... than to cavil, disbelieve or explain it away, because such a doctrine contradicts the conclusions of your reasoning mind? You censure Arminians for saying that they cannot receive election because it contradicts their first notions, their primary, fundamental principles, both of the justice and love of God... To reject [scriptural doctrine] merely because it contradicts some of your preconceived opinions is most dangerous ground to take, and is to set up your authority against that of the word of truth' (Philpot: *Eternal Sonship* pp22-25). In fact, Philpot went even further than *seeming* contradictions: '"The will of God" may be divided into two branches; there is the revealed will of God, and there is the secret will of God; and these two are often contradictory' (Philpot: *Selected* p54). See my *Offer* pp57-134. Reader, please excuse the constant refrain 'see my *Offer*', but I see no point in repeating arguments I have already made. As I will make clear, this book is meant to be a Supplement to the other.

[2] But there is a misunderstanding about 'logic' and the free offer. (Take, for instance, Allen Baird: 'Calvin' p3). I do not deny that things 'may be deduced by good and necessary consequence from Scripture', but if we are convinced that two statements are, each of them, scriptural, then we have to accept both, even if they appear to contradict each other; we have to accept both and admit the paradox. This is not an 'absurdity'. Quite the reverse; it is wisdom. If, instead, we apply our reason to either statement to twist it to say what it does not say in order to gain logical consistency, this, far from being a 'good and necessary' deduction from Scripture, is, in fact, an unwarranted imposition upon Scripture, and, therefore, utterly wrong. (I acknowledge, of course, one man's *imposition* may be another's *interpretation*). We must face all Scripture, and take full cognisance of all its teaching, even if we find it difficult to fit into our system. Indeed, if necessary we should relax our system to accommodate the seeming paradox, and put up with the taunt of illogicality, rather than warp Scripture. John Davenant: 'If... two decrees seem to anyone to oppose each other, [the reader] ought rather to acknowledge the weakness of his own understanding, than to deny any of those things which are so plainly contained in the holy Scriptures' (Davenant p163). See Philpot below. Andrew Fuller: 'There are, doubtless, many questions that might be started by a curious mind which it would be difficult, and perhaps impossible, to solve. Nor is this to be wondered at. The same difficulty attends us, in our present state, respecting almost all the works of God. No man could solve one half of the difficulties that might be started concerning God's goodness in

creating the world, when he knew all that would follow. The same might be said of a thousand things in the scheme of divine providence. Suffice it for us, at present, that we know our littleness; that when we come to see things as they are, we shall be fully convinced of all that has been told us, and shall unite in the universal acclamation, HE HAS DONE ALL THINGS WELL! That there is a consistency between the divine decrees and the free agency of men I believe; but whether I can account for it is another thing. Whether it can be accounted for at all, so as to enable us clearly to comprehend it, I cannot tell. Be that as it may, it does not distress me: I believe in both, because both appear to me to be plainly revealed' (Fuller: *Philanthropos* p229, emphasis his). There is also a misunderstanding about a paradox and unreliability. I was asked by e-mail (3rd Oct. 2005): 'The problem here for me is, how do I know which parts of the Bible are reliable and which parts contain paradoxes?' I replied: 'All the Scripture is reliable. The seeming paradox is reliable. All I have to do is ask myself on any particular issue – can I interpret this passage in light of other Scripture? If I cannot reconcile what I genuinely see as true, then I must resign myself to the fact that one day all will be revealed – and now go on with the tension (but not the unreliability) of the seeming contradiction'.

[3] 1 Cor. 2:4 does not militate against it. Although Paul did not preach using the techniques of the worldly-wise 'with persuasive words of human wisdom', by the Spirit of God he did persuade men, the very thing he set out to do. See my *Septimus Sears*.

[4] 'An *offer* is a presenting for acceptance, a proposal to give or do something, a proposal of marriage'. 'To *offer* is to tender for acceptance or refusal, to hold out to a person to take if he will, to make a proposal, to present for sale, to propose or express one's willingness to do something, conditionally on the assent of the person addressed'. 'To *proffer* is to put before a person for acceptance, to offer, present, tender, to propose or offer to do something'. 'To *propose* is to put forward for acceptance, to make an offer of marriage, to put before another something which one offers to do or wishes to be done'. 'To *tender* is to offer or advance in due terms, to offer in exact fulfilment of an obligation, to present for approval and acceptance, to proffer'. 'To *invite* is to ask a person graciously, kindly, to come to, to try to attract or induce, to present inducements to a person to do something or to proceed to an action'. 'To *beg* is to ask as a favour, to ask humbly or supplicatingly, to entreat'. 'To *entreat* is to plead for, to ask earnestly for, to request earnestly, to beseech, to implore, to persuade by pleading'. 'To *beseech* is to seek after, to try to get, to beg earnestly for, to ask earnestly' (*Shorter*). I am convinced all these catch the spirit of

the way sinners are addressed with the gospel in Scripture. I cite the *Shorter* because the Puritan (in particular) use of 'offer' is sometimes said to be historically and classically restricted to 'present', 'set before' or 'exhibit' (Engelsma p48; Baird: *Westminster* p9; Watts and Buss p58, for instance). This does not stand scrutiny. A glance at the *Shorter* will easily demonstrate that the warmer use of 'offer' was current in Puritan times and long before. The Puritans knew what they were saying, *and meant it.* Just a couple of Puritan examples must suffice. John Owen: 'This is the gospel, this is the work of it – namely, a divine *declaration* of the way of God for the saving of sinners, through the person, mediation, blood, righteousness and intercession of Christ. This is that which it *reveals*, *declares*, *proposes* and *tenders* unto sinners – there is a way for their salvation... This way of saving sinners being *proposed*, *offered* and *tendered* unto us in the gospel, true and saving faith receives it, approves of it, rests in it, renounces all other hopes and expectations, reposing its whole confidence therein... It is *proposed* unto us as that which we ought practically to close withal, for ourselves to trust alone unto it for life and salvation' (Owen: *Grounds* in *Works* Vol.5 pp410-411, emphasis mine). And David Clarkson, Owen's successor: 'Suppose a man should *offer* to restore sight to another upon condition that he would not wilfully shut his eyes... The case is like here; Christ *offers* to [reveal] to a sinner the things that concern his peace... he *offers* to [reveal] himself to him, if he will not turn his back on Christ when he is *presented* to his view... A prince *offers* to adopt a man for his son... The Lord *offers* to adopt a sinner for his son... Christ *offers* to restore sinners... Christ *offers* to be reconciled to you, to delight in you, to make you beautiful and lovely, if you will but part with your leprosy, your deformity, sin, which makes you nasty and loathsome to him... Christ meets the sinner, *offers* to bring him home, to bring him to heaven... Those whose hearts now quarrel with [these terms]... will be struck dumb... when they stand before the judgement seat of Christ... he shall then demand why they refused him when he *offered* upon terms so easy... I question not but the apprehension does wound those damned souls with more anguish than any pang of death, when they remember that they refused Christ when he was *offered* upon such easy... terms' (Clarkson pp118-119, emphasis mine). Reader, try replacing 'offer' with 'present'; it is impossible. Some may not like it, but the truth is the Puritans offered Christ to sinners in the warmest sense of the word. This does not mean they were necessarily right, but it will not wash to try to make out that they spoke in a detached way and merely presented Christ to sinners, and left it at that! As can be seen, Clarkson did use the word 'present' – of course, Christ has to be presented! – but he also has to be *offered* to sinners. Above all, reader, peruse the Puritans (and many of their successors) for yourself – see my *Offer* pp122-124 for some sources – and get a sense of the tenor of their addresses to sinners. It is not merely the word 'offer'; it is the whole tone of their passionate appeals to, and pleadings with, sinners that I am talking about. Finally, although he was not a Puritan, could anybody argue George Whitefield had not imbibed their spirit? Read his sermon: 'Christ The Best Husband, or An earnest invitation to young women to come and see Christ' (Whitefield: *Sermons* pp77-87). It is nothing if not the most passionate proposal of marriage to Christ given to 'A Society of Young Women in Fetter Lane'. Never again could anyone who has read this sermon say that Whitefield did not offer Christ and the gospel to sinners – and I mean *offer*.

[5] John Calvin on John 10:27: 'Let [faithful teachers] do their utmost to bring the whole world into the fold of Christ', even though 'they that are not sheep... do not obey the gospel. For God effectually calls all whom he has elected', and 'it is no small consolation to faithful teachers, that though the greater part of the world do not listen to Christ, yet he has his sheep'. Further, when faithful teachers have done their utmost to bring the world to Christ, and yet still 'they do not succeed according to their wish, let them be satisfied with this single consideration, that they who are sheep will be gathered by their agency' (Calvin: *Commentaries* Vol.17 Part 2 p415). The two parts of Calvin's counsel here are spot on. But they must be taken together – a full trust in God's sovereign grace, *and* a full commitment to bring as many as possible to Christ. Calvin again: 'Ministers are here [2 Cor. 6:1] taught, that it is not enough simply to advance doctrine. They must also labour that it may be received by the hearers... For as they are messengers between God and men, the first duty devolving upon them is, to make offer of the grace of God; and the second is, to strive with all their might, that it may not be offered in vain' (Calvin: *Commentaries* Vol.20 Part 2 p245). Take Acts 2. Peter repeatedly called for his hearers' attention (Acts 2:14,22); having got it, he aimed for their minds, declaring and explaining the facts of the case, taking away misunderstandings and setting out biblical truth (Acts 2:14-36); he applied the truth to his hearers (note the 'you') in a most personal way, pressing home their sin and responsibility (Acts 2:22-23,36); he spoke with open confidence and authority (Acts 2:29); he drew conclusions from his arguments (Acts 2:36); he called for – commanded – his hearers to repent and be baptised (Acts 2:38), encouraging them so to do (Acts 2:38-39). In short, 'with many other words' he solemnly testified, kept on exhorting, and warned, pleaded, commanded and tried to persuade them to come to Christ (Acts 2:40).

Take Acts 3. Peter questioned the crowd (Acts 3:12), clearing away their misunderstandings (Acts 3:12). Having declared the truth (Acts 3:13-26), he was personal and pointed (note the 'you') in showing them their sin, responsibility, ignorance and opportunity (Acts 3:13-26), commanding them to repent and believe (Acts 3:19), encouraging them, but warning them also (Acts 3:19-26). See my *Offer* pp67-68, and below, for God's desire in Acts 3:26.

[6] Philpot's review of James Wells: *The Moral Government of God...*, in the *Gospel Standard* 1841 pp52-53. As Philpot later said: If the exhortations of the Scripture were confined to the elect, 'Mr Wells would have had no need to write his book, nor we to trespass so much upon the patience of our readers' (*Gospel Standard* 1841 p180). As for 'unreasonable length', and trespassing upon the patience of others, I acknowledge my continued predilection for generous extracts. No doubt some will say over-generous – see Morden pp82-83 for Fuller's criticism of Abraham Booth's 'extremely heavy use of quotation', even though, in his *Worthy*, Fuller himself 'quoted liberally... extensively' from the Puritans whom he 'cited often' (Morden pp26,30-33,99)! Of course, Fuller 'often deployed quotations from ['Owen and other Puritans'] to support positions *he had already arrived at*' (Morden p32, emphasis mine). I will return to this. Speaking for myself, I know how much I appreciate extensive quotes. I can only ask the indulgence of readers who do not. And there is a further point. I am conscious of the truth of the remarks of Davenant's 21st century publisher: 'Often in debate, each side has shown misunderstanding of the other's position and presented a caricature of it which convinces no one but themselves. This is no less true in the debates surrounding the extent and efficacy of the death of Christ' (Davenant xxi). While the use of extensive extracts will not avoid this danger entirely, it will, at least, allow those I quote to have a fair crack of the whip, and make it more difficult for me to build men of straw.

[7] Davenant p3.

[8] I echo the (21st century) Publisher's Foreword to Davenant, though I would put it more strongly: 'It is also hoped that it will result in the free offer of salvation in Christ being more freely made to those who walk in darkness' (Davenant xxi).

[9] Davenant p3.

[10] I do not accept that the passages in question teach universal redemption. I hold to particular redemption; see my *Offer* and below.

[11] 'The simple truth is that Christ died for everyone, as many scriptures state very plainly. I see no references to these verses in your index. Why is that?' (Clifford's e-mail to me, 26th Jan. 2005).

[12] And, after 'completing' the mss, with Davenant's work, recently republished.
[13] Arminians do not see what all the fuss is about: Christ died for all equally, and the gospel is to be freely offered to all, all of whom can respond if they wish. So they say.
[14] I am defining a 'four-pointer' as a Calvinist who holds to general redemption. This, I admit, is simplistic. See below.
[15] Unlike some others, I take 'atonement' and 'redemption' as virtually interchangeable. See Douty p12.
[16] And worse! See Ella: 'Brief' pp16-18.
[17] 'Calvin (and Amyraut) grounded the free offer in a universal atonement. Once you allow a universal aspect to an atonement otherwise efficacious for the elect alone your case will be perfect and the picture complete' (Clifford's letter to me, 21st Jan. 2005).
[18] In using 'irresistible grace', Owen's comment should be kept in mind: 'We do not affirm grace to be irresistible, as though it came upon the will with such an overflowing violence as to beat it down before it, and subdue it by compulsion to what it is no way inclinable [unto]. But if that term must be used, it denotes... only such an unconquerable efficacy of grace as always and infallibly produces its effect' (Owen: *Display* in *Works* Vol.10 p134). Philpot spoke of '[Augustus] Toplady... and other good men... [who] have objected to the use of the expression "irresistible" influences of the blessed Spirit, and have preferred the term "invincible"' (Philpot: *Meditations* p384). This may be a question of words (Clifford: *Atonement* pp115,123,242). See Edwards: *Freedom* pp87-88.
[19] God commands all sinners to both believe and repent; the two cannot be divorced. In addition to what I have said on Ella's claim that only the repentant may be commanded to believe, that repentance must come first (see my *Offer* pp5-13), consider Calvin: 'That repentance not only always follows faith, but is produced by it, ought to be without controversy... Those who think that repentance precedes faith instead of flowing from, or being produced by it as the fruit of the tree, have never understood its nature' (Calvin: *Institutes* Vol.1 pp509-510). Owen connected this with the notion of 'duty': 'After the angels had sinned, God never once called them to repentance... He has no forgiveness for them, and therefore would require no repentance of them. It is not, nor ever was, a duty incumbent upon them to repent. Nor is it so unto the damned in hell. God requires it not of them, nor is it their duty... Assignation then, of repentance, is a revelation of forgiveness. God would not call upon a sinful creature to humble itself and bewail its sin if there were no way of recovery or relief... What, then, does God aim at

in and by [various scriptures]?... It is to bring [the sinner] to repentance... [And] no repentance is acceptable with God but what is built or leans on the faith of forgiveness... [For God] to prescribe repentance as a duty unto sinners, without a foundation of pardon and forgiveness in himself, is inconsistent with... all [the] glorious excellencies and perfections of the nature of God... Repenting is for sinners only... It is for them, and them only. It was no duty for Adam in Eden, it is none for the angels in heaven, nor for the damned in hell... [In] Isa. 55:7, [God] speaks... to men perversely wicked, and such as make a trade of sinning. What does he call them unto? Plainly, to repentance, to the duty we have insisted on' (Owen: *Psalm 130* in *Works* Vol.6 pp437-440). Going back to the first point, note Owen's: 'No repentance is acceptable with God but what is built or leans on the faith of forgiveness'.

[20] 'Since you hold to a universal free offer, what exactly is on offer to all? Your answer [because you believe in particular redemption] really must be: "Nothing". When unbelievers reject the gospel, what exactly are they rejecting?' (Clifford's e-mail to me, 3rd Feb. 2005; see also Clifford: *Atonement* pp74,112-114,156). Clifford has missed a point here. The free offer involves duty faith – which Clifford gave a somewhat derogatory mention – 'in [Owen's] view the gospel offer *merely* declares the duty of sinners to believe' (Clifford: *Atonement* p113, emphasis mine) – and when sinners refuse the offer, they are in fact refusing to obey a command (and accept an invitation). As for the link between the offer and duty, Owen was clear: 'The external *offer* is such as from which every man may conclude his own *duty*; [but] none [may conclude] God's purpose, which yet may be known [by a man] upon performance of his *duty* [that is, a man may know God's election of him and Christ's redemption of him, but only after he believes]... [God's] *offer* in the preaching of the gospel is not declarative to any [man] in particular... of what God has done nor of what he will do in reference to him, *but of what [the man] ought to do*, if he would be approved of God and obtain the good things *promised*' (Owen: *Death* in *Works* Vol.10 p300, emphasis mine).

[21] My *Offer* pp118-119. See below for Fuller's criticism of Booth over addresses to sinners.

[22] 'I think we often are not as full, earnest and uninhibited as we should be in urging sinners to repent and turn to Christ, with the certainty that if they do they will find a full, perfect and eternal salvation in him. I think the trouble is holding this free offer together with our understanding of the limited extent of the atonement' (Walford H.Catling's letter to me, 4th May 2005). '"If Christ died only for the elect, and not for all",

ministers "are puzzled to understand how they should proceed with the calls and invitations of the gospel"' (Thomas Chalmers quoted by Clifford: *Atonement* p88).

[23] What I say in this book applies equally to unconditional election. The two cases are parallel. My position is that both election and redemption are unconditional, determining and absolute. And neither contradicts the free offer – quite the reverse.

[24] I do not want to be too big for my boots, but I think of Robert Hall's *Help to Zion's Travellers* (1781), expanded from his sermon at Northampton two years before. 'An attempt', he said it was, 'to remove various stumbling-blocks out of the way, relating to doctrinal, experimental and practical religion' (Underwood p160). And so it proved.

[25] 'Provide' is a word which casts a long shadow. There is a great deal of inconsistency in its use, even by those who are against the idea! See, for example, Fuller: *Philanthropos* pp223-224; *Reality* p247; Booth: *Reign* pp82,107; *Glad Tidings* p40; Hodge: *2 Corinthians* p147; Owen: *Psalm 130* in *Works* Vol.6 p523; Gill: *Cause* p165; Haldane pp36,112; Ella: *The Free Offer* pp9,13,16,22,52,53. I try to avoid it in connection with Christ's redemption. See my *Offer* p138. But since it is ubiquitous, I have to use it in extracts – without approval! The suggestion that Christ has made redemption merely 'available', falls far short of Scripture; it is, to me at least, abhorrent; Christ died to *accomplish* redemption. (Davenant did not seem to use 'provisional', but 'applicable'; Christ's death is 'applicable to all mankind'). What about 'provided' in Scripture? The notion that Christ has 'provided' redemption is unknown in Scripture, as far as I can see; the word is not used in that way. True, the NIV has: 'He provided redemption for his people' (Ps. 111:9), but I can find no support for this translation. In: 'God's abundant provision of grace' (Rom. 5:17 NIV), the gratuitous inclusion of 'provision' weakens Paul's reference to 'abundance of grace'. 'After he had provided purification for sins' (Heb. 1:3 NIV), is not a happy translation. Rather, Christ was the author of the purification; he caused it, brought it about. See Thayer, AV, NKJV, NASB. See also the translation of *poieō* in the preceding verse, Heb. 1:2 (God made, created, the universe). I admit the word is, uniquely in Scripture, translated 'provide' in Luke 12:33 (AV, NKJV, NIV), but Arndt & Gingrich called this a 'specialised expression', and the NASB has 'make'. What of: 'God having provided something better for us' (Heb. 11:40)? The word, *problepō*, means 'foresee' (Thayer). Owen: 'The word properly signifies "foreseeing". But God's prevision is his provision, as being always accompanied with his preordination: his foresight with his decree' (Owen: *Hebrews* Vol.4

Part 2 p216). In other words, God has planned and determined something better for us. See NIV.

[26] I categorically reject (i) that I 'deny that it was at Calvary that the ransom was paid once and for all time', and (ii) that 'the predominant theology of the free-offer sect is based on an unfinished work of Christ on the cross' (Ella: *The Free Offer* pp39,46). When Christ cried out: 'It is finished' (John 19:30), he meant it! All was finished, accomplished; he has 'put away sin by the sacrifice of himself' (Heb. 9:26), and by his 'one offering he has perfected for ever those who are being sanctified' (Heb. 10:14).

[27] Clifford: *Atonement* pp69-166; *Amyraut* pp12-15,17-18,29-30,32-37,44-45,49; 'Evangelicalisms' p13.

[28] See the Appendix for comments on Clifford: *Atonement* pp142-166. I appreciate the force of Clifford's e-mail to me (17th Nov. 2005), quoting Richard Baxter: 'When God says so expressly that Christ died for all [2 Cor. 5:14-15], and tasted death for every man [Heb. 2:9], and is the ransom for all [1 Tim. 2:6], and the propitiation for the sins of the whole world [1 John 2:2], it beseems every Christian rather to explain in what sense Christ died for all, than flatly to deny it'. See Clifford: *Atonement* p82. The same goes for Norman F.Douty quoting Davenant: 'For what purpose, I ask, is it that the Spirit of God, in speaking of the death of Christ, frequently makes use of general terms, extending it to all, while in mentioning the divine predestination, he always uses restrictive terms, limiting it to few, if the death of Christ, and the predestination of God as to mankind, had an equal and altogether same extent?' (Davenant pp88-89; Douty p11). In reply, I ask: If the death of Christ is an equal provision for all, what need of passages (Matt. 1:21; John 10:11,15; 11:51-52; Acts 20:28; Rom. 5:8; 8:32; Eph. 5:23,25-27; Tit. 2:14; 1 Pet. 1:18-21; 1 John 2:2; 4:10, for instance), which speak of particular redemption? This, of course, is at the heart of what we are thinking about. As for the passages Baxter raised, I have explained why I am not expounding them at this time, but in short I will say again what I understand by them: Christ died as a substitute for all for whom he stood. This means, and I freely admit it, I gloss the 'all' words in the passages Baxter quoted. But this is no different to Baxter (and Clifford); they gloss the 'for' and the 'redemption'. Every believer glosses. By 'gloss' I mean: 'An explanatory word or phrase inserted between the lines or in the margin of a text... a comment, explanation, interpretation or paraphrase'. I do not, I hope, mean: 'Read a different sense into; explain away' (*Concise*). I freely admit, of course, that one man's *explanation* is another man's *explaining away*. Consequently we have to

gloss 'gloss'! See the Appendix for more on glossing. The tiny word 'for', it should be noted, plays a big part in this discussion.
[29] See *The Three* pp43-45; Lumpkin pp158,260-263; Owen: *Display* in *Works* Vol.10 pp87-100; *Death* in *Works* Vol.10 pp139-479; Gill: *Cause*; *Body* Vol.2 pp159-190; Fuller: *Philanthropos* pp223-233; *Reality* pp247-255; Boston: *Marrow* pp102-104; Dabney: *Systematic* pp500-545; Dagg pp324-331; Cunningham pp323-343; Scott pp59-82; Berkhof pp373-399; John Murray: *Redemption* pp59-75; *Collected* Vol.1 pp74-80; Vol.2 pp123-131,142-150; Cheeseman pp78-92; Nettles pp297-321; Packer; Tom Wells; *etc.* I do not endorse every argument used by every writer in this list. I certainly do not agree with Philpot's remarks on the texts in question: 'Such texts seem left in the sacred word as tests of [for] the believing and obedient, and as stumbling blocks to the unbelieving and disobedient' (Philpot: *Answers* p155). This strikes me as bizarre – and worse. Did he get the idea from Berridge: 'The wise are taken in their own craftiness... Hear how the Lord takes them. Gins and snares are scattered in his word to catch a subtle scribe; just as traps are laid by us to catch a fox... Every fundamental doctrine meets with something which seems directly to oppose it; and these seeming contradictions are the traps which are laid' (Berridge pp287-288).
[30] But, reader, do not misunderstand me. What the Scripture teaches is absolutely fundamental to what I say, but I see no point in repeating arguments – arguments which have been excellently set out elsewhere – to establish particular redemption, when this is not my present purpose in writing. In addition, let me return to a point I made in my *Offer* (x, p39); I do not quote men to *prove* what I say – the Scriptures must do that; I quote men to *support* what I say, and to encourage the hesitant by reminding them of that which countless Calvinists have asserted.
As did Fuller (Morden pp32,36-38,45-51,63,66,89,96-97,102,172-175,181,183).
[31] Other problems would immediately arise, of course!
[32] Interestingly, while there has been a long debate about the extent of the **atonement**, few, as far as I am aware, have raised the extent of the **resurrection**. Christopher Ness was one who spoke about it: 'The benefits of Christ's death and resurrection are of equal extent in their objects; but the benefit of Christ's resurrection is not extended to all. That the benefit of Christ's resurrection is not extended to all and everyone alike, but is peculiar to believers [the elect], is acknowledged even by the Arminians. That the death and resurrection of Christ are of equal extent in their objects is evident from Rom. 8:34 (they are both put together)... Those for whom Christ died and rose again for cannot be condemned... (Rom. 4:25). Those that have the fruit of Christ's battle

have the fruit of his victory also; but this cannot be said of all men, for on some the wrath of God abides (John 3:36)' (Ness p46).

Let me explore this a little. Christ died *for* sinners and was raised again *for* those same sinners (Rom. 4:25 AV, NIV; see John Murray: *Romans* Vol.1 pp154-156). *For* whom? Paul could tell believers: 'If Christ is not risen... you are still in your sins' (1 Cor. 15:17). 'But God, who is rich in mercy, because of his great love with which he loved us, even when we were dead in trespasses, made us alive together with Christ... and raised us up together, and made us sit together in the heavenly places in Christ Jesus' (Eph. 2:4-6). Christ died *for* – and was raised *for* – the elect, 'for us'. Not only so. The elect died *with* – and were raised *with* – Christ. This takes us to the vital doctrine of union and identification with Christ in his death *and* burial *and* resurrection *and* ascension. The elect died with Christ when he died, *and* were buried with him when he was buried, *and* were raised with him when he was raised, *and* were taken into glory and seated with him (Rom. 6:2-11; 7:4-6; 2 Cor. 5:14-18; Gal. 2:19-20; Eph. 2:1,4-6; Col. 2:11-15,20; 3:1,3; 1 Pet. 2:24; see also John 14:19; Rom. 8:34; 1 Thess. 5:10; 1 Pet. 1:3). Christ 'was delivered up because of our offences, *and was raised for our justification*' (Rom. 4:25), the 'our' being, of course, the elect. 'The efficacy of the death of Christ *and of his resurrection* lies on the face of the text. As Jesus rose again in order to guarantee our justification, so he was delivered up in order to deal effectively with our trespasses' (John Murray: *Romans* Vol.1 p156, emphasis mine). In short, as James Haldane put it: 'In the resurrection of Christ, all the redeemed were justified. They died and rose in him; and none can now lay anything to their charge' (Haldane p172). All this speaks of particularity and definiteness. See the Appendix.

And what about the extent of the **intercession** of Christ? 'It is Christ who died, and furthermore is also risen, who is even at the right hand of God, who also makes intercession for us' (Rom. 8:34). Note the unbreakable link between Christ's death, resurrection and intercession – and all 'for us'. Jesus 'the forerunner has entered [behind the veil] *for us*'; 'he is... able to save to the uttermost *those who come* to God through him, since he always makes intercession *for them*'; 'Christ has... entered... into heaven itself, now to appear in the presence of God *for us*' (Heb. 6:20; 7:25; 9:24). All this, without question, is particular and efficacious, not merely sufficient or provisional, nor universal, contrary to Davenant. He started well: 'The death, resurrection and intercession of Christ are joined together in indissoluble union'. Quite! But he was soon careering off the tracks: 'If we consider the whole human race, that is, each and every man, then we say, not only the death, but the

resurrection and intercession of Christ regards them, as to the *possibility* [emphasis mine] of their enjoying these benefits'. Incredible! How Davenant could fairly deduce this from Rom. 4:25; 8:34 is, for me at least, hard to see. As he himself said: The 'whole discourse in Rom. 8 is not designed to console any description of persons in any condition, but the elect; nor the elect merely as such, but the elect now called, justified, sanctified... Nor does [the apostle] simply and universally affirm that God freely gives all things to all men for whom Christ died, but to all *of us* [emphasis Davenant's] to whom the present discourse relates; that is, to all the predestinated who are believing in Christ... If anyone desires to apply the aforesaid reasoning to any persons whatsoever setting aside the consideration of predestination, calling and justification, in this manner: "Christ died for you, or Christ gave himself a ransom or sacrifice to God to expiate your sins...", I say, that he extends this argument beyond its limits, contrary to the mind of the apostle, who confined it to certain persons; namely, the predestinated, and to them as placed in a certain condition; namely, of justification and adoption'. As Davenant said, it is 'the elect [only who have]... the infallibility of enjoying' these benefits. Of course, all sinners may be (and should be) offered Christ, but to allege from this that the benefits of the death, resurrection and intercession of Christ are provisionally provided for them is a totally unwarranted deduction from the two verses, which so definitely speak of Christ dying, being raised and interceding *for us*, the elect, as Davenant himself admitted and so adamantly argued (Davenant pp49,59-60). As Roger Nicole put it: 'The clear-cut particularity of intercession becomes... a telling argument for the equal particularity of the atonement' (Nicole pp288,301-302;323).
The death of Christ is basic to *all* these benefits; the concept of priesthood demands it – the priest offers the blood he has sacrificed, and on that basis pleads for those he represents. 'With his own blood he entered the Most Holy Place once for all [time], having obtained eternal redemption... Once, at the end of the ages, he has appeared to put away sin by the sacrifice of himself... Christ was offered once to bear the sins of many' (Heb. 9:12,26,28). I have dealt with the suggestion that all this is provisional for all men, but what of the suggestion that the purpose of Christ's death is universal and provisional, yet his resurrection and intercession is particular and efficacious? This, too, is incredible in the light of Rom. 8:34; it is even more incredible in the context.
Bearing in mind his view on the atonement (but see Nicole p328), and its effect in Scotland (see below), the following from John Brown is significant: 'The perfection of [Christ's] atonement is the ground of his exaltation, and of his unbounded saving power... He appears before the

throne of God *for us*, as our representative, as our advocate, making intercession on the ground of his all-perfect atonement... Having made an all-perfect atonement, he now, henceforward and for ever, makes appearance for us as our advocate' (Brown: *Hebrews* pp396,425, emphasis his; I would also stress the '*for us* as *our* advocate'). Owen: 'The discharge of Christ's priestly office is the way designed to save us by, or to effect this great work of salvation... The efficacy of this intercession as it is sacerdotal depends wholly on the antecedent oblation [previous offering] and sacrifice of himself... The sure foundations of our eternal salvation were laid in his death and resurrection... It is such an act and duty of our high priest as supposes [is based upon] the offering of himself a sacrifice for sin antecedently... for it was with the blood of the expiatory sacrifices offered before on the altar that the high priest entered into the holy place. It has therefore regard unto his antecedent sacrifice, or his offering himself in his death and blood-shedding unto God... It supposes the accomplishment of the work of the redemption of the church... He thus appears there for us' (Owen: *Hebrews* Vol.3 Part 2 pp526,541,543; Vol.4 Part 1 pp383-384; see also Vol.3 Part 2 pp285-291,521-546; Vol.4 Part 1 pp379-386; *Death* in *Works* Vol.10 pp174-200, not that I agree with every comment Owen made – see the Appendix).

Haldane: 'All the sacrifices enjoined by the law had a definite object... Atonement and intercession are inseparable; they are component parts of the priestly office, and cannot be disjoined; consequently, to represent Christ as dying for the world, while he expressly disclaims praying for the world, is evidently most unscriptural... The sword of justice could not smite both the shepherd and the flock; the surety, and those whom he represented. In Christ's death, all the members of his mystical body died... It is impossible that payment should be demanded both of the surety and those who cause he undertook... It is evident that the offering and the intercession must be of equal extent; they are component and inseparable parts of the priestly office, and it is consequently given as the reason for Christ's ability to save to the uttermost them that come unto God by him, that he ever lives to make intercession for them (Heb. 7:25)... The atonement and the intercession were necessarily co-extensive... As the names of the tribes of Israel were engraved on the breastplate of the high priest, so were the names of his people on the heart of Jesus... Considering the atonement and intercession as component and inseparable parts of the priest's office, our Lord's declaration that he prays not for the world, affords a demonstration that the atonement was made exclusively for the church... The priesthood of Christ includes the sacrifice which he presented to God on earth, and the intercession which he carries on in heaven... Speaking of the sacrifice of the sin offering on the great day of atonement... there was a symbolical transference of the guilt of the transgressor to the victim... The symbol was fulfilled in the sacrifice of Christ; for the Jewish sacrifices served "unto the example and shadow of heavenly things". If there was a symbolical transference of the guilt of Israel according to the flesh on the great day of atonement, when the high priest laid his hands on the head of the scapegoat, confessing the sins of the people, there must have been a real transference of the guilt of the true [spiritual] Israel [to Christ] when Jesus hung upon the cross. The Gentiles had no concern with the Jewish expiation. [It was] the names of the twelve tribes, not of the Gentile nations, [which] were inscribed on the breastplate of the high priest. The sacrifice was for Israel alone, and the truth of the figure consists in the type being fulfilled in that sacrifice by which all the true [spiritual] Israel are justified... Christ is the surety of the new covenant (Heb. 7:22), and, consequently, only of the children of that covenant. But if Christ was the surety of all men, all received a discharge in his resurrection, and thus universal atonement conducts us to its necessary consummation; [namely,] universal salvation; for Christ was raised for the justification of all those for whose offences he was delivered (Rom. 4:25). Be they few or many, they were justified by his blood, and much more shall be saved from wrath through him. "If when we were enemies, we were reconciled to God by the death of his Son, much more, being reconciled, we shall be saved by his life" (Rom. 5:10). If there was not another explicit declaration in Scripture, this would be conclusive in proof of the atonement having been made only for the heirs of salvation. Those for whom the death of the Son of God was an atonement or reconciliation shall MUCH MORE be saved through his life, for he is at the right hand of God, making intercession for them, and the Father hears him always... The work of Christ is one. The atonement, the intercession and the final blessing are component parts of the same wonderful plan, just as the duty of the high priest in Israel, on the great day of atonement, was one continued action. He first offered the sacrifice, then burnt incense, and afterwards blessed the people. So Christ, having offered the great sacrifice, entered heaven with his own blood to make intercession for those whose sins he had borne. The fruit of this intercession is their receiving repentance unto life [plus all the other benefits and merits of his person and work]; and he will at last appear to bless them, and receive them to himself. These are inseparable links of the same chain... Christ disclaims making intercession for any but his people; he will bless none other, and it would be passing strange if the sacrifice – which is the only remaining part of the priestly office –

was offered for those for whom he does not intercede, and whom he does not bless, because, as he tells them, he never knew them. That church which he purchased with his own blood, Christ calls, and justifies and glorifies' (Haldane pp75,80-82,134,249,251,316,323-324,350, emphasis his).

J.K.Popham: 'Yet another irrefragable argument for a limited redemption and assured results, lies in the priesthood of Christ. It need not be remarked that Israel alone was interested in, and benefited by, the Levitical priesthood. [The] surrounding nations were "strangers from the covenants of promise". To the Jew alone belonged the advantage of possessing the oracles of God and [the] ordinances of divine worship. Whatever the Levitical priesthood meant was confined to Israel. Can the glorious, antitypical priesthood of Christ answer to this, and yet be stretched to every man... in the world?... Vicarious... is a definite, limited, inclusive word. It excludes all and sundry not included in the vicariate. And this is scriptural. Christ "loved the church, and gave himself for it" (Eph. 5:25)... [See also] 2 Cor. 5:21... 1 Pet. 2:24. Surely the Holy Ghost does not use ambiguous words; he is not wont to use limited terms with an unlimited intention' (Popham p61).

Calvin could not have more strongly linked the death of Christ and his intercession for the elect, those whom 'he had... previously embraced... with free favour': 'With his own blood [Christ] expiated the sins which rendered them hateful to God, by this expiation satisfied and duly propitiated God the Father, by this intercession appeased his anger, on this basis founded peace between God and men' (Calvin: *Institutes* Vol.1 p435); or (in the translation quoted by Helm pp14-15): 'As intercessor he has appeased God's wrath [and] on this foundation rests the peace of God with men'. Calvin knew that Christ interceded as mediator for the elect only: 'Christ [here in John 17] prays for the elect only' (Calvin: *Commentaries* Vol.18 Part 1 p173). Again, commenting on: 'He bore the sin of many, and made intercession for the transgressors' (Isa. 53:12): 'Because the ratification of the atonement, with which Christ has washed us by his death, implies that he pleaded with the Father on our behalf, it was proper that this should be added. For, as in the ancient law, the priest, who "never entered without blood", at the same time interceded for the people, so what was there shadowed out is fulfilled in Christ (Ex. 30:10; Heb. 9:7). *First*, he offered the sacrifice of his body, and shed his blood, that he might endure the punishment which was due to us; and *secondly*, in order that the atonement might take effect, he performed the office of an advocate, and interceded for all who embraced this sacrifice by faith; as is evident from... John 17:20' (Calvin: *Commentaries* Vol.8 Part 2 pp131-132). Indeed, Calvin went so far as to say: 'God justifies us

through the intercession of Christ' (Calvin: *Institutes* Vol.2 p39; see also Vol.1 p450).
John Gill: 'Universal [redemption] separates the works [in truth, it is one work] of Christ, the work of redemption and the work of intercession, and makes them to belong to different [beneficiaries]; whereas they are of equal extent, and belong to the same [beneficiaries]; for whom Christ died, for them he rose again from the dead... For the same [beneficiaries] he entered into heaven... and appears in the presence of God for them, and ever lives to make intercession for them; and for the same [beneficiaries] for whom he is an advocate, he is the propitiation, for his advocacy is founded upon his propitiatory sacrifice. Now those for whom he prays and intercedes, are not all men... John 17:9. Yet, according to the universal scheme, he died for them for whom he would not pray; which is absurd and incredible' (Gill: *Body* Vol.2 p176).
William Gouge: 'As [Christ] came down from heaven for our good, so for the same end he entered into heaven again. Indeed, for us, and for our good, he did and endured all that he did and endured... Christ has entered thither *for us*, that we should be made partakers of the happiness there enjoyed... Christ's excellences made him an all-sufficient priest... Christ was able and meet to accomplish what he undertook... The salvation which Christ brings is full and perfect... This... "for us"... shows the especial end of Christ so manifesting himself, even for our sakes, to make us partakers of the benefit of his intercession' (Gouge pp464,529,657, emphasis his). Charles Hodge: 'Christ continues since his resurrection and exaltation to secure for his people the benefits of his death; everything comes from God through him, and for his sake' (Hodge: *Romans* p290; Lloyd-Jones: *Final* p437). See also Manton pp137-146, especially pp142-144,146.
So much for the death, resurrection and intercession of Christ, but what of the **return** of Christ? As Christ said: 'I go to prepare a place for *you*. And if [since] I go and prepare a place for *you*, I will come again and receive *you* to myself; that where I am, there *you* may be also' (John 14:2-3). 'To those who eagerly wait for him he will appear a second time... for salvation' (Heb. 9:28). True, when Christ returns, he will have a purpose for all; he will raise all the dead, and all the dead will have to appear before him. But his *saving* purpose in his death, resurrection, intercession – and return – is particular to his elect, and only to them; the purpose in his return, as it concerns the non-elect, is *condemning*.
Marcus Rainsford: John 17:9 'is... an illustration... of the intercession [Christ] is now carrying on for us at the right hand of God... What Aaron did upon the great day of atonement on earth, the greater than Aaron has done in the temple of heaven... and there... "he appears

in the presence of God *for us*"... He appears "*for us*", he came "for us", he lived "for us", he died "for us", he rose "for us", ascended "for us", entered into the highest heavens "for us", presents his blood "for us", intercedes "for us", prepares a place "for us", claims the mansions "for us", has caused holy Scripture to be written "for us", has sent down the Holy Ghost "for us", and will come again "for us"' (Rainsford pp141-142, emphasis his).

To sum up this lengthy excursus: The question of 'extent' cannot be confined – as it usually is – to the death of Christ. The doctrine of union with Christ means that whatever is said – in regard to 'extent' – about the death of Christ, must be said about his resurrection, intercession and return. If Christ died for the elect, he was raised for the elect, he intercedes for the elect, and will return for the elect; if Christ died for all, he was raised for all, he intercedes for all, and will return for (the salvation of) all. And this because of the doctrine of union with Christ: Those for whom Christ died, rose and entered heaven, died, rose and entered heaven *in and with* him. This can only be particular for the elect. Once again, see the Appendix.

Haldane: 'The atonement is founded upon the union [Haldane sometimes used 'unity'] of Christ and his people, with whom he took part in flesh and blood... Heb. 2:11-15... The deliverance is not universal... It is not said he took on him the seed of Adam, the father of mankind [that is, Christ did not take upon him every man]; but the seed of Abraham, the father of believers [that is, the elect]... On the union of Christ and his people... is founded the atonement made for them on the cross... John 17:20-23. Upon this glorious truth the atonement rests... The doctrine of the union of Christ and his people... goes to the root of... the atonement... Were it not for the union of Christ and his people, justice instead of being magnified, would have been violated in his substitution... In order to purge our sins, in order to ransom his church, Christ must so entirely unite himself with his people, that their sins should become his sins, that his suffering should be their suffering, and his death their death... Christ is not only the substitute, but the surety of his people... The union of Christ and his people is the foundation of the atonement... [Without] the union of Christ and his people, he could have made no atonement for them, for he that sanctifies, and they that are sanctified, must be all of one... The union between Christ and his people... upon this union hangs the whole scheme of salvation' (Haldane pp47-64,134,209-210,341; see also pp196-197,320). May I repeat Haldane's excellent observation: 'Were it not for the union of Christ and his people, justice instead of being magnified, would have been violated in his substitution'.

---

[33] 'When we speak of the atonement we must always have in view... obedience, sacrifice (expiation), propitiation, reconciliation and redemption. The question of extent is bound up with that of nature. For the question is: For whom did Christ *vicariously* render obedience, offer sacrifice and make propitiation? Whom did he reconcile to God and redeem by his blood?... The topic is sometimes spoken of as the design of the atonement. There is... an advantage in the term "extent"... Who are embraced in that which the atonement actually accomplished? For whom were the obedience, sacrifice, propitiation, reconciliation and redemption designed?' (John Murray: *Collected* Vol.1 pp62-63, emphasis his). See Nicole pp303-304,479.

[34] 'The extent of the atonement is involved in its nature and essence... When men are agreed about the nature of the atonement, they will soon be at one respecting its extent. When a real atonement, expiation or satisfaction for sin is admitted, it must of necessity be restricted to those whose guilt it cancels' (Haldane p74).

[35] There are various nuances and some movement between some of these, but I am trying to be fair and yet make things as simple as I can. See Beaton pp35-51.

[36] Short of extending this book inordinately, I do not know how I can justify my conclusion about this being a minority view. I simply state it with apologies to those (like Clifford) who feel that Amyraut's view is authentic Calvinism. The dispute is not germane to what I am saying.

[37] Amyraut was a student of John Cameron, from whom he derived his system – which became known as Amyraldianism; it should, perhaps, have been known as Cameronianism (compare John Glas and Robert Sandeman, and Sandemanianism). Cameron has had a large influence on Scottish theology, and further afield. See Macleod pp60-62,244-251,293; Davenant pp203-204; Iain Murray's note in Brown: *Hebrews* v. But for Brown and Amyraldianism, see Nicole p328.

[38] See, for instance, Nettles pp297-321. Other names will become apparent as we proceed. Davenant was mistaken when he said that the formula – sufficient for all, effective for the elect – is 'the commonly received distinction among *all* divines' (Davenant p175, emphasis mine). It is, perhaps, among *most Calvinists*.

[39] Despite what some have said, I do not believe 'there was a special atonement' for the elect, 'and a universal atonement securing a possibility of salvation to all' (Williams pp37,41). That was Amyraut's position. Let me deal with the use of adjectives. As far as I am concerned, the adjective 'efficacious' is a tautology when applied to redemption. Redemption is efficacious or it is nothing. See Clifford: *Atonement* pp125,135; Davenant p78. Compare 'free grace'; how can

grace be anything but *free*? The more scholastic and further away from Scripture we get, the greater our use of (what should be) redundant or invented (and often wrong) adjectives. For instance, *Christian/Jewish* church, *believer's/infant* baptism, *gospel/Old-Testament* church, and so on. But I know I too live in this particular glasshouse. And I realise that adjectives have to be introduced to counter error. There would be no talk of 'believer's baptism' if 'infant baptism' had not been thought of, for instance. See Clifford: *Atonement* pp120-121 for his justification of certain adjectives. But what now of his attitude to glossing? See below and Appendix.

[40] Fuller: *Reality* p247, emphasis his. 'The doctrine of a limitation of design in the death of Christ stands or falls with that of the divine purposes' (Fuller: *Philanthropos* p229). Hence, 'particular redemption' is better than 'limited atonement'. Some have preferred 'definite atonement' (see Beaton p30). 'Limited' is an unfortunate choice. It implies a negative approach to the atonement, a defensive restriction of something greater and more glorious than words can describe. It is also unfortunate in another way. As I have said, all – apart from Universalists – impose some limit on the atonement – including Arminians. But it is the Calvinist who is left with the 'offending' word in his hand. Although Arminians are willing to mock this, they should remember that they too impose a limit on the atonement. In fact, their limit ruins the atonement! While the Calvinist proclaims God's limit to the atonement's extent, the Arminian destroys its very nature. But whatever the rights and wrongs of 'limited', in this book I am left with no choice but to use it. It would be interesting, however, to see what would happen if 'definite atonement' took over from 'limited atonement'. As Nicole (pp431-433) pointed out, it would remove the unnecessary contrast between the seeming generosity of those who hold to general redemption and the corresponding grudging-ness of those who hold to particular redemption. The latter would assert a definite redemption; what would the former assert? an indefinite redemption? This would effectively place the negative note of protest where it rightly belongs – with the Arminians not the Calvinists.

[41] The design or intention of God in Christ's redemption is *the* vital point. Owen rightly opened his treatise on the subject: 'By the *end* [purpose] of the death of Christ, we mean in general, both, *first*, that which his Father and himself *intended* in it; and *secondly*, that which was effectually fulfilled and accomplished by it' (Owen: *Death* in *Works* Vol.10 pp157-158, emphasis mine; see also, for instance, pp222-223,247,250,315). He also hinted that another work might be called for – specifically dealing with 'the *cause* of [the] sending [of] Jesus Christ'

(Owen: *Death* in *Works* Vol.10 pp231,245,395, emphasis mine). 'What... did Christ do in his death? What did he *aim* at and *design*? what was his *intention* in submitting unto and undergoing the will of God in these things?' (Owen: *Psalm 130* in *Works* Vol.6 p493, emphasis mine). Fuller's first question to Dan Taylor (Philanthropos) showed the same concern: 'Had our Lord Jesus Christ any absolute *determination* in his death to save any of the human race?' (Fuller: *Philanthropos* p224, emphasis mine; Nettles p123). Booth: 'To be voluntary in suffering, to bear imputed sin, and to *intend*, in dying, to make reconciliation, were essential to [Christ's] death as a sacrifice and atonement' (Booth: *Divine Justice* in *Works* Vol.3 p80, emphasis mine). See Edwards: *Freedom* p88; Scott pp59-60.

[42] All Calvinists believe Christ's atonement is sufficient, but sufficient for whom? and for what? and why? That is the issue. Clifford said that 'no seventeenth-century divine seriously questioned the idea' of sufficiency (Clifford: *Atonement* p27), but, as he pointed out, the Westminster Confession says nothing about it, even though its compilers were well aware of the controversy over the idea (Clifford: *Atonement* pp26-27,75,87). Some 17th century theologians, it seems, did not want to assert sufficiency. Was it that they realised there is no need to travel this road since it serves no purpose other than to try to justify God with human logic? Or did they not want to get embroiled in a (fruitless) argument over the word? After all, Owen and Baxter both held to sufficiency, but meant different things by it. Widening the discussion, the same could be said of Calvin, Amyraut, Booth and Fuller; they all asserted the infinite sufficiency of Christ's redemption, but did not mean the same thing by it. As Clifford said: 'An element of ambiguity in the term "sufficient" permitted all schools to attach their own meaning to it' (Clifford: *Atonement* p74). For a discussion of the nuances of 'this phrase [which] is ambiguous', see Beaton pp30-31, where he rightly observed, and as I have already noted, the real question is the atonement's 'design or intention'. 'Sufficiency', this chameleon-like word, is, in the end, meaningless in this debate. I will return to the point.

[43] I use the phrase in the sense of a 'fine or subtle' distinction 'requiring careful thought or attention' (*Concise*).

[44] : If the ground of the offer is the extent of the atonement, then in preaching to sinners all this has to be thoroughly explained to them. Nonsense. Sinners do not need to be able to argue the ins-and-outs of the extent of the atonement before they can be invited or come to Christ. In the name of God, on the authority of God's command and promise, sinners need to be persuaded to come to Christ as the perfect, only and all-sufficient Saviour, and be assured of a welcome if they do. John

Bonar addressed 'the ground on which sinners are... called and invited, and the warrant they have for instant compliance with that call. Two things are... required in order that these calls may be warrantably addressed to all, and all may have full warrant to comply with them. 1st, That there should be a Saviour provided... 2nd, That that Saviour being provided, his salvation should be freely offered to us'. As for the first, 'Christ is an all-sufficient Saviour – having all that sinners can need'. As for the second, 'Christ as thus all-sufficient is freely offered to all – *and this offer of Christ is conveyed to us upon the testimony of God*' (John Bonar p16, emphasis mine). We have to preach 'the readiness of Christ to receive every sinner... that shall come unto him. And hereof we have the highest evidences that divine wisdom and grace can give unto us' (Owen: *Meditations* in *Works* Vol.1 p423). To look at this issue, is, of course, my reason for writing this book.

[45] Owen: *Death* in *Works* Vol.10 pp295,315; see also *Psalm 130* in *Works* Vol.6 pp500-501.

[46] Bunyan: *Jerusalem* in *Works* Vol.2 p474; *Reprobation* in *Works* Vol.3 p282. But Bunyan went further than this at times, and there I part company with him: God would have all invited, 'and the reason is, because Christ died for all... The offer of the gospel cannot... be offered any further than the death of Jesus Christ goes; because if that be taken away, there is indeed no gospel, nor grace to be extended... There is a sufficiency of life and righteousness laid up in Christ for all men, and this [is] tendered by the gospel to them without exception' (Bunyan: *Reprobation* in *Works* Vol.3 pp281-282).

[47] 'The use of more words than are needed to give the sense' (*Concise*).

[48] Gill: *Sermons* Vol.2 pp5-6,15-16; see the entire sermon.

[49] 'An all-sufficient Saviour – a Saviour, the infinite worthiness of whose person, as the incarnate Son of God, and the absolute perfection of whose work, in obedience and in sufferings, as our voluntary sponsor, magnify the law which we have dishonoured, display the justice of God, in the tremendous punishment of sin, and exhibit the riches of sovereign mercy in the free pardon of deservedly condemned criminals' (Booth: *Divine Justice* in *Works* Vol.3 pp43-44; see also *Divine Justice* pp82,94-95). 'What encouragement, then, has the miserable sinner to look to [the obedience of the Lord Redeemer!] How safely may he confide in it, as all-sufficient to justify his ungodly soul!... Nor can it seem strange that the work of Christ should be thus efficacious. For God the Son performed it, in the capacity of a substitute. God the Father declares his delight in it... And it is the principal business of God the Holy Spirit... to testify of it... In this most perfect obedience, believers are now exalted, and the saints in heaven triumph. For the work of Christ finished on a

cross is the [theme] of their songs. But who can point out all its beauties? Who can show forth half its praise? After all that has been written or said about it, by prophets or apostles here on earth; after all that has been sung or can be conceived, by saints or angels in the world of glory; considered under its divine character... it exceeds all possible praise. The inhabitants of the heavenly world must be conscious that their loftiest strains... fall vastly short of displaying all its excellence' (Booth: *Reign* pp267-268; see also *Reign* pp139-140). 'The all-sufficiency of that grace which is revealed in Jesus Christ... What a wonderful exhibition is here, of sovereign, free and all-sufficient mercy!... Here we have, not only the apostles of Christ, but Christ himself, and, in his ambassadors, even the divine Father, inviting, persuading, entreating the polluted, impoverished, perishing wretches, to regard the vicarious work of Jesus, as the only ground of their justification; and the plentiful provisions of divine grace, as containing all that is wanted for their complete happiness... The grace revealed is rich, abundant, exceedingly abundant, and all-sufficient... Preaching the gospel... is preaching Christ himself... as the only, the all-sufficient, the absolutely free Saviour of the condemned – the worthless – the lost... The gracious gospel, considered as a complete warrant for the ungodly to believe in Jesus, encourages the most profligate, and the most criminal, to regard the atonement of Christ as all-sufficient... Let him [the sinner] remember... that pardon is entirely through the atoning blood of Jesus; that justification is merely by his imputed righteousness; that salvation is absolutely in a way of sovereign grace; and that Christ, with all his fullness of spiritual blessings, is exhibited in the glad tidings, as equally free for him, as for the most virtuous character on earth... that the gracious gospel, by revealing an almighty Saviour, forbids despair... He being revealed... as perfectly suitable to [sinners'] wants, and as completely free for their acceptance, they are presented, by sovereign grace, with an all-sufficient Saviour for their immediate dependence... the comfort [arising]... from that grace which the gospel reveals, and from the all-sufficiency of Jesus in whom they trust... Christ... is completely able to save the chief of sinners' (Booth: *Glad Tidings* in *Works* Vol.2 pp5,28,40,66,78,204-207,214; see also *Works* Vol.3 pp296-297). See also John Bonar pp17-19.

[50] Booth, while he avoided the sufficiency formula, mistakenly got close to it (but rightly sheered off), in words just preceding the above-quoted extract: 'While cheerfully admitting the sufficiency of Immanuel's death to have redeemed all mankind, had all the sins of the whole human species been equally imputed to him, and had he, as the universal representative, sustained that curse of the law which was due to all

mankind, yet we cannot perceive any solid reason to conclude that his propitiatory sufferings are sufficient for the expiation of sins which he did not bear, or for the redemption of sinners whom he did not represent as a sponsor when he expired on the cross'. Such speculation about 'sufficient for all' – as opened this extract from Booth – should be dropped.

Similarly for Haldane: 'With regard to the infinite value of the sacrifice of Christ considered in itself, there is no dispute. Had it pleased God that all mankind should be saved, no more suffering than Christ endured would have been necessary; and had it been the divine purpose that but one solitary individual of Adam's race should obtain salvation, there would have been no abatement of what Jesus endured upon earth... Whoever said the atonement was not, in itself, sufficient to secure the salvation of all mankind?... If it had been God's purpose to save all mankind by the blood of the cross, no further suffering on the part of the surety of the new covenant would have been required' (Haldane pp124,337). I have no doubt that this is right, but I know of no scripture which says it. Neither Booth or Haldane advanced their cause – which was good – biblical, indeed – by speculating in this way. Use of: 'Had it pleased God that...' could lead to all sorts of conjecture. Let us stick to what we know *has* pleased God!

Having thus criticised Haldane, I record my gratitude to Donald Macauley for his recommendation of Haldane's book on the atonement. Although I came across it very late – my wife and I were checking the mss in preparation for typesetting! – as is obvious, I simply had to use his work. Not all of it, however. Much as I admire Haldane's book, I do not agree with his stance against the offer, his stance against God's general love to all men leading to his revealed desire to see all sinners saved, and his view that the elect were never the object of God's wrath (Haldane pp106,122-124,143-150,182-183,239-240,329,351-352). For a summary of Haldane's position, see Alexander Haldane: *The Lives of Robert and James Haldane*, The Banner of Truth Trust, Edinburgh, 1990, pp638-651, even though I disagree with his (Alexander's) speculation about the benefits of Christ's death for the non-elect. As he himself said: 'The question as to the bearing of the atonement on the finally impenitent is surely... merely a speculation'. What is more, he aptly quoted Robert Candlish: 'We proclaim no general amnesty or indiscriminate jail delivery, purchased for men at large by Christ; but we set before you Christ himself, and all that come to him we assure of pardon, peace and eternal life. We do not merely tell you of the infinite amount of merit and atoning virtue which there is in the obedience and death of Jesus. But we tell you of Jesus himself, who will clothe you –

any of you – all of you – who will only come unto him, with a robe of perfect righteousness, and wash you in a fountain that will make you all clean. And we tell you further, that with any questions as to what there may be in Christ – for you or for any – while not coming unto him, you have no concern. It is presumption to ask such questions; it would be vain and useless to have them answered. Come unto Christ; come and see; taste, and see that the Lord is good. This is his present call; this is your present duty, admitting of no evasion and of no delay. Come to Christ, and he will make all clear to you. Come unto him, and he will give you rest'. This extract contains the seeds of much of what I want to say. As for references, since I have not cited Alexander Haldane anywhere else in this book, I have not included his work in the Source List; furthermore, in the text, by 'Haldane', I have meant and continue to mean James Haldane. Finally, this good man was no mere theorist. Donald Macauley told me that if the minister had not preached the gospel in the service, James Haldane had the courage to put the matter right and preach at the gate as the congregation left the building.
To return, for a moment, to Booth. He quoted the 'words of an old Nonconformist': 'If any man be bound to believe Christ's satisfaction [is] sufficient to justify him for whom it was never paid, he is bound to believe an untruth – God will never make it any man's duty to rest for salvation on that blood that was never shed for him, or that satisfaction which was never made for him' (Booth: *Divine Justice* in *Works* Vol.3 pp61-62). I am not sure what Booth (and 'the old Nonconformist') meant. It is no part of the free offer to tell sinners that Christ died for them, nor is it their duty to believe it. Thus far I agree with the extract. But it is the duty of all sinners to trust Christ (see my *Offer* pp1-55). Did Booth believe in duty faith? I record, with sadness, it seems he did not. As Fuller observed: 'Mr Booth has (to all appearances, designedly) avoided the question: Whether faith in Christ be the *duty* of the ungodly?... In the course of his work, he describes the gospel message as full of kind invitations, winning persuasions and importunate entreaties; and the messengers as commissioned to persuade and entreat sinners to be reconciled to God, and to regard the vicarious work of Jesus as the only ground of their justification... But how [what] if they should remain unreconciled, and continue to disregard the work of Christ? How [what] if they should, after all, *make light* of this "royal banquet", and prefer their farms and their merchandises to these "plentiful provisions of divine grace"? Are they guiltless in so doing, and free from all breach of duty? I am persuaded, whatever was Mr Booth's reason for being silent on this subject, he will not say they are' (Fuller: *Worthy* p156, emphasis his). Again: 'Mr Booth is partial to the term *warrant*, and seems to have

studiously kept the idea of obligation out of sight' (Fuller: *Reviews* p964, emphasis his). I will return to this when looking at Fuller's criticism of Booth's actual addresses to sinners.

[51] Fuller: *Sermons* pp624-625.

[52] Fuller: *Awakened* p878. See also Fuller: *Worthy* p153. Hodge: 'The death of Christ has been accepted [by God] as an expiation for sin, of infinite value and efficiency' (Hodge: *2 Corinthians* p145). But to say that Christ's sacrifice is of infinite worth is not, as I have explained, the same as saying it is sufficient for all, and that this 'sufficiency for all' is to be preached to sinners.

[53] Brown: *Hebrews* pp102-103.

[54] See Thayer. D.Martyn Lloyd-Jones: 'If we could but see what is in Christ! But it is unsearchable, untraceable... The riches that are in Christ are unsearchable in this respect, that no man, not even a Christian, can ever fully comprehend them. As Paul continued in the Christian life he was more and more amazed at these riches. He may have thought at times that he had been to every room in this great treasury, but then he found another. There is always some further inner room, and yet another and another. We shall spend our eternity in discovering fresh aspects and facets of the unsearchable riches of Christ. Unsearchable, untraceable! Another meaning of this term is that the riches can never be fully described... The riches of Christ are inexhaustible; they can never fail. Though men and women for centuries have been drawing from them, there is still as much remaining as there was at the beginning. They can never be diminished... Christ has everything I need... Christ himself is the riches... It is in Christ that riches abound... He offers to all who believe in him his "unsearchable riches"' (Lloyd-Jones: *Unsearchable* pp60-66).

[55] Clifford: 'Introduction' xii.

[56] *The Three* p30.

[57] Interestingly, Clifford was very strong against Owen for his use of the Schoolmen (Clifford: *Atonement* pp95-110), but the scholastic sufficiency-efficiency formula is basic to his own case. A pity he did not follow Hugh Latimer, of whom he quoted with approval: When he 'began to smell the word of God [he] forsook the School-doctors and such fooleries'. A pity, too, that both Clifford and Owen did not take Owen's own medicine, to which also Clifford referred with approval: 'If those theological determinations that make up at this day among some men the greatest part of those assertions, positions, or propositions... which are not delivered in the words that the Spirit of God teaches, but in terms of art, and in answer to rules and notions which the world might... without any great disadvantage [have] been unacquainted with

unto this day had not Aristotle found them out or stumbled on them... innumerable causes of strife and contentions would be taken away; but... small hopes have I to see any such impression and consent befall the minds of concerned men' (Clifford: *Atonement* p106; Owen: *Vindication* in *Works* Vol.14 p315). A pity, I repeat, that Owen had not taken this line when writing his *Death*. (It is, of course, necessary to remember that Owen's *Death* was published 16 or 17 years *before* his *Vindication*). But neither was Amyraut immune to scholasticism; as an advocate of his theological position has admitted, Amyraut, depending on philosophy, had 'rationalistic tendencies', and was prepared to make 'rationalistic statements' (Jenkins pp13-17). See also Clifford: 'Introduction' xv.

[58] Clifford: *Atonement* pp74-75; *Amyraut* pp20-21; Cunningham p332; Owen: *Death* in *Works* Vol.10 p296; Davenant pp18,175,186.

[59] Lloyd-Jones: *Life* pp145-146.

[60] Millions of worlds? Would they be men? In light of Heb. 2:10-18; 4:15-16, 'how... could the obedience unto death of the Son of Man, atone for the sins of a separate race?' (Haldane p160).

[61] Boston: *Beauties* pp183-186.

[62] John Murray: *Redemption* p 64; *Collected* Vol.1 pp62-63,68. Clifford, referring to this, did not point out that Murray immediately went on to say: 'It must, however, be marked with equal emphasis that these fruits or benefits all fall short of salvation' (Clifford: *Atonement* p91).

Some comments on: 'Many benefits accrue to the non-elect, from the redemptive work of Christ'. This is often said, but I have seen no convincing proof of it. For Baxter's view of 'other ends' in Christ's redemption, for instance, see Clifford: *Atonement* pp101-102. But, as with John Murray just quoted, it is also said by others who hold to particular redemption. C.H.Spurgeon, for instance, was another: 'We do not believe in general redemption, but... there are many passages in the Scripture which seem to show that Christ's death had a universal bearing upon the sons of men. We are told that he tasted death for every man. What does that mean? Does it mean that Jesus Christ died to save every man? I do not believe it does, for it seems to me that everything which Christ intended to accomplish by the act of his death he must accomplish... Those whom Christ died to save I believe he will save effectually, through his substitutionary sacrifice. But did he in any other sense die for the rest of mankind? [I think] he did. Nothing can be much more plain in Scripture, it seems to me, than that all sinners are spared as the result of Jesus Christ's death, and this is the sense in which men are said to trample on the blood of Jesus Christ. We read of some who denied the Lord that bought them. No one who is bought with blood for eternal salvation ever tramples on that blood; but Jesus Christ has shed his blood for the reprieve of men that they may be spared... You can hold that doctrine without holding universal redemption, or without at all contradicting that undoubted truth, that Jesus laid down his life for his sheep, and that where he suffered he suffered not in vain. Now, sinner, whether you know it or not, you are indebted to him that did hang upon the tree, for the breath that is now in you. You would not have been on praying ground and pleading terms with God this morning if it had not been for that dear suffering one' (Spurgeon: *Metropolitan* Vol.11 pp526-527). As above, I am not aware of any biblical proof of these assertions. Spurgeon cited Heb. 2:9. Bearing in mind Brown's view of the atonement – which I noted earlier – his comments on the verse are valuable: 'The universality here specified is plainly a limited universality. The word in the original is not "every man", "every human being"; it is "every one" – a word that naturally leads you on to ask: "Every one of whom?" And when you look into the context you find a particular class of persons mentioned – "the heirs of salvation" – the "many sons" of God – the "sanctified" ones – the "brethren" of Christ – the "children" of Christ, "whom God had given him". It was for "every one" of these that Jesus, when he became mortal, laid down his life. He died *for* them' (Brown: *Hebrews* p102, emphasis his). See also Owen: *Death* in *Works* Vol.10 pp349-350. Spurgeon also cited 2 Pet. 2:1. See the Appendix for my comments on that verse.

Robert L.Dabney also thought 'Christ died for all sinners in some sense'; God designed 'a combination of results from' Christ's death. It not only purchased 'the full and assured redemption of all the elect, or of all believers', but, in addition, for the still-born 'it has purchased heaven', for the non-elect who are not still-born it accomplished 'a [temporary] reprieve of doom... postponement of death and perdition, secular well-being, and the bounties of life... sincere offers of a salvation on terms of faith... a justly enhanced condemnation of those who reject the gospel... [and] a disclosure of the infinite tenderness and glory of God's compassion... to all rational creatures' (Dabney: *Systematic* pp527-529; see also 'God's' p310). Apart from the complete redemption of the elect – which is clearly scriptural – all the rest (apart from the offer – this is why I am writing this book) might well be right, but once again I know of no scripture which says it. Dabney offered none. As for the offer, was Dabney not contradicting what he had said earlier (Dabney: *Systematic* p523, see below; see also 'God's' pp283-284)?

Clifford cited Matt. 18:11; 20:28, Luke 13:34; John 1:11; 3:16; 6:32; 2 Cor. 5:19; 1 Tim. 1:15, rightly saying: 'Christ is said to have come even for those who eventually rejected him'. But he made a leap too far when he immediately deduced: 'In short, his atoning death provided grace for

a greater number than those who actually receive it' (Clifford: *Atonement* pp97,107). See John Murray: *Collected* Vol.4 p110, to which I will return. It is freely granted that God has a universal love for all men, and makes a free offer to all, but this does not mean he has atoned for all. And Christ's 'coming' to men need not refer to his death. Take, for instance, Acts 3:26 & Eph. 2:17. As I have shown (see my *Offer* pp67-68), such passages refer to the external call of the gospel; that is, God's desire to see sinners saved, and his commanding them to repent and believe, and his offer of Christ and salvation. Christ himself came to men in his lifetime; he comes today by his Spirit. Clifford was wrong to say that Acts 3:26 – 'God... sent [Jesus] to bless you, in turning away everyone of you from your iniquities' – teaches: 'All were... embraced in the divine *intention*' (Clifford: *Atonement* p121, emphasis mine). Were all who heard Peter that day, turned? Of course not. 'Many of those who heard the word believed' (Acts 4:4); many, but not all. Even so, God sent his Son to turn them from their sins; that is, he *desired* them to turn. Whoever God *intends* to turn, will turn: 'As many as had been appointed to eternal life believed' (Acts 13:48). But he *desires* all to turn, which *desire* he expresses through his servants. John the Baptist preached Christ, 'that all through him might believe' (John 1:7); that is, this was John's (and God's!) *desire* and their *duty*. 'John indeed baptised with a baptism of repentance, saying to the people that they should believe on... Christ Jesus' (Acts 19:4). Paul spoke 'to the Gentiles that they may be saved' (1 Thess. 2:16); that is, he preached with this *desire*.
But some, even though sympathetic to the Amyraldian position, have distanced themselves from saying that the death of Christ benefits all men. Douty, for instance: 'If Christ died for those who go to hell, what benefit have they from his death?... We may as well ask: What good did the bitten Israelites get from the brazen serpent to which they refused to look? None of course' (Douty p91). True – but a remarkable statement for one with his view of the atonement – see below.
As far as I am aware, the Scriptures only ever speak of the spiritual blessings in Christ 'for us'; that is, the elect. As I have mentioned, it is noticeable, as far as I have read, that when men write in fulsome terms of the spiritual benefits obtained by Christ's death for all men, most do not supply a passage to prove it or to tell us what they are. Davenant was a notable exception (Davenant pp31-33). Even so, while it is an enormous privilege to preach the gospel (Rom. 10:15), and to hear it (John 6:68; Acts 5:20; Tit. 2:11), and not to have the gospel is the severest punishment (Matt. 21:43), and rejecting it brings a curse (Luke 10:11; 2 Thess. 1:8), none of this, it seems to me, establishes Davenant's case. Again, Heb. 6:4-6 does not seem to prove the point. And John

1:16; 1 Cor. 12:11; 2 Cor. 4:7; Eph. 6:7 all apply to the elect. Furthermore, Davenant misquoted Luke 24:46-47; it does not say Christ died and rose 'that repentance and remission of sins should be preached' – that is, 'it was necessary that Christ should die *so that* the gospel might be preached'; rather, 'it was necessary for the Christ to suffer and to rise from the dead the third day, and that repentance and remission of sins should be preached' (NKJV, AV, NASB) – that is, 'it was necessary for Christ to die and rise, *and it was also necessary that* the gospel should be preached'. As for the Fathers and their claim that 'the death of Christ is... applicable to the non-elect... because... it was applied in baptism for the remission of original sin to every baptised infant', words fail. (They fail here – but I have written plenty of words about it in my *Infant*).
Replying to Baxter, Owen, in what may be considered as an Appendix to his *Death*: 'If by "benefit" [men] understand that which... is intentionally so... condemned persons... surely receive no benefit by Christ, for they are condemned... [Furthermore,] the delay of the condemnation of reprobates is no part of the purchase of Christ. The Scripture says no more nor less of any such thing, but peculiarly assigns it to another cause, Rom. 9:22' (Owen: *Death* in *Works* Vol.10 p462).

[63] See *The Three* p43; Owen: *Death* in *Works* Vol.10 pp294-298,383-384; Edwards: *Freedom* p88; *Christ* p215; Fuller: *Button* p207; *Philanthropos* pp223-233; *Reality* pp247-255; *Three Conversations* pp314-317; *Six Letters* pp320-324; *Sermons* p597; Sheehan pp108-117; Oliver pp209-221; Dabney: *Systematic* pp523-529; 'God's' p310; Berkhof pp393-394,397-399; Pratt pp165-166; Hodge: *1 Corinthians* p149; Clifford: *Amyraut* pp20-25,59-64; Davenant; and so on.

[64] Contrary to the (21st century) Publisher's Foreword to Davenant: 'It is partly with a concern that opponents would understand *the* "sufficient for all, effective only for the elect" position that this work [Davenant's] has been republished' (Davenant xxi, emphasis mine). There are *two* such positions, not one. 'Both... say that Christ's death was sufficient for all men, but [they] do not mean the same thing... [Owenites] repeat the dictum of the Schoolmen... [but] they do not mean what those divines meant. They only mean that his death, in its intrinsic value, was sufficient for all; they deny that Christ intended to suffer it for all' (Douty pp35-36). Davenant, at Dort, was an Anglican advocate of a 'modified form' of what would become the Amyraldian position (Davenant was advocating his view at Dort in 1618 when Amyraut was only 22; Cameron was at that time at Saumur, Amyraut only becoming Professor of Theology there in 1633; see Douty pp111,116) – as far as I have read, his Dissertation is the fullest account of that position – and, consequently, I disagree with much (but not all) of what he said, as will

become clear. Douty was a 20th century Calvinistic Baptist minister, whose book, though simpler than Davenant's, was well-researched – although he did not seem to recognise that some who believe in particular redemption, and preach the free offer, do not use the sufficiency formula. Davenant distinguished the two forms of the sufficiency formula as 'mere sufficiency' and 'ordained sufficiency' (Davenant p72); Douty did it by asking the question: 'Was Christ's atonement possessed of a *bare* sufficiency (a mere adequacy to cover all human sin whatsoever), or of an *ordained* sufficiency (being divinely appointed for everybody)?' His own answer was very clear: 'A moment's reflection ought to be enough to show that a bare sufficiency is of no practical use to sinners' (Douty p35, emphasis his). While I agree with Douty's assessment of a 'bare sufficiency' (Owen's position) – which I call meaningless (for my reasons, see the main body of my book) – I disagree with him over an 'ordained sufficiency' (Amyraut's position). Davenant claimed that what would become the Owenite position was a novelty – 'it never occurred to the Schoolmen to defend this sufficiency only, and to deny absolutely that Christ died for all' (Davenant p52). Douty agreed: 'This transferring of the term "sufficiency" from the intention of [Christ's] dying to the mere intrinsic value of [his] death *per se*, [was] something novel' (Douty p36).
As for Douty himself, he can be regarded as a modified Amyraldian (Douty p112). Even so, his view on the subject in hand amounted not to Amyraldianism but to Arminianism: 'We maintain... that Christ's propitiation propitiates, his reconciliation reconciles, his redemption redeems, and his atonement atones so far as its own intrinsic efficacy is concerned, but not with reference to any sinner, unless he repents and believes... We hold that these same benefits are equally provided for the non-elect [as the elect]... I, too, am a limited atonement man', said Douty, 'if I am permitted to apply the adjective to [the] atonement's possession, rather than to its provision' . But this much could be said by any non-Universalist – including Arminians. Nevertheless, I agree with Douty when he said: 'The transaction of Calvary was a single transaction, instead of being one for the elect and another for the non-elect'. I do not agree, however, when he went on to show his agreement with the Amyraldian stance: 'But... there was a double intention in that single transaction, according to which the one, all-comprehensive, provision of salvation was intended to be effectually applied to the elect, but not to the non-elect. A single transaction with a double intention' (Douty pp43,48). I will develop these points as we go on.

[65] It is more complicated (hair-splitting) than this, at least in Owen's presentation of it, as I will explain.

[66] As for Calvin, on 'sufficient for all' he was definite. Although he did not think it was the right interpretation of 1 John 2:2, it was his view that 'Christ suffered sufficiently for the whole world, but efficiently only for the elect' (Calvin: *Commentaries* Vol.22 Part 2 p173; Clifford: *Atonement* pp86,155). But whether or not Calvin thought Christ provided redemption sufficient for all by God's design, or that the sufficiency arose out of Christ's intrinsic worth, is not at all clear – at least, to me. If Clifford could have cited Calvin plainly stating the former, he would have done so. Clearly, Calvin would have been an Amyraldian!
On which side did Dort fall? As above, Dort stated that 'the death of the Son of God is the only and most perfect sacrifice and satisfaction for sin; and is of infinite worth and value, abundantly sufficient to expiate the sins of the whole world' (*The Three* p43). Clifford, as others, tried hard to read *design* and intention into this, but it is not convincing; what he called Dort's 'ambiguity' was, in fact, its 'silence'. Dort did not say that God designed and Christ accomplished a provisional redemption for all. As for Dort and Calvin, Clifford asserted that Dort went beyond Calvin, moving from the Amyraldian (that is, according to Clifford, the Calvinistic) position to the Bezan (Owenite) position (Clifford: *Atonement* pp70-75; 'Introduction' xii,xvi,xvii). This seems borne out by Dort: 'This death derives its infinite value and dignity from [among other 'considerations']... the person who submitted to it' (*The Three* p43) – Owen's view. For the difficulty in maintaining Beza's alleged part in moving beyond Calvin, see Nicole p304.
What about Owen's view of Calvin on the question? Interestingly, Clifford pointed out, Owen never 'referred to Calvin's precise views on the extent of the atonement'. Either Owen thought Calvin and he believed the same (Clifford's suggestion; see Clifford: *Atonement* pp11,72), or else, perhaps, Owen felt Calvin had not been detailed and careful enough on the issue.
If the latter, the quarrel over the extent of the atonement, and its connection with its nature, it must not be forgotten, only came to life about 40 years after Calvin's death. Similarly, the free-offer controversy started to rage 100 years later still, and this after Owen's death. Doctrinal statements are usually (invariably) precisely defined *against* something perceived as error (see John Murray: *Collected* Vol.1 p317, not that precision in itself precludes error, see Clifford: *Atonement* p85). The error has to arise first. But once it has arisen, we have to respond. Clifford admitted the point (Clifford: *Atonement* p120). And as for Calvin, great though he was, some, not excluding Clifford (despite his own protestation – Clifford: *Atonement* p243), give me the impression

that they want to prove him totally consistent at all costs. But Calvin was human, therefore fallible, therefore inconsistent. Given the length of time of writing, his vast output, much of it preached when under the pressure of daily events, his breaking of new ground, his (like all mortals) fallible memory, his poor health – why not simply admit the fact and go on?

[67] Quoted by Clifford: *Amyraut* pp11,31.

[68] Clifford: *Amyraut* pp18-19,48-49. Clifford had 'according to both Amyraut and Calvin'. This is a bone of contention between Clifford and many other Calvinists. See Goold p140. I do not wish to enter this dialogue – as I have said, it has no effect on my thesis. For an overview of both Calvin's view of the extent of the atonement, and the Amyraldian controversy, see Nicole pp283-330.

[69] Clifford's e-mail to me, 9th Feb. 2005. Davenant: 'We do not contend that God by his absolute will (which not only predetermines the ordination of means to an end, but also the infallible production of the end) intended actually to procure the salvation of each and every man through the death of Christ; but that he appointed, willed and ordained that the death of his Son should be, and should be esteemed, a ransom of such a kind that it might be offered and applied to all men individually'. 'Christ died for all *sufficiently*, but for the elect *effectually*' (Davenant pp63,175, emphasis his).

[70] But what do we know of God's *decree* concerning the *non*-elect? We know God 'has mercy on whom he wills, and whom he wills he hardens... God, wanting to show his wrath and to make his power known, endured with much longsuffering the vessels of wrath prepared for destruction... The elect have obtained it [salvation by grace], and the rest were blinded' (Rom. 9:18,22; 11:7-10; see also John 12:39-40; 1 Pet. 2:8). The context of Rom. 9:18,22 is to do with God's will – that is, his determining decree – concerning fallen man. Indeed, Rom. 9:18 is a direct consequence (note the 'therefore') of Rom. 9:14-17 where God speaks of his sovereign determining decree in the affairs of men (Ishmael, Isaac, Jacob, Esau, Pharaoh, for example), whether to show mercy or to harden. Paul declares God's sovereign rights in all this: 'Does not the potter have power [a/the right, AV, NASB, NIV] over the clay, from the same lump to make one vessel for honour and another for dishonour?' (Rom. 9:21). It is, of course, 'from the same lump', from fallen humanity, that God chooses and forms elect or reprobate vessels. 'Paul is not now dealing with God's sovereign rights over men *as men* but over men *as sinners*' (John Murray: *Romans* Vol.2 pp26-32, emphasis mine). 'The mass of *fallen men* are in [God's] hands, and it is his right to dispose of them at pleasure' (Hodge: *Romans* p319,

emphasis mine). 'The potter does not create the clay; he starts with it, it is there in front of him on the bench... The apostle is not dealing here at all with God's purpose in the original creation of man, or with what God does with human nature as such. He is dealing with God's relationship to *fallen humanity*' (Lloyd-Jones: *Romans 9* pp199-200, emphasis mine). These excellent observations contradict Calvin who went too far in ascribing Paul's statement, not to fallen humanity, but to men as creatures; see Calvin's comments and his editor's correcting notes in Calvin: *Commentaries* Vol.19 Part 2 pp366-367,417-418.

All humanity, elect and reprobate, are at birth 'by nature children of wrath' (Eph. 2:3), of 'the same lump'. So, in dealing with sinners, although God has shown his desire in his revealed will to save all men, in his secret decree he has determined to save some and condemn the rest. 'It is not the desire of God that any should perish; indeed it is the desire of God that all should come to repentance. But it is not God's will [decree] that all should come to repentance' (Lloyd-Jones: *Romans 9* p216). In order to save the 'some', therefore, God decreed to give his Son to die for the elect to bring them to glory. They were part of the sinful clay; he 'makes' them vessels for honour; he has determined to redeem them, decreed mercy for them, decreed Christ to die for them. As for the sinners which made up the rest of the clay, he determined not to elect them, but to harden them; he did not decree mercy for them, he did not decree Christ to die for them. Nevertheless, God desires the salvation of all, even though he has decreed neither the end nor the means; that is, he has not decreed to give Christ to die for them all, nor the Spirit effectually to call them all, and so on. Dabney: 'The only merciful volition ['the exercise of the will, the power of willing' (*Concise*); that is, 'decree'] of God in Scripture is that towards the elect; and "the rest he hardens"... It is inevitably delusive to represent an omniscient and omnipotent agent as having any kind of volition [decree] towards a result [in this case, 'to provide expiation for all men, and to receive them all to heaven, provided they would believe on him'] when, [i] foreseeing that the sinner will certainly not present the essential condition thereof – faith – he himself distinctly purposes not to bestow it; [ii] that the hearing of the gospel (Rom. 10:14) is as [a] means equally essential, and [yet] God providentially leaves [a vast number of] all the heathen without this; and [iii] that it is derogatory to God's power and sovereignty to represent any volition [decree] of his, that is a volition [decree] as failing in a multitude of cases' (Dabney: 'God's' pp283-284, citing François Turretin's refutation of 'hypothetical universalism'. Dabney, however, rightly went on to expose the wrongness of the assumption often adopted by 'the Reformed divines of Turretin's school'; namely, that since God has not secretly decreed to save all men, he can have no revealed desire to save all). Concerning the non-elect, Amyraldianism ends up with a *real* contradiction in God's *decree*; namely, God in his secret will *decreed* to (sufficiently) redeem them on condition of faith, yet *decreed* not to elect them to redemption, but to harden them. (But do Amyraldians, in fact, speak of God hardening the non-elect? I will return to this). The biblical position is that there can be a *seeming* contradiction between God's decree and his desire, between his secret will and his revealed will, *but not a real contradiction in his decree*.

[71] See my *Offer* pp57-134. Fuller: 'That there is a conformity between God's revealed will and his decrees I admit... There is no contradiction in these things, in themselves considered, however they may appear to short-sighted mortals. That there is, however, a real distinction between the secret and revealed will of God is not very difficult to prove'. Fuller showed from Scripture that, on the one hand, 'the will of God is represented in Scripture... as that which can never be frustrated', but also, on the other, 'as that which may be frustrated or disobeyed... The former belongs unto God, being the rule of his own conduct, and to us is secret; the latter belongs to us and to our children for ever being the rule of our conduct... and this is fully revealed' (Fuller: *Philanthropos* p230; see also p232). Jonathan Edwards: 'The Arminians [and hyper-Calvinists] themselves must be obliged, whether they will or no, to allow a distinction of God's will, amounting to just the same thing that Calvinists intend by their distinction of a secret and revealed will' (Edwards: *Freedom* p79; Scott pp17-18). Edwards gave his reasons.
Philpot: 'God's open will is made known to us in the Scriptures... But besides this open or express will, God has a secret will, not revealed, at least not plainly and clearly revealed, as is his positive will in the word of truth... But as all our readers may not see the distinction we make between the open and the secret will of God, let us explain our meaning a little more distinctly... It was God's open or expressed will that when he sent his dear Son, Israel after the flesh should believe in him as the promised Messiah; but his secret will was, that his people by outward covenant should reject him, and nail him to the accursed tree, that redemption by atoning blood might be accomplished, and also that the Gentiles should be the firstfruits of the Saviour's finished work... Now... the secret will of God thus sometimes differs from his open will'. Philpot cited Deut. 29:29 (Philpot: *Meditations* pp305-306). In fact, as I have already shown, Philpot went even further: '"The will of God" may be divided into two branches; there is the revealed will of God, and there

is the secret will of God; and these two are often contradictory' (Philpot: *Selected* p54).
I do not agree with J.L.Dagg's way of putting it: 'According to God's secret will, or will of purpose, redemption is secured by the death of Christ to all the elect; according to his revealed will, it is secured to those only who believe' (Dagg p326). The secret aspect of God's will, in this matter, lies in who the elect are; it is *that* which, to us, is the unknown; God knows, for he has determined who they are. The revealed aspect of God's will, in this matter, is that Christ died for the elect, and only those who believe will receive redemption; there is nothing secret about *that*. As Haldane expressed it: 'We are ever to distinguish between the revealed will of God and his secret purpose. It is his revealed will that salvation should be preached to all who are brought under the sound of the gospel, but it is his purpose to save only those whom he has chosen in Christ... For whom the atonement was actually made is a secret thing which belongs to God; but to us it is revealed, that, in calling on the name of the Lord, the vilest shall be saved... Election [that is, those who are elect] is a secret thing which belongs to God, but [the fact of] the salvation of all who believe, without exception, is revealed to us' (Haldane pp115,261,288-289).
[72] Davenant spoke of 'this conditional decree of God' (Davenant p92). The Amyraldian might well protest he believes Christ has wrought but one redemption – sufficient for all on condition of faith. The fact that some – the elect – believe, and therefore the atonement is effective for them – is to be ascribed to God's election and not Christ's redemption. But this does not answer. The saints in glory, in their song of praise to Christ, are prepared to speak of the distinction Christ made in his redemption, with no mention of election: 'For you were slain, and have redeemed us to God by your blood out of every tribe and tongue and people and nation' (Rev. 5:9). I am not, I hasten to add, driving a wedge between election and redemption; it is the Amyraldian who has raised the issue. God, in his one decree, elected the elect *and* determined Christ to redeem them. As they say in their song: 'You... have redeemed *us*', the elect. The Amyraldian does end up with two secret wills in God concerning Christ's redemption; on the cross, Christ fulfilled these two secret wills, dying under one will for all men, and under the other for the elect. But, as above, how can God *decree* to redeem (sufficiently) the non-elect on condition of faith, yet *decree* not to elect but to harden them? Furthermore, if any are saved by the conditional redemption, it means Christ has two sorts of redeemed people; one sort having been redeemed effectively, the other, conditionally. Will they know which is which? And if so, what will it mean for their relations with one another?

If no sinner is saved on the conditional scheme, why did God design and decree it? I will return to this.

[73] Durham pp183.

[74] The purpose, the end, which God intended in the death of Christ, was the salvation of the elect, including their eternal glory in Christ. The supreme and ultimate end of all things, of course, is God's own glory (Rom. 11:33-36; 1 Cor. 15:28; Eph. 1:3-14). See Owen: *Death* in *Works* Vol.10 p162.

[75] As for Heb. 10:5-10, God's 'desire' or 'pleasure' is spoken of in the passage, but the will in question is God's decree, and that, as the context shows, is here all to do with the redemption Christ wrought. 'By that will we have been sanctified through the offering of the body of Jesus Christ once for all' (Heb. 10:10). Owen: 'The will of God is taken [in] two ways: *First*, for his eternal purpose and design, called "the counsel of his will" (Eph. 1:11); and most commonly his "will" itself – the will of God as to what he will do, or cause to be done. *Secondly*, for the declaration of his will and pleasure... It is the will of God in the former sense that is here intended; as is evident from [Heb. 10:10] where it is said that "by this will of God we are sanctified"'. I agree, of course, with Owen, that 'neither is the other sense absolutely excluded; for the Lord Christ came so to fulfil the will of God's purpose, as that we may be enabled to fulfil the will of his command. Indeed, and he himself had a command from God to lay down his life for the accomplishment of this work... He fulfilled the will of his purpose, by obedience to the will of his command... It was the will, that is, the counsel, the purpose, the decree of God... Our Lord Christ knew that this was the will of God, the will of the Father... Wherefore the will of God here intended... is nothing but the eternal, gracious, free act or purpose of his will, whereby he determined or purposed in himself to recover a church out of lost mankind, to sanctify them unto himself, and to bring them to the enjoyment of himself hereafter' (Owen: *Hebrews* Vol.4 Part 1 pp470-471,479). Davenant, on the other hand, wrongly spoke of a twofold 'ordination of God' in the death of Christ. *First*, what he called 'the evangelical covenant confirmed with the whole human race through the merit of [Christ's] death, and of the divine *ordination* depending upon it, according to which, under the possible condition of faith, remission of sins and eternal life is decreed to be set before every mortal man who will believe it, on account of the merits of Christ... Through the merit of the death of Christ, a [*sic*] new covenant was entered into between God and the human race'. Citing Gal. 3, Davenant contrasted 'this covenant': 'Believe, and you shall live', with 'the legal command: "Do this, and you shall live"... This evangelical covenant [is] confirmed by the death

of Christ'. *Secondly*, 'But it is to be confessed, that there is also another *ordination* of God, secret and absolute, regarding certain definite persons, and founded likewise on the death of Christ, which obtains the name of the "new covenant"... Christ by his death not only established that conditional covenant... but also that secret and absolute covenant' (Davenant pp71-75, emphasis mine). This is wrong, I say. Note Davenant's twofold 'ordination'. Note also his confusion between '*a* new covenant' and '*the* new covenant'; one conditional, the other absolute. Yes, the Bible does speak of *a* new or better covenant (Jer. 31:31; Heb. 8:6,13), but it does so in reference to *the* new covenant – not a different covenant altogether. *There is only one new covenant.* And this leads to the final point: As for a gospel covenant with the entire human race – I know of no scripture which speaks of it; it is pure conjecture.

[76] If it is said that the non-elect *were* united to Christ in his death, but only 'provisionally', 'conditionally' or 'sufficiently' united to him, what would *that* mean? As I have said, the doctrine of union with Christ, being 'in Christ', is key; the elect died with and in Christ. To imagine that, at the same time, the non-elect died provisionally (or conditionally or sufficiently) with and in Christ, is incredible. A man is in Christ, or he is not; he died with and in Christ, or he did not. As I have pointed out, these considerations apply equally to the resurrection, ascension, exaltation, intercession and return of Christ.

[77] See Helm pp38,48.

[78] Haldane: 'If... salvation is limited to those whom the Father's electing love gave to his Son [as it is – even as Amyraldians agree], how could the Son go beyond the purpose of him whose will he came to do? How could he give his life for those whom the Father never knew, whom the Holy Spirit will never sanctify, whom the Son himself will for ever reject, when, beholding his blood-bought sheep – the members of his body the church, "he shall see of the travail of his soul, and be satisfied"? The unity of the will of Christ with that of the eternal Father is of itself conclusive on the subject of the extent of the atonement; it demonstrates that the atonement was made only for the church... The sword of justice could not smite both the shepherd and the flock; the surety, and those whom he represented. In Christ's death, all the members of his mystical body died... [We must not] lose sight of the unity of the Father and [the] Son. The plan of salvation was the eternal purpose of God... Each of the divine persons performed a special part in the accomplishment of the great design. The Father chose the heirs of salvation in Christ... the Son appeared... to redeem them... according to his Father's will... Having finished the work, he entered into his glory,

and received power over all flesh that he might give eternal life to as many as the Father had given him. This he accomplishes by quickening them by the Holy Spirit, which, as the great head of the body, he has received without measure. [Since] the Son can do nothing of himself, there must ever be the most perfect harmony among the divine persons, for they are one... The plan of salvation is the fullest disclosure of all the divine attributes; it harmonises what appears irreconcilable – the justification of those who had incurred God's righteous condemnation; but all is marred by the figment of universal atonement; which is no atonement, for it does not prevent [many] of those for whom it was made going down the broad road to destruction... The eternal purpose of God, his choosing his people in Christ, is always kept in view in connection with the plan of salvation... [Without] the union of Christ and his people, he could have made no atonement for them, for he that sanctifies, and they that are sanctified, must be all of one... The priesthood of Christ includes the sacrifice which he presented to God on earth, and the intercession which he carries on in heaven... But according to [the Amyraldian] system, Christ acted as a priest to *all* mankind in offering the sacrifice, and only to a *part* of mankind in making intercession... Is Christ then divided?' (Haldane pp80-81,167-169,182,210,316, emphasis his). This is the distinction I made a few moments ago. While there is a seeming contradiction between God's revealed desire and his secret decree, this is very different to the Amyraldian view that God has two wills, two purposes in Christ's atonement. Very different!

[79] I agree with Calvin (and Clifford) on 'the supreme paradox of God's inscrutable purpose and [his] revealed will' (Clifford: *Atonement* pp74,86), but which will did Christ die under? This is the nub of the issue between me and Clifford. He thinks the extent of election is the concern of the decree only, but the extent of redemption is the concern of both the decree and the revealed will. I think the extent of both election and redemption is the concern of the decree; it is the freeness of the universal invitation which is the revealed will.

[80] Davenant talked of it, as I noted earlier. But to suggest it would seem to be getting very close to 'open theism'. Would this twofold decree apply to election? In other words, has God elected all sinners, decreeing they all shall be saved, but some absolutely decreed and the rest conditionally? Would it apply to irresistible grace? What is a conditional irresistibility?

[81] See my *Offer* pp89-100. Davenant was weak: 'There is some kind of ordination or good pleasure of the divine will' (Davenant pp62,73).

[82] Booth: *Reign* p59.

---

[83] 'Christ died for all who believe' (*The Banner of Truth*, March 2004, p14) is not a happy expression. In this context, it is wrong; it puts the cart before the horse. All for whom Christ died will believe. It all starts with election; faith is conditional on it. 'You do not believe, because you are not my sheep', said Christ (John 10:26); consequently, they who are Christ's sheep, and only they, will believe. This cannot be dismissed as an 'indirect reference to election' (Clifford: *Atonement* p144). True, it is a *figurative* reference, but nonetheless it is a reference to election. In John 10, 'the sheep' could sometimes be replaced by 'believers' (John 10:3-5,14,27), yes, but sometimes 'the sheep' can only be understood as 'the elect'; Christ did not give his life for believers (John 10:11,15) ('Christ died for the ungodly [not for *believers*]... while we were still sinners [*unbelievers* – indeed, for most, as yet unborn!], Christ died for us', Rom. 5:6,8); he did not have other believers to bring into his fold (John 10:16). Again, John 10:28-29 is far better understood as speaking of 'the elect', rather than 'believers'. In any case, John 10:26 would be reduced to rank tautology if 'the sheep' is understood as 'believers': 'You do not believe because you are not believers'! Furthermore, when Jesus speaks of his sheep hearing his voice and following him (John 10:3-4,16,27), is he talking of believers obeying him, or of his elect hearing his effectual call in the gospel in their conversion? In at least some of the verses, the latter is included. Hence, 'the sheep' are 'the elect'.
Davenant: 'In predestination to faith, the application of the death of Christ was infallibly destined for some certain persons; and we say that this faith is not prepared for believers, as such, but for unbelievers, that through it they may become believers'. He rightly linked John 10:15; 11:51-52; Acts 20:28; Eph. 1:22-23; 5:23,25-26; Tit. 2:14 to say 'that by the names of "sheep, the church, the children of God, the body of Christ", are intended the sheep, the children of God, and members of Christ, not as *actually* united to him by faith *already* received, but as by the counsel and design of God *to be* united by faith *to be* received... He so loved his sheep, his children, his church, that he determined by his death effectually to derive to [that is, convey to, or obtain for (*Shorter*, the former in use by 1526; the latter by 1561)] them faith and eternal life... He is the Saviour and Redeemer of his sheep, his church, his body; in short, of the predestinated children of God, inasmuch as by his special design he has destined and procured this remedy to be applied to them... that by faith they might possess Christ effectually united and applied to them... Faith, when it is first given, is not given to a believer, but to an unbeliever' (Davenant pp166,168-170,183,187-189,192,194, emphasis mine). This last sentence would seem self-evident; the elect are

unbelievers before they are given faith. And they are given faith because they are elect.
Gill: 'Should it be said, as it is, that by God's elect are meant true believers, it should be observed, that they are not denominated God's elect from their being true believers, but they become true believers in consequence of their being God's elect' (Gill: *Cause* p101; see also *Sermons* Vol.5 pp106-107,109). Haldane: 'The gospel is the touchstone by which the elect are distinguished from those who die in their sins. Those for whom no atonement was made, who are not of Christ's sheep, for whom the good shepherd did not lay down his life, do not receive him as their Saviour; in other words, are not made partakers of precious faith; but his sheep hear his voice, he knows them, they follow him, and he gives them eternal life... The gospel is addressed indiscriminately to all who come under its sound; to the non-elect it comes in *word*; to the elect in *power*. The former, like the deaf adder, stop their ears, and will not listen to the voice of the charmer; the latter set to their seal that God is true, by trusting in the blood of [the] atonement... Pardon and salvation through faith in Christ are proclaimed [to all] in the gospel; and, by means of its gracious invitations, [those] ordained to eternal life are gathered in'. And the reason is, as Haldane had explained: 'Men are the sheep of Christ by election, not by faith: "Other sheep I have, which are not of this fold; them also I must bring, and they shall hear my voice" (John 10:16)' (Haldane pp117,184,243, emphasis his).
Fuller, citing Matt. 11:25; John 6:37; 15:16; Acts 13:48; 18:10; Rom. 8:29; 9:15,29; 11:5,7; Eph. 1:3; 2 Thess. 2:13; 2 Tim. 1:9; 1 Pet. 1:2, said: 'God eternally purposed in himself that they [the elect] should believe and be saved' (Fuller: *Philanthropos* p225; Nettles p125). Again: 'The connection in which the death of Christ is here introduced [Eph. 5:25-27], namely as being "for his church", or, which is the same thing, for his elect people, teaches us that all which he did and suffered was with a view to their salvation... If we will allow the Scriptures to speak out on all occasions, and form our principles by them, taken as a whole, we must conclude that it was his intention, design or purpose to save those, and only those, by it, who were given to him of the Father. In other words, it never was his intention to impart faith, and other succeeding benefits, to any other than his elect: "Whom he did predestinate them he also called". We are saved and called, "not according to our works, but according to his own purpose and grace, which was given us in Christ Jesus, before the world began"' (Fuller: *Sermons* p597). If not, it must be that God saves sinners on account of their faith. But their redemption was purposed before the foundation of the world when the Father gave them to Christ, and this, of course,

before their existence – let alone their believing. Nor did God elect them because he foresaw they would believe; they are saved according to, because of, his own purpose and grace, given them in Christ Jesus before time began (2 Tim. 1:9). 'He indeed was foreordained before the foundation of the world' (1 Pet. 1:20). See Booth: *Reign* pp61-62.
As for Clifford's use of 'indirect', such a use would not weaken the point Christ was making in John 10; rather, it would strengthen it. Notice how the Jews rightly deduced that Christ was claiming to be God (John 10:33), *even though he did not directly say as much!* See also John 6:35-37,44,65; 8:43,47; 18:37; 1 John 4:6. See below & the Appendix. Asides and indirect 'proofs' are often more powerful than the direct; allusions are often more powerful than statements. Consider, for instance, the many asides and incidental remarks in Scripture where – if Christ is not God, if there is no trinity – the writers and speakers have been irresponsible, culpably unguarded and misleading. Four examples must suffice. 'The same Spirit... the same Lord... the same God' (1 Cor. 12:4-6; see 3-11); 'Ananias, why... lie to the Holy Spirit...? You have not lied to men but to God' (Acts 5:3-4); note the singular verb in: 'May our God and Father himself, and our Lord Jesus Christ, *direct* our way to you' (1 Thess. 3:11); and note both the order ('our Lord Jesus Christ... and our God and Father') and the singular verbs (he 'has loved... and given', may he 'comfort... and establish') in: 'Now may our Lord Jesus Christ himself, and our God and Father, who has loved us and given us everlasting consolation and good hope by grace, comfort your hearts and establish you in every good word and work' (2 Thess. 2:16-17). Compare Isa. 41:4; Rev. 1:8,11; 20:6; 21:6; 22:13. See also John 5:16-27; 14:28; Rom. 1:7; 1 Cor. 1:3; 2 Cor. 1:2; Gal. 1:1,3; Eph. 1:2; Phil. 1:2; 1 Thess. 1:1; 2 Thess. 1:1-2; Jas. 1:1; 2 Pet. 1:2; 1 John 1:3; 2 John 3,9; Rev. 1:2 *etc.* 'Grace to you and peace from God our Father and the Lord Jesus Christ'. Imagine reading: 'Grace to you and peace from God our Father ***and*** *Joe Bloggs*'. Its utter ludicrousness, its sheer blasphemousness, shouts to the skies. I do not pretend that all this constitutes *proof* of Christ's Godhood, and I admit the argument could be used against me; see 1 Tim. 5:21, for instance. But even here, note the two 'ands'; the phrase could be punctuated: 'God and the Lord Jesus Christ, and the elect angels'. Furthermore, try the above substitution. And see also 1 Tim. 6:13. As I say, I do not offer this as proof of Christ's Godhood, but simply point out that the writers have done nothing (to put it mildly) to stop me drawing the inference from their words. For more on 'indirect or incidental testimonies of Scripture to the divinity of Christ', see Charles J.Brown: *The Divine Glory of Christ*, The Banner of Truth Trust, Edinburgh, 1982. (Since I have not cited

Charles J.Brown anywhere else in this book, I have not included his work in the Source List). Similarly, consider the force of 'if it were not so' (John 14:1-4), and 'who cannot lie' (Tit. 1:1-3).

[84] Haldane: 'If the atonement was made for the [ultimately] lost as well as for the saved, no man is saved by *it*; his salvation rests on some other foundation. It may be replied: "Salvation is of faith". It is so; but whence is faith?' (Haldane p75, emphasis mine). This is an important point, which will come up again. The elect are saved *through* faith it is true (Eph. 2:8), but not *because* of their faith. They are saved, however, *because of the redemption Christ accomplished for them*. To say that Christ died for sinners, but in his death did not purchase the gift of faith for them, yet even so they will be saved only on condition that they believe, is biblically wrong, and leads, therefore, to dreadful consequences. I will return to this.

[85] 'Election is... the parent of faith'. Faith, rightly according to Calvin, holds 'second place' to election (Calvin: *Institutes* Vol.2 pp222-223; see also Vol.1 pp257-258).

[86] But do they really go even this far? Amyraut, according to Clifford, saw 'predestination and election' merely 'as the final *explanation* of the success of the preaching of the gospel, rather than as its dominating idea' (Clifford: 'Evangelicalisms' p8, emphasis mine). This is woefully inadequate. While I am not saying God's decrees are to be at the forefront of our addresses to sinners, they certainly dominate – indeed, they determine – the entire matter. I will come back to this.

[87] Fuller had reservations about the idea of 'purchase': Some 'have considered the death of Christ as purchasing repentance and faith, as well as all other spiritual blessings, on behalf of the elect. [I] never could perceive that any clear or determinate idea was conveyed by the term "purchase" in this connection; nor does it appear to [me] to be applicable to the subject, unless it be in an improper or figurative sense. [I have] no doubt of the atonement of Christ being a perfect satisfaction to divine justice; nor of [Christ] being worthy of all that was conferred upon him, and upon us for his sake; nor of that which to us is sovereign mercy being to him an exercise of remunerative justice. But [I wish] it to be considered: Whether the moral governor of the world was laid under such a kind of obligation to show mercy to sinners as a creditor is under to discharge a debtor, on having received full satisfaction at the hands of a surety?' If so, Fuller thought, it robbed God's forgiveness of its freeness (Fuller: *Witness* pp38-39). Fuller again: 'If the atonement of Christ were considered as the literal payment of a debt – if the measure of his sufferings were according to the number of those for whom he died, and to the degree of their guilt, in such a manner as that if more

had been saved, or if those who are saved had been more guilty, his sorrows must have been proportionately increased – it might, for aught I know, be inconsistent with indefinite invitations. But it would be equally inconsistent with the free forgiveness of sin, and with sinners being directed to apply for mercy as *supplicants*, rather than as claimants. I conclude, therefore, that an hypothesis which in so many important points is manifestly inconsistent with the Scriptures cannot be true' (Fuller: *Worthy* p170, emphasis his; see also *Three Conversations* pp312-314; *Antinomianism* p344; *Satisfaction* pp998-999; Naylor p200). This gets us close to the problem with Fuller and the atonement. I will return to it; see Morden pp84-85; Haykin pp107-128; Macleod p247; Haldane pp44,49,58,126-127,166-170,191-193. Fuller wrote as he did because he wanted to safeguard the freeness of grace. He had no need to worry! And, in any case, he was persuaded of the main point I am making: 'The Lord Jesus Christ made such a provision by his death, thereby procuring the certain bestowment of faith, as well as all other spiritual blessings which follow upon it' (Fuller: *Philanthropos* p223). The fact is, speculation about how much suffering Christ needed to endure (and that is what it is – speculation) ought to be dropped. Joseph Swain: 'No nearer we venture than this,/ To gaze on a deep so profound;/ But tread, whilst we taste of the bliss,/ With rev'rence the hallowèd ground' (*Gospel Hymns* number 298). If I may use God's words to Moses: 'Do not draw near this place' (Ex. 3:5). As I have already noted, Christ gave *himself*. What more can be said? What more *should* be said?

As for purchase, *agorpazō* is the root word for Christ's redemption in 1 Cor. 6:20; 7:23; Gal. 3:13; 4:5; 2 Pet. 2:1; Rev. 5:9; 14:3-4, with the idea of buying in the market place, and *peripoieō* (Acts 20:28) is 'to acquire, obtain', 'to get for one's self, purchase' (Arndt & Gingrich; Thayer). Calvin: 'That Christ, by his obedience, truly purchased and merited grace for us with the Father, is accurately inferred from several passages of Scripture. I take it for granted, that if Christ satisfied for our sins, if he paid the penalty due by us, if he appeased God by his obedience; *in fine*, if he suffered the just for the unjust, salvation was obtained for us by his righteousness; which is just equivalent to meriting' (Calvin: *Institutes* Vol.1 p455).

Davenant: 'Although it is of the mere good pleasure of God that he is willing to grant... effectual grace and salvation, yet this good pleasure is not accomplished otherwise than through the merits of Christ... Although every work of special grace which is done in the elect is done on account of the merits of Christ being specially applied to them, yet in their justification and salvation is seen the true way of mercy, and not of justice; because Christ with his merits, with this very mode of meriting and offering his merits, some special regard being had to the elect, the whole of this... derives its *origin* from the gratuitous good will of God towards them... Christ laid down his life for the elect... in order to *purchase* his church' (Davenant pp193-194,198, emphasis mine).

Of course, as with all such figures, this can be pushed too far (see Clifford: *Atonement* pp127-141; Cunningham Vol.2 pp305-311). As Fuller said: 'The blood of Christ is indeed the price of our redemption... but this metaphorical language... may be carried too far, and may lead us into many errors'. Fuller gave another example – the mediation of Christ: 'Probably there is no similitude fully adequate to the purpose'. His conclusion? In general, in using analogies of truth, 'it is not always safe to reason from the former to the latter; much less is it just to affirm that the latter has for its basis every principle which pertains to the former' (Fuller: *Three Conversations* p312; *Witness* pp37-38). Exactly! Think, for instance, of how the likening of the second coming of Christ to a thief could be misused. Fuller, however, forgot this principle when, trying to grapple with an infinite spiritual truth – the atonement – revealed and illustrated in everyday terms, he probed 'purchase' where he ought not. Even so, as he said: 'Sins are called debts, not properly, but metaphorically'. Having cautioned against over-working the illustration, he went on: 'There is a sufficient resemblance, however, between them, to justify the use of the term' (Fuller: *Exposition* p492). Haldane: 'All figurative language, and symbolical illustrations, even when found in Scripture, are to be used cautiously, but let us beware [that we do not] reject the truth which they express' (Haldane p192).

Fuller, when dealing with the hyper-Calvinistic emphasis upon eternal justification to try to maintain justification on the basis of grace and not works, said: 'They [hyper-Calvinists] seem to have supposed that if God justified us before we had any existence, or could have performed any good works, it must be on the footing of *grace*'; that is, hyper-Calvinists have thought they defend the freeness of grace by their view of eternal justification. Not so, said Fuller: 'Yet these divines maintained that some men were ordained to condemnation from eternity; and that, as a punishment for their sin, which God foresaw. But if an eternal decree of condemnation might rest upon foreseen evil, who does not perceive that an eternal decree of justification might equally rest upon foreseen good?' In other words, the hyper-Calvinists have failed to defend the freeness of grace by their insistence of eternal justification. Fuller concluded: 'The truth is, the freeness of justification does not depend upon the date of it' (Fuller: *Appendix* to *Worthy* p183, emphasis his). Excellent! A pity Fuller did not see that a biblical view of the scriptural doctrine of 'purchase' does not destroy the freeness of grace in the atonement. I will say more about the date of justification in my *Septimus Sears*.

Clifford's sane remarks on the subject were spoiled somewhat by his use of 'credit facilities'. Nor do I like the cheap-sounding: 'It's yours for the taking' (Clifford: *Atonement* pp113,127,156; but see Macleod p246; Spurgeon: *Around* p13); and if the 'it' means 'Christ's death for you', I strongly disagree.

[88] Particular election leads to particular redemption. 'Universal atonement [allowing it for sake of argument] introduces a fundamental disjunction between the universal intent of the Son who [supposedly] gave himself for all, and the particular purpose of the Father who elected only some'. 'To attempt to combine universal redemption with particular election... is to introduce an intolerable disjunction in the divine purpose' (Nicole pp304,324). '*Intent... purpose*', I stress. As I have explained, there is a seeming contradiction (disjunction) between God's decree and his revealed desire, but there is no disjunction in his decree. Clifford, to my mind, failed to grapple with this in his reply to Nicole (Clifford: *Calvinus* pp42-43).

[89] The elect before conversion are as unbelieving as the non-elect. If Christ earned the gift of faith as much for the latter as the former, then all must be saved. But not all will be saved. The elect, and only the elect, come to salvation through faith. Christ, therefore, could not have earned the gift of faith as much for the non-elect as the elect. If, however, the Amyraldian is right, and Christ's redemption is sufficient for all, why are all not saved? 'Sufficient' must mean sufficient for salvation, comprising everything required for salvation. So, why are any damned? On what basis? If (as it is) because of unbelief – is that unbelief not a sin? It certainly is; it is the damning sin (John 3:18-19,36). But the blood of Christ cleanses from all sin (1 John 1:7), *every* sin, including the sin of unbelief. If, therefore, Christ died for all men, and thereby earned, merited and provided salvation sufficient for all men, then this 'sufficiency' must include the gift of faith for all; it must deal with the sin of unbelief for all. Consequently, on this 'sufficiency' basis, those who are damned, are damned even though a sufficient redemption has been made for all their sin, including their unbelief. They are, therefore, damned unjustly – God's wrath having been propitiated and his justice satisfied sufficiently, covering every sin for such sinners – including their unbelief – yet still they are damned. See Durham p184; Macleod p61; Booth: *Divine Justice* in *Works* Vol.3 pp84-85,87. To sum up: If Christ earned the gift of faith for any, since he did not accomplish two redemptions (one involving the gift of faith, the other not), he earned it

for the elect only, since only the elect come to faith; consequently, Christ died for the elect only. Of course, what I called 'the cardinal question' remains: Did Christ earn the gift of faith? As I now seek to prove, he did. Christ did not redeem any sinner on condition of faith. All this applies, of course, to repentance also.

[90] As many have said. Owen: 'Christ did not die for any upon condition, [namely] if they do believe, but he died for all God's elect, that they should believe... Christ being not to be received without faith, and God giving faith to whom he pleases, it is manifest that he never intends Christ to them on whom he will not bestow faith... He died not for believers as believers, though he died for all believers; but for all the elect as elect, who, *by the benefit of his death*, do become believers'. Again, later, answering Baxter's response to *Death*, and referring to sections in it: 'Faith... is itself *procured by the death* of Christ for them for whom he died, to be freely bestowed upon them... The Lord Jesus, *by the satisfaction and merit of his death* and oblation, made for all and only his elect, has actually and absolutely *purchased* and *procured* for them all spiritual blessings of grace and glory, to be made out to them, and bestowed upon them, in God's way and time, without dependence on any condition to be by them performed [which is] not absolutely procured for them thereby... God having appointed that his eternal love, in the fruits thereof, should be no otherwise communicated but only in and by Christ, all right thereunto must of necessity be of his *procurement* and *purchasing*... all those good things which he before purposed and willed... to them... being *purchased and procured*... by that *satisfaction and merit... in that death of Christ*... All such conditions (if spiritual blessings) [not excluding faith] are part of the *purchase of the death* of Christ... What Christ has *merited* for us... we have a right to... But this right... is from the *merit* of Christ alone... faith itself being of the number of those things so *procured*... All the fruits of the death of Christ are *obtained* and *procured* by his *merit* for them for whom he *died*... (2 Pet. 1:1)... It is a righteous thing with God to give faith to them for whom Christ died, because thereby they have a right to it. Faith being among the most precious *fruits of the death* of Christ, by virtue thereof [it] becomes their due for whom he died... What spiritual blessings soever are bestowed on any soul... they are all bestowed... for Christ's sake; that is, they are *purchased* by his *merit*, and *procured* by his intercession thereupon... God's reckoning Christ... is the imputing of Christ to ungodly, unbelieving sinners for whom he died... and to bestow faith and grace upon them for his sake... The Lord... for his sake gives them faith... Our actual conversion, the efficient [cause] whereof is the Spirit, is the immediate *procurement* of *the merit* of Christ' (Owen:

Death in *Works* Vol.10 pp235,314,420,450,457-458,464,467-470,473, emphasis mine). In this, I have omitted Owen's arguments in his reply to Baxter – which see – including the references to his earlier work.

Davenant (as did Dort) certainly thought Christ by his death merited and purchased faith for the elect: 'Faith, like all other saving gifts, is conferred upon men on account of Christ and through his merit'. He quoted the 'words of the divines of the Palatinate [which were]... in their judgement exhibited at... Dort': 'The faith of the elect does not precede, but follows the death of Christ, because *his death is the cause* [but not the *primary* cause – see below] *of faith*, on account of which the elect are given to Christ, and [as?] the object of faith, which [object] it [faith] beholds and embraces' (Davenant p40, emphasis mine). Dort was explicit: 'As many as truly believe, and are delivered and saved from sin and destruction through the death of Christ, are indebted to this benefit solely to the grace of God, given them in Christ from everlasting... For this was the sovereign counsel, and most gracious will and purpose of God the Father, that the quickening and saving efficacy of *the most precious death of his Son should extend to all the elect,* ***for*** *bestowing upon them alone the gift of justifying faith*, thereby to bring them infallibly to salvation; that is, that it was the will of God, that Christ by the blood of his cross... should effectually redeem... all those, and those only, who were from eternity chosen to salvation, and given to him by the Father; that he should confer upon them *faith* which together with all other saving gifts of the Holy Spirit, *he purchased for them by his death*... The Synod rejects the errors of those who teach... that *Christ by his satisfaction merited* neither salvation itself for anyone, nor *faith*, whereby this satisfaction of Christ unto salvation is effectually appropriated' (*The Three* pp43-44, emphasis mine).

Davenant argued the point over many pages (the following is but a sample): 'Christ... had... as conscious of the divine predestination, *a special intention* conformed to the secret and eternal good pleasure of the Father; namely, *that he might obtain through the merit of his death* for his sheep, who were given to him according to the decree of election, *and might give them faith, salvation and all things*. And *with this special intention* it is said that *he laid down his life* for his own peculiar people; that is, for certain individual persons. [And this salvation including the necessary faith] comes to certain persons *from* the *death* of Christ'. 'Repentance, faith, regeneration and sanctification... are given to some because the special mercy of God *procures* them'. Davenant rightly would not speculate on the order of God's decrees (see below). Even so: 'Conceive... first... the decree concerning the election of certain persons to salvation; that afterwards was the decree concerning the destination [designation?] of Christ to the office of mediator, yet you could never so separate these, *as that the passion of Christ, which was specially offered and accepted for them, should not be the* ***cause*** [but not the *primary* cause – that being election – see following note] *of preparing and giving to those elect persons both effectual grace and salvation...* Those, therefore, who are specially given to Christ by election, *always derive faith, remission of sins, sanctification and salvation from the death of Christ...* that *Christ crucified* should not become to them a stumbling-block or foolishness, but the power and wisdom of God, *effectually to work in them faith and salvation...* But he so loved his sheep, his children, his church, that he determined *by his death effectually to derive to them faith* and eternal life... It was... decreed by God *on account of the death of his Son, to give faith to some persons... that they should believe and be converted... through and on account of the mediator... Whatever of spiritual and saving good* the Spirit of Christ produces in any persons, *the blood-shedding of Christ merited it for them*: But the Spirit of Christ produces in some certain persons, *repentance and faith*, and through *faith and repentance* the infallible application of his death: Therefore he *merited* these special benefits for those persons: Therefore he *intended to merit* them when *he made himself a sacrifice on the cross*'. In speaking of this gift of faith, Davenant rightly linked the death of Christ with his intercession: 'Whatever Christ obtains for individual persons by his special intercession, that he *merited* for them with the Father by the offering of himself[,] which pertained to them especially; but *by his intercession he obtains for the elect, faith, perseverance and salvation itself*; therefore he specially *offered himself* for them, that he might infallibly *procure* for them these benefits... Since *saving faith itself*, which is peculiar to the elect, is to be placed among the chief spiritual blessings, it ought to be granted that it is given *on account of* the merits of Christ to all those to whom it is actually given... *Faith...* is given to the elect *on account of* the merits of the mediator' (Davenant pp68,137,165-184,194-199, emphasis mine). I have quoted Davenant extensively on this point because he was a proto-Amyraldian.

William Rushton: 'There is a necessary connection between the vicarious death of Christ, and the conversion of those for whom he died, which cannot be the case if the atonement be indefinite' (Rushton p125; see also Rushton pp34,121).

Clifford's (Amyraut's and Baxter's) position is far weaker, and weakening. Whereas once he said: 'The gift of faith is *rooted in* the atonement; it is so indirectly', later it became: 'The gift of faith is *related to* the atonement; it is so indirectly' (Clifford: *Atonement* p115; *Amyraut* p39, emphasis mine). Note the 'indirectly'. This is wrong. The elect are not granted faith independently of the death of Christ, nor even 'indirectly' through it. Christ earned it, and God bestows it through the death of Christ. The distinction between the saved and the rest does not arise in election, disappear in the atonement, and re-appear in irresistible grace; it is as dominant in the atonement as in the other two. (To put it another way: It is not credible to think that the Father, the Son and the Spirit do not have an absolute unity of purpose; see Nicole pp300,304,324, and my earlier note on Clifford's inadequate reply to the point about 'purpose'). In saying this, I do not attempt the impossible, and fix a temporal order to the decrees. Here I agree with Baxter, Dabney and Clifford, disagreeing with Amyraut (Clifford: *Atonement* p154). God's purpose is 'an eternal purpose' (Eph. 3:11), which he determined before time began, being 'from the beginning of the ages... hidden in God' (Eph. 3:9). Therefore, though the decrees might appear to us to have a time sequence, this is simplistic. Indeed, although I have often referred to 'the decrees', in truth I should have always said 'the decree'. As Davenant put it: 'Although, to sustain the weakness of the human understanding, we are compelled to conceive of some of the eternal decrees of God as prior and some as posterior, yet it seems to me a slippery and very dangerous thing to contend about these imaginary signs of our reason, as to undertake to establish and refute from them questions of faith. It ought, indeed, to be placed beyond all doubt, that those decrees of God, which are thought by us according to the order of prior and posterior, with respect to God himself, consist of an equable eternity of infinity; neither can or ought any separate moment to be granted, in which one decree having been established, it can be rightly supposed that the other is not yet foreseen and established' (Davenant pp164-165).

Getting back to the question in hand: Unbelief is a sin (John 3:18-19). Christ died for all the sins of the elect; he therefore died for their unbelief (see Owen: *Death* in *Works* Vol.10 pp173-174); which is the same as saying he died to earn for them the gift of faith. Thus saving faith was purchased for the elect by Christ in his death, not simply decreed for them by God. Of course, just because Owen (and many others, including Davenant) thought it (and many still think it), it does not make it right (as Clifford pointed out, Clifford: *Amyraut* p38), but I believe I establish the point in what follows. And when Clifford said Christ 'had a "special" intention to die for the elect, granting them "special" grace and thus enabling them to fulfil the conditions' (Clifford's e-mail to me, 25th Feb. 2005), it appears to me he was getting very close to saying Christ's death merited the bestowal of faith to the elect. What does this 'special grace' involve, if not the gift of faith?

[91] Clifford: *Amyraut* p39; see also *Atonement* p115. As Davenant said: 'We confess that the death of Christ is infallibly applied to the elect alone, because the certainty of the application depends, *as to the [its] primary cause*, on the secret and eternal act of God in predestinating' (Davenant pp68,137,146-162, emphasis mine).

[92] 'The sacrifice of Christ was designed by the trinity to effect precisely what it does effect – all this, and no more. If [since] God regulates all his works by his decree, and is sovereign and omnipotent in them all, then the historical unfolding of his providence must be the exact exposition of his purpose' (Dabney: 'God's' p310).

[93] In Scripture (take Isa. 53:11-12; 1 Cor. 15:3; Gal. 2:20; Eph. 5:26; Tit. 2:14; Heb. 10:12), salvation is attributed not (merely) to the *electing* purpose of the Father, nor (merely) to the *application* of redemption by the Spirit, but also to its *accomplishment* by the Son. One example: 'For God did not appoint us to wrath, but to obtain salvation through our Lord Jesus Christ, who died for us' (1 Thess. 5: 9-10). Of course, salvation comes from election by the Father, through effectual calling by the Spirit: 'God from the beginning chose you for salvation through sanctification by the Spirit and belief of the truth' (2 Thess. 2:13). But it comes no less through the Son's work. And all three works – the Father's, the Son's and the Spirit's – are as particular as each other; all have the same intention and design; all accomplish the same end; and all depend entirely on each other to complete the plan. The elect are 'elect according to the foreknowledge of God the Father, in sanctification of the Spirit, for obedience and sprinkling of the blood of Jesus Christ' (1 Pet. 1:2). As for faith, certainly 'the bestowal of faith [is attributed] to divine election and predestination', and, yes, it is given by 'the influence of the word and Spirit of God' (Clifford: *Amyraut* pp39-40), but, as I will show, it is also directly earned and merited for the elect in Christ's redemptive work, along with all the other means and benefits of redemption. Faith is not an exception; at least, Scripture never says it is.

[94] Note the '*in* Christ'. This phrase, 'in Christ', is no vague sentiment. See, for example: John 14 – 17; Rom. 6:2-11; 7:4-6; 8:1; 1 Cor. 1:30; 2 Cor. 5:14-18; Gal. 2:19-20; Eph. 2:1,4-6; Col. 2:10-15,20; 3:1,3; 1 Pet. 2:24. See also such phrases as 'in him' and 'in me'. Note also 'in Christ' and 'Christ in us'. This theme of 'in Christ' pervades the New Testament. God's people are blessed 'with every spiritual blessing... *in Christ*'; that is, in union with him from eternity (in God's decree), in time (in his death, burial, resurrection and ascension), in experience now (by the operation of the Holy Spirit), and for ever after his return in the

consummation of all things. In other words, they are blessed 'with every spiritual blessing' through God's election, Christ's person and work (including, not least, his redeeming work), and the Spirit's operations, and it is all 'in Christ'. Redemption is not an exception to the 'in Christ', and faith is not an exception to the 'every spiritual blessing'. See the note immediately following for more on this last point. Lloyd-Jones: 'If you leave out the "in Christ" you will never have any blessings at all. This is, of course, pivotal and central in connection with the whole of our Christian faith. Every blessing we enjoy as Christian people comes to us through the Lord Jesus Christ' (Lloyd-Jones: *Ultimate* p58). And this must, at the very least, involve his redemption. So when Clifford said Eph. 1:3; Phil. 1:29; Heb. 12:2 'support the notion [that the atonement includes the specific purchase of faith] *at best* only inferentially' (Clifford: *Amyraut* p38, emphasis his), he missed the point. What does 'in Christ' mean, if not (at the very least) by God's election 'in Christ's death'? Paul states categorically that every spiritual blessing we receive is received 'in Christ'. What else can it mean but that (at the very least) these blessings come 'in and through the *merit* of his death'? Fee, commenting on 1 Cor. 1:2,30: 'The phrase *en Christō Iēsou* is probably not locative, but semi-instrumental. By what God has accomplished "in Christ Jesus" they have become his children' (Fee p85). As Davenant, whom Clifford himself quoted, said (on Col. 1:14): 'The apostle does not say we have redemption by the Son of God, but *in* him... *in* him the elect and faithful alone have effectual redemption, because they alone are *in* him' (Clifford: 'Introduction' ix, emphasis Davenant's; see also Davenant p137). I will return yet again to the question of union, and make no apology for doing so. It is, as I have stated, the key to all this discussion. See also the Appendix.
As for Heb. 12:2, part of the root meaning of *archēgos* is 'furnishing the first cause or occasion' (Thayer). Owen said the word here speaks 'of procurement and real efficiency. [Christ] by his obedience and death procured this grace for us' (Owen: *Hebrews* Vol.4 Part 2 p238). I do not say that this exhausts the meaning of Heb. 12:2, but it certainly is a part of it.

[95] *Every* spiritual blessing. The elect are 'the called according to his purpose. For whom he foreknew, he also predestined to be conformed to the image of his Son... Moreover whom he predestined, these he also called; whom he called, these he also justified; and whom he justified, these he also glorified' (Rom. 8:28-30). Not one link in this chain is missing. And it is all for the same people, the 'us'. Gill: The elect 'are chosen unto... all spiritual blessings – adoption, justification, sanctification, belief of the truth, and salvation by Jesus Christ... Both

means and end are sure to the chosen ones, since this is an act of God's immutable will; these are redeemed by the blood of Christ; he died for their sins, and made satisfaction for them; they are justified by his righteousness, and no charge can be laid against them; they are effectually called by the grace of God; they are sanctified by his Spirit; they persevere to the end, and cannot totally and finally be deceived and fall away, but shall be everlastingly glorified' (Gill: *Sermons* Vol.5 pp107-108). Calvin: 'Now seeing we are created in Jesus Christ [Eph. 2:10], it is the same as saying that all the righteousness, all the wisdom, all the virtue, and all the goodness that is in us we draw from that [same] source, and God does not pour them out haphazardly here and there, but has put the fullness of all things belonging to our salvation into Jesus Christ (John 1:16; Col. 1:19; 2:9)' (Calvin: *Sermons* p165; see also *Institutes* Vol.1 p452). 'From the fullness of [Christ's] grace we have all received one blessing after another' (John 1:16 NIV). 'The office of Christ... contains within itself an abundance of all blessings, so that no part of salvation must be sought anywhere else' (Calvin: *Commentaries* Vol.17 Part 2 p50). See Owen: *Display* in *Works* Vol.10 pp100-108; *Death* in *Works* Vol.10 pp222-236,240-258,311-313; Booth: *Divine Justice* in *Works* Vol.3 p87, on Rom. 5:8; Dagg pp332-335; Nettles p313.

[96] 'Is not faith comprehended among the spiritual riches of which... Paul makes mention? Indeed, and (what is more) it is the chief of them... Faith continues always chief of all the spiritual benefits that God bestows upon us. Now let us well remember... Paul's order. He says that God has given us faith *as well as any [all?] of the rest*, according to his election of us' (Calvin: *Sermons* p28, emphasis mine; see also *Institutes* Vol.1 pp255-258,465-466,499-501). And, of course, election led to redemption (Eph. 1:3-7); that is, election led to redemption which led to faith. And it is all 'in Christ' from eternity to eternity, not excluding the cross. As I have noted, election is the primary cause.

[97] 'The anger of the Father has been appeased by the sacrifice of the Son, and... the Son has been offered up for the expiation of the sins of men on this *ground* – because God, having compassion upon them, *determined* that this death should be the pledge *and means by which he would receive them* into favour... Paul makes [the intervention of Christ's sacrifice] the commencement and *cause* of reconciliation, with regard to us' (Calvin: *Commentaries* Vol.20 Part 2 p238, including footnote, emphasis mine). The 'means' and the 'cause... with regard to us' must include faith.

[98] On Eph. 2:8, it matters not if the gift is faith, grace or salvation; the gift of salvation (the greater) includes the gift of grace and the gift of

faith. Calvin was sure which it was: 'Many persons restrict the word "gift" to faith alone. But [Paul's]... meaning is, not that faith is the gift of God, but that salvation is given to us by God, or, that we obtain it by the gift of God' (Calvin: *Commentaries* Vol.21 Part 1 pp228-229). Lloyd-Jones had it right: 'Is it possible to settle the dispute? It is not. It is not a question of grammar, it is not a question of language... It is a question that cannot be decided. And there is a sense in which it really does not matter at all, because it comes to much the same thing in the end' (Lloyd-Jones: *Way* p135). See Gill: *Commentary* Vol.6 p427.

[99] Phil. 1:29 has an interesting construction: 'To you it has been granted on behalf of Christ, not only to believe in him, but also to suffer for his sake'. Clearly both faith and suffering are God's grant or gift to the elect. But does the 'on behalf of Christ' govern the faith as well as the suffering? *huper* here means 'of the impelling or moving cause; on account of, for the sake of' (Thayer). Was Paul saying the elect are granted faith on account of Christ? for the sake of Christ? or concerning, centring on Christ? Matthew Henry: 'Faith is God's gift on the behalf of Christ, who purchased for us not only the blessedness which is the object of faith, but the grace of faith itself; the ability or disposition to believe is from God'. Matthew Poole: It was 'upon the account of Christ's merit and mediation... that they did... believe on him' (Poole p686). Note Poole's use of 'merit and mediation'; see my earlier remarks on the co-extensive nature of Christ's death and intercession.

[100] The 'faith' here no doubt includes objective faith – *what* the believer believes; but it also speaks of the faith *by which* he believes – see verse 5. See Calvin: *Commentaries* Vol.22 Part 2 p366; Lillie p352.

[101] Consider this circle: Only the elect believe (John 10:26); those who believe have everlasting life (John 3:16); Christ came so that they might have this life by dying for them (John 10:10-11,15) under the Father's command or charge (John 10:18), completing the work he gave him to do (John 4:34; 5:36; 17:4; 19:30) – that is, by his death he earned it for them; he gives it to them (John 10:28) – that is, having earned it, he has the power and right to give them life upon their believing; more, he brings them in faith to himself (John 10:16); and the circle is completed in John 17:2, where Christ makes clear that he gives eternal life to all the elect. The circle? Yes indeed. Through the eternal purpose of the Father, the elect come to faith and receive eternal life through Christ; that is through his redemption. In short, he died that the elect might believe, come to him and be saved. For Christ to 'give' eternal life to all the elect, must mean he accomplished all that was necessary for that life, including the bestowing (giving) of it to them, and all that was necessary for them to receive that life. In other words, Christ accomplished

redemption for the elect, *and its application to them*. This must involve their believing.

Take 1 Pet. 1:20-21. 'He indeed was foreordained before the foundation of the world, but was manifest in these last times for you who through him believe in God, who raised him from the dead and gave him glory, so that your faith and hope are in God'. Here we have God's purpose in eternity, and the coming of the Redeemer, in time, to die. But Peter was not saying that Christ died for those who would believe on him, as though faith rules the roost. Faith comes by election (as Amyraldians will agree). Peter, therefore, was saying that Christ came into the world to die for the elect. What is more, their believing is not left to 'chance'. Christ died, and God raised him from the dead and gave him glory in order that the elect might be given the faith to believe, that they might be brought to God (1 Pet. 3:18). Septimus Sears: 'Every poor sinner brought to the foot of the cross... has scriptural ground to believe that his being *brought to* the blood is the result of his being *bought by* the blood. It is *"the ransomed of the Lord"* who "return and come". The sheep are *bought*... The sheep are *brought*' (*Sower* 1877 p301, emphasis his).

As for John 10:18, Christ, according to Calvin, here 'recalls our attention to the eternal purpose of the Father... and Christ himself, who came into the world to be in all respects obedient to the Father, confirms the statement, that he has no other object in view than to promote our [the elect's] benefit' – that is, their salvation (Calvin: *Commentaries* Vol.17 Part 2 p410). Gill noted that Christ was loved of the Father 'on various accounts', including 'as his own Son... also as mediator, engaging for, and on the behalf of his chosen people... as suffering in their room and stead... The bruising of him was a pleasure to him... because hereby his counsels and decrees were accomplished... and the salvation of his people obtained' (John 10:17). Christ 'so readily exerted his power, both in laying down his life, and taking it again, because it was his Father's command and will, and which he received from him, with the utmost pleasure; his and his Father's love, good will, gracious ends, and views towards the elect, herein being the same' (Gill: *Commentary* Vol.5 pp699-700). In short, Christ, according to the will of his Father, accomplished the salvation of the elect – *including all the means of that salvation*, as well as its end. And this includes the vital gift of faith.

[102] 'He... received from the Father the promised Holy Spirit' (Acts 2:33 NIV). See also Luke 24:46-49; John 7:39; 14:16-18,26; 15:26; 16:5-15; 20:21-22; Acts 1:4-5,8; 5:30-32; Eph. 4:8. Calvin: 'God... [having] placed Christ in his princely seat... by this means ['poured out'] the force

and fruit of Christ in his death and resurrection is sealed' (Calvin: *Commentaries* Vol.18 Part 2 p110).

[103] Why would Christ give repentance, but not faith? Did he purchase the gift of repentance and the right to bestow it – but not do the same for the gift of faith?

[104] I remind you, reader, of Amyraut's words about the elect – which I quoted at the start of this chapter: 'Jesus Christ died for... the elect... effectually... His intention was to die for... the elect... in respect of... [the] quickening and saving virtue and efficacy [of his satisfaction]... This was the most free counsel and gracious purpose both of God the Father, in giving his Son... and of the Lord Jesus Christ in suffering the pains of death, that the efficacy thereof should particularly belong unto all the elect, and to them only'. I draw attention to Amyraut's use of 'quickening... and efficacy'. What else can his words mean other than that Christ in his death, according to the purpose of his Father, earned all the necessary means of salvation – including the gift of faith – for the elect?

[105] There is no suggestion of doubt in the 'might'. The verse teaches that the sufferings of Christ were as a punishment, substitutionary and atoning, with a specified end in view, all by design and intention, with purpose. See Brown: *1 Peter* pp123-189.

[106] Take John 11:50-52. As John explained, Caiaphas prophesied far more than he knew, using phrases which were true in a far greater sense than he could have envisaged or intended, the meaning of which would be revealed by the Spirit only after the death of Christ, and here set out by John. Caiaphas predicted that Jesus would die; that he would die for (*huper*) some, not all; that he would gather all these together into one. For (*huper*) whom would he die? For two groups – Israel, 'the people... the whole nation... the nation... that nation', and 'the children of God scattered abroad'. Without extending this note to explore all my reasons (including the way to interpret the prophets – see my *Christ is All*), I am convinced Caiaphas (without realising it) prophesied Christ dying for all the elect – some of whom are in Israel (Jews) and some of whom are scattered abroad (Gentiles). Caiaphas prophesied that Christ would die for a limited number, the elect; that he would die for them in order to gather them all into one. In other words, he predicted Christ's definite, particular (or limited) atonement for the elect; not to make the gathering of all men a *possibility*, but *actually to gather* those for whom he died; Jesus would die, and in his death he would save all for whom he died. He would 'bring them to God'. This must involve the gift of faith. See Pink Vol.2 pp219-223.

[107] See Eph. 2:13-18; Col. 1:21-22. Note, as before, brought near *by the blood of Christ*, not simply by election and effectual calling.
[108] Durham p186. Fuller: 'Some have asserted that Christ by his satisfaction accomplished this only: "That God now, consistently with the honour of his justice, may pardon (returning) sinners if he wills so to do". This is, doubtless, true, as far as it goes; but it makes no provision for the return of the sinner. This scheme, therefore, leaves the sinner to perish in impenitence and unbelief, and the Saviour without any security of seeing of the travail of his soul. For how can a sinner return without the power of the Holy Spirit? And the Holy Spirit, equally with every other spiritual blessing, is given in consideration of the death of Christ' (Fuller: *Witness* pp38-39). The Amyraldian position – God decreed that Christ should die for all – is worse than the one Fuller wrote against, since, as I have already noted, we know that, for the reprobate, God has not merely decreed not to elect them, not to redeem them effectually, not to give them faith, *but to harden them.*
[109] I can detect nothing tentative or conditional about such passages as Rom. 8:29-34; Eph. 1:1-14; 5:25; 1 Thess. 5:10; 2 Thess. 2:13-14; 2 Tim. 1:9-10, dogmatic statements about a definite, accomplished redemption for the elect, in which every accusation against them is answered by Christ's death (Rom. 8:33-34). Note the past tense in Rom. 8:29-30: 'For whom he *foreknew*, he also *predestined* to be conformed to the image of his Son, that he might be the firstborn among many brethren. Moreover whom he *predestined*, these he also *called*; whom he *called*, these he also *justified*; and whom he *justified*, these he also *glorified*'. Note, I say, the past tense, *even when speaking of the glorification of the elect!* All is certain! In addition, note the repeated 'also'. As above, not one link is missing. Consider: 'As by one man's disobedience many were made sinners, so also by one man's obedience many will be made righteous' (Rom. 5:19). Note the direct comparison between Adam and Christ, their works, and the consequences to their seed. There was nothing provisional about the consequences of Adam's disobedience; nor is there anything provisional in the consequences of Christ's obedience. 'Made' is too weak; in Adam, all men are 'constituted' sinners; in Christ, all the elect are 'constituted' righteous. Imputation and union are at the heart of this. See John Murray: *Romans* Vol.1 pp205-206; Lloyd-Jones: *Assurance* pp209-210,271-280. I repeat the point; there is nothing tentative or conditional here. The elect are constituted righteous in Christ, and it happened in Christ because God decreed it. 'Since by man came death, by man also came the resurrection of the dead. For as in Adam all die, even so in Christ shall all be made alive' (1 Cor. 15:21-22). All (who are) in Adam die; all (who are) in

Christ live. All for whom Adam stood, die; all for whom Christ stood, live. See the Appendix.

[110] Clifford rightly cited Rom. 8:32 as an atonement 'efficacious' for 'the elect' (Clifford: 'Evangelicalisms' p13), conceding its predestination context. Even so, because Paul did not say that Christ died for us *alone*, Clifford could still contemplate a universal provisional atonement in the verse (Clifford: *Atonement* pp147-148). Similarly, he ruled out particular redemption because Scripture does *not* state: 'Christ died *only* for his people, his sheep, his friends, his church and for us' (Clifford: *Calvinus* p41, emphasis mine). He was, however, clutching at a straw. As Haldane said: 'No doubt Christ laid down his life for his sheep, but it is not said *only* for them. [But] such a supplement was quite unnecessary; it is plainly implied, although not expressed. [Consider, for instance, 1 Tim. 2:5, where] it is said: "There is one God and one mediator between God and men", but the word *only* is not added; now, upon the same principle that men [(such as Clifford) use to] argue in favour of universal atonement, because it is said to have been made for the sheep – and not for the sheep *only* [emphasis mine] – it might be alleged that there was more than one mediator. Again, our Lord says: "There shall be one fold, and one shepherd" (John 10:16), but because it is not said *only* one, it might [on Clifford's argument] be alleged that there was more than one' (Haldane p243, emphasis his, except where stated). Such conclusions, it need not be said, are ridiculous. The premise, therefore, likewise. Above all, take the context of Rom. 8:32. Note the repeated 'us' – God for *us*; God gave up his Son for *us*; God gives *us* all things; Christ interceding for *us*; nothing shall separate *us*; *we* face death; *we* are considered; *we* are more than; he loved *us*; nothing shall separate *us*. Since this was written to believers, to the predestinated, speaking to them personally, the 'us' and 'we', therefore, must be limited to the elect. How can any of it be provisionally for all? If it is, how can we tell which is which? For 1 John 2:2, where John extends what he says to 'the whole world', see the Appendix.

[111] Haldane p118. In essence there is only one gift – Christ. All the other gifts are inextricably and inevitably bound up with him, and encompassed him, and it is impossible to separate them. Christ is *the* gift and with him and in him comes everything. 'Christ is all and in all' (Col. 3:11).

[112] The whole tone of Scripture cries out that Christ in his death accomplished all the means and all the ends of salvation for the elect. Take Galatians: 'Our Lord Jesus Christ... gave himself for our sins, that he might deliver us from this present evil age, according to the will of our God and Father... I through the law died to the law that I might live

to God. I have been crucified with Christ... I live by faith in the Son of God, who loved me and gave himself for me... God sent forth his Son... to redeem... that we might receive the adoption as sons. And because you are sons, God has sent forth the Spirit of his Son into your hearts... Therefore you are... a son... an heir of God through Christ... I... boast... in the cross of our Lord Jesus Christ, by whom the world has been crucified to me, and I to the world. For in Christ Jesus... [we are] a new creation' (Gal. 1:3-4; 2:19-20; 4:4-7; 6:14-15). Christ, according to the will of his Father, died for the elect *in order to* redeem and deliver them, make and adopt them sons and heirs of God – they, having died with him, being made a new creation to live in and with him. To think that the gift of faith might be excluded from such a list is incredible. Davenant: 'Faith and a saving knowledge of Christ, is a special gift, granted to some [the elect]... So likewise as to repentance, faith, regeneration [and] sanctification, all of which are given to some [the elect] because the special mercy of God procures them' (Davenant p137). How else did the special mercy of God 'procure' these gifts and graces – other than in and through the death of Christ? Did not Christ procure, purchase, earn them in his death?

[113] That is, we end up with another absurdity (or worse); God did not elect the sinner, but the sinner – by his believing – elected God! 'Two errors are here to be avoided. Some make man a fellow-worker with God in such a sense, that man's suffrage ratifies election, so that, according to them, the will of man is superior to the counsel of God. As if Scripture taught that only the power of being able to believe is given us, and not rather faith itself. Others... make election dependent on faith, as if it were doubtful and ineffectual till confirmed by faith' (Calvin: *Institutes* Vol.2 p242). Once again, since election led to redemption, what Calvin said about election applies equally to the latter. Although Clifford stressed election, at times he seemed to place even more emphasis upon faith. For Amyraut, he said, as I noted above, election merely explains gospel success (Clifford: 'Evangelicalisms' p8), when, as I have pointed out, it dominates it. See Nicole p300). For John Wesley, salvation 'is only efficacious to believers' (Clifford: *Atonement* p99). This is true, of course, but men only become believers because they are elect.

[114] A nice distinction must be maintained here. Justification comes *through*, *by* faith; but NOT *on account of*, *because of*, faith. Faith is its means, not its cause. Amyraldianism tends (to put it no stronger) to blur this distinction. See previous note, and earlier.

[115] Durham pp180-186. See Gill: *Cause* p99. This takes us back to the second point above – God's will of decree is not conditional; it is not 'suspended' on anything.

[116] See Fuller: *Philanthropos* pp225-226; Nettles p125; Macleod p62. 'Who shall bring a charge against God's elect?... Who is he who condemns?' The relief – and ground of assurance – for the accused believer, is all to do with Christ and his work. The answer to a charge against one of God's elect is not the believer's faith, nor even God's election of him. It is *not*: 'I am elect; I have believed'; but: 'It is *Christ* who died, and furthermore is also risen, who is even at the right hand of God, who also makes intercession for us' (Rom. 8:33-34; see also 5:18-19).

In Eph. 2, Paul, spelling out many of the believer's blessings, ascribes all to Christ, his blood, his cross, his resurrection, his ascension, and our union with him. It is all received by faith (Eph. 2:8), yes, but the ground of these benefits is not our faith, nor God's work in bringing us to faith, but the work of Christ: We 'have been brought near *by the blood of Christ*, for *he himself* is our peace, who has made both one, and has broken down the middle wall of separation, having abolished *in his flesh* the enmity... so as to create *in himself* one new man from the two, thus making peace, and that *he* might reconcile them both to God in one body *through the cross*... For *through him* we both have access by one Spirit to the Father' (Eph. 2:13-18). Note, *first*, it is by Christ and in Christ that all these things are accomplished: 'Christ, he, he...' *Secondly*, note the certainty, the definiteness of Paul's statements: Christ *has* brought us near, he *is* our peace, he *has* made both one, he *has* broken down the separating wall, he *has* abolished the enmity, he *has* created a new man, he *has* made peace, and he *has* reconciled. *Thirdly*, note the tense of the verbs; all was accomplished at the cross – not at our believing. And, *fourthly*, note the verbs: Christ brought, made, broke down, abolished, created, reconciled. There is nothing merely provisional or sufficient, nothing conditional or 'suspended' about this; it is God's 'eternal purpose which he accomplished in Christ Jesus' (Eph. 3:11). 'It is finished [accomplished]!' (John 19:30).

Booth: 'They [atonement, redemption and satisfaction] are all represented, in the volume of revelation, as proceeding *immediately from the death* of our all-sufficient Sponsor, or as flowing in the blood of the Lamb, being all procured for miserable sinners by the same penal sufferings, and at the same time' (Booth: *Divine Justice* in *Works* Vol.3 pp94-95, emphasis his). The theme of 'union' will continue to recur.

[117] See Rushton p125; see also Rushton pp127-129. While Rushton here accused Fuller of teaching that faith, not Christ's obedience, is imputed for righteousness, he had to admit this 'is not openly avowed in his writings', but that he, Rushton, had 'deduced' it from them. I think it

more properly lies at the door of the Amyraldian, which I do not think Fuller was. But see below.

[118] Of course, sinners have to believe to receive salvation. I do not deny it for a moment! But, granted God's election, since, as I have explained, Christ by his death earned faith for the elect, Christ's death must be and is *the* condition of the fulfilment of God's decree. If the Amyraldian is right, the believer's faith is the ultimate condition – unthinkable!

[119] Booth: *Reign* pp135,263; see also *Reign* pp133-141.

[120] Clifford's e-mail to me, 19th Feb. 2005. I prefer Booth: 'In this forgiveness, grace reigns, and the riches of grace are displayed. It is an absolutely perfect pardon; and to make it so, three things are required. It must be full, free and everlasting. That is, it must extend to all [the] sin [of the elect]; it must be vouchsafed without any conditions to be performed by the sinner; and it must be absolutely irreversible' (Booth: *Reign* p 115).

[121] I said I would return to this.

[122] Clifford's e-mail to me, 25th Feb. 2005.

[123] Clifford's e-mail to me, 9th Feb. 2005.

[124] True, Christ offers himself *to* all in the preaching of the gospel, but on the cross he offered himself to God *for* the elect only. The invitation to sinners may be unsuccessful (Matt. 22:1-10; 23:37; Luke 13:34; 14:16-24), but the sacrifice for sinners, never. This may seem illogical to human reason, but human reason has to bow to God's revelation. Joseph Bellamy had taken Clifford's view two hundred years before: 'If Christ did not design by his death to open a door for all to be saved conditionally, that is upon condition of faith, then there is no such door opened; the door is not opened wider than Christ designed it should be; there is nothing more purchased by his death than he intended; if this benefit was not intended, then it is not procured; if it be not procured, then the non-elect can not any of them be saved, consistently with divine justice' (quoted by Oliver p217). While there is muddled thinking here, note the proper emphasis upon 'intention'. What was Bellamy's muddle? The non-elect will never be saved! But the real point he was making was that if Christ has not died for all, then the non-elect cannot be offered salvation: 'Bellamy... retained a belief in the doctrine of election but rejected particular redemption on the ground that it choked the free offer of the gospel' (Oliver p217). Once again, Bellamy was muddled; as I have said, if particular redemption 'chokes the free offer', so does unconditional election. But neither does! Clifford quoted Bellamy, himself quoting Twisse: 'Everyone who hears the gospel, (without distinction between elect and reprobate) is bound to believe that Christ died for him, so far as to procure both the pardon of his sins and

the salvation of his soul, in case [in the event that] he believes and repents'. Clifford quoted Wesley: 'For what should [all men under heaven] believe? Ought they to believe that Christ was given for them? Then he was given for them' (Clifford: *Atonement* pp89,153). I disagree with Clifford, Bellamy, Wesley and Twisse. Where is the scripture for their claim? Where are we told that every sinner is duty-bound to believe that Christ died for him?

[125] As I have pointed out, God's decree concerning the non-elect is to harden them (John 12:39-40; Rom. 9:18,22; 11:7-10; see also 1 Pet. 2:8). What do Amyraldians say about this? I cannot find Clifford dealt with the question. And Davenant showed his weakness on it. True, he did say: 'From the ordination of God... he determines that faith... should be infallibly given to certain persons and not given to others'; that is, God determines that faith should *not* be given to some – the non-elect. So far, so good. But Davenant watered it down to 'permission': 'Nor is it contrary to the divine wisdom to appoint and sometimes to confer upon men means ordained and applicable to [that is, means provided for] a certain end, and at the same time to *permit* many men to fail of attaining that end'. On, 'whom he wills [God] hardens' (Rom. 9:18), Davenant on one occasion weakened it by misquotation as '*leaves* hardened', and even when he quoted the verse properly, he still diluted it: 'It depends on the divine election that the effects of the merits of Christ are mercifully applied to any, while, through the impediment of their own unbelief, they are not applied to others'. 'Scripture... refers... the communication of saving grace... to God, who loves and pities one more than another... Repentance, faith, regeneration [and] sanctification... are given to some because the special mercy of God procures them, but are denied to others, because the same mercy does not unfold its riches to them' (Davenant pp40-41,63,97,121,135,137, emphasis mine). All true enough, but not getting to grips with 'whom he wills [God] hardens'. And Davenant said nothing at all on 'the vessels of wrath prepared for destruction... the elect have obtained it, and the rest were blinded' (Rom. 9:22; 11:7). *kataptizō*, 'to fit out, equip, put in order, arrange, adjust... men whose souls God has so constituted that they cannot escape destruction' (Thayer). See also 'perfected, ordained, prepared' (Matt. 21:16 NKJV/AV, NIV, NASB, respectively); 'framed, prepared, formed' (Heb. 11:3 NKJV/AV, NASB, NIV, respectively).

Davenant was taking a similar line to Dort: 'We believe that all the posterity of Adam being thus fallen into perdition and ruin, by the sin of our first parents, God did then manifest himself such as he is; that is to say, merciful and just: Merciful, since he delivers and preserves from this perdition all whom he, in his eternal and unchangeable counsel of mere goodness, has elected in Christ Jesus our Lord, without any respect to their works: Just, in *leaving* others in the fall and perdition wherein they have involved themselves... The cause or guilt of this unbelief... is no wise in God, but in man himself, whereas faith in Jesus Christ, and salvation through him is the free gift of God... (Eph. 2:8; Phil. 1:29)... That some receive the gift of faith from God, and others do not receive it, proceeds from God's eternal decree... According to which decree, he graciously softens the hearts of the elect, however obstinate, and inclines them to believe, while he *leaves* the non-elect in his just judgement to their own wickedness and obduracy. And herein is especially displayed the profound, the merciful, and at the same time the righteous discrimination between men, equally involved in ruin; or that decree of election and reprobation, revealed in the word of God, which though men of perverse, impure and unstable minds wrest to their own destruction, yet to holy and pious souls affords unspeakable consolation... Election is the fountain of every saving good; from which proceed faith, holiness and the other gifts of salvation, and finally eternal life itself... (Eph. 1:4)'. Dort rejected those who say 'that God, simply by virtue of his righteous will, did not decide either to *leave* anyone in the fall of Adam and in the common state of sin and condemnation, or to *pass* anyone *by* in the communication of grace which is necessary for faith and conversion... (Rom. 9:18)' (*The Three* pp28,38-39,42, emphasis mine). As far as I can see, Dort was content to speak of God *leaving* or *passing by* sinners, failing to do justice to *harden*. I cannot discover that Dort cited or dealt with Rom. 9:22; 11:7-10.

Not so Calvin: 'The word "hardens", when applied to God in Scripture, means not only permission, (as some washy moderators would have it), but also the operation of the wrath of God; for all those external things, which lead to the blinding of the reprobate, are the instruments of his wrath; and Satan himself, who works inwardly with great power, is so far his minister, that he acts not but by his command' (Calvin: *Commentaries* Vol.19 Part 2 p362). I agree. Of course, with Calvin's editor: 'Why some were hardened and others were softened, is what must be resolved altogether to the will of God' (in Calvin: *Commentaries* Vol. 19 Part 2 p418). Calvin again: 'As God had resolved to destroy [Sihon (Deut 2:30)], the hardening of his heart was the divine preparation for his ruin'. 'See how [Paul in Rom. 9:18] refers both [God having mercy and hardening] to the mere pleasure of God. Therefore, if we cannot assign any reason for his bestowing mercy to his people, but just that it so pleases him, neither can we have any reason for his reprobating others – but his will. When God is said to visit in mercy or harden whom he will, men are reminded that they are not to seek for any

cause beyond his will... Those... whom God passes by he reprobates, and that for no other cause but because he is pleased to exclude them from the inheritance which he predestines to his children... Paul does not... labour anxiously to defend God, by calling in the aid of falsehood; he only reminds us that it is unlawful for the creature to quarrel with its Creator... (Rom. 9:22-23)... The hidden counsel of God is the cause of hardening... Foolish men raise many grounds of quarrel with God, as if they held him subject to their accusations... Therefore, when it is asked why the Lord did so, we must answer: Because he [is] pleased [so to do]. But if you proceed further to ask why he [is] pleased [so to do], you ask for something greater and more sublime than the will of God, and nothing such can be found... Why he willed it is not ours to ask, as we cannot comprehend, nor can it become us even to raise a controversy as to the justice of the divine will'. Note, Calvin, as Davenant and Dort, rightly talked in terms of 'passing by' the reprobate, but *he* did not leave it there. As I have shown, he was against those 'washy moderators' who try to limit reprobation to 'permission', when 'they recur to the distinction between will and permission'. Even so, he was clear: 'Though [the] perdition [of the reprobate] depends on the predestination of God, the cause and matter of it is in themselves'. Calvin was very strong against those who blame God for their sin, and those who try to pry into his secret will. In concluding his discourse on the matter, Calvin said: 'Finally, after all that has been adduced on this side and on that, let it be our conclusion to feel overawed with Paul at the great depth, and if petulant tongues will still murmur, let us not be ashamed to join in his exclamation: "No but, O man, who are you that replies against God?" (Rom. 9:20). Truly does Augustine maintain that it is perverse to measure [the] divine [justice] by the standard of human justice' (Calvin: *Institutes* Vol.1 p268; Vol.2 pp223-229,232-233,251-258).
Jerom Zanchius: 'We, with the Scriptures, assert that there is a predestination of some particular persons to life for the praise of the glory of divine grace, and a predestination of other particular persons to death, which death of punishment they shall inevitably undergo, and that justly, on account of their sins... This future death they shall inevitably undergo, for, as God will certainly save all whom he wills should be saved, so he will as surely condemn all whom he wills shall be condemned... The reprobate shall undergo this punishment justly and on account of their sins. Sin is the meritorious and immediate cause of any man's damnation. God condemns and punishes the non-elect, not... as men, but as sinners... God did, from all eternity, decree to leave some of Adam's fallen posterity in their sins, and to exclude them from the participation in Christ and his benefits'. I pause. Zanchius quite rightly,

as Davenant and Dort, used the word 'leave'. But he, like Calvin, did not let it go at that: '[They] were, from all eternity, not only negatively excepted from a participation of Christ and his salvation, but positively ordained to continue in their natural blindness, hardness of heart... and that by the just judgement of God... The non-elect were predestinated, not only to continue in final impenitency, sin and unbelief, but were likewise, for such their sins, righteously appointed to infernal death hereafter... As the future faith and good works of the elect were not the cause of their being chosen, so neither were the future sins of the reprobate the cause of their being passed by, but both the choice of the former and the decretive omission of the latter were owing, merely and entirely, to the sovereign will and determining pleasure of God'. Zanchius explained: 'We distinguish between... bare non-election, which is a purely negative thing, and condemnation or appointment to punishment; the will of God was the cause of the former, the sins of the non-elect are the reason of the latter. Though God determined to leave, and actually does leave, whom he pleases in the spiritual darkness and death of nature, out of which he is under no obligation to deliver them, yet he does not positively condemn any of these merely because he has not chosen them, but because they have sinned against him... God is the creator of the wicked, but not their wickedness; he is the author of their being, but not the infuser of their sin... [But] the condemnation of the reprobate is necessary and inevitable... The non-elect could not be condemned [were] it not the divine pleasure and determination that they should, and if God wills and determines their condemnation, that condemnation is necessary and inevitable. By their sins they have made themselves guilty of death, and as it is not the will of God to pardon those sins and grant them repentance unto life, the punishment of such impenitent sinners is as unavoidable as it is just... Nor does it follow... that God forces the reprobate into sin, and thereby into misery, against their wills, but that, in consequence of their natural depravity (which it is not the divine pleasure to deliver them out of, neither is he bound to do it, nor are they themselves so much as desirous that he would), they are voluntarily biased and inclined to evil; [indeed], which is worse still, they hug and value their spiritual chains, and even greedily pursue the paths of sin, which lead to the chambers of death. Thus God does not... compel the wicked to sin... So that though the condemnation of the reprobate is unavoidable, yet the necessity of it... does not in the least interfere with the rational freedom of their wills, nor serve to render them less inexcusable... The punishment of the non-elect [is, however,] not the ultimate end of their creation, but [that ultimate end is] the glory of God' (Zanchius pp85-87,104-122). Zanchius developed his scriptural arguments, of course, which, for lack of space, I have omitted. Amyraldianism does not come to terms with this doctrine of God's decree concerning the non-elect or reprobate. It is not enough to say that God *leaves* the non-elect in their sins; he *hardens* them (John 12:39-40; Rom. 9:18; 11:7-10). Haldane: 'If the doctrine of election is admitted, what difficulty do we get rid of by asserting that Christ died for all? The elect alone obtain salvation, and the rest are blinded' (Haldane p38; see also pp120-121,240-241).

In all this, I am not, of course dismissing the scriptural use of 'permit' or 'allow' – see for instance Acts 14:16; 16:7; 1 Cor. 10:13; 16:7; Heb. 6:3 – as applied to the will of God. But, as Calvin noted – see above – this does not imply any diluting of the positive aspect of God's decree. To describe the outcome of events, as we see them, in terms of God allowing or permitting certain things to happen, is, as Owen put it, to speak 'of our absolute dependence on [God]... [that] all our affairs... are in the hand of God, and at his disposal... Jas. 4:13-15'. It is not the same, however, as 'a mere naked permission in God' (Owen: *Hebrews* Vol.3 Part 2 pp65-66).

[126] Quoted by Nettles p307.

[127] Douty, in quoting Owen here, did not distinguish between God's decree and his desire (Douty p30).

[128] Owen: *Death* in *Works* Vol.10 p149.

[129] Gill: *Cause* p164. Both the Amyraldian and the Owenite say that in some sense Christ died for all men but not 'with the "intention" of rendering his atonement the means of salvation to all men, else all men must be saved. What difficulty then is got rid of by universal atonement?' If it is said that 'it throws the responsibility of rejecting it on the sinner', the reply is at hand: 'Who denies this?' (Haldane p318). To return to an earlier point, and to anticipate a criticism of what I am saying: In the free offer, there is a *seeming* contradiction between God's decree and his desire, but this is very different to the Amyraldian position, which has a *real* (not merely a seeming) contradiction in God's decree. Also, it is utterly wrong to give the slightest suggestion of any need for God to justify his actions. As I will show, the Amyraldian and the Owenite join hands at this point with the hyper-Calvinist and the Arminian; all – for the best of motives – try to provide a logical justification for God. This mistake, though well-meant, is nevertheless serious. God needs no justification whatsoever from man for his actions.

[130] Davenant contradicted himself on the atonement. On the one hand: 'This reconciliation, this not imputing of sins... is considered as performed on the part of God and Christ, as soon as Christ is understood to have laid down his life for the sins of the world'. On the other: 'We

do not undertake the cause of those who declare that Christ by his death obtained remission of sins, reconciliation with God, and a state of salvation for each and every man... God is so far pacified by the death of Christ that he is now ready to receive into favour...' (Davenant pp28,37,43,107). I dare say Davenant's supporters will plead he was making a very fine distinction. If so, the distinction is too fine for me, I am afraid. Did the death of Christ pacify God or make God pacifiable? Did it reconcile him or make him reconcilable? Davenant thought 'we can truly announce to every man that his sins are expiable by the death of Christ according to the ordination of God' (Davenant p49). Expiable? Christ *expiated* the sins of those for whom he stood; he did not make their sins *expiable*. Christ was given the name of Jesus as he came into the world because he would, by the 'ordination of God', save sinners (Matt. 1:21; 1 Tim. 1:15) – not make them saveable.

[131] See above; Macleod pp61-62.

[132] Substitution is at the heart of redemption which, therefore, must be particular. Booth: 'If, in his perfect obedience and penal death, [Christ] acted and suffered as the substitute of all mankind, they are all redeemed; but if, as the representative of the elect only, redemption must be considered as exclusively theirs. For, to imagine that the death of Christ, as the price of deliverance from the curse of the law, redeemed any for whom, as a substitute, he did not suffer; and to suppose that any of those, for whom as a surety, he sustained the penalty of death, are not redeemed, seems equally indefensible and absurd... The substitution of Christ, and the imputation of sin to him, are essential to the scriptural doctrine of redemption by our adorable Jesus' (Booth: *Divine Justice* in *Works* Vol.3 pp60-62; see also *Divine Justice* pp78-89). Robert W.Oliver: 'The strictly substitutionary view of the atonement require[s] either that the sins of the elect were imputed to Christ and he atoned for these alone, or that he died for all and saved all, which [is] universalism' (Oliver p217). Substitution was the nub of the contention between Booth and Fuller, Booth holding to strict substitution, and thinking that Fuller was weakening on it and in danger of adopting the New England theology which, after the death of Edwards senior, jettisoned particular redemption. Fuller denied this (Fuller: *Six Letters* pp317-325). See Oliver pp217-221. But see Haykin pp124-126; Macleod p247.
Rushton called it a 'fallacy' to say the atonement 'is sufficient... for all mankind [but] intended only for the elect'. 'The Scriptures always ascribe the salvation of a sinner, not to any abstract sufficiency, but to the vicarious nature of the death of Christ. The atonement, therefore, is in no sense sufficient for a man unless Jesus died *for* that man... To this the Scripture always traces our salvation. "For God has not appointed us

to wrath, but to obtain salvation by our Lord Jesus Christ, *who died for us*". I conclude, therefore, that it is much less absurd to affirm, with the Arminians, that Christ died for all mankind, than to maintain... that the atonement is sufficient for the salvation of those for whom it was not intended, and for whom the Saviour did not die' effectually (Rushton pp23-24, emphasis his). Rushton was here attacking Fuller on the atonement, but his comments apply to all who hold the sufficiency formula – in either of its forms; they have to face Rushton's just assessment. As for attacks on Fuller over the atonement, it is hard to be precise about Fuller's views on these matters – little wonder considering how much he wrote over many years, and his own admitted change (see below). See Haykin pp107-128; Macleod p247; Haldane pp44,49,58,126-127,166-170,191-193.

Amyraldianism fatally weakens substitution. James Macgregor, quoted by John Macleod, noted the first of what he called 'the more malignant aspects of Amyraldianism': 'The notion of any saving purpose of God that does not infallibly determine salvation... is not only... unscriptural, but... offensive... Nor does the notion [improve]... when transferred from God's eternal decree to the execution of that decree in time on the cross. For the notion of any substitution of Christ that does not infallibly secure by purchase the salvation of all for whom he died, is deeply dishonouring to the personal work of the adorable substitute' (Macleod p250). This is *the* point. 'Atonement [is] by sacrifice; in other words, by substitution and vicarious suffering', as Haldane put it. 'If Christ was the substitute for all, then all must be saved... What kind of substitution is that of Christ, if those for whom he stood as their vicarious head, remain, after all his sufferings, under the guilt, and consequently, under the dominion of sin? If the atonement was sufficient, it cannot be consistent with justice to punish the offender, by whose substitute this atonement was made. If Christ was the substitute of all mankind – if he bore their sins in his own body on the tree, that they being dead to sin, might live unto righteousness, then either they are become dead to the law by the body of Christ, and therefore must be saved, or the penalty must be twice inflicted. Thus it appears that the doctrine of the universality of the atonement sets aside Christ's vicarious and substitutionary sufferings, of which... the Bible is full... The whole sacrificial system [of the Old Testament] proceeds upon the principle of substitution... All the sacrifices of Israel kept the doctrine of substitution before them... The lamb of the morning, and the lamb of the evening, offered up on the altar, kept the doctrine of substitution constantly before the people... How is it possible that sin should be imputed both to the substitute and to him whom he represented; both to the surety and to

him in whose behalf he had been accepted?' (Haldane pp104,131-133,289).
In short: 'An "indefinite atonement"... if the whole world is not saved, is no atonement; it is... a complete failure... An atonement for all mankind, while it is applied only to the elect, and all perish who are not thus distinguished... vindicates neither the justice nor the truth of God' (Haldane pp104,185). Popham: 'A redemption which leaves some of the redeemed in the power of the slave master... is not redemption. It is an immitigable blot on the character of God... A universal redemption, leaving myriads of sinners slaves to sin and under divine punishment, is no redemption. The assertion of such a redemption is a reproach, a dishonour to Jehovah, a denial of law, of justice, of purity, and a travesty of holy Scripture' (Popham pp60,63).

[133] As I have said before, the elect died with Christ, were buried with him, were raised with him, and are seated with him in glory (Rom. 6:2-11; 7:4-6; 2 Cor. 5:14-18; Gal. 2:19-20; Eph. 2:1,4-6; Col. 2:11-15,20; 3:1,3; 1 Pet. 2:24). This was decreed in eternity, accomplished at Calvary, and is experienced by faith. But the central point is that which I stress here; all was accomplished in Christ's death at Calvary, and in his resurrection and ascension.

[134] Although Fuller was not dealing precisely with Amyraut – insofar as Amyraut held a conditional redemption for all the non-elect, Fuller's words apply.

[135] Not so. It is the mistake I am tackling in this book.

[136] Fuller: *Philanthropos* pp224-225; see Nettles p125. See below for changes in Fuller's views. See also Kennedy pp51-57.

[137] To repeat them in summary: 1. God does not have a twofold decree in Christ's redemption. 2. God's decree is not conditional. 3. Christ earned the gift of faith for the elect. 4. *The* condition of redemption is Christ's death, not faith. 5. No good purpose is served by any supposed redemption for the non-elect. 6. The Amyraldian scheme fatally weakens the atonement.

[138] 'I see nothing as yet of the least efficacy or force to dissuade me [of this], and am bold to tell those concerned therein, that their conditional satisfaction, or their suspending the fruits of the death of Christ upon conditions... is a vain figment, contrary to the Scriptures, inconsistent in itself and destructive of the true value and virtue of the death of Christ' (Owen: *Death* in *Works* Vol.10 p450).

[139] See Dabney's 'several objections' to the system, and his reasons for saying 'the advantage proposed to be gained by it appears illusory' (Dabney: *Systematic* pp519-520; see also 'God's' pp282-313). As before, what is said about faith, is to be understood of repentance.

[140] Booth (according to Oliver pp219-220 & Morden p86) was answering Fuller's view of the atonement, though he did not name him. See Rushton p3. Booth had done a similar thing a few years earlier on another issue (Morden p79). It seems to me, however, Booth was actually dealing with (more or less) Amyraldianism – which as far as I can judge, Fuller never held. But see Macleod p247. See below. Rushton attributed Fuller's view to Arminianism: 'If the nature of that sufficiency for all men, which Mr Fuller ascribes to the atonement, be further sifted, it will appear to be nothing more than a conditional sufficiency, such as the Arminians attribute to their universal redemption' (Rushton pp24-26; Randalls pp21-22 cited Rushton p27, but his edition may be later). Yet, in the same place, Rushton distinguished between Fuller and the Arminian. As I say, Fuller was neither Arminian nor Amyraldian, but came to believe in particular redemption with the usual sufficiency formula attached. Even so, because of his changes over the atonement, I cannot say he came to the 'Owenite position'. On the question in hand, I do not know where, precisely, he ended up. See Haykin pp107-128; Clifford: *Atonement* p88; Morden pp84-97.
A hundred years ago, an interesting little episode was played out in the pages of the *Gospel Standard*. First, the editor, Enoch Feazey, quoted with approval John Newton: 'The efficacy of [Christ's] atonement is indeed greater than the actual application, and sufficient to save the whole race of mankind if they truly believed on the Son of God'. This contradiction of his own Articles being pointed out to him, Feazey twice printed a retraction: 'John Newton... makes the atonement of Christ infinitely more extensive than the application thereof, which... we cannot possibly believe without scripture proof. This erroneous doctrine has been held by certain persons under various names, but some have embraced it in this century, Fullerism' (*Gospel Standard* 1900 p426; Indices vi). This sweeping generalisation was, and remains, simplistic – and wrong. It scoops into the net many who hold to duty faith (me included), daubs them with the notion of 'sufficient for all' – not taking care to distinguish between Calvin, Amyraut, Owen, Newton, Fuller and the rest – and throws their views into the waste-paper bin labelled 'Fullerism'. But whether intentionally or not, by pressing the right button – 'Fullerism' – Feazey effectively diverted his readers' attention away from his own gaffe.
[141] Booth, of course, was not suggesting Christ did make an atonement for all mankind; he was dealing with those who wanted to say this and, at the same time, hold to some form of particular redemption.
[142] See above, where I note that this is the chief point.
[143] Emphasis mine.

[144] Emphasis mine.

[145] Note once again the consistency in God's decree – which consistency Amyraldianism at least undermines.

[146] Rushton said it amounted to the same (Rushton p24), but he overstated the case. Booth's accusation dates from 1802, after Fuller and he had met. Fuller, tracing the rumours about his 'Arminianism' back to Booth, wrote to him to ask him to own up to the misrepresentation. While Booth did not reply to Fuller, he admitted to Ryland that Fuller was not an Arminian. Booth thought Fuller had become a Baxterian – whom Clifford linked with Amyraut, as did Macleod (Clifford: *Amyraut* p62; Macleod pp60-62,246-247) – but Fuller abhorred the thought of being lumped with Baxter on the atonement (Fuller: *Six Letters* pp317-319,323-324; Haykin pp107-108,127-128). 'Mr Baxter pleads for "universal redemption"; I only contend for the *sufficiency* of the atonement... for the redemption and salvation of the whole world' (Fuller: *Six Letters* p324, emphasis his). Digressing just for a moment: Booth knew that a true gospel preacher always leaves himself open to the (false) accusation of being an antinomian or an Arminian: 'Does a minister of the gospel display the absolute freeness, the infinite riches, and all-sufficiency of that grace which is revealed in Jesus Christ, as an immediate ground of encouragement for the vilest of sinners to confide in him? the doctrine will be stigmatised, by multitudes, as manifestly licentious' (Booth: *Glad Tidings* in *Works* Vol.2 p5). It is, in fact, an acid test of preaching. This, of course, though relevant to the free offer, is not the point being made above.

[147] Amyraldians might well protest that they believe Christ made an effectual redemption for the elect, but a sufficient redemption for all. But this will not answer Booth's charge. Christ shed his blood once only. According to Amyraldians, he shed his blood equally for all; that is, sufficiently for all; he did not shed his blood differently for the elect and non-elect; the fact that Christ's blood is effective for the elect, has nothing to do with the redemption itself; it is election which determines the extent of the application of that redemption. Booth's charge against Amyraldianism stands.

[148] Booth: *Divine Justice* in *Works* Vol.3 pp78-95, emphasis his, excepted where stated. See the whole section for all his arguments. Again: 'It was necessary... to be determined... who in particular should be interested in this wonderful work, and saved by it. Their persons... must be known to [Christ] and distinguished from others. For it is absurd to suppose that he should engage as a substitute to perform obedience and pour [out] his blood, to lay down his life as a ransom to satisfy justice, and all this for persons unknown... Nor does it appear that the

design of God in the salvation of sinners, by the incarnation and death of his own Son, could have been certainly answered on any other hypothesis. Supposing, for instance, that it had been the divine purpose to save, by the mediation of Jesus, all who should ever believe; without ascertaining the persons who should thus embrace the Redeemer, it would have remained dubious whether any would be finally saved, because uncertain whether any would ever believe. But if it were certain that some would believe, this certainty must arise from the purpose of God; for, on any other foundation, nothing future can be absolutely certain. If it was determined that some should believe, the divine appointment must be considered as extending to every individual whose faith and salvation are supposed to be certain. For faith is a gift of grace, and could not be foreseen in any but these on whom the great dispenser of every favour had determined to bestow it. Hence we may safely infer that the death of Christ was absolutely certain, in virtue of a divine purpose, and the everlasting compact between the Eternal Three; so [that] all the individuals that should ever be saved by the undertaking of Jesus were chosen of God, were distinguished from others, and consigned to the great shepherd as his peculiar charge'; that is, given to him so that he should die for them as their substitute and redeem them, earning every grace and gift necessary for their complete salvation (Booth: *Reign* pp58-59).

[149] Haldane p38, emphasis mine.

[150] It appears that I am inserting the 'not' to change Gill's meaning entirely. It is not so. Gill, replying to Dr Whitby, was making the point that he agreed with him in this respect: 'The distinctions... for my own part, I can no more admit of than himself'.

[151] Gill: *Cause* p98.

[152] Gill: *Cause* p172. Amyraldians say that the elect *will* believe, so their faith is not 'precarious'. But since no sinner can know he is one of the elect, before coming to faith, this leaves all in the 'precarious' condition Gill described.

[153] The answer – in case there is any doubt – is a resounding NO!

[154] Haldane pp127,337, emphasis mine.

[155] In addition to what I have already said on the question, and bearing in mind my reference to the power of the indirect, take: 'The Son of God has come and has given us an understanding, that we may know him who is true' (1 John 5:20). *This* 'coming' of Christ must include his death: 'God... loved us and sent his Son to be the propitiation for our sins' (1 John 4:10). *This* 'understanding' must include 'life': 'God has sent his only begotten Son into the world that we might live through him' (1 John 4:9). *diavoia* involves 'understanding, feeling, desiring'

(Thayer). In short, God sent his Son into the world to die so that the elect might be regenerated, brought to faith (that is, come to Christ) and given eternal life (John 3:14-16,36; 4:10; 5:21,24,40; 6:27,40,47,51,53,57,63; 7:38; 8:24; 10:10-11,28; 11:25-26; 17:2-3; 1 John 5:11). The bringing of the elect to faith, please note, is at the heart of this. Note the chain of election, redemption, the Spirit, and spiritual understanding including faith, in 1 Cor. 1:17 – 2:16.

[156] I remind you, reader, of Clifford's statement which I quoted earlier: 'The gift of faith is *related to* the atonement; it is so indirectly' (Clifford: *Amyraut* p39, emphasis mine). This is so weak a link, it seems hardly worth making. Whatever form of words is used, unless the Amyraldian agrees that the gift of faith was purchased by Christ absolutely for the elect, then the gift of faith *is* given to them in God's decree independent of Christ's death.

[157] Lloyd-Jones: *Life* pp145-146; Boston: *Beauties* pp183-186. See also Cunningham p331.

[158] Moreover, it was 'sufficient in itself for the redeeming... of other worlds also, if the Lord should freely make them, and would redeem them'.

[159] 'This sufficiency of his sacrifice has a twofold rise: *First*, The dignity of the person that did offer and was offered. *Secondly*, The greatness of the pain he endured, by which he was able to bear, and did undergo, the whole curse of the law and wrath of God due to sin. And this sets out the innate, real, true worth and value of the blood-shedding of Jesus Christ. This is its own true internal perfection and sufficiency'.

[160] 'Owen's... idea of "intrinsic" or "innate" sufficiency relates to the person of Christ rather than a redemptive provision' (Clifford's e-mail to me, 31st Jan. 2005).

[161] 'Embraced and used by various Protestant divines, though by others... rejected'.

[162] I add the word 'merely' because, as I have shown, Owen has already stated that 'the sacrifice of Christ... was in itself of infinite value and sufficiency to have been made a price to have bought and purchased all and every man in the world... The value and fitness of it to be made a price arises from its own internal sufficiency'. See his 'merely' in the extract below.

[163] Owen: *Death* in *Works* Vol.10 pp295-296, emphasis mine.

[164] Owen: *Death* in *Works* Vol.10 p296.

[165] Owen: *Death* in *Works* Vol.10 p441. Somewhere in all this logical twisting and turning lies the self-contradiction I spoke of. According to Owen, although God did not intend that Christ should redeem all, he did intend that Christ's redemption would be sufficient for all if he had

intended to redeem all, which he did not. But did that sufficiency lie in the intrinsic worth of the person of Christ? or in God's intention in the sacrifice, and not the intrinsic worth of it? To my mind, Owen wanted it both ways.

[166] Owen, to put it mildly, did not think much of Amyraut's treatise. See Owen: *Death* in *Works* Vol.10 p479.

[167] But when Owen said: 'There is a sufficiency in the merit of Christ to save them if they should believe' (Owen: *Death* in *Works* Vol.10 p383), I fail to see much difference between him and Amyraut.

[168] I remind you, reader, that 'efficacious' is a tautology when speaking of redemption. It is either efficacious or it is nothing.

[169] Owen: *Death* in *Works* Vol.10 p383.

[170] Although Owen turned to logic, he was illogical! Compare the space I have had to devote to Amyraut – with that which I have allocated to Owen. Both the Arminian and hyper-Calvinistic schemes are logical from a human point of view.

[171] As on another, related topic, 'we are in danger of intruding into those things which do not belong to us. If the Holy Scriptures teach us nothing on the subject, we should not seek to be wise above what is written. The Scriptures, so far as I know, contain no proof of the hypothesis' (Dagg p329).

[172] To avoid any misunderstanding, let me make my position clear yet again: I am not for a moment suggesting any deficiency in the infinite worth of Christ's person or sacrifice. Nor am I belittling in any way whatsoever the indescribable greatness of his sufferings. I apply the word 'meaningless' entirely and only to Owen's logical (to my mind, self-contradicting) gymnastics in trying to defend 'sufficient for all'.

[173] Clifford: *Atonement* pp74,112-113. Clifford attributed this to Owen's 'commercial theory of the atonement'.

[174] As Davenant said: 'They will never rightly defend the alone-sufficiency of the death of Christ as to all, unless they confess at the same time that it is applicable to [in Davenant's terms, provided for] all for salvation, according to the appointment of God... It is foolishly and falsely asserted that he died for all sufficiently, who is affirmed to have died only for the elect, because the word "sufficiently" is not a diminishing term... Nor can it easily be explained how, without evident contradiction, it can be affirmed that Christ died or was offered up sufficiently for all, and at the same time be altogether denied that he was unwilling to die or be offered up for many [that is, the non-elect]'. By saying that Christ 'died for all sufficiently' (on account of the intrinsic worth of his person and sacrifice), but that he 'died for the elect alone', the Owenites, as Davenant observed, 'entirely extinguish the first part of

the sentence'; namely, that Christ died sufficiently for all men. 'Common sense refuses that it should be granted that he died sufficiently for all, who is denied to have died... for some'. Davenant rightly dismissed the 'Owenite' distinction (which he called 'hypothetical' – a further complication of the terminology since some call the Amyraldian position 'hypothetical') as 'evidently frivolous and vain' (Davenant pp31,52,71,76-78). Such use of the formula seems little more than a limbering-up exercise in scholasticism, and ought to be dropped.

[175] See earlier note.

[176] See below; Nettles pp304-305. Thomas J.Nettles' reference to the feeding of the 5000 (Nettles p308) was unfortunate. While his explanation of the baskets of leftovers was ingenious, to argue that Christ provided 'just enough food to satisfy' the crowd 'plus another day's provision for the disciples', was speculation and did nothing to strengthen the case. Rather, Nettles was adopting the sort of logic he was exposing. Baxter rightly called Owen's approach an 'absurdity': The Schoolmen's sufficiency-efficiency formula 'cannot without absurdity be interpreted to mean that [Christ's] death is sufficient for all if it had been a price for them, and [at the same time say it is] not a sufficient price for them. For that were to contradict themselves' (Clifford: *Atonement* p121). Compare, as above, Davenant's use of 'foolishly', 'evident contradiction', against 'common sense', 'evidently frivolous and vain', and such like. For the kind of debate engendered by a scholastic approach to the atonement, and the posing of conundrums which should not be raised and cannot be solved, see Macleod pp184-185.

[177] The answer – as before – in case there is any doubt – is a resounding NO!

[178] Haldane pp127,337, emphasis mine.

[179] 'If God makes proposals of mercy to men, who he foresees will certainly reject them and perish, and whom he immutably purposes to leave without effectual calling, how can his power and wisdom be cleared, save at the expense of his sincerity? or his sincerity at the expense of his wisdom or power? This is obviously the point in the Reformed or Augustinian theology most difficult of adjustment... It is against this point that the most persistent attacks of Arminians are still made' (Dabney: 'God's' p282). And, as for effectual calling, so particular redemption.

[180] As I have pointed out, talk of 'sufficiency' weakens substitution, imputation, propitiation, and union and identification with Christ.

[181] See earlier note on the mistaken search for a justification of God's actions. Amyraldians argue it from first principles, whereas Owenites

seem to feel the need of a logical expedient in order to answer objections. But they are mistaken. The right course is to state the truth (in this case, the paradox) and ride out the (in this case, the hyper/Arminian) storm. Scripture gives many examples of men having to do such a thing. See for instance 1 Kings 22:13-28; Jer. 1:7-8,17-19; Ezek. 2:6-7.

[182] For instance: 'There must be... a certain universalism belonging to the redemptive events that lays the basis for and warrants the universal proclamation' (John Murray: *Collected* Vol.1 pp62-64). Fuller, in *Worthy*, second edition, 1801: 'If the atonement... is in itself equal to the salvation of the whole world, were the whole world to embrace it – and if the peculiarity which attends it consists not in its insufficiency to save more than are saved, but in the sovereignty of its application – no such inconsistency [between the free offer and particular redemption] can justly be ascribed to it... Christ, by his death, opened a door of hope to sinners of the human race as sinners; affording a ground for their being invited, without distinction, to believe and be saved'. Again, in his *Six Letters*: 'I... contend for the sufficiency of the atonement... for the redemption and salvation of the whole world; and this affords a ground for a universal invitation to sinners to believe' (Fuller: *Worthy* pp170-171; *Six Letters* p324). Besides contradicting himself (see the extract below from Fuller: *Philanthropos* pp226-227), this weakens the doctrine of the atonement – particularly the substitution aspect – and takes us back towards the Amyraldian view – which Booth exposed (see above). But there is a problem with Fuller's position. By the time he published the second edition mentioned above, he said his views had changed from when he had answered Taylor. When writing against Taylor, Fuller owned he had not studied the extent of the atonement deeply. Later, writing to Ryland, Fuller admitted this had caused him difficulties in trying to answer Taylor, but after studying the writings of earlier Calvinists, he had now adopted the sufficiency formula, and come to think this is 'the ground of gospel invitations'; nothing else, he thought, would do (Fuller: *Philanthropos* p223; *Six Letters* p322). So far this seems clear. But I still find a difficulty. Although Fuller said to Ryland that he had 'tried to answer [Taylor] without considering the sufficiency of the atonement in itself considered, and of its being the ground of gospel invitations' (Fuller: *Six Letters* p322), he *had*: 'There is in the death of Christ a sufficient ground for indefinite calls and universal invitations... These views of the subject accord with my own'. Taylor replied to Fuller's reply to Philanthropos (who, as I have explained, was Taylor himself). Fuller replied to this reply, but, not wanting to prolong the controversy for a public who he feared might be growing tired of his

voice, he used the pseudonym Agnostos. Fuller, therefore, as Agnostos: 'I have admitted the necessity of a universal provision as a ground of invitation; and that in two respects. 1. A provision of pardon on behalf of all those who shall believe in Christ. 2. A provision of means and motives to induce them to believe. And if no more than this were meant by the term "provision", I should not object to it. And if by Christ dying for the whole world were meant no more than this, I should not wish to have any dispute about it' (Fuller: *Philanthropos* p223; *Reality* pp235,247). See the following note; Oliver pp217-219; Haykin pp124-126.

[183] 'The fact... that an infinite satisfaction was made for imputed guilt', even allowing this to be a proper way of speaking of the atonement, 'does not seem to be a sufficient ground for offering the benefits thereof to those whose sins were never imputed' (Dabney: *Systematic* p523). Dabney gave his reasons. (This is the contradiction which I noted a moment or two ago). Fuller: 'There have been and now are many considerable writers, who are far from disowning the doctrine of particular redemption, (or that the salvation of those who are saved is owing to an absolute and consequently limited design in the death of Christ), who yet apprehend that a way is opened for sinners, without distinction, being invited to return to God with the promise of free pardon on their return. And they suppose that the... general expressions ["all men", "world", "whole world", *etc*.] are intended to convey to us this idea. For my part, though I think with them in respect to the thing itself [that is, I agree with the free universal invitation], yet I question if these general expressions are so to be understood. The terms "ransom", "propitiation", *etc*., appear to me to express more than this, and what is true only of those who are finally saved. To die *for us* appears to me to express the design or intention of the Redeemer. Christ's death effected a real *redemption, through which we are justified*. He *redeemed* us... Such a meaning, therefore, of the general expressions above mentioned does not appear to me agreeable' (Fuller: *Philanthropos* pp226-227, emphasis his). Fuller here seems to contradict what he said in the extract in the previous note.

[184] Gill in Crisp Vol.1 p114.

[185] See the Gospel Standard Articles, especially Article 33. The Articles will not allow 'duty faith', 'duty repentance' or 'offers of grace'. See also my *Septimus Sears*.

[186] Engelsma p61.

[187] Herman Hoeksema (quoted by Engelsma p61).

[188] Ella: *The Free Offer* pp13-15, under 'The Free Offer Dissected and Analysed', in a section entitled 'Evangelical Arminianism'. Again:

'[John] Murray [with the free offer] seems to be saying... that all might repent through the merits of a universal atonement'. 'The Calvinistic quarter... has always insisted, until the days of Fuller at least, on a particular atonement... and on the fact that Christ's atonement was not in vain and those whom he aimed to save are saved. The faulty theory of the atonement which underlies the entire reasoning of Wesley, but to a greater extent Fuller, Gay and [John] Murray [that is, the free offer], emerged in the Dark Ages of Rome' (Ella: *The Free Offer* pp23,31). While I am flattered to be bracketed with Fuller and Murray, I hope I have it made clear that I do not view the atonement in precisely the same way as the former. What is more, I am arguing for a different basis for the free offer than the one he (and Owen and others) adopted.

[189] Peter Meney (Ella: *The Free Offer* p6). For more of the same, see my *Offer* pp137-144.

[190] Clifford's e-mail to me, 9th Feb. 2005. In case there is any doubt, my answer is: No!

[191] Owen: *Death* in *Works* Vol.10 pp297-298,383,420; see also pp344,410. See Fuller: *Philanthropos* p223; *Reality* p247; *Three Conversations* p314; *Six Letters* pp321,324.

[192] Owenites might well reply that they do not *deny* the free offer on the basis of particular redemption, but, as above, that the offer requires or is based upon a universal sufficiency. For the reasons I set out, this is wrong, and needs to be put right. While I will not repeat this note, it applies every time the point comes up.

[193] Several of the extracts which follow are relevant to more than one of these general principles.

[194] In effect, 'the Father elected you, Christ died for you, the Holy Spirit will work in you'.

[195] Kennedy p35. I do not agree with Kennedy, however, when he said we cannot tell sinners God loves them – see my *Offer* pp57-134. 'God so loved the world' (John 3:16). I am not saying that God loves all men with the love he has for his elect, but he has a general love for them and does desire their salvation.

[196] See the earlier note on Twisse and Bellamy.

[197] See my *Offer* p3.

[198] If saving faith is to believe 'Christ died for me', then no sinner will ever be saved, because no unsaved sinner can believe that Christ died for him. He must first trust Christ for salvation, then he will know Christ died for him. Duty faith comes in at this point also. It is not the duty of a sinner to believe Christ died for him; his duty is to trust Christ. Conversely, sinners are condemned for not trusting Christ – which they ought to do even though they have no power to do; they are not

condemned for not believing that Christ died for them – since such knowledge, such faith, is impossible for an unsaved sinner. See Fuller: *Worthy* p152; Naylor pp194-195.

[199] See Owen: *Death* in *Works* Vol.10 pp315,409-410. Owen: 'Some... make [faith] to be a full persuasion of the forgiveness of our sins through the mediation of Christ; or, that what Christ did and suffered as our mediator, he did it for us in particular: and a particular application of special mercy unto our own souls and consciences is hereby made the essence of faith; or, to believe that our own sins are forgiven seems hereby to be the first and most proper act of justifying faith'. If so, consequences follow, said Owen: 'Hence it would follow that whosoever does not [so] believe, or has not a firm persuasion of the forgiveness of his own sins in particular, has no saving faith – is no true believer'. As Owen tersely observed: 'Which is by no means to be admitted'. The fact is, as Owen pointed out, to take this line is to confuse saving faith and assurance. Even though – and, as Owen noted, understandably so – the early Reformers, recoiling from their struggle with Rome, sometimes tended to make this mistake, 'but yet... I never read any of them (I know not what others have done) who affirmed that every true and sincere believer always had a full assurance of the special love of God in Christ, or of the pardon of his own sins'. Yet this must follow if assurance is the essence of saving faith. But as Owen pointed out – arguing from Isa. 50:10 – not all believers have this assurance. In any case, as he said: 'The belief of the pardon of their own sins in particular... is not proposed unto [sinners] in the first preaching of the gospel' (Owen: *Justification* in *Works* Vol.5 pp83-85,96).

[200] See 1 Thess. 1:4-10, for instance. Calvin: 'No man is truly persuaded that he is of God until he has embraced his offered favour' (Calvin: *Institutes* Vol.1 p510). Owen: Christ died 'for all the elect as elect, who, by the benefit of his death, do become believers, and so obtain assurance that he died for them... Though Christ died for them, yet we deny that they can have any assurance of it while they continue [unbelievers]' (Owen: *Death* in *Works* Vol.10 p420). 'But is this the first thing that we are... to propose to the soul of a sinner... that *Christ died for him in particular*? Is that the beginning of our message to him?... No; but... this is the "beginning of the gospel of Jesus Christ"; this is "the voice of one crying in the wilderness: Prepare the way of the Lord": "There is a way of reconciliation provided. 'God is in Christ reconciling the world to himself'. There is a way of acceptance; there is forgiveness with him to be obtained". At this threshold of the Lord's house do the greatest part of men to whom the gospel is preached fall and perish, never looking in to see the treasures that are in the house itself, never coming into any

such state and condition wherein they have any ground or bottom to enquire whether Christ died for them in particular or not. They believe not this report, nor take any serious notice of it. This was the ministry of the Baptist, and they who received it not, "rejected the counsel of God" concerning their salvation (Luke 7:10), and so perished in their sins. This is the sum of the blessed invitation given by Wisdom (Prov. 9:1-5). And here men stumble, fall and perish (Prov. 1:29,30)' (Owen: *Psalm 130* in *Works* Vol.6 p523, emphasis his). See my *Septimus Sears*.

[201] I repeat the point I have made before: The free offer is not simply an offer; it contains an invitation; and it involves a command. While sinners are to be invited to come to Christ, and encouraged with the promises of God attached to the free offer, they are also commanded to come in faith and repentance.

[202] Noah's obedience of faith 'condemned the world' (Heb. 11:7), but since he was 'a preacher of righteousness' (2 Pet. 2:5), may we not believe he commanded sinners to join him in faith and repentance? Did he not warn them to flee from the wrath to come? Did he not promise them salvation if they came? Of course he did. God's 'longsuffering waited patiently' (1 Pet. 3:20, including footnote) in those days, and we know what *that* means (Gen. 6:3; Rom. 2:4; 1 Tim. 1:16; 2 Pet. 3:9,15) – even in light of Rom. 9:22, on which, Gill: 'God... externally calls them, but they refuse... and therefore are inexcusable... after all this patience, indulgence and forbearance' (Gill: *Commentary* Vol.6 p81). But can we imagine Noah engaging with unbelievers in a discussion about whether or not they were elect, about the size of the ark and whether it could contain all if all came? Would he have been bothered about any seeming contradiction between the size of the ark and the breadth of his invitation? Would the fact that God was going to condemn the world, and establish his covenant with him (Gen. 6:7,13,17-18; 7:4), hinder his preaching? To ask such questions is to answer them. Would any Israelite who needed to avoid vengeance (Num. 35:6-34; Josh. 20), debate within himself the size of the city of refuge, and whether or not he could find a lodging in the place? Would any friend of his encourage him so to debate? Run, he would tell him, run for your life! And run he would! Likewise in the gospel; we have to call sinners to flee to Christ for refuge (Heb. 2:3; 6:18), not discuss the extent of the atonement with them. The sinners of Noah's day were not concerned about election and particular redemption, and their interest, or otherwise, in it; they were totally consumed with the carnal. And so it is today, and will be throughout this age (Matt. 24:37-39).

Lest my comments on Noah's preaching be dismissed as too speculative, consider Calvin and Gill on Gen. 6:3. Calvin: 'For as long as the Lord suspends punishment, he... invites [the world] to repentance. In this way he had striven already... with the world... And now, as if wearied out, he declares that he has no mind to contend any longer. For when God, by inviting the unbelievers to repentance, had long striven with them, the deluge put an end to the controversy... [The 120 years] refers... to a time of repentance to be granted to the whole world. Moreover, here also the admirable benignity of God is apparent, in that he, though wearied with the wickedness of men, yet postpones the execution of extreme vengeance for more than a century' (Calvin: *Commentaries* Vol.1 Part 1 pp241,243). Gill spoke of 'God himself [saying]... there shall not always be contention within me concerning man, whether I shall destroy him, or have mercy on him... Or rather... that the Spirit of God which had been litigating and reasoning the point... with these men in the court, and at the bar of their own consciences by one providence or by one minister or another, particularly by Noah, a preacher of righteousness, in vain, and to no purpose; therefore he determines to proceed no longer in this way, but pass and execute the sentence of condemnation on them... [The 120 years] designs the space that God would give for repentance, before he proceeded to execute his vengeance on [them]' (Gill: *Commentary* Vol.1 p37).

[203] If I may apply Prov. 11:22 to the case, to debate with an unbeliever the extent of election and particular redemption, seems like putting 'a ring of gold in a swine's snout' – not the place for it! Lloyd-Jones: 'You... do not, must not, debate or discuss these matters [the gospel (Lloyd-Jones) – let alone the decrees (DG)] with them on an equal standing. To do so is to deny the initial Christian postulate... This whole notion of having a debate or a discussion or exchange of views concerning these matters is something that is contrary to the very character and nature of the gospel itself' (Lloyd-Jones: *Preaching* pp50-51).

[204] 'Do not... cast your pearls before swine, lest they trample them under their feet, and turn and tear you in pieces' (Matt. 7:6). If I may apply Matt. 15:26: 'It is not good to take the children's bread and throw it to the little dogs'.

[205] 'There was no necessity for the apostles to publish the divine purposes to mankind in their addresses to them. These were not designed as a rule of action, either for the preachers or the hearers. It was sufficient for them both that Christ was ready to pardon and accept... any sinner whatever that should come unto him. It was equally sufficient, on the other hand, if, after people believed, they were taught those truths which relate to the purposes of grace on their behalf... Hence it is that the chief of those scriptures which we conceive to hold forth a limitation

of design in the death of Christ, or any other doctrine of discriminating grace, are such as were addressed to believers' (Fuller: *Philanthropos* p226).

Spurgeon explained his position in his sermon of 28th Feb. 1858: 'When first it was my duty to occupy this pulpit, and preach in this hall [Royal Surrey Gardens], my congregation assumed the appearance of an irregular mass of persons collected from the streets of this city to listen to the word. 'Twas then simply... preaching to many who had not heard the gospel before. By the grace of God, the most blessed change has taken place... It has been my wont to address you from the simple truths of the gospel; I have very seldom, in this place, attempted to dive into the deep things of God... There are many high and mysterious doctrines which I have often taken the opportunity of handling in my own place [New Park Street], that I have not taken the liberty of introducing here, regarding you as a company of people casually gathered together to hear the word. But now, since the circumstances are changed, the teaching will be changed also. I shall not now simply confine myself to the doctrine of faith, or the teaching of believer's baptism; I shall not stay upon the surface of matters, but shall venture, as God shall lead me, to enter into those things that lie at the basis of the religion that we hold so dear. I shall not blush to preach before you the doctrine of God's divine sovereignty; I shall not stagger to preach in the most unreserved and unguarded [Spurgeon did not mean 'thoughtless'] manner the doctrine of election... I shall not withhold that undoubted truth of Scripture, the effectual calling of God's elect... Seeing that many of you have now "tasted that the Lord is gracious", we will endeavour to go through the whole system of the doctrines of grace, that saints may be edified and built up in their most holy faith. I begin this morning with the doctrine of particular redemption. "He gave his life a ransom for many". The doctrine of redemption is one of the most important doctrines of the system of faith. A mistake on this point will inevitably lead to a mistake through the entire system of our belief' (Spurgeon: *New* pp129-130).

[206] 'Were anyone to address the people thus: "If you do not believe, the reason is, because God has already doomed you to destruction", he would not only encourage sloth, but also give countenance to wickedness. Were anyone to give utterance to the sentiment in the future tense, and say, that those who hear will not believe because they are reprobates, it were imprecation [a spoken curse] rather than doctrine. Wherefore, Augustine not undeservedly orders such, as senseless teachers or sinister and ill-omened prophets, to retire from the church' (Calvin: *Institutes* Vol.2 p238).

[207] Clifford was wrong to say: 'Once the guilty sinner is informed of his duty to repent, the knowledge that Christ has died for him provides encouragement to believe' (Clifford: *Atonement* p114). Clifford gave no scripture to show any preacher giving such encouragement to an unbeliever, nor did he give any example of a sinner who trusted Christ because he knew Christ had died for him. The apostle, when telling the jailer to believe, encouraged him, not by saying 'Christ died for you', but assuring him that if he believed he would be saved (Acts 16:31). What I am saying is underlined when, allowing hyper-Calvinistic terms for the moment, it is remembered that the jailer was 'a sensible sinner', and therefore one of the elect and redeemed by Christ, one who (in hyper terms) can be invited to come to Christ. As I have made clear – see my *Offer* and my *Septimus Sears* – this hyper-Calvinistic limitation of the invitation is wrong. Nevertheless, if Paul had thought Clifford's suggestion is the way to encourage any sinner to believe, he could – he surely would – have adopted it in the jailer's case. But he did not.

[208] As I explained in my *Offer* pp145-166, the sinner needs no preparation before he is invited to Christ. He certainly does not need to have a knowledge of the decrees and his personal interest in them. And a good job too! For such knowledge, as above, is unattainable. Nor does the preacher need to know it – and for the same reason. 'As many as had been appointed to eternal life believed' (Acts 13:48) does not mean that it was those who knew they had been elected who trusted Christ. No! It was those whom God had (secretly) ordained to salvation who believed. It was only after their believing that they could know they had been elected. 'The faith of Jesus is not the persuasion that we are of the elect, or that our sins are pardoned. Neither of these can be ascertained previous to our believing. We are exhorted to make our calling and election sure. The latter can only be ascertained by the former. We are never required to believe anything but what is true, independently of our belief... Faith is the manifestation of election; the two are inseparably connected. We can only know our election by our calling (2 Pet. 1:10)' (Haldane pp114,157).

Judging by his comment (Randalls p30), Andrew G.Randalls seemed to get this the wrong way round. Robert Hawker was wrong to say that when 'the apostles discovered any of the Lord's chosen ones present' in a congregation, they then used their apostolic power to plead with them to receive Christ at once (quoted by Randalls p47). May we be given an example of such a case? Note the 'if perhaps' in Acts 8:22 & 2 Tim. 2:25. It was only after evidences of saving faith that the apostles knew their hearers were elect. I have already referred to 1 Thess. 1:4-10. Randalls was arguing that 'no minister since the age of the apostles has

had the same power to... command sinners to do spiritual acts [such as repent and believe]... We find no authority in the Bible to make the invitations of the gospel indiscriminately to all men without distinction... Have today's ministers the same power to exhort sinners as Peter?... [No, Randalls claimed,] we should preach the necessity of faith and repentance as essential to salvation, not insist that our hearers are under obligation to perform spiritual acts [that is, repent and believe] which they are incapable of out of Christ' (Randalls pp36,41-42). But this is wrong. The apostles did not preach merely the *necessity* for faith and repentance; they called on sinners to repent and believe (Acts 2:38; 3:19; 8:22; 16:31; 17:30; 19:4). As Randalls admitted, the apostles did command sinners to do spiritual acts – repent and believe, for example. (See above for Philpot's recognition of the fact). But the point is, the apostles did not do this because they were apostles, nor because they knew their hearers were elect, *but because this is the way to preach the gospel to sinners*. See my *Offer* pp1-55,135-136,145-166; *Septimus Sears*; Fuller: *Strictures* p257.
Booth: 'Did the apostles preach Jesus Christ, or did they proclaim pardon and peace through his blood, to those only whom they considered as really penitent, and as having a holy turn of heart? The reverse is a fact... they were commissioned to proclaim glad tidings to the profligate, impious and wicked world... When Paul was preaching to his Jewish [countrymen], of whom he had a painful suspicion that, while they wondered at his testimony, they would reject it and perish in their unbelief – even those Jews who are said to be "filled with envy", to "contradict and blaspheme", his language was: "Be it known unto you, therefore, men and brethren, that through this illustrious Jesus is preached unto YOU the forgiveness of sins; and that by him all that believe are justified from all things, from which you could not be justified by the law of Moses". Now, [just] as it would be a dangerous mistake to suppose that Paul declared the sins of those ungodly Jews to be already forgiven, and their persons justified, so it would be inconsistent with the nature of his gracious declaration to imagine that he did not consider them as authorised, by his infallible testimony, immediately to believe in Christ for pardon and acceptance with God' (Booth: *Glad Tidings* in *Works* Vol.2 p79). In fact, of course, Paul was calling them to it. What is more, if we do not have biblical warrant to preach the gospel as we are shown in Scripture, what is our warrant for doing as Randalls asserted and 'preach the necessity of faith and repentance as essential to salvation'? Who gives us this authority – and where?

[209] The elect were chosen, and Christ was appointed to be slain, from the beginning, before time and the foundation of the world (Eph. 1:4; 2 Thess. 2:13; 2 Tim. 1:9; Tit. 1:2; 1 Pet. 1:20; Rev. 13:8; 17:8).
[210] John Murray: *Collected* Vol.1 p84.
[211] I cannot see how this can be dismissed, unless we turn Amyraldian, by saying 'nothing substantial is really on offer to all', and then, in light of that slur, deduce that 'ungrateful unbelief is quite meaningless' (Clifford: *Atonement* p156). Jesus did not see it that way: 'You are not willing [that is, you refuse] to come to me that you might have life' (John 5:40). Nothing substantial? 'Life' is on offer!
[212] John Murray: *Collected* Vol.1 pp82-83,128; see also *Redemption* p65.
[213] Booth: *Glad Tidings* in *Works* Vol.2 p78. There is, however, more to preaching that 'bearing public testimony to... proclaiming... exhibiting Jesus'. I use the above because Booth properly expressed *what* is to be preached. See below for a better statement from him on *how* the gospel is to be preached, where he included 'inviting, persuading, entreating'. Similarly for Haldane: 'The gospel tells no [unconverted] man his sins are atoned for, but it tells every man who hears it, that it is a faithful saying, and worthy of all acceptation, that Christ came into the world to save the chief of sinners; and that by him, all who believe are justified from all things, while the wrath of God abides upon unbelievers' (Haldane p36; see also Haldane pp107-108). As with Booth, the facts are right – but there is more to preaching than telling sinners the facts.
[214] Clifford quoted Owen: *Death* in *Works* Vol.10 pp173-174 to try to expose the conundrum: Are sinners condemned for unbelief or not? (Clifford: *Atonement* pp111-112). Of course they are (John 3:18-19). Owen: 'Is not unbelief the great damning sin, where faith is required? (John 3:36)?' (Owen: *Death* in *Works* Vol.10 p406). Here we meet another of the many paradoxes in Scripture. As I have pointed out, the ultimate cause of salvation is God's electing decree in the redemption accomplished by Christ, but the immediate cause of damnation is the sinner's unbelief. As always, the former (the decree) is not the sinner's concern, but the latter (his unbelief) is. God is sovereign, Satan has his finger in the pie, but man is responsible: 'The coming of the lawless one is according to the working of Satan... among those who perish, because they did not receive the love of the truth, that they might be saved. And for this reason God will send them strong delusion, that they should believe the lie, that they all may be condemned who did not believe the truth but had pleasure in unrighteousness' (2 Thess. 2:9-12). William Hendriksen: 'This coming of the final antagonist... has the effect of deceiving... those who are perishing... The cause of their perishing lies not in God but in themselves. They are perishing because they did not

accept... the love for the truth... When the gospel is proclaimed, the hearers are urged to accept Christ and all his benefits... Those hearers who perish do so because they have rejected what they have been urged to accept... The purpose of their accepting it would have been "that they might be saved". It is true that in his own power no man can accept "the love for the truth". That, however, is not the emphasis here. Here what is stressed is *man's guilt*. When man is lost, it is ever his own fault, never God's' (Hendriksen p185, emphasis his). Haldane: 'It is true that since Christ did not die for all mankind, all shall not be saved; but it is equally true that the reason why all are not saved is that all have not faith. Had it been given to every individual of the human race to believe in Christ, not one would have perished. None who trust in Christ shall be lost through [any supposed] insufficiency of the atonement. The rejection of Christ's salvation, from the love of darkness and hatred of the light, will be the ground of the condemnation of all who have heard and rejected the gospel. None who come to Jesus shall be cast out because no provision was made for their salvation' (Haldane pp111-112).
Why should refusal of Christ be such a damning sin? Because of the worth, the greatness, of the person and work of Christ. The greatness of the sin can only be measured by the greatness of the offer. 'He who does not believe God has made him a liar, because he has not believed the testimony God has given of his Son' (1 John 5:10). Edwards: 'Unbelievers set at nought the glory and excellency in Christ. They set at nought the excellency of his person. Christ is a great and glorious person, a person of infinite worthiness... infinitely esteemed and loved of the Father, and is continually adored by the angels. But unbelievers have no esteem for him... They set nothing by his infinite majesty; his glorious brightness and greatness excite not any true respect or reverence in them... An unbeliever sets no value at all upon the infinite grace of Christ. Neither do unbelievers set anything by [his] excellent virtues... They set at nought his excellency in his work and office. They are told how glorious and complete a mediator he is, how sufficient to answer all our necessities, and to save sinners to the uttermost; but they make light of it all; indeed, they make nothing of it... They make no account of the excellency of this way of salvation... The unbeliever... hears much of the dying love of Christ to sinners, how wonderful it was that so glorious a person, who is infinitely above angels, should so set his love on such worms of the dust, as to come and be made a curse for them, and die a cruel and ignominious death in their stead; but he [the unbeliever] sets nothing by all this. This dying love of Christ is of no account with him; those great things that Christ has done and suffered are with him light matters. Unbelievers not only set *little* by the glory

and excellency of Christ, but they set *nothing* by these things... What has been said may show why unbelief is spoken of as a heinous sin (John 3:18; 16:9; 1 John 5:10). For thereby all the glory of Christ is set at nought... Natural men in their unbelief cast contempt on all this glory, and tread it under foot, as being nothing worth. Their unbelief treats the excellency of Christ as being of less value than the meanest earthly enjoyments'. Edwards went on to warn unbelievers, repeatedly using the second person. 'You', he said, 'may be convinced of the greatness of your guilt... of your danger... You may hence be led to see how worthless many of those things in yourselves are, that you have been ready to make much of. Particularly, if you set nothing by all the glory of Christ... how justly God might for ever refuse to give you an interest in Christ' (Edwards: *Unbelievers* pp61-64, emphasis his). See below for Edwards reasoning on another occasion with sinners over the point, and pleading with them to come to Christ. See also Edwards: *Christ* pp216-217.

One of the great ends of both the preaching of the gospel, and the final judgement, is the glory of Christ: 'The Father... has committed all judgement to the Son, that all should honour the Son just as they honour the Father. He who does not honour the Son does not honour the Father who sent him' (John 5:22-23). 'God... has highly exalted him and given him the name which is above every name, that at the name of Jesus every knee should bow, of those in heaven, and of those on earth, and of those under the earth, and that every tongue should confess that Jesus Christ is Lord to the glory of God the Father' (Phil. 2:9-11). Here we see both God's desire in the preaching of the gospel, and his decree for the final day. God will have his Son glorified by all – and in this, he himself will be glorified.

[215] Gill: *Cause* pp102,164,166. Again: 'In Christ... there is salvation; the reason therefore of these men's perishing [2 Thess. 2:10-12] is not the decree of God... but their rejection and contempt of [the gospel]... that they might be condemned and punished with everlasting destruction from the presence of the Lord... that they may be damned, since they received not the love of the truth that they might be saved... neither the word of truth, the gospel of salvation, nor Christ, who is truth itself; and therefore were [will be] righteously given up to believe a lie; and whose damnation is just, according to the declaration of Christ – he that believes not shall be damned' (Gill: *Commentary* Vol.6 p579).

Some hyper-Calvinists disagree with Gill. Terry Bellamy, omitting the 'immediate', dismissed my, 'the immediate cause of damnation is unbelief' (my *Offer* p53), and attributed the sinner's damnation to 'Adam's sin' (Terry Bellamy p25. As for Bellamy, this is my only

reference to Terry; every other is to Joseph). As did James Wells: 'I do not hold it to be sinful for a man not to have saving faith... Man is lost by original sin, not by anything that he has done [or failed to do]. No man was ever lost yet by anything he has personally done [or failed to do]. We are lost in the first Adam; that is where judgement has come upon all men unto eternal condemnation' (James Wells pp276-277). Even though Watts and Buss could say: 'Unbelief... is the chief of sins', they could also declare it to be an error to say 'a person can be saved or lost depending on whether he accepts or rejects the invitations which appear in Scripture'. Reader, are sinners saved or damned *independently* of their response to the invitation? If so, they are mere sticks or stones devoid of responsibility; and this contradicts the plain word of Christ (John 3:18-19). I fail to see how stressing a sinner's responsibility and accountability for his unbelief leading to his damnation can be said 'grossly to undervalue the precious invitations of the gospel and make salvation contingent upon the will or decision of man'; or be said to 'imply that when Christ died, he did not know precisely for whom he died' (Watts and Buss pp32,48).
The hyper-Calvinist John Foreman: 'Men are damned for law-breaking, not for failing to savingly believe... Men holding duty faith will say that the natural man ought to believe, and that it is his duty; and many [including me, DG], if not all of them, will go so far as to say: "That though the natural man has not the power to believe unto salvation, yet that he will be damned for not believing"! But this is charging God foolishly, and turning the precious gospel of the grace of God into a... self-inconsistency... and is consequently ungodly and untrue... And so for any man to be damned to hell for not believing unto salvation, the very idea appears to me to be as silly as it is false... I know it is written: "He that believes not, shall be damned" (Mark 16:16), but the gospel does not bring that condemnation upon the unbeliever; nor does the lack of faith, or the non-believing of the gospel unto salvation, create, make, cause or bring that damnation' (Foreman pp16-18). Really? Foreman's comment on Mark 16:16 seems silly to me! If Foreman was right, what *does* Mark 16:16 mean? Surely the principle is: If a man will not eat, he will die, and the immediate cause of his death will be his refusal to eat; his refusal brought it about. Of course, since he was born in Adam, he had to die in some way or another according to God's sovereign appointment, but this particular man died because he refused to eat. And what is true physically, is no less true spiritually – see John 6:26-59, for instance. Foreman, here at least, failed to mention John 3:18-19, on which Gill commented: '"And this is the condemnation"... of him that believes not in Christ; that is, this is the matter and cause of his

condemnation' (Gill: *Commentary* Vol.5 p621). As Fuller remarked: 'Dr Gill, in general, opposed [duty faith], yet frequently, when his system was out of sight, he established [it]'. He certainly did! As Fuller reasoned: 'Unbelief is expressly declared to be a sin... John 16:8-9. But unbelief cannot be a sin if faith is not a duty' (Fuller: *Worthy* p163).
Owen had it right: 'Upon our acquiescing in this testimony [of the gospel], on our approbation of this way of saving sinners, or our refusal of it, our eternal safety or ruin does absolutely depend... The receiving and embracing of this testimony, with an approbation of the way of salvation testified unto [us], is that work of faith which secures us of eternal life'. Lest anyone should misunderstand Owen's view of saving faith, as he explained, 'the principal genuine acting of saving faith... consists in the choosing, embracing and approbation of God's way of saving sinners by the meditation of Jesus Christ, relying thereon, with a renunciation of all other ways and means pretending unto the same end of salvation' (Owen: *Grounds* in *Works* Vol.5 pp405-406).
And Clarkson expressed it pithily: 'Salvation or damnation depend upon faith and unbelief. No salvation but by faith. Nothing but damnation by unbelief. Faith is the principal saving grace, and unbelief the chief damning sin. No sin can damn without this, and this will damn without any other sin: John 3:18, "is condemned"... All are condemned, and shall be executed, except they believe... Unbelief is the symptom of eternal death' (Clarkson pp63-64).
[216] Whatever adjective is put in front of 'redeemed' – whether 'particularly', 'definitely', 'absolutely', 'conditionally', 'hypothetically', 'applicably' or 'sufficiently'.
[217] 'The invitations of the gospel... are addressed to sinners, as sinners' (Fuller: *Sermons* p597). Corresponding to three kinds of sinners, 'there are *three* kinds of blessings... which God... bestows upon men: *First*, he sends forth the gospel of salvation, accompanied with a free and indefinite invitation to embrace it, and an assurance that whosoever complies with the invitation... shall have everlasting life. This favour is bestowed on *sinners as sinners*. God "gives the true bread from heaven" in this way to many who never receive it. He invites those to the gospel supper who refuse and make light of it (John 6:32-36; Matt. 22:4-5). *Secondly*, he bestows his Holy Spirit to renew and sanctify the soul; gives a new heart and a right spirit, and takes away the heart of stone. "Christ is exalted to give repentance" (Acts 5:31). "Unto us it is given, in behalf of Christ, to believe in him" (Phil. 1:29). "We have obtained like precious faith through the righteousness of God, and our Saviour Jesus Christ" (2 Pet. 1:1). This favour is conferred on *elect sinners*. See Acts 13:48; Rom. 8:28-30. *Thirdly*, through the same medium is given

the free pardon of all our sins, acceptance with God, power to become the sons of God, and the promise of everlasting life. "Your sins are forgiven you for his name's sake" (1 John 2:12). "God for Christ's sake has forgiven you" (Eph. 4:32). "We are accepted in the beloved" (Eph. 1:6). By means of his death we "receive the promise of eternal inheritance" (Heb. 9:15). This kind of blessings is conferred on *believing sinners*' (Fuller: *Witness* p39, emphasis his). But the invitations, I repeat, are to be addressed to sinners as sinners.

[218] As always, I am not saying election and particular redemption have nothing to do with the gospel. Certainly not! They determine who will come to Christ and be saved. But they impose no limit on those who should be invited and commanded.

[219] But the sinner must come only as a sinner. 'Nothing in my hand I bring'. He does not come because he knows he is a repentant sinner, an elect sinner, a sensible sinner, a redeemed sinner or a prepared sinner. So stands the testimony of Scripture. But, as Fuller observed, 'when the revealed will of God is disregarded as a rule of life, it is common for the mind to be much occupied about his secret will, or his decrees, as a substitute for it. It is thus that men stumble upon the dark mountains, and fall into many dangerous errors... To what other cause can it be attributed that the invitations of the gospel, instead of being addressed to sinners considered merely as guilty and miserable, should be confined to sensible sinners, or to persons who, though they have never yet come to Christ, taken his yoke, or learned his spirit, are nevertheless supposed to be in possession of something that proves them to be of the elect, and therefore entitled to have the invitations addressed to them? Who can trace the delusion which must arise from such a doctrine? [In this hyper-Calvinistic system,] if a sinner is ever invited to come to Christ, it is when he is considered as sufficiently sensible of his lost condition; and this is held up, not merely as that which is necessary in the nature of things to his coming, but as giving him a warrant to come. Thus the sinner is taught to think himself one of God's elect, while as yet he has neither repentance toward God, nor faith toward our Lord Jesus Christ' (Fuller: *Antinomianism* p345). See my *Offer* pp145-166; *Septimus Sears*. Booth: Christ 'invites us by the name of sinners. As sinners, therefore, miserable, ruined sinners, we must come to him for life and salvation. The gospel of peace is preached to such, and them the gospel calls, even those who are not conscious that they are the objects of any good disposition. Yes, disconsolate sinner, be it known to you, be it never forgotten by you, that the gospel with all its blessings, that Christ with all his fullness, are a glorious provision made by the great sovereign, and by grace as reigning, for the guilty and the wretched – for such as have

nothing of their own on which to rely, and utterly despair of ever being able to do anything for that purpose... He... who believes in Christ, relies on him as the justifier of the ungodly. Nor does he consider himself in any other light... If he did, he could not believe on him as the justifier of such. The only encouragement a sinner has to apply to Christ for all that he wants, consists – not in a consciousness of being possessed of any pious disposition, of having come up to terms, performed any conditions, or as being in any way different from what he was before – but in that grace which reigns, and is proclaimed in the gospel. Yes, the free declarations of the gospel, concerning Jesus, contain a sufficient warrant for the vilest sinner, in the most desperate circumstances, to look for relief at the hand of Christ... These free declarations are founded in the glorious undertaking and finished work of Christ... [The following] divine testimonies [Isa. 45:22; Matt. 9:12-13; 11:28; 22:4; Luke 5:31-32; 19:10; John 3:16; 6:37; Rom. 5:8,10; 1 Pet. 3:18] are only a specimen of what might be produced... and they, together with others of the same import, are the proper ground of our faith in Christ, or dependence on him, for everlasting salvation... The sinner who is effectually called of God, is not led by the Holy Spirit to believe in a dying Redeemer under a persuasion of his being now distinguished from his ungodly neighbours and former self... No, the divine Spirit... [bears] witness to... the all-sufficiency, suitableness and absolute freeness of Christ, and all the blessings included in his mediation. The basis of a believer's hope, and the source of his spiritual joy, are... the truth he believes and the Saviour on whom he relies... The divine Redeemer and his finished work being the object of faith, and the report of the gospel its warrant and ground, to believe [therefore] is to trust entirely and without reserve on the faithful word which God has spoken, and on the perfect work which Christ has wrought. Such is the faith of God's elect... Yes, blessed be God! The unerring word warrants me to assert that this righteousness is absolutely free. It was wrought for the sinner; it was designed for the sinner; and is freely bestowed on the vilest of sinners... It is not... proposed on certain conditions... but it is a free gift' (Booth: *Reign* pp107-109,181-182,264-265; see also *Glad Tidings* in *Works* Vol.2 pp200-201). None of this must be taken to mean that I am saying sin does not matter, that a sinner, after coming to Christ, can go on in sin. My intended book on the law will spell out what I think about sanctification. But here I am dealing with sinners coming to Christ.

[220] See my *Offer* pp145-166.

[221] Kennedy p41, emphasis mine.

[222] Bunyan: *Reprobation* in *Works* Vol.3 pp281-282, emphasis mine.

[223] Fuller: *Worthy* p171, emphasis his.

[224] Owen: *Psalm 130* in *Works* Vol.6 p523, emphasis mine. See my *Offer* p158. Although Clifford suggested that Owen was not always clear on the free offer (Clifford: *Atonement* pp134,140), see my *Offer* pp46-48 for examples of Owen stressing duty faith and the invitations of the gospel, which, as I have said, are vital aspects of the free offer.
[225] Election is the ground of salvation, but not of the offer.
[226] You can see at a glance, reader, how ridiculous these suggestions are when applied to the other matters.
[227] See Iain Murray: *Spurgeon* p73. As before, I am not saying, of course, that God's decrees in Christ's redemption and the Spirit's application of that redemption are not behind the free offer. But the warrant we have for making the free offer does not lie in these secret matters, but in God's revealed will of command in Scripture. I will not repeat this caveat every time this theme recurs, but it always applies.
[228] William H.Goold: 'Among Calvinists that adhere to the doctrine of a definite atonement, it has been a matter of debate, not whether the gospel should be universally offered [sadly, this is no longer true], but on what basis – the simple command and warrant of the word, or the intrinsic and infinite sufficiency of the atonement – the universal offer of the gospel proceeds'. Owen, unfortunately, chose the wrong one. Unfortunately, also, Goold was weak in dealing with this: 'Perhaps this point was never formally before the mind of [Owen], but he intimates that the "innate sufficiency of the death of Christ is the foundation of its promiscuous proposal to the elect and reprobate"' (Goold p141). As I have shown, Owen more than 'intimates' it; there is more than a grain of truth in Clifford's allegation that Goold 'attempts to excuse Owen' on the issue (Clifford: *Atonement* p10).
[229] See my *Offer* pp1-55,111-124,145-166. As before, in saying this, I am not, of course, claiming we have apostolic powers (see Randalls; the Gospel Standard Articles numbers 32 & 33). But if we are not to obey the commands of God in Scripture and follow apostolic practice, if 'it would be unsafe, from the brief records we have of the way in which the apostles, under the immediate direction of the Lord, addressed their hearers in certain special cases and circumstances, to derive absolute and universal rules for ministerial addresses in the present day under widely different circumstances' (Article 32), what yardstick, according to the *Gospel Standard*, can we use? Gill, Huntingdon, Hawker, Gadsby and Philpot? See my *Septimus Sears*.
[230] Owen: *Death* in *Works* Vol.10 pp311-312,315.
[231] Booth was dealing with preparationism – see my *Offer* pp145-166.
[232] Booth: *Glad Tidings* in *Works* Vol.2 pp40,66,213, emphasis mine, except where stated; see also *Reign* pp264-268.

---

[233] Cunningham pp347-348, emphasis mine. I agree with Cunningham – we must distinguish between encouragements to believe and the warrant to believe.
[234] Durham p186, emphasis mine.
[235] Haldane p311.
[236] That is, the gospel *invites* sinners to trust Christ; it does not try to explain to unbelievers how this fits in with election and particular redemption. Of course not. In order to be saved, sinners have to trust Christ, not be able to understand all the minutiae of God's decrees. A good job too!
[237] Haldane pp102,114,116-117.
[238] Elliot pp45-46, emphasis mine.
[239] As I explained in the Preamble, this was my position in my *Offer*; hence I said little about the objection to the free offer based on particular redemption. Let me remind you, reader, of how I there defined the free offer: 'The free offer is the invitation to all sinners to believe on the Lord Jesus Christ, promising them salvation if they do, even though Christ's atonement was neither intended for all, nor accomplished for all'. If this is a reasonable definition of the free offer, then, as can be seen, any and every objection to the free offer based on the extent of the atonement is specifically ruled out.
[240] Contrary to Fuller: 'The invitations of the gospel... are founded on the *sufficiency* of Christ's atonement for the pardon of all the sins of the whole world, were they to believe in him' (Fuller: *Sermons* p597, emphasis his). 'Mr Baxter pleads for "universal redemption"; I only contend for the *sufficiency* of the atonement... for the redemption and salvation of the whole world; and this affords a ground for the universal invitation to sinners to believe; which was maintained by Calvin, and all the old Calvinists' (Fuller: *Six Letters* p324, emphasis his). He cited Matt. 22:4; John 3:16; 2 Cor. 5:19-21 as proof-texts to show that the invitation is based upon universal sufficiency (Fuller: *Reality* p247; *Three Conversations* p314; *Six Letters* p321). Of Fuller's proof texts, 2 Cor. 5:19-21 seems the most powerful to me – so I will say more on it. As for Matt. 22:4, if 'all things are ready' is taken to mean that all sinners have to be told that Christ has died for them, this being part of the '*all* things' which are 'ready', presumably all sinners will have to be told that they are all elect, and that God has decreed that the Spirit will effectually call them all, and poured out his Spirit in order to do it. Are they to be told that *all* these are provisionally provided for them, that these things are 'ready' for them? As for John 3:16, it is not relevant to this particular debate. See the Appendix.

As for 2 Cor. 5:19-21, although I do not pretend to have untied all the knots: *First*, what is this 'reconciliation'? *katallagē* 'has two sides. It is first a reconciliation [by which God] laid aside his holy anger against our sins, and received us into favour, a reconciliation effected for us once for all by Christ upon his cross; so 2 Cor. 5:18-19; Rom. 5:10... But *katallagē* is secondly and subordinately the reconciliation... under the operation of the Holy Spirit, of the enmity of the [sinner] toward God... (2 Cor. 5:20)... All attempts to make this secondary [meaning] to be indeed the primary meaning and intention of the word, [suffer from two fundamental flaws; they] rest not on an unprejudiced exegesis [that is, they are based not only on a prejudiced exegesis], but on a foregone determination to get rid of the reality of God's anger against the sinner. [The truth is,] with *katallagē* is connected all that language of Scripture which describes sin as a state of enmity... with God (Rom. 8:7; Eph. 2:15; Jas. 4:4), and sinners as enemies to him and alienated from him (Rom. 5:10; Col. 1:21); which sets forth Christ on the cross as the peace and the maker of peace between God and man (Eph. 2:14; Col. 1:20); [and] all such invitations as this: "Be reconciled with God" (2 Cor. 5:20)' (Trench p292). In other words, reconciliation is primarily the objective work God accomplished in Christ to deal with his wrath against sinners in order to receive them into his favour. God in Christ reconciled all for whom Christ died. Christ, therefore, reconciled the elect; he died for *them*. For, as with redemption, design or intention is the key to reconciliation: 'It is impossible to think of the reconciling action apart from the design' (John Murray: *Collected* Vol.4 p107; see also *Redemption* pp33-42).
Secondly, as for 'world', in addition to what I have said elsewhere throughout this book, and the sources I have specified for more detailed comment – which see – I observe that 2 Cor. 5:19-21 is part of Paul's argument which starts in verse 11. Note the repeated 'for' or 'therefore' (verses 11,12,13,14,16,17), not forgetting the 'now' (verses 18,20), and 'that is' (verse 19) – all words of reasoned argument. Especially note how Paul immediately follows verses 14-15 (for my comments on these verses, see the Appendix); his 'therefore' has to be accounted for: '*Therefore*, from now on, we regard no one according to the flesh. Even though we have known Christ according to the flesh, yet now we know him thus no longer' (verse 16). 'According to the flesh', 'after the flesh', here means, 'by what he is in the flesh' (NASB margin); 'we do not judge a man by his nationality, background or status'; 'we do not boast in appearance' (see verse 12); 'we do not form our opinion of another on the basis of flesh – neither his or ours'. But why 'therefore'? and why 'from now on'? Before conversion, Paul used to judge – evaluate –

every thing and every man from a Jewish standpoint; he viewed things through Jewish spectacles; he thought only for Jews; he had no time for Gentiles. But being converted, his eyes are now opened. He has come to see that God loves all men in general, and savingly loves his elect – both Jew and Gentile. Indeed, he knows that Christ died for all the elect whether Jew or Gentile. Therefore, says the apostle, we now view all things through these new-covenant spectacles. We think no longer in Jewish/Gentile terms. In particular, since Christ has redeemed his people (whether Jew and Gentile) by his precious blood, how can we let our approach to men – unbelievers – be coloured by nationality, background, class, wealth, or anything other than the fact that they are sinners? And, of course, as for Paul and his attitude towards sinners, so for all believers. 'For the love of Christ compels us' since we have now come to think, realise ('we judge thus'): 'One died for all' the elect, whether Jew or Gentile (verse 14; as I say, see the Appendix for my arguments). So much for the 'therefore' and 'from now on' of verse 16. But Paul has not finished with his use of 'therefore' – he has not come to the end of these consequences; the 'therefore' continues into the next verse: '*Therefore*, if anyone is in Christ, he is a new creation; old things have passed away; behold, all things have become new' (2 Cor. 5:17). And one of these 'new' things is this consideration of the lost. We don't think of them as Jews or Gentiles – they are sinners, men. This theme of 'humanity', as I noted earlier, starts (if not with 2 Cor. 2:12) with 2 Cor. 5:11 ('We persuade' – we try to persuade – '*men*'), and continues throughout the passage until 2 Cor. 6:2, if not 2 Cor. 6:10, and beyond. See 2 Cor. 4:2,15 (NASB, NIV); 5:19 (NIV); 8:21; 9:13. So when Paul here talks about 'the world' (2 Cor. 5:19), he means the world as men, humanity, Jews and Gentiles, not merely Jews; in short, sinners. Paul was the apostle who was given 'the clear insight that [Christ's] atonement nullifies all other grounds for relationship with God, so that Gentile and Jew together are accepted freely by grace' (Fee p722). Just so! Christ 'is our peace, who has made both [Jew and Gentile] one, and has broken down the middle wall of separation, having abolished in his flesh the enmity, that is, the law of commandments contained in ordinances, so as to create in himself one new man from the two, thus making peace, and that he might reconcile them both to God in one body through the cross, thereby putting to death the enmity. And he came and preached peace to you who were afar off and to those who were near. For through him we both have access by one Spirit to the Father' (Eph. 2:14-18). See also Acts 10:44-46; 11:15-18; 15:7-18; Rom. 1:16; 1 Cor. 1:20-24; 12:13; Gal. 3:28-29; Eph. 2:11-13; 3:6-10; Col. 1:20-23,28;

3:11-12; Heb 2:14-17; Rev. 5:9. 'The world' in 2 Cor. 5:19 means men as sinners.

Thirdly, I move on to the idea of 'sufficiency'. The reconciliation God accomplished in Christ, I note, is not said to be merely 'sufficient'. There is not a hint or whisper of 'sufficiency' about it. It reads as an absolute accomplished reconciliation, all of a piece with those other passages of Scripture which, as I have said, have nothing tentative about them whatsoever (Rom. 8:29-34; Eph. 1:1-14; 5:25; 1 Thess. 5:10; 2 Thess. 2:13-14; 2 Tim. 1:9-10). As for 2 Cor. 5:19-21, to those for whom Christ died, in his death, on the cross, God was not imputing their trespasses, because he made the sinless Christ sin for all of them, and made them – all of them – righteous in the Redeemer. He did not do it sufficiently; *he did it!* And he did it for all of them and to all of them. The notion of 'sufficiency' grievously diminishes the reconciliation here described; imputation and substitution are at its heart; that which Christ wrought is effectual or nothing. It can, therefore, be only for the elect. Haldane: '"God has made him to be sin for *us*" (who [now] believe); *we* are made the righteousness of God in him. The two clauses are co-extensive; those for whom Christ was made sin are made the righteousness of God in him. If we understand *us* for whom he was made sin, to include all, it necessarily follows that *we* who are made the righteousness of God in him, must likewise include all mankind' (Haldane p261, emphasis his). John Murray: 'The death of Christ as reconciling action cannot be interpreted as something broader in its scope and intent than the final outcome of reconciliation bestowed'. Murray argued his case (John Murray: *Collected* Vol.4 p110). Clifford was wrong to say: 'God is reconcilable to all, even if all are not actually reconciled' (Clifford: *Atonement* pp126,135). *Reconcilability* is *not* what the passage teaches; *reconcilability* is *not* what Paul said. On the cross, God was reconciling the world to himself – not making himself reconcilable to the world; that is, in Christ, he was removing the offence, not merely making it possible to have the offence removed. Davenant, accordingly, was mistaken to say: 'To "have reconciled the world" generally [note the gloss] can mean nothing else than to have ordained and granted to the world that universal remedy or propitiatory sacrifice of the death of Christ, which is applicable to [Davenant's phrase for 'provided or sufficient for'] all'. Certainly not! Christ accomplished *reconciliation* – not a *sufficient* or *applicable* reconciliation. As Davenant himself rightly declared: 'This reconciliation, this not imputing of sins... is considered as performed on the part of God and Christ, as soon as Christ is understood to have laid down his life' (Davenant p28). 'It is finished' (John 19:30); it is (see Thayer)

---

performed, executed, completed, fulfilled, accomplished according to God's appointment.

Fourthly, we must not confuse Paul's *explanation* of that reconciliation, as here (2 Cor. 5:18-21) given to the Corinthian *believers*, with what he *actually preached* to *unbelievers*. Let me emphasise this by stressing the obvious but easily-forgotten fact; *these verses were written to believers*; these verses are Paul's explanation – for them – not only of how he preached to sinners, what he aimed for in that preaching, and of how God used him and worked through him in it, but also of Christ's reconciliation which they – the believers – had experienced. We must be careful to distinguish the two. The apostle was not for a moment implying that this explanation was a part of his addresses to the ungodly, that he had lifted these words straight out of one of his discourses to unbelievers. This is no 'cut-and-paste' job. He was not saying – or even implying – that he included the sinners who heard him – those whom he implored to come to Christ – that he included *them* in the 'us', in the reconciled. He would have had no way of knowing such a thing! Paul did not say that in his preaching he told sinners that Christ had reconciled *them* (not even sufficiently or provisionally). Rather, he told the Corinthians, we – as 'ambassadors for Christ' (verse 20) – we have been given 'the ministry or word of reconciliation' (verses 18-19), 'the message of reconciliation' (verse 19 NIV). What is this 'word of reconciliation'? It is, as he explained, 'as though God were pleading through us: we implore you on Christ's behalf, be reconciled to God' (verse 20; see below for the 'you'). This is a description of his 'ministry'; this is what he was about – his ministry as a fellow-worker with God (2 Cor. 6:1), God in Christ working through him (2 Cor. 5:20; 13:3), pleading with sinners, imploring them to come to Christ and be reconciled to God. This is what he aimed for in his preaching – sinners to be converted.

But what did he preach in this ministry? What did he say to sinners? Not: 'For he made him to be sin for us, that we might become the righteousness of God in him' (verse 21). This is *not* what the apostle told unbelievers; this does *not* form 'part of the word of reconciliation' (contrary to Alford p278). Nor even as Hodge, that verse 21 'is designed to *enforce* the preceding [verse 20]. "Be reconciled to God, for [even Hodge admitted the 'for' is 'doubtful' – it should, however, be omitted; see Vincent Vol.2 p824; Alford p278; NASB; NIV] an abundant and trustworthy provision has been made for your reconciliation [to] and acceptance [with God]"' (Hodge: *2 Corinthians* p147, emphasis mine). No! Paul was not here *enforcing* his preaching to *sinners*; rather, he was *explaining* to *believers* what God in Christ has accomplished for *them* –

indeed, for *us*, the elect of God – that on the cross, Christ was made sin for *us* that *we* might become the righteousness of God in him, that he might reconcile *us* to himself. Colin Kruse: 'This is the way Paul (in this letter) describes the basis upon which God reconciled us to himself'. As Kruse went on to say: 'From this statement we get some idea why the cross... had such a great motivating power in the apostle's life' (Kruse p128). Hodge: 'The apostle states in this verse [21] what God has done for the justification of men' (Hodge: *2 Corinthians* p147); that is, done for the justification of the elect.

We must be clear: Paul did not tell sinners that Christ was made sin for *us*, in the sense of including *them*; that *they* along with *us* have become the righteousness of God in Christ; that *they* were reconciled to God in Christ, that *their* sins had been imputed to Christ, and so on. Certainly not! Paul would never had told unbelievers that they were included in verses 19 & 21 – as I have pointed out, he would not have known such a thing – could not have known such a thing – until they had come to faith; in which case, of course, they would not have been unbelievers. That he spoke to unbelievers (as in verse 19) about the atonement, yes (1 Cor. 1:18,21,23; 2:2; Gal. 3:1; 6:14; see also 2 Cor. 4:5); and that he pleaded with them to 'be reconciled to God' through that atonement (verse 20), yes; but that he assured them that Christ had been made sin for them in order that they might become the righteousness of God in him, so that their sins were never to be imputed to them, cannot be proved. Indeed, to tell them such a thing would have been downright wrong. Not all who heard Paul preaching were saved (Acts 17:32; 24:24-27; 26:24-32; 28:24-29, for instance) – could they go away claiming that Paul had told them they had been reconciled to God, that they had been made the righteousness of God in Christ? that their sins would never be imputed to them since Christ had borne them? and that Paul had assured them of all this? The suggestion is patent nonsense. We have no scriptural example of any preacher saying such a thing to unbelievers. See the earlier extract from Fuller: *Philanthropos* p226. For treatment similar to this on 2 Cor. 5:18-21, see 1 Cor. 15:1-11; the summary, 'the creed', given there, does not set out *verbatim* what the apostle preached to sinners (compare Acts 18:4-5). See Fee pp717-737.

In other words, I am suggesting the passage (2 Cor. 5:18-21) consists of a twofold series of parallel statements:

(i) The reconciliation itself: 'God has reconciled us to himself through Jesus Christ' (first part of verse 18). What is this 'reconciliation' (the last word of verse 18, in the Greek as well as the English)? Paul's explanation (note the 'that is', 'to wit' (AV), 'seeing that', 'because', or 'namely') follows immediately in the first part of verse 19: 'That is, that

---

God was in Christ reconciling the world to himself, not imputing their trespasses to them'. As Hodge said: 'This verse [19] is an explanation and confirmation of what precedes... It is an explanation of... the "reconciliation"' (Hodge: *2 Corinthians* p143). This reconciliation is further explained by the apostle: 'For he made him who knew no sin to be sin for us, that we might become the righteousness of God in him' (verse 21). So much for 'the reconciliation' itself. We must be careful, however, not to confuse the reconciliation *itself* with the *ministry* of that reconciliation: 'Our reconciliation to God is not the ministry of reconciliation' (Hodge: *2 Corinthians* p143).

(ii) The ministry of reconciliation: 'God... has given us the ministry of reconciliation' (second part of verse 18), 'the word of reconciliation' which he 'has committed to us' (second part of verse 19); that is, 'we are ambassadors for Christ, as though God were pleading through us: we implore you on Christ's behalf, be reconciled to God... We... plead with you not to receive the grace of God in vain... Behold, now is the accepted time; behold, now is the day of salvation' (2 Cor. 5:20; 6:1-2).

If this suggestion of a twofold series of statements is right, the first part of verse 18 is explained and expanded in the first part of verse 19, and in verse 21; this comprises 'the reconciliation', *that which Christ accomplished.* And the second part of verse 18 is repeated in the second part of verse 19, in verse 20, and in 2 Cor. 6:1-2; this comprises 'the ministry of reconciliation', *that which Paul did and aimed for in his preaching*. See John Murray: *Collected* Vol.4 pp108-110.

In other words, if **A** is **the reconciliation** and **B** is **the ministry of reconciliation**, the passage may be set out like this:

A: 'God... has reconciled us to himself through Jesus Christ' (verse 18).

B: 'God... has given us the ministry of reconciliation' (verse 18).

A: 'God was in Christ reconciling the world to himself, not imputing their trespasses to them' (verse 19).

B: 'God... has committed to us the word of reconciliation... We are ambassadors for Christ as though God were pleading through us: we implore you on Christ's behalf, be reconciled to God' (verses 19-20).

A: '[God] made him who knew no sin to be sin for us, that we might become the righteousness of God in him' (verse 21).

B: 'We then, as workers together with him also plead with you not to receive the grace of God in vain... Behold, now is the accepted time; behold, now is the day of salvation' (2 Cor. 6:1-2).

Or, to collate the statements:

A: **What God has done**: 'God... has reconciled us to himself through Jesus Christ... God was in Christ reconciling the world to himself, not

imputing their trespasses to them... he made him who knew no sin to be sin for us, that we might become the righteousness of God in him'.
B: What God has given us to do: 'God... has given us the ministry of reconciliation... God... has committed to us the word of reconciliation... We are ambassadors for Christ as though God were pleading through us: we implore you on Christ's behalf, be reconciled to God... We then, as workers together with him also plead with you not to receive the grace of God in vain... Behold, now is the accepted time; behold, now is the day of salvation'.
Objection: This does not take proper account of the 'you' in verse 20, and in 2 Cor. 6:1. Surely, if what has been suggested here is correct, Paul would have said to the Corinthians: 'We are ambassadors for Christ, as though God were pleading through us: we implore *them – unbelievers* – on Christ's behalf, be reconciled to God... We then, as workers together with him, also plead with *them* not to receive the grace of God in vain'. He would not have said: 'We implore *you...* be reconciled to God... we plead with *you*'.
Answer: Paul did not use 'you' in verse 20. His exact words are: 'For Christ therefore we are ambassadors, as it were God exhorting by us, we beseech for Christ: Be reconciled to God'. Paul did not say: 'As though God did beseech *you* by us; we pray *you* in Christ's stead' (AV) – the *you* has been added by the translators (AV, twice; NKJV, NASB, NIV, once). I do not say the translators were wrong in this – Paul would have used 'you' in his preaching (see my *Septimus Sears*) – but, for the reasons I have given, we must distinguish between, on the one hand, Paul's explanation of Christ's reconciliation, and, on the other, Paul's explanation of his ministry, especially his desire in that ministry. In short, verse 20 is a report or record of how and what he preached to sinners. When he preached, he would have used 'you', but in his report of that preaching, even if he had used 'you' (which he did not in verse 20), the Corinthians would have understood he was not addressing them! As I have said, verse 20 (which has no 'you' in it) could quite properly be translated: 'As though God did beseech *men* (sinners) by us; we pray *them* to be reconciled to God', parallel to: 'We persuade *men*' (2 Cor. 5:11). The same goes for 2 Cor. 6:1 where Paul *did* use 'you' – once, but not twice (AV). None of this, of course, applies to the apostle's use of 'us' and 'we' in verse 21 – as I have explained, this forms part of his explanation, for the Corinthians, of Christ's reconciliation of the elect. See James pp2-3; Fuller: *Worthy* p162; Haldane p260.
To sum up this long excursus: A detailed exposition of the first part of verse 19 expanded by verse 21 *is not* what we have to preach to sinners, but is an explanation for believers of what Christ accomplished for the

elect. It is also that which encourages us and compels us (2 Cor. 5:14) to discharge our responsibility in the preaching of the word of reconciliation to sinners. Of course, we have to preach the atonement to sinners, but there is no call to labour its extent when addressing them, since there is no apostolic precedent for so doing. I say it yet again: Yes, we have to preach the decrees, and the particular and substitutionary nature of Christ's redemption – but not as hindrances to sinners coming to Christ. Above all, for my purpose in this excursus, 2 Cor. 5:19-21 does *not* teach us that we have to preach Christ's redemption as sufficient for all, nor that such a supposed sufficiency is the basis and ground of making the free offer. For more on the passage, see my *Septimus Sears*. For more on its effect on preaching to sinners, see John Murray: *Collected* Vol.4 pp111-112; *Redemption* pp41-42.

[241] Owen: *Death* in *Works* Vol.10 p313.

[242] John Murray: *Collected* Vol.1 p84.

[243] See my *Offer* pp57-134; Iain Murray: *Spurgeon* pp73-75. Whatever opponents may say, even though we cannot resolve every difficulty, this does not mean that there is no defence whatsoever. In fact, the boot is on the other foot. 'Those who wish to point to a disparity between the universality of the offer and the definiteness of the atonement should be prepared to show that on these terms something is lacking that must be rated an indispensable component of any well-meant offer' (Nicole p337). For this reason, with respect I urge you, reader, not to forget the points already made in this section of my book under the questions: 1. What is *not* offered in the free offer? 2. What *is* offered in the free offer? 3. To whom is the offer made? 4. What is the warrant for the free offer? There is nothing in what I have said under these heads which demands universal atonement or precludes particular redemption (or total depravity, unconditional election or irresistible grace). Nicole spelled out his version of what is required for a sincere offer: 'That if the terms of the offer be observed, that which is offered be actually granted. In connection with the gospel offer the terms are that a person should repent and believe. Whenever that occurs, salvation is actually conferred. There is not a single case on record in the whole history of mankind where a person came to God in repentance and faith and was refused salvation'. Nicole citing John 6:37 in both its parts, went on: 'Far from undermining the sincere offer of the gospel, the doctrine of definite atonement undergirds the call' (Nicole p340).

[244] 'We do not understand, for God has not explained, how he can offer to all that salvation which is ordained only for some. But we do not need to understand; we need simply to believe and to act upon the fact. We are expected to do so, moreover, without the slightest hesitation. Far

from inhibiting the sincere offer of the gospel to all, the definiteness of the atonement undergirds it. For what is offered is not a potential but an actual salvation, irrevocably secured, "redemption accomplished"... There is salvation for everyone who comes' (Donnelly p5).

245 ''Tis vain to offer that to man,/ Man has no will or power to take' (hyper-Calvinistic hymn quoted by Randalls in his prelims). If this is true, then 'tis vain to tell the unconverted anything except 'the elect have obtained it, and the rest were blinded' (Rom. 11:7). However, it would only be 'vain' to offer salvation to sinners, commanding them to come to Christ, if God had not warranted us to do it, but since he has, it must be anything but 'vain'; and not to do it, disobedience. See below and my *Offer* pp1-55. Hawker's statement (quoted by Burrows p24): 'The free offer presupposes that man, in his natural state, is not so far dead in trespasses and sins, as to be unable to fall in with these tenders, invitations and offers; but that he is able to do this, which is both pleasing and acceptable to God', is, of course, completely untrue. The free offer presupposes the exact opposite; sinners are utterly dead in sin and totally unable to respond to the gospel in their natural state. Hawker went on: 'The free offer must presuppose this [ability in the sinner] or [else] these offers are inefficient, futile and vain'. According to human logic, Hawker was right, but according to Scripture he could not have been further from the truth.

246 Fuller: 'Objections to the foregoing principles, from the doctrine of election, are generally united with those from particular redemption; and, indeed, they are so connected that the validity of the one stands or falls with that of the other' (Fuller: *Worthy* p170). And reprobation, but this, of course, does not appear in the five points. According to hyper-Calvinists, 'the well-meant offer is... in conflict with... total depravity, particular redemption and unconditional election. But it contradicts none of these other doctrines so plainly as it does the doctrine of reprobation. Reprobation means exactly and explicitly the opposite of the well-meant offer' (Hanko p7). It does not. Take Rom. 9:18-22; 11:7-10 with Rom. 10:21, for instance.

247 Meney: 'All free-offer preachers... generally ignore anything to do with God's electing decrees, the divine source of repentance and faith, the purposely limited extent of the atonement and the necessity of Holy Spirit regeneration' – or worse! (Ella: *The Free Offer* p6). For more of the same, see my *Offer* pp137-144. How can this sort of thing be said in light of what I have written, plus the copious citations and extracts I have supplied from Owen, Bunyan, Edwards, Whitefield, Booth, Fuller, Spurgeon and the like?

---

[248] See Owen: *Death* in *Works* Vol.10 pp409-410; Edwards: *Freedom* pp87-88. Take but just one example of the sort of thing I am talking about. God, through Ahijah, told Jeroboam he would use him to tear Israel apart after the death of Solomon. God promised Jeroboam that if he then obeyed his commands, he would build him a house as lasting as David's (1 Kings 11:29-39). God told him his duty – to obey his commands; and he set out the promised benefit – the enduring kingdom of Israel. God, it goes without saying, was sincere in this command and promise given to Jeroboam through Ahijah. But all the while, he knew (to put it no stronger), that Jeroboam would turn out to be a notorious sinner, would not obey his commands, and would not get an enduring kingdom. But none of this comprised the original command and promise. Again, there is no reason to doubt Ahijah's sincerity in what he said, but, of course, he was unaware of what the outcome would be. As before, none of this compromised the original command and promise or hindered him addressing Jeroboam in this way. So it is with the gospel offer.

[249] We should go only as far as the Bible warrants us, and not resort to philosophy and speculation (see my *Offer* pp80-81). As above, see 1 Cor. 4:6. The believer 'should avoid indulging his curiosity by plunging into questions that God in his wisdom has not seen fit to answer' (Nettles p281). Calvin warned against 'human curiosity, which cannot be restrained from wandering into forbidden paths, and climbing to the clouds'. As he said: 'The word of the Lord is the only way which can conduct us to the investigation of whatever it is lawful for us to hold with regard to him – is the only light which can enable us to discern what we ought to see with regard to him'. Keeping this in mind 'will curb and restrain all presumption'. 'Let us not be ashamed to be ignorant in a matter in which ignorance is learning. Rather let us willingly abstain from the search after knowledge, to which it is both foolish as well as perilous, and even fatal to aspire. If an unrestrained imagination urges us, our proper course is to oppose it' (Calvin: *Institutes* Vol.2 pp203-204). Davenant: The reason 'why [God] should give [faith] to some and not give it to others, ought not to be enquired [of], since it cannot be solved; but must be referred to the secret will of God... [From Acts 13:38,46,48, we learn that] the death of Christ is proposed and offered to mankind without distinction... [but] faith... is produced in them that believe through the special favour of a merciful God. And here the mystery of election at length presents itself... But why, in dispensing the treasure of the merits of Christ... [God] acts so unequally with persons in equal circumstances, we ought not to enquire, since we cannot ascertain, but with the apostle acquiesce in the secret will of God' (Davenant

pp24,27,40,54-56). Irfon Hughes: 'It may seem to us that there is an inconsistency between believing that Christ died for the elect, and offering the hope of the gospel indiscriminately to all... but the secret purposes of God are not our concern' (Hughes p21). See Donnelly p7.

[250] In particular, a universally sufficient or provisional atonement, allowing it for the moment, would fail to justify the free offer in light of total depravity, unconditional election and irresistible grace. Take Davenant: 'God is not bound to procure the [actual] application of his remedy to any individual to whom he has willed that it should be applicable [that is, provided for]... The death of Christ... may be both announced and applied to [that is, preached as provided for] every individual of the human race for the remission of sins, yet God is not bound by any promise to procure that it should be announced and actually applied to every individual' (Davenant p47). In other words, God may provide redemption for every man yet not make it effective to every man; but this does not preclude the free offer. While I do not accept Davenant's premise – a provisional redemption for all – his argument is right; the free offer is not hindered by God's decree in election, particular redemption or effectual calling. We may not be able to understand it – but that is not our business. See Nicole pp334-342.

[251] According to the Amyraldian, 'unbelievers are also rejecting redemption provided. Otherwise, the gospel command is a command to make bricks without straw! God only commands us to accept what is given in Christ. Your definition of "particular redemption" entails that God commands unbelievers to accept something which turns out to be nothing' (Clifford's e-mail to me, 9th Feb. 2005). Again: 'It is clear that unbelievers are guilty of rejecting nothing if Christ was not given for them; unbelief surely involves the rejection of a definite provision of grace... If nothing substantial is really on offer to all, then ungrateful unbelief is quite meaningless' (Clifford: *Atonement* pp112,156; see also *Atonement* pp74,113-114). No! I have answered this before. Unbelievers are guilty of defiance – they will not submit to God in repentance and faith; they are guilty of despising the promise of Christ and full salvation. Again, the gospel command *is* a command to sinners 'to make bricks without straw', in the sense of demanding the impossible. I made this clear in my *Offer* pp1-55. Ezekiel's call to the dry bones, Christ's command to the man with the withered arm, to the paralytic, his call to the dead Lazarus, Jairus' daughter and the corpse at Nain, all illustrate the point.

Here, as I have said, is the root of this entire debate – the clash between human logic and God's word. Human logic says that since all men are offered salvation, Christ must have died provisionally for them all

(Amyraldianism), or Christ's redemption must be sufficient for all (Owenism); but God in his word teaches that Christ has died for his elect only, and absolutely for them, yet all men must be offered salvation. Again, human logic says that since the sinner is commanded to repent and believe, he must have the ability to respond (Arminianism), or since he has no power to respond, the sinner must not be commanded (hyper-Calvinism); but God in his word teaches that the sinner is dead, yet must be commanded! As Randalls rightly pointed out: 'Man has as much ability to come to Christ as the dead have to sit up in their coffins!' (Randalls p28), but in preaching to sinners, as Christ illustrated by the very case (Luke 7:11-17), we *have* to preach to dead sinners commanding them to repent and believe – and when a sinner by God's grace is regenerated and converted, this is precisely what happens – the dead live! We do not command sinners to come to Christ because they have the power 'to sit up in their coffins', but because God calls us to do it, and because he gives power through his preached word to enable sinners to come to Christ. Christ in the gospel does the impossible: 'Then the eyes of the blind shall be opened, and the ears of the deaf shall be unstopped. Then the lame shall leap like a deer, and the tongue of the dumb sing' (Isa. 35:5-6). That which Christ did physically (Luke 7:22), he accomplishes by (what the natural man would call the foolishness of) using preachers to preach his gospel to the spiritually dead, blind, deaf, lame and dumb; that is, using those, who have no power in themselves to effect the change required, to preach to those who have no power in themselves to respond.

Spurgeon, preaching on Christ's command to the corpse of the young man at Nain: Christ 'spoke as if the man had been alive. This is the gospel way. He did not wait until he saw signs of life before he bade him rise; but to the dead man he said: "Arise". This is the model of gospel preaching: in the name of the Lord Jesus, his commissioned servants speak to the dead as if they were alive. Some of my brethren cavil at this, and say that it is inconsistent and foolish; but all through the New Testament it is even so. There we read: "Arise from the dead, and Christ shall give you light". I do not attempt to justify it; it is more than enough for me that so I read the word of God. We are to bid men believe on the Lord Jesus Christ, even though we know that they are dead in sin, and that faith is the [gift] of the Spirit of God. Our faith enables us in God's name to command dead men to live, and they do live. We bid unbelieving man believe in Jesus, and power goes with the word, and God's elect do believe. It is by this word of faith which we preach that the voice of Jesus sounds out to men. The young man who could not rise, for he was dead, nevertheless did rise when Jesus bade him. Even so, when the Lord speaks by his servants, the gospel command: "Believe and live", is obeyed, and men live' (Spurgeon: *Metropolitan* Vol.34 p33; see also Vol.30 p492). If I may use Spurgeon's words, as to the seeming contradiction in all this: 'I do not attempt to justify it'.

Philpot: 'Some of the dry, hardened, letter Calvinists deny [human] responsibility, because, according to their opinions, it is inconsistent with God's eternal decrees and the doctrine of predestination... To which we answer: If we take the Scriptures as a divine revelation, we must receive them implicitly, without questioning or cavilling, but in the spirit and temper of a little child. Now the doctrines of divine predestination and of human responsibility each stand as separate truths on their own individual basis. We may not be able fully and clearly to reconcile them, as we may not be in possession of, or in our present state be able to comprehend a third truth, which would reconcile them completely... [uniting] two apparently discordant links. So there may be, and doubtless is an intermediate link between divine predestination and human responsibility, which God has not seen fit to reveal, either for the exercise of our faith, or because it surpasses our present comprehension' (Philpot: 'Review' p55). Would that all Philpot's pupils had followed their teacher!

All ***non-****'dry, hardened, letter Calvinists' (to use Philpot's phrase) have to admit a seeming contradiction somewhere in the chain of redemption.* All of them, I say. Consistent hyper-Calvinists don't – Philpot was inconsistent with his creed here – but all other Calvinists do. The Amyraldian places it where election and the free offer meet; the Owenite, where particular redemption and the free offer meet. I place it – where I argue the Bible does – in the twofold will of God; namely, the decree to save the elect and the desire to save all. While I dissent from Davenant's view that Christ died to provide salvation sufficient for all, nevertheless he was right to say of the seeming clash with the doctrine of election: 'But let us not by an unreasonable and too deep speculation into an awful [that is, full of awe] subject, draw a veil over that divine philanthropy from which has emanated... [as he saw it, a provisional redemption sufficient for all] though certainly effectual only to all those who believe' (Davenant pp27-28). If I may paraphrase: Let us not, by speculation, reject the twofold will of God which is so clearly revealed in Scripture, and thus bury the free offer under a mound of human logic.

[252] Is it not patent that every article of the faith ends defeating our poor minds? Who can understand and explain (by human logic) the trinity, creation, redemption, the resurrection, eternity and all the rest? It is 'by faith we understand that the worlds were framed by the word of God' (Heb. 11:3).

[253] 'I confess these things [Fuller was speaking of another issue, but the principle applies] may look like contradictions... and, perhaps... we shall never be fully able, in the present state, to explain [them]... but... the fact is revealed abundantly in Scripture; and it does not distress me, if in this matter I have, all my life, to walk by faith, and not by sight' (Fuller: *Philanthropos* p231; see also p229). On reconciling the free offer with particular redemption, Fuller said: 'Whether I can perfectly reconcile these statements with each other... I believe they are both taught in the Scriptures'. Then he added, somewhat ironically: 'But I acknowledge that I do not at present perceive their inconsistency' (Fuller: *Six Letters* p321). Neither do I. As he said: 'There is no contradiction between this peculiarity of design in the death of Christ, and a universal obligation on those who hear the gospel to believe in him, or a universal invitation being addressed to them. If God, through the death of his Son, has promised salvation to all who comply with the gospel... [then] exhortations and invitations to believe and be saved are consistent; and our duty, as preachers of the gospel, is to administer them, without any more regard to particular redemption than to election; both being secret things, which belong to the Lord our God, and which, however they be a rule to him, are none to us. If that which sinners are called upon to believe respected the particular design of Christ to save them, it would then be inconsistent; but [the truth is] they are neither exhorted nor invited to believe anything but what is revealed, and what will prove true, whether they believe it or not' (Fuller: *Worthy* p171). 'Neither does it belong to me to show how... a limitation of design is consistent with universal invitations; but I believe it to be so, because he that has ordered the one has, in effect, declared the other. Vain men may ask: "Why then does he yet find fault; for who has resisted his will?" But if, instead of "replying against God", they were to throw themselves at the feet of sovereign mercy, and seek forgiveness in the name of Jesus, it would turn to a better account' (Fuller: *Sermons* p597).
Edward Donnelly: 'The objectors to a universal gospel offer have been seduced into error by spurious logic, and we must not allow what seems reasonable to our little minds to intimidate us into placing limitations upon the kindness of God' (Donnelly p3). Kennedy: 'Why, if God designed only the salvation of some, does he address the gospel call to all without distinction?... How can an earnest call be addressed by God to those whom he does not [electingly-savingly] love?' Kennedy said of these questions: 'Many a fool's attempt has been made to answer... The gracious design of God, in the preaching of the gospel, is the salvation of the elect through faith in Christ... Why then, it is asked, is the gospel preached to all? The answer must be, that "so it seemed good" in the

sight of God... The difficulty felt by many minds in dealing with the second question... is one of their own creation... All, who hear the gospel, are required by God, to believe in Christ, in order that the promise of salvation may be theirs in him' (Kennedy pp45-47).

[254] Christ preached in this way: 'No one can come to me unless the Father who sent me draws him' (total depravity); 'all that the Father gives me' (unconditional election), 'will come to me' (irresistible grace); 'this is the work of God, that you believe in him whom he sent' (duty faith); 'the one who comes to me I will by no means cast out... he who believes in me has everlasting life' (the promise) (John 6:22-59). (I believe also that particular redemption is in the passage, but it would be too much of a digression to establish it here – see the Appendix for indications of my approach). In light of the attitude of the hearers shown by their (sneering) questions, note Jesus' repeated emphasis upon duty faith (John 6:29,35-37,40,45,47,50-51,53-58,64). See my *Offer* pp26-39. See below for Matt. 11:25-30.

Bunyan offered Christ to all, both elect and reprobate (Bunyan: *Reprobation* in *Works* Vol.3 pp279-291), not baulking at issues such as: 'Whether eternal reprobation in itself, or in its doctrine, is in very deed a hindrance to any man in seeking the salvation of his soul?... Whether God would, indeed and in truth, that the gospel, with the grace thereof, should be tendered to those that yet he has bound up under eternal reprobation?... Seeing then that the grace of God in the gospel is... to be proffered to sinners as sinners, as well to the reprobate as the elect, is it possible for those who indeed are not elect, to receive it, and be saved?' Of course, the non-elect cannot, will not, be saved – but since no preacher or any sinner knows who (prior to believing) is elect (and who is not!), all are to be offered salvation, all are to be commanded to trust Christ. Those who come to Christ will demonstrate that they were the objects of God's eternal saving grace and love. Bunyan was unequivocal: 'The gospel is to be tendered to all in general, as well to the reprobate as to the elect, to sinners as sinners; and so they are to receive it, and to close with the tenders thereof'.

[255] As Booth, replying to those who cavil at unconditional election: 'Without paying the least compliment to the learning, sagacity or character of any who dare to arraign the divine conduct, [Scripture] repels their insolence in the following blunt manner: [Rom. 9:20]' (Booth: *Reign* p56). 'It is the LORD. Let him do what seems good to him' (1 Sam. 3:18).

[256] See my *Offer* pp57-134. Just after issuing a promiscuous command (or invitation) to sinners to come to Christ for salvation (Isa. 55:1-7), God declares: '"For my thoughts are not your thoughts, nor are your

ways my ways", says the LORD. "For as the heavens are higher than the earth, so are my ways higher than your ways, and my thoughts than your thoughts"' (Isa. 55:8-9). Edward J.Young: 'The ways and thoughts of God are incomprehensible to man. Even though God reveal them to man, he cannot fully understand them; to him they are incomprehensible' (Young p383); that is, even if God did reveal them, man could not understand. Rom. 11:33-36 sums it up.

[257] Douty: 'It is impossible to explain why we are commanded to preach the gospel... to all, if Christ did not die for all. If he did not die for all, there is no good news for all'. I disagree with the second sentence, but agree with first – even though Douty himself was dismissing the free offer 'if Christ did not die for all'. I agree that 'it is impossible to explain' – but the fact is we have no need or warrant to try to find an explanation. God has commanded us to preach the gospel, so we do it. I agree with Douty: 'The two ideas, of limited atonement and universal offer, create a tension too great for the ablest of particular redemption men to relieve'; that is, by human logic. But I disagree with him when he went on: 'How can God authorise his servants to offer pardon to the non-elect if Christ did not purchase it for them?' (Douty pp40-41). I have answered this. Take, for instance, the episode with Ahijah and Jeroboam, mentioned earlier. On Douty's premise, how could God offer Jeroboam the kingdom when he had not decreed he should have it? The mistake, of course, is to ask the question. Rom. 9:20!

[258] 'Many cannot be satisfied with this. In the pride of their heart, they say God could not call unless man could comply – indeed, that it would be unjust in God to exhort, call and urge, to what man had yet to get the help of God to do; and, increasing in boldness as they advance in this course, they ask whether it is not a mockery, unworthy of God, to call dead men to walk, and impotent to rise, and all to do what he knows no man can do without his special grace given to them?... [To this] *first* of all, we would say, however startling it may appear at first sight, that God *can* command what men are utterly unable to fulfil... else God's right of sovereignty would be measured by man's willingness to comply with it... *Secondly*... God *can* blame and punish man for not doing what... he cannot do – else the more depraved man became, the less blameable he would become... A proud objector will triumphantly say, and a trembling soul will sometimes also anxiously ask: How can you consistently offer what is not really designed to be given?... You offer what is not there; there is nothing in your system except an offer; there is nothing behind it; there is no reality. But where is it, we ask, that there is nothing?... Is it in the work of Christ that there is nothing? There is [a] glorious sufficiency in it. The atonement is complete; nothing needs to

be [done], nothing can be added to it... Is it in the offer that there is nothing? There is the most blessed certainty – the largest, the fullest extent in it – and what could there be more of in any offer? But, still, proud man... asks: How can you sincerely offer what you say... may not be God's design actually to bestow?... How can God offer that to all which is not meant for all? This, instead of an offer of mercy, is but mocking and deceiving man... No! God neither mocks nor deceives anyone... There is no deceit... Whosoever believes [the promise], and claims [better, pleads] the fulfilment, to him shall it be made fully and gloriously good, and good for ever... Putting down, then, all such contendings against God... let us... rejoice in the full warrant which every minister has to offer Christ to all – and the full warrant which each [sinner] has to receive Christ for himself' (John Bonar pp12-16,18-19, emphasis mine). Moreover, God not only *can* command sinners to do what they cannot do, and punish them for not doing it – he *does* and *will*. In quoting this from Bonar, let me remind you, reader, that to say Christ is all-sufficient, is not the same as saying his redemption is sufficient for all.

Lloyd-Jones on the issue of the sinner being under the wrath of God: 'If you believe that the Bible is divinely inspired, then you must not say: "But I don't understand". You are not asked to understand. I do not understand it, I do not pretend to understand it. But I start from this basis, that my mind is not only finite but is, furthermore, sinful, and I cannot possibly understand fully the nature of God and the justice and the holiness of God. If we are going to base everything on our understanding, then we might as well give up at this point... The business of preaching is not to ask people to understand'. Again: 'Ah, you say, I do not understand that, I cannot grasp that, it seems to me almost immoral. Of course you do not understand it. Who can understand such things? It is not a question of understanding, it is a question of whether you believe the Scriptures or not' (Lloyd-Jones: *Way* pp54,57).

[259] Nettles p306; see also p274. I do not agree with Nettles when he extends this to calling. God has revealed that he does have a twofold will in calling – the general, outward, universal call (his will of desire), and the particular, inward, effective call (his will of decree). Election and the atonement are, however, to do with God's will of decree, and this is single. God's decrees are secret, within himself; his desires are open, revealed.

[260] How many unbelievers actually raise the problem of squaring the free offer and particular redemption? If they do, is it because their preachers have been teaching them the ramifications of particular redemption, and

thus raising the problem for them? If so, what biblical example do we have of a preacher doing such thing? As I explained in my *Offer* xii-xiii, pp112,114, we should not so preach the decrees as to stifle the offer. As for unbelievers asking the question, I suspect it is far more commonly raised by (hyper) Calvinists, over-anxious about what they think unbelievers *ought* to feel! and when unbelievers do ask it, it is because their teachers have given them the problem in the first place!

[261] See Owen: *Death* in *Works* Vol.10 pp404-410; my *Offer* p3; *Septimus Sears*. Kennedy: 'How vain is [the] faith that reaches not the living Christ of God! And does that faith not stop short of [Christ] which merely grasps a statement regarding the love of God or the death of Christ, and on that warrant [thinks he] appropriates the promise of salvation?' (Kennedy p48). To digress for a moment. This, I fear, is getting close to what is wrong with much preaching today. We must not stop at explaining facts to sinners; our responsibility is to try to persuade them, because of those facts, to repent of their sin and believe in Christ. I will come back to this. It is at the heart of what I am writing for.

[262] See Owen: *Death* in *Works* Vol.10 pp404-421.

[263] Donnelly p6.

[264] To those who objected that the doctrine of election hindered them in coming to Christ, Booth had this to say (his words apply equally to particular redemption): 'This objection, however plausible it may seem, or however much the conscience of an awakened sinner may be harassed by it, is weak and impertinent. It supposes that a person must know the divine appointment concerning him; that he must, as it were, peruse the eternal roll of God's decrees, and read his name in the book of life, before he can upon solid grounds apply to Christ for salvation. But this is a grand mistake... It is very evident that he has no business to enquire about any further right to partake... Complete provision is made for the certain salvation of every sinner, however unworthy, who feels his want and applies to Christ. The gospel is not preached to sinners, nor are they encouraged to believe in Jesus, under the formal notion of their being elected [or redeemed]. No; these tidings of heavenly mercy are addressed to sinners, considered as ready to perish... The order established in the economy of grace... does not require perishing sinners to prove their election [or particular redemption] before they are permitted, or have encouragement, to trust in Christ for complete deliverance; but seeing their state, they have all the encouragement which the word of Jehovah can give, without hesitation to rely on the Saviour; and all the assurance which the oath of God can impart... These things are evident from the tenor of divine revelation; and to conceive otherwise proceeds on a mistake of the doctrine, and is followed by an

abuse of the truth. Consequently it [unconditional election; the same goes for particular redemption and irresistible grace] administers no real occasion to discouragement or fear to the inquiring soul or the sensible sinner' (Booth: *Reign* pp81-83). Note Booth's use of 'impertinent', even when dealing with the *anxious* sinner. I will return to this in a moment. But in one respect I would go further than Booth; sinners are not only permitted and encouraged to trust Christ – they are commanded.

[265] See earlier note on the *anxious* sinner.

[266] 'He that believes in Jesus Christ must believe in him as he is revealed in the gospel, and that is the Saviour of sinners. It is only as a sinner, exposed to the righteous displeasure of God, that he must approach him' (Fuller: *Worthy* p171). A sinner has to 'come' to Christ (Matt. 11:28; John 6:37,44,65), not 'strut' to him. 'Whoever does not receive the kingdom of God as a little child will by no means enter it' (Mark 10:15; Luke 18:17).

[267] See my *Septimus Sears*.

[268] '"He that will know his own particular redemption before he will believe," says [Elisha Coles], "begins at the wrong end"' (Fuller: *Worthy* p171).

[269] 'What the natural man needs above everything else is to be humbled. This is essential before we can do anything with him. The ultimate trouble with the natural man is his pride. This point is worked out in [1 Cor. 1:18-31]: "Where is the wise? Where is the scribe? Where is the disputer of this world?" And the apostle's argument is that what God does to this man is not to have a discussion with him but to make him look foolish. He has to be humbled because he glories in himself, whereas the Christian position is that "he who glories, let him glory in the LORD". The first thing to be done with the man who does not accept the Christian faith is to humble him. That is the first essential. "Has not God made foolish the wisdom of this world?" Or as our Lord himself put it: "Unless you are converted and become like little children, you will by no means enter the kingdom of heaven" (Matt. 18:3)... [See] Matt. 11:25-27' (Lloyd-Jones: *Preaching* pp49-50).

[270] This is the point I made just now. Hyper-Calvinists make a rod for their own back; worse, they take sinners into a bondage unknown in Scripture.

[271] See my *Offer* pp1-55. Robert Murray M'Cheyne: 'Perhaps you cannot explain why your names are not in the book of life [if indeed they are not!], and yet you are invited to come. But this is not the reason why you will not come. What then is the reason?... In the day of judgement... Christ will say: "I [would] have often gathered you as a hen gathers her brood under her wings, and you would not". I sent you my ministers...

but yet you would not come to me. I converted many by your side, and yet you would not come. O what will you say to the Lord of glory when he puts these accusations to you?' As M'Cheyne had said in an earlier sermon: 'Some will say, why did he not save Jerusalem, if he was willing? To this I answer, that you must take the gospel as you find it. It is not your business nor mine to enquire into anything of the sort. It is sufficient for us to know that he is willing to save. He said: "If any man thirsts, let him come unto me and drink". "He that comes to me I will in no wise cast out"' (M'Cheyne pp96,140).
Whatever ought to be made of Calvin's comments on Heb. 9:28, he put the responsibility for not being saved where it belongs: 'Their unbelief prevents them' (Calvin: *Commentaries* Vol.22 Part 1 p220). 'You are not willing to come to me that you may have life' (John 5:40). 'Some were convinced by what [Paul] said, but others would not believe' (Acts 28:24 NIV). No man will be able to excuse himself by saying 'Christ did not die for me! I was not elected!'. The ball is firmly in the sinner's court. So when Clifford asked: 'If unbelievers are guilty of rejecting Christ, whence their guilt, if Christ was not given for them?' (Clifford: *Atonement* p100), the answer is that Clifford has raised a *non-sequiter*. True, not all are saved, because not all are elect and redeemed – but this belongs to God's secret decree. As God's revealed will has made clear, not all are saved, because not all will believe. And for this, they are culpable. All who are damned, are damned because they did not, they would not, believe. 'In the gospel, salvation is offered promiscuously to all those to whom it is preached... This salvation which is... offered to men in the gospel, is neglected and repelled by many... [and] this neglect and unbelief is the true cause which prevents the ungodly from obtaining the rest of the Lord; that is, which deprives them of eternal life offered to them in Christ' (Davenant p30). I will return to this quotation from Davenant when dealing with his claim that universal redemption is the basis of the offer. As far as I have quoted him here, he was right.

[272] 'O sinner: Christ is the way, the truth and the life; there is no other by whom you can be saved; flee to him then as for your life; and let not Satan hinder you, by diverting you to impossibilities and *impertinences*. Comply with the call and offer of the gospel. This is [your] present and pertinent duty, and trouble not yourself about the secrets of God' (Boston: *Beauties* pp156-159, emphasis mine).

[273] I do not agree with Randalls' view of Rom. 10:21 (Randalls p57). God is not here stretching out his hands in judgement, but in mercy. The context is conclusive. See Calvin: *Commentaries* Vol.19 Part 2 p407; John Murray: *Romans* Vol.2 p63. Toplady, quoted by Philpot: 'The gospel of grace may be rejected, but the grace of the gospel cannot.

God's written message in the Scriptures, and his verbal message by his ministers, may or may not be listened to; whence it is recorded: "All day long I have stretched forth my hands unto a disobedient and gainsaying people" [Rom. 10:21]. But when God himself comes, and takes the heart into his own hands; when he speaks from heaven to the soul, and makes the gospel of grace a channel to convey the grace of the gospel, the business is effectually done' (*Gospel Standard* 1858 p52). Gill said the passage refers to 'the ministry of the prophets one after another to them, the preaching of John the Baptist, of Christ and his apostles among them', but they refused all these calls (Gill: *Commentary* Vol.6 p93). Did these preachers make no overtures of mercy? In any case, does God stand *all day* calling sinners to judgement? When God calls a sinner to judgement, he calls but once! Can any sinner refuse God's call to judgement? As for the reference to Prov. 1:24-33, yes, there is such a thing as God's judgement against those who... against those who do what? Against those who refuse his overtures of mercy, and calls to return (Prov. 1:24-25). See Isa. 65:2,12; 66:4; Jer. 6:10-34; 7:13-16; Zech. 7:4-14.

[274] Nor must it dampen our desire to see sinners saved. 'Paul, as has been already observed, believed and taught the doctrine of election; yet in the same epistle, indeed, in the same chapter, he declared his most anxious solicitude for the salvation of his unbelieving "brethren and kinsmen according to the flesh" [Rom. 9:1-3; 10:1]. And why? Because he desired anything contrary to the will of God? No; but not knowing what was the secret will of God respecting individuals, he was satisfied with obeying his commandments. God he well knew would regulate his own conduct by his wise and righteous decrees, but they could be no rule to him, inasmuch as they were utterly beyond his knowledge. It was for him to obey the precept, and to leave the issue to his disposal who "works all things after the counsel of his own will"' (Fuller: *Antinomianism* p345).

[275] Rushton, while steering well clear of the free offer, nevertheless made a most interesting comment. Naturally, he disagreed with Fuller, but he also distanced himself from Gill's view of Acts 3:19, in which he, Gill, tried to make out that Peter was there calling for attendance to ordinances, external repentance and such like (see also my *Offer* pp4,38,146-147). Allowing that Rushton restricted the way to approach sinners, nevertheless he admitted: 'While I firmly maintain eternal election and particular redemption... these doctrines are by no means inconsistent with the free exhibition of Christ to sinners as such, nor with the solemn calls and invitations of the gospel. So far from being inimical to scriptural warnings addressed to the unconverted, I think that

no minister of Christ is clear from the blood of all men who does not use them freely. How such calls are consistent with particular redemption, it does not lie upon me to explain, further than to observe that the publication of the gospel is the Lord's appointed means of gathering in his redeemed, and that as both these branches of divine truth are exhibited in the Scripture, they are perfectly concordant, whether we can point out the consistency or not. The gospel, in all its parts, is one grand harmonious whole, but... such are its heights and depths, that it can never be confined within the bounds of a human system... It becomes us to receive the kingdom of God as little children, to sit at the feet of Jesus, to learn of him, and to become fools, that we may be wise' (Rushton pp124-125). Randalls and Ella described Rushton's book as 'excellent' (do they attach the word to these sentiments?); Philpot gave him a mixed press (Randalls p98; Ella: *Gill* p306; Dix p103. But see Haykin p108).

[276] Dagg p330.

[277] Let us never forget some simple facts, so often overlooked: Sinners are saved by believing, not by understanding; preachers, too, are believers, not understanders of all the wonders of the gospel – and they are persuaders, not mere explainers. I am not, of course, in making these comments, belittling understanding or explaining the gospel. But the point stands. Sinners are called upon the repent and *believe*; and preachers must be able to adopt the apostle's language: 'We... *believe* and therefore speak' (2 Cor. 4:13). The centurion's attitude (Luke 7:1-10) must be ours. He trusted Christ's command, and staked his all upon it, confident that what Christ said, by his authority he would accomplish. In the Gospels, it is recorded that Christ marvelled at two things only; this man's faith (Luke 7:9), and the unbelief of the crowd (Mark. 6:6). See the earlier comment from Lloyd-Jones on 'understanding'.

[278] Dagg pp319,330-331, emphasis mine. John Bonar: 'If [since] all men are dead in trespasses and sins, and yet all men are called – if [since] Christ died for his people, to redeem them to God, yet salvation is offered to all – it follows necessarily that an obligation to spiritual duty is not inconsistent with total spiritual inability, and that a universal offer neither rests upon nor implies a universal atonement. Many think otherwise, and many who do not, are yet greatly perplexed by what such advance' (John Bonar p11).

[279] My *Offer* p97. I re-emphasise the point; as it *seems* to us.

[280] Iain Murray: *Spurgeon* pp74-75. I am pressing the need for our 'trust' and 'resolve' in this matter.

[281] Take total depravity. Using 'can' with precision – namely, 'has the power and ability necessary' – if the sinner is told he *must* come to

Christ and *can* come (Arminianism), he is deluded and puffed up, and God is robbed of his glory. If a sinner is told he *cannot* come, yet not told he *must* come (hyper-Calvinism), he is given the excuse to be complacent and blame God for his end. If a sinner is told he *cannot* come, but *must* come, yet only *God* can bring him (the biblical free offer), he is shut up to God, stripped of any feeling of merit, and God is glorified. See Duncan's speech quoted in John Bonar p16.

[282] See my *Offer* xi. James Henley Thornwell was most earnest with sinners; throughout his preaching there was 'a continual call to conversion, and an instant urging to faith and repentance... At the same time, it is important for us to realise that Thornwell's earnest and tender calls for conversion were solidly based upon a well-balanced understanding of the scriptural order of salvation. He continually emphasises the priority of the sovereign and gracious God in his free election of sinners to be awakened from their death-like slumbers so that they may place their trust in [God in Christ]. Thornwell's preaching has in common with his fellow Calvinists, [John] Girardeau, [Benjamin Morgan] Palmer and [Daniel] Baker, the frequent teaching of the scriptural order of salvation. Unlike some today who are afraid that a robust Calvinism will turn sinners away, and so [they] become Arminian in their methods (and in their message – by leaving some important truths unsaid), these [men] regularly and enthusiastically taught the facts of redemption from a God-centered perspective – and saw thousands converted' (Kelly pp76-78). This illustrates the point I have tried to make. The decrees need not be preached as hindrances to sinners. The very reverse!

But I fear, as Andrew Bonar noted, 'the Calvinistic doctrines... have [been] so preached... that... these truths have become little better than dry theses'. 'In admirable contrast', however, '[Asahel] Nettleton's preaching... set these high truths before his hearers, on all occasions, in a most thoroughly practical form. They saw in them the God of majesty, glory, grace, dealing with rebels, and were bowed down before him'. Using John's gospel to bring out the doctrines of election, particular redemption, irresistible grace (John 1:13; 6:37,39,44-45,65; 10:11,28-29; 17:2,6,9,11-12; 18:9) – 'John, he who so fully opens up to view the love of God' – Bonar turned to 'Whitefield and Edwards and Nettleton [who] never found themselves, nor those they addressed, hindered by these great truths; they were helped by them, not hindered. No wonder; for do not each of these doctrines at once turn our eye upon God himself, and cause us to hear his voice...? They lead us to the fullest and freest gospel... It declares that this gospel call, this invitation of rich, boundless love, need never fall on any man's ear in vain, however depraved, hardened, desperately wicked he may be, since the same God of holy love who sends it has the power to turn that heart in the very moment the invitation comes to it. Love is so unlimited that it can sweep away the very unwillingness of the sinner to whom it addresses its message of grace! Is not this glad tidings? – free unlimited love, a flood that is not turned aside into another channel by meeting the rock in its way, but that [flood] rises... till its waters pour over it in a cataract! Nor let us fail to notice that all the doctrines of grace are beams from the glorious person of Christ... election... particular redemption... special grace... irresistible grace... The person of Christ (associated, of course, with what he wrought) being... the centre and core of all the doctrines of grace, we have a brief and satisfactory answer therein to those who allege that they cannot disentangle the sinner's free access to the offered salvation from the difficulties that beset some of these doctrines. We point... to the centre doctrine of all – the person of Christ... that God commands you to go to him... a bottomless fountain of grace; and every child of Adam is warranted at once to approach to this and use it. Deal with him here, if other truths perplex you; and solve all questions as to whether or not you were specially intended when this fountain was opened for sinners, by drinking of it; or, in other words, by willingly receiving Christ himself, and putting your soul at his disposal'. As for 'these doctrines of grace' blunting zeal, Bonar had a ready reply; they are, he said, 'most assuredly... fitted to lead a man and a minister of Christ... to be zealous of good works, and zealous for souls – bent upon God's glory, and bent upon the salvation of men' (Andrew Bonar ix-xv).

[283] How can total depravity, unconditional election, limited atonement and distinguishing grace enforce the free offer? Before I answer, I repeat that it is the *Scriptures* which must be preached; this, of course, will have a doctrinal framework, but doctrine, as mere doctrine, must not be preached. Nor should the decrees be preached as hindrances to the offer. With these caveats in mind, I suggest that *total depravity* brings home to the sinner his desperate plight, his personal responsibility and accountability, humbles his pride, and strips him of any hope in himself, his self-sufficiency (see earlier note); *unconditional election* humbles the sinner, and drives him to look to God's grace alone in hope of mercy; *limited atonement* points the sinner to the glorious Redeemer and the absolute certainty and fullness of the redemption he wrought; and *irresistible, distinguishing grace* humbles the sinner, exposes his inadequacy and shuts him up to God. Note the emphasis on humbling the sinner; see above for my comments on this. These are just some of the ways in which these doctrines, when biblically preached in the presence of sinners, enforce the free offer. True enough, at first glance

they seem to be at variance with it, but they are not. See John Murray *Collected* Vol.1 pp126-129; Booth: *Reign* p56; John Bonar pp14-20; Calvin: *Institutes* Vol.2 p237; Zanchius p133. See Owen: *Meditations* in *Works* Vol.1 pp419-432, for the way Owen, having set out 'the glory of Christ', offered him to sinners. See my *Offer* xii-xiii. For Nettleton's sermon on the decrees, see Andrew Bonar pp199-204; for Edwards on Rom. 9:18, and the way he appealed to sinners not to make the doctrine of God's sovereignty an excuse for 'presumption and discouragement', see Edwards: *Seventeen* pp849-854.

Haldane: Concerning 'the doctrine of election' (and effectual calling), 'whatever canons may be laid down by divines as to the proper method of preaching the gospel, it is well for us to be guided by the example of the Lord and his inspired apostles [see John 6:37,44; 10:26; Acts 2:23; 3:18; 4:27-28]... Man's utterly ruined state is most fully exhibited in the doctrine of election. Not only is he incapable of saving himself, but when a free salvation is preached to him, he continues to spurn it, till it is brought home to his heart with divine power and energy. Here, then, we have the fullest exhibition of the awful state and circumstances of fallen man; and should it be concealed from those whom we address? Shall we hide from them their true situation, in the hope of beguiling them into the faith of Christ? Shall we be afraid to tell them how absolutely dependent they are upon him who made them? "No", says the apostle, "we have renounced the hidden things of dishonesty, not walking in craftiness, not handling the word of God deceitfully"... This doctrine shuts men up to absolute dependence on God's mercy' (Haldane pp109-111).

[284] John Murray: *Redemption* p65, emphasis mine. 'Bound up with a limited extent is the real nature of the salvation and of the Christ offered. If we universalise the extent of the atonement we must limit its efficacy, and when we limit its efficacy, it is an impoverished and truncated salvation that the ministers of evangelism have to offer... [But] somehow or other [some (many? DG) Calvinists] have begun to fear that the full, free and unfettered overture of Christ in the gospel to all men without distinction, and the pressing upon men lost and dead in sins the claims and demands of that free overture, would impinge upon other truths such as sovereign election, definite atonement, and efficacious grace. Consequently, while indeed avowing the doctrine of the free offer, they have not been successful in bringing it to bear upon men with spontaneity and without any reserve [that is, though they have agreed with the principle they have failed to preach it. See below, where I re-make this very important point concerning incipient hyper-Calvinism]. This is a grave failure. And the failure gathers the proportions of [a]

tragedy when we remember that if [since] it is the Reformed faith that has given the most consistent expression to the whole counsel of God, then it is only on the basis of the Reformed conception of salvation and of grace, of Christ and of his work, that a full, free and unfettered overture of Christ can be presented. It is only with the definiteness and particularism which characterises our Reformed faith that Christ can be presented in all his fullness and freeness as a Saviour. It is a grave sin against Christ and his gospel not to realise that it is precisely the definiteness of the redemption which he accomplished that [is an integral part of – I disagree with Murray who had 'grounds and validates'] the fullness and freeness with which he is offered to all men in the unrestricted overtures of his grace. And if we have any reserve or lack of spontaneity in offering Christ to lost men, and in presenting the claims which inhere in the glory of his person and the perfection of his finished work, then it is because we have a distorted conception of the relation which the sovereignty of God sustains to the free offer of Christ in the gospel. It is on the crest of the wave of divine sovereignty that the full and free overtures of God's grace in Christ break upon the shores of lost humanity'. Murray went on to say that a lack of freedom in making the offer hinders sinners being saved: 'If we fail to appreciate what the free offer of the gospel is, and if we fail to present this free offer with freedom and spontaneity, with passion and urgency, then we are not only doing dishonour to Christ and his glory, but we are also choking those who are the candidates of saving faith... It is not the belief that we have been saved, not even the belief that Christ died for us, but the commitment of ourselves to Christ as unsaved, lost, helpless and undone, *in order that we may be saved*. This is the specific character of that act of faith whereby we respond to the free overture of Christ in the gospel... Christ in all his fullness and freeness as the all-sufficient, all-suitable and perfect Saviour. Faith is the engagement of person to person, the engagement of a lost sinner to Christ, in the commitment of faith. How can there be such engagement and entrustment except as lost and helpless sinners are confronted with the Saviour[?] And they are confronted with him in the full, free and unfettered overture which he makes of himself in the gospel of his grace' (John Murray: *Collected* Vol.1 pp128,145-147, emphasis his).

[285] John Murray: *Collected* Vol.1 pp81-82, emphasis mine.

[286] See my *Offer* pp145-166. As above, this may seem illogical to fallen men, but not to Christ!

[287] Calvin: *Commentaries* Vol.16 Part 2 pp37,40-41.

[288] I use 'tandem' advisedly. The decrees lead; the free offer follows.

[289] Gill: *Commentary* Vol.5 pp100-101.

---

[290] Griffin, I am sure, had no thought of the usual connotations of 'chance'.
[291] Griffin Vol.2 pp545-548,555.
[292] I apologise for the measure of repetition in what has gone before *and in what follows*, but I want each of these 'answers' to stand on its own. Having nearly finished my mss, I was much encouraged to read Douty's words: 'If anyone objects to the repetitive character of this treatise, let him try to handle the subject himself. He will soon discover that his treatment will be as repetitive as mine, and, if he does any research, he will see that mine is no more so than those which support the other view' (Douty p13). Haldane evidently found the same difficulty, as a glance at his book will confirm.
[293] See Acts 2:24,31-33; 3:15,26; 4:2,10,33; 5:30-31; 10:40; 13:30,33-37; 17:3,18,31-32; 23:6; 24:15,21. Yet, although the resurrection is frequently preached to unbelievers in Acts, not once did any preacher tell them that Christ has been raised *for them*. Here is a clear parallel with the atonement. As I have made clear, the atonement and the resurrection cannot be separated. See also the Appendix.
[294] Paul gave some explanatory details in Rom. 10:1-21; 1 Cor. 1:17-25; 2:1-10; 2 Cor. 4:5; 5:18-21; 6:1-2; Gal. 6:14; Col. 1:27-28 *etc*.
[295] I am trying to be fair to those who disagree with me. I contend that Paul never said it to anybody, because it is not true. (For my comments on seemingly 'universal' texts, see earlier notes and the Appendix). But at this point I am dealing with the approach to unbelievers. I repeat my challenge. Will those who disagree, cite a preacher in the Bible who based the gospel invitation upon universal redemption? Take Isa. 45:22. In the context, God gave many supporting arguments to encourage all sinners without exception to look to him and be saved – his uniqueness, sovereignty, power, revelation of himself, promise of salvation, and so on – but not universal atonement. Universal judgement, universal accountability, yes; universal atonement, no. See my *Offer* pp18-25.
[296] See Tom Wells pp96-103. I am not suggesting that we should never preach the atonement to sinners. Of course not! I am just observing that the apostles did not deal with the question: 'For whom did Christ die?', when preaching to sinners. The reason is obvious. No unbeliever, as I have explained, can know he is elect, and that Christ died for him; and no preacher can know it for any unbeliever. So why would a preacher spend his time on a detail he is ignorant of, when addressing unbelieving sinners who cannot be anything but ignorant of what he is talking about? and which is none of their business? If sinners want to know all about the grace of God, and their interest in it, they must be told: 'Taste and see' (Ps. 34:8), just as Christ who, being asked where he was staying,

did not go into minute descriptive details, but succinctly replied: 'Come and see' (John 1:38-39). Philip did the same to Nathaniel (John 1:46).
[297] Ella: *The Free Offer* p16.
[298] This is not *one* class; both the Amyraldian and the Owenite in their differing ways take this line, but it applies far more to the former. Strictly speaking, as I have explained, the Owenite does not think Christ offered his sacrifice for the non-elect; only that it was innately sufficient for them. As I have made clear, I am not dealing with the Universalist or the Arminian. Furthermore, I am taking Haldane's 'as well as' to mean 'in addition to', not 'as much as'. Neither the Amyraldian or the Owenite thinks Christ died for the ultimately lost 'as much as' he died for the elect; that, once again, is either Universalism or Arminianism.
[299] Haldane pp38,112,125-126.
[300] Note the repeated 'dare'. Ralph Erskine: 'The offer is universal to all that hear the gospel... Let Arminians maintain, at their peril, their universal redemption; but we must maintain, at our peril, the universal offer. Necessity is laid upon us, and woe is us, if we preach not this gospel to every creature' (M'Millan pp133,183). Echoes here of my note about riding the storm.
[301] John Bonar pp11-21.
[302] Gouge p668. Gouge's conclusion – 'that... they for whom Christ was indeed given might believe, and others made inexcusable' – is ambiguous. If he meant that God offers Christ to all *so that* the non-elect might be made inexcusable, I disagree with him. The offer is made sincerely. Of course, unbelievers are inexcusable for their refusal of Christ (John 3:18-19), but I do not believe the offer is made with the *intention* of making them inexcusable. At least, I do not know of any scripture saying it is so. (I fully accept that it is an inevitable consequence for those who refuse. The preacher cannot avoid this – he is the aroma of both death and life (2 Cor. 2:16). The sower inevitably treads the ground even as he sows). But Gouge may have been simply stating a fact; Christ is offered to all so that the elect might believe; as for the rest, they will not believe and so are made inexcusable. In other words, the 'that' governs the effectual calling, but not the making of the non-elect inexcusable.
[303] Owen: *Death* in *Works* Vol.10 p300.
[304] Precisely my point about going outside Scripture to try to resolve the paradox.
[305] Cunningham pp344-348.
[306] See above and my *Offer* pp57-134.
[307] Moody-Stuart p145.
[308] Note, the offer is conditional; Christ's redemption is not.

[309] Shepard pp62,231-232, emphasis mine. George Gillespie: 'If it is objected... but God works faith only in the elect, and I know not whether I am elected or not – I answer, you are discharged (in this case) to run [from running] back to election (which is God's secret), and are commanded to obey the revealed command, according to... Deut. 29:29' (Gillespie pp121-122).
[310] Kevan p114.
[311] 'It is undeniable that the atonement makes a universal provision for universal gospel preaching (Mark 16:15)' (Clifford: *Amyraut* p49). I disagree. Mark 16:15 does not prove it.
[312] 'In the gospel, salvation is offered promiscuously to all those to whom it is preached... This salvation which is... offered to men in the gospel, is neglected and repelled by many... [and] this neglect and unbelief is the true cause which prevents the ungodly from obtaining the rest of the Lord; that is, which deprives them of eternal life offered to them in Christ. But none of these things can be said truly and seriously unless it is presupposed that salvation through the death of Christ is applicable to [that is, in Davenant's terms, provided for] all men, according to the appointment of God' (Davenant p30). Clifford: 'If you define "particular redemption" as "Christ died for the elect alone", then how can the "offer" be wider? You have nothing to offer to the world in general. If "Christ and salvation" are "on offer", then he died (with intent) for those to whom he made it available. Therefore, why not simply accept the Amyraldian position: Christ died (with dual intent) for all "provisionally" but for the elect "receptively". We believe in a "particular efficacious redemption" as well as a "general sufficient redemption". Can't you accept this too? It makes sense of all the universalist verses of Scripture' (Clifford's e-mail to me, 9th Feb. 2005). 'Christ had a "general" intention to die for all, thus providing a "general" salvation conditional on repentance and faith. This is the basis of gospel preaching' (Clifford's e-mail to me, 25th Feb. 2005). Clifford rightly owned the duty of sinners to repent and believe – for which he provided scriptural support – but also argued that 'the knowledge that Christ has died for him provides encouragement [for the sinner] to believe' – for which, significantly, he offered no scriptural support (Clifford: *Atonement* p114). There is none.
[313] Dagg: 'An unrestricted invitation to all who hear the gospel, to come to Christ for life, *seems to imply* that universal provision has been made in him; and in order to the making of universal provision, *it appears necessary* that he should have borne the sins of all men'. Dagg produced his arguments to show that this is not so (Dagg pp326-331, emphasis mine). I return to an earlier quotation from Dabney: 'If God makes

proposals of mercy to men, who he foresees will certainly reject them and perish, and whom he immutably purposes to leave without effectual calling, how can his power and wisdom be cleared, save at the expense of his sincerity? or his sincerity at the expense of his wisdom or power? This is obviously the point in the Reformed or Augustinian theology most difficult of adjustment. The excogitations of the scheme of the "Hypothetic Universalists" among a part of the French Reformed, and the intricate discussions between them and the Genevans, evince the fact' (Dabney: 'God's' p282). And what Dabney said about effectual calling applies of course to particular redemption. Clifford thought Arminians, not Amyraldians, are the real 'hypothetic universalists' (Clifford: *Atonement* p154). I would say Arminians are the *consistent* hypothetic universalists. In passing, of course, note that many of the objections to Amyraldianism apply to Arminianism – although the latter is not my concern in this present work.

[314] Haldane pp115-116.

[315] Haldane pp119-120.

[316] As before, Haldane was not talking about Arminians; he was dealing with those who hold to universal atonement while believing in election. His words apply, therefore to Amyraldians and Owenites, but more to the former than the latter.

[317] Haldane pp240-241,288-289.

[318] See earlier note from Lloyd-Jones on the need for the sinner to be humbled.

[319] I repeat my earlier note. A nice distinction must be maintained here. Justification comes *through*, *by* faith; but NOT *on account of*, *because of*, faith. Faith is its means, not its cause. Amyraldianism tends (to put it no stronger) to blur this distinction.

[320] See my *Offer* p149.

[321] 'If one is preaching evangelistically, my emphasis (whoever is present) is on the universality of redemptive provision' (Clifford's e-mail to me, 2nd Mar. 2005). In other words, in a mixed congregation, Clifford as an Amyraldian addresses his hearers as all potentially, sufficiently but conditionally, redeemed. This, it seems to me, inevitably leads the believing sinner to regard his own faith as making the difference between him and the unbeliever. And if the preacher at the same time, explains that – although the provision is universal – only the elect can come, only the elect are effectively redeemed, the original 'problem' – which the Amyraldian thinks he has solved – remains.

[322] I am, for the moment, leaving aside the fact that the latter is the biblical position.

[323] 'If Christ died only for the elect, does it not become necessary for enquirers to discover their election before they come to Christ?' (Clifford: 'Evangelicalisms' p14). The answer is: No, as I have shown. The sinner does not have to concern himself with the extent of election or the atonement before he trusts Christ. But if the Amyraldian persists with his objection, should he not take his own medicine? Since he rightly argues that the sinner can believe only if he is elect, does the sinner not have to know he is elect before he believes? The biblical answer is, of course, as before: No! But consistent Amyraldian logic must reply: Yes! A similar point can be made against the Owenite system. See below. The fact is, the hyper-Calvinist, the Amyraldian and the Owenite put this question of election into the sinner's mind at the point of faith. In the biblical free offer, no such question is put into the sinner's mind – all the sinner has to be concerned about is coming to Christ.
[324] Macleod pp246,250-251, emphasis mine.
[325] Gillespie was mistaken here; as we have seen, (at least some) Amyraldians do not go even this far.
[326] Was Gillespie conceding too much here? See above, where I raised the question of Amyraldianism and God's decree concerning the non-elect.
[327] Gillespie pp117-118. Of course, as I have explained, unbelief is the damning sin – but Gillespie was showing how Amyraldianism fails to solve the seeming contradiction involved in encouraging or commanding all sinners to trust Christ.
[328] Kennedy pp51-57.
[329] Of course, in preaching the gospel, we do command spiritually dead sinners to believe. Haldane, it goes without saying, was not referring to *that*; he was illustrating the paucity, the ineffectualness, of Amyraldian claims.
[330] I am defining the 'two systems' as the Amyraldian and the one I am putting forward.
[331] Haldane pp108,290-291,293-297,325-326, emphasis his. 'There is not the shadow of inconsistency in holding that the atonement was made for the elect alone, and that they are separated from others by the general calls and invitations of the gospel' (Haldane p361).
[332] Haldane pp39-40. This is very important. We should shun all talk of sufficiency as the basis of the free offer.
[333] To return to the nice point I made earlier, I do not dissent from Owen when he spoke of the all-sufficiency of Christ for all believers (Owen: *Death* in *Works* Vol.10 pp344,383,410,420), (although I cannot go all the way with him in the way he expressed it). Nevertheless, 'the ground

and basis' of the free offer is not the sufficiency (however described) of Christ's redemption, but the plain command and example of God's word.

[334] Peter Naylor quoted Joseph Ivimey's disagreement with Fuller's use of 'sufficiency' to justify the free offer: 'It would be much more easily supported, and be better understood, by a reference to the manner in which the Lord Jesus and his inspired apostles preached the gospel. Who can deny but that those infallible specimens support the practice of calling on the unconverted to "repent and believe the gospel"'. Reader, not only is it 'more easily supported' in this way, it is *biblically* supported in this way. And, applying Naylor's comment concerning Fuller to the Owenite position in general: 'It seems that Fuller was struggling in order to provide *unnecessary* justification for the practice of preaching the gospel to the unconverted' (Naylor 199-202, emphasis mine). This is the point I am making. The Owenite interpretation of the formula is unnecessary; indeed, as I have said, it is meaningless.

[335] When Cunningham said: 'Now it is evident that these two things are not, as the language of some orthodox divines might lead us to suppose, contrasted with, or opposed to each other', he should have been more precise. Which 'two things' was he referring to? If he meant that which he had raised earlier in the paragraph – namely, 'limited atonement', on the one hand, and 'unlimited or indiscriminate offers of pardon and acceptance... unlimited or indiscriminate invitations and commands to come to Christ and to lay hold on him', on the other – he was perfectly correct. But if one of the two was Owen's claim of 'sufficient for all', then, as Cunningham himself observed, there is no biblical warrant for such a view. As I have explained, it is right to say Christ's sacrifice is 'all-sufficient', but it is speculation to say it is 'sufficient for all', and that such a sufficiency is the basis of the offer.

[336] Cunningham pp344-348. I draw attention to Cunningham's use of 'design' in the above. Baird badly misquoted Cunningham on this issue. Whereas Cunningham wrote: 'Calvinists, while they admit that pardon and salvation are offered indiscriminately to all to whom the gospel is preached, and that all who can be reached should be invited and urged to come to Christ and embrace him, deny that this flows from, or indicates, any *design* or purpose on God's part to save all men' (Cunningham p396), Baird had 'any *desire* or purpose on God's part' (Baird: 'Amyrauldianism' p26). This, of course, was a serious misquotation. God does not decree, design or purpose the salvation of all, but he certainly desires it. See my *Offer* pp57-166. In a later article, although he did correctly quote Cunningham this time (as he ought, having taunted John Brentnall – 'has he read [Cunningham] carefully?'), Baird

misrepresented the free offer by conflating desire and intention; it is no part of the free offer to say 'that God may be properly said to *desire or intend* the salvation of all men' (Baird: 'Calvin' p2, emphasis mine). But Hanko did the same: 'The well-meant offer [teaches] that God in the gospel *intends and desires* the salvation of all who hear' (Hanko p7, emphasis mine). This kind of misrepresentation shows either gross ignorance of the free offer, or malice.

[337] Dabney called Cunningham's view 'thoroughly short-sighted' (Dabney: *Systematic* p529), but I think his own eyes here ranged beyond scriptural warrant. See earlier notes on Dabney, and Dabney: *Systematic* pp518-535.

[338] 'If God designed that Christ die only for the elect, how can the infinite worth of his death, by itself, afford ground for offering salvation to all men? However valuable his sacrifice, it cannot furnish salvation for the non-elect, if it was designed exclusively for the elect' (Douty p35).

[339] Rushton p28; Pink Vol.2 pp219-223. To be fair to Fuller, he did not always(!) get it wrong: 'Let us enquire what it is, in the redemption of Christ, to which the Scriptures ascribe its efficacy. Justification is ascribed to his blood, and to his obedience... His obedience unto death was more than the means of salvation; it was the procuring cause of it. Salvation was the effect of the "travail of his soul"... Christ was "the author of eternal salvation". (The redemption of Christ is not the cause of the Father's grace; but that in consideration of which it is exercised)... What is there... in... his obedience unto death...?... We are "redeemed – with the precious blood of Christ – the blood of Jesus Christ, his Son, cleanses us from all sin... when he had by himself" expiated "our sins...". If there be any meaning in language, the efficacy of the sufferings and work of Christ is here ascribed to the dignity of his person; and that dignity amounts to nothing short of his proper deity... the strength by which he was borne up in his sufferings, and his resurrection from the dead, to the power of the Father... When the value, or virtue, of his interposition is spoken of, it is ascribed to the intrinsic glory of his person, as the Son of God... Justification stands connected, in the Scriptures, with union with Christ' (Fuller: *Sermons* pp610-611). This important extract from Fuller links much of what I have said. Christ accomplished redemption; there is nothing merely sufficient or conditional about it; Christ is an all-sufficient Saviour, because of who he is; redemption is ascribed to Christ and his work, not our faith; and union and identification with Christ is key.

[340] All three objectors – the hyper-Calvinist, the Amyraldian and the Owenite – make the sinner think in terms of preparation, and his part in

God's decrees – 'Am I elect? Has Christ died for me?' – when he ought to be trusting Christ. See above.
[341] It is a case of Isaac Newton's Third Law of Dynamics: 'To every action there is an equal and opposite reaction'. Clifford argued that '*high* Calvinism too easily gives Arminians the excuse to reject *authentic* Calvinism' (Clifford: 'Evangelicalisms' p12, emphasis his), remarkably, in my view, classifying Owen and Whitefield as high-Calvinists (Clifford: 'Evangelicalisms' pp12,14; *Calvinus* p7 – watch the edition; *Amyraut* pp13-14). My view is that hyper-Calvinism and Arminianism are the true opposites, and each has encouraged the other to reject Calvinism. Owen and Whitefield I would classify as Calvinists.
[342] It never speaks of it at all!
[343] Haldane pp101-105,124-127, emphasis mine.
[344] Quoted by Fuller: *Six Letters* p321. Fuller did not give the writer's name, except that it was not Booth. Fuller did not agree with the suggestion, of course. I do!
[345] The 'nice' point I have repeated from time to time.
[346] In general: 'He who comes to God must believe that he is, and that he is a rewarder of those who diligently seek him' (Heb. 11:6). In particular, the coming sinner must believe Christ can and will receive him, and save him. The leper had no doubt about Christ's ability; it was his willingness which worried him. He had no need to fear: 'I am willing', said the Saviour (Mark 1:40-41).
[347] But, of course, just as God's saving mercy does not extend to all, neither does the all-sufficiency of Christ's sacrifice mean he died for all.
[348] Gillespie pp118-122. Other encouragements Gillespie spoke of were Christ's dying for all sorts of sinners and all manner of sins, that Christ receives all who come to him, and that God is the giver of faith.
[349] John Murray: *Collected* Vol.1 p62.
[350] I am not, of course, saying we should limit our preaching to these texts! I am just illustrating the difference between the way we ***should*** address *unbelievers* and the way we ***can*** address *believers*. In our preaching, we should make it clear to all our hearers, in their respective conditions, to whom the words of the particular passage apply, and how.
[351] See my *Offer* pp51-52,115-122; and above. I do not exclude myself from this challenge and rebuke.
[352] Booth made his position clear enough in the substance and subtitle of his *Glad Tidings to Perishing Sinners: The Genuine Gospel a Complete Warrant for the Ungodly to Believe in Jesus*. Fuller was 'happy' with Booth – 'that great and good man' (Fuller: *Sermons* p690) – on 'the complete warrant which every sinner who hears the gospel has to believe in Christ for the salvation of his soul, antecedent to all holy

qualifications or dispositions whatever' – a truth which, Fuller went on to say, 'leaves all unbelievers without excuse... and affords a plain direction to gospel ministers to invite their auditors, without distinction, to a participation of eternal life. This important truth, though plentifully taught in the... Scriptures, and generally, if not universally, embraced by the Reformers, Puritans and Nonconformists, has been much opposed in the present century [the 18th; the sluices would be opened in the 19th]. Those writers who have laboured to set aside the gospel offer, as inconsistent with the doctrines of grace, have with it explained away the free invitations of the gospel as they respect the unregenerate; considering them as addressed only to sinners made sensible of their sin, and thirsting after spiritual blessings; and contending that no other descriptions of men have any warrant to embrace them. This notion Mr Booth has successfully combated, proving, beyond all just contradiction, that the invitations of the gospel are addressed to sinners *as sinners*' (Fuller: *Reviews* p964, emphasis his).

[353] Fuller: *Six Letters* p323.

[354] I have found Booth addressing sinners in the cautious way adopted by those who are not entirely free of all traces of hyper-Calvinism (see my *Septimus Sears*); that is, going as far as to *describe* the freeness of the gospel, *warning* sinners, *praying fo*r them, *wishing* they would believe, *questioning* them, *lamenting* their unbelief, *trembling for* them, and so on (Booth: *Reign* pp51-52,95,107-109,111,118,149,181-182,184,264-265,286-288; *Glad Tidings* in *Works* Vol.2 pp5,41,204-206,213-214; *Divine Justice* in *Works* Vol.3 pp75-77; *Works* Vol.3 pp236-237,242-252,257-259,264-266,274-275,277-280,301-304,321). See above for my note on Booth and 'duty'. The comments of the writer of his *Memoir* should also be borne in mind, although I acknowledge there are differences of opinion about 'high' (I prefer the term 'hyper') Calvinism: Booth was 'a Calvinist, and in some particulars approaching what is called high Calvinism; but he has sometimes declared, as many other great men have done, that he never saw any human system which he could fully and entirely adopt' (*Memoir* in Booth: *Reign* p32; see also Morden pp12,77-78,83,92-93). I am not a 'great man', but it must be obvious from this book that I, too, do not find any human system to have all the answers, nor even to have asked all the questions! In particular, therefore, although I agree with much that Booth wrote on this subject, I cannot go with him all the way, while sometimes I go further.

[355] If I have misrepresented Fuller (or Booth), and if any reader can supply references, I shall be more than pleased to correct my comments. But, as far as I have discovered, yes, Fuller directed ministers as to how they should preach the gospel: 'Christ wept over sinners, and so must

we'. We have to 'bring [sinners] to Christ', he said, 'the gospel is a feast, and you are to invite guests... Dwell on the freeness, and fullness, and all-sufficiency of his grace, and how welcome even the worst of sinners are'. 'If we are true ministers of Christ, we shall love the souls of men as he loved them' (Fuller: *Sermons* pp688,691,708). But what of his own preaching? How did he actually address sinners? True, he declared 'sinners, even the greatest of sinners, have encouragement to repent and believe in Jesus'. 'There is the utmost encouragement for the most guilty and unworthy to return to God by Jesus Christ'. 'A way is opened, by the death of Christ, for any sinner to return to God and be saved... The servants of Christ, as though God did beseech by them, pray [beg – see my *Offer* pp116-117] men in Christ's stead, saying: "Be reconciled to God"'. 'The world and Christ are in competition for our choice, and we are required to give a decisive and immediate answer. Choose this day whom you will serve... If any refuse [Christ], and prefer the present world before him, be it known to them that, as is their choice in this world, such will be their portion in that which is to come'. 'We are sinners... and there is but one refuge for us to seek to – and if we seek him with all our heart and soul, we shall find mercy'. 'Thus life and death are set before you; which will you choose?... If you enter the strait gate, and walk in the narrow way, an abundant entrance will be ministered unto you, into the everlasting kingdom of our Lord Jesus Christ; but if found pursuing the broad way, you shall hereafter strive to enter into that kingdom, and shall not be able'. 'My dear hearers, you have heard much of the gospel... but do not forget one thing; do not... forget to ask... Am I a Christian? Do I repent of my sins? Do I believe in the Son of God for the salvation of my soul?' 'You have got to die, and it is a very serious matter whether this sentence [Heb. 9:27-28] be executed upon you in its terror: it must – it will – if out of Christ' (Fuller: *Sermons* pp604,617,620,658-659,665,670,677,679). But this falls short of preaching the free offer. The fact is, Fuller seemed to stop with this advice to preachers: 'Souls are perishing around you... publish [the atonement]... and, receiving and exhibiting this atonement, you may hope to save yourself and them that hear you' (Fuller: *Sermons* p694). As I have made clear, there is far more to preaching the gospel than this. Fuller got closer in an extended passage in which he powerfully questioned and warned, spelled out the promises of the gospel and Christ's demand that ministers should compel sinners to come in, and so on. He spoke of Christ's atonement, saying: 'To this you are *invited*, and that in the most pressing terms' (Fuller: *The Great Question* pp871-874, emphasis his). And the best I have found is: 'Jesus invites you to come to him. His servants beseech you, in his name, to be reconciled to God.

The Spirit says: Come; and the bride says: Come; and "whosoever will, let him come, and take of the water of life freely". An eternal heaven is before you in one direction, and an eternal hell in the other. Your answer is required. Be one thing or [the] other. Choose you, this day, whom you will serve' (Fuller: *Worthy* pp175-179). Even so, it is hardly a *pressing* invitation in his own words! See my *Septimus Sears*.
[356] Fuller: *Sermons* p687, emphasis his.
[357] I am not claiming that either man would have agreed with my thesis in this book. But since neither of them here addressed sinners based on the sufficiency formula – even though they rightly preached the all-sufficient Christ – I feel justified in using these extracts.
What about Whitefield? What was his position? As I have noted, Clifford bracketed him with Owen as a high (hyper) Calvinist – a remarkable claim if ever there was. But, granted Whitefield's free preaching, was he really even a Calvinist? Without doubt! As evidence, I call upon his letter to Wesley in response to the latter's publication against the doctrine of predestination. In this letter, Whitefield set out his firm belief in God's decrees of election and reprobation, and in the preaching of them; he very strongly opposed universal redemption, maintaining that Christ died only for the elect to purchase salvation for them; but still he held to the free promiscuous preaching of the gospel to all. Let him speak for himself.
'Has not God, who has appointed salvation for a certain number, appointed also the preaching of the word, as a means to bring them to it?... And since we know not who are elect, and who [are] reprobate, we are to preach promiscuously to all... By these means... as many as the Lord has ordained to eternal life shall certainly be quickened and enabled to believe... None living... can know that they are not of the number of God's elect. None, but the unconverted, can have any just reason so much as to fear it... What if the doctrine of election and reprobation does put some upon doubting? So does that of regeneration. But is not this doubting a good means to put them upon searching and striving; and that striving, a good means to make their calling and election sure? This is one reason among many others, why I admire the doctrine of election, and am convinced that it should have a place in gospel ministrations, and should be insisted on with faithfulness and care. It has a natural tendency to rouse the soul out of its carnal security. And therefore many carnal men cry out against it. Whereas universal redemption is a notion sadly adapted to keep the soul in its lethargic sleepy condition, and therefore so many natural men admire and applaud it'.

'Do not they who believe God's dooming men to everlasting burnings, also believe that God looked upon them as men fallen in Adam? and that the decree which ordained the punishment, first regarded the crime by which it was deserved?... After Adam fell, and his posterity in him, God might justly have passed them all by, without sending his own Son to be a Saviour for anyone. Unless you heartily agree to both these points, you do not believe [in] original sin aright. If you do own them, then you must acknowledge the doctrine of election and reprobation to be highly just and reasonable... And, if you would be consistent, you must either give up the doctrine of [the] imputation of Adam's sin, or receive the amiable doctrine of election, with a holy and righteous reprobation as its consequent. For whether you can believe it or not, the word of God abides faithful: "The election has obtained it, and the rest were blinded"... When considered as fallen in Adam, were [all men] not objects of [God's] hatred? And might not God, of his own good pleasure, love or show mercy to... the elect, and yet at the same time do the reprobate no wrong?'

'The doctrine of universal redemption... is really the highest reproach upon the dignity of the Son of God, and the merit of his blood. Consider whether it is not rather blasphemy to say... "Christ not only died for those that are saved, but also for those that perish"... How can all be universally redeemed, if all are not finally saved?... Consider how you dishonour God by denying election... [Without it] Jesus Christ would not have had the satisfaction of seeing the fruit of his death in the eternal salvation of one soul. Our preaching would then be vain, and all invitations for people to believe in him, would also be in vain. But, blessed be God, our Lord knew for whom he died. There was an eternal compact between the Father and the Son. A certain number was then given him, as the purchase and reward of his obedience and death. For these he prayed (John 17 [verses 9 & 20]), and not for the world. For these, and these only, he is now interceding, and with their salvation he will be fully satisfied' (Whitefield: 'A Letter to... Wesley' pp563-588).

If further evidence should be wanted, the letters Whitefield wrote on his voyage to America in the autumn of 1739 amply provide it – letters he penned just as he was coming to clearer views on the doctrines of grace. While these letters show his delight in those doctrines, and his determination to be more explicit in including them in preaching the whole counsel of God, they also show his desire for the salvation of sinners, his willingness to probe the unconverted with the pressing command to believe, and the urging of the converted to join him in doing the same in their turn. See Whitefield: *Letters* pp65-120. And this is typical of many references in the rest of that volume, showing that,

while firmly convinced of God's electing grace, and determined against universal redemption, Whitefield could hardly have been more eager for the salvation of sinners.
Reader, I ask your indulgence as I cannot resist including a few more extracts. The man who said: 'I... utterly detest Arminian principles', had already confessed: 'My soul is athirst for the salvation of poor sinners'. Was Whitefield persuaded of the doctrines of grace? Judge him by this letter to a believing lady: 'I rejoice to hear that you are enabled to see not only the freeness but eternal duration of God's grace... He loved me freely, he went before me by his grace; he chose me from eternity, he called me in time, and I am persuaded will keep me till time shall be no more. This consideration makes my faith to work by love... The Lord Jesus will not suffer to be lost the purchase of his blood. He knew for whom he died, and neither men nor devils shall ever pluck them out of his hands... I am persuaded were the effects of our Lord's redemption to depend on man's own compliance, or was the continuance of God's grace to depend solely on man's [own unaided] improvement [use of it], Jesus Christ would have died in vain... Adam could not stand in paradise when left to his own free will; how then can we? No, blessed be God, our salvation is put into better hands than our own. Jesus Christ has purchased not only wisdom, righteousness and sanctification, but also eternal redemption for us' (Whitefield: *Letters* pp145-146,396,406).
Whitefield, I acknowledge, did occasionally use questionable expressions. But, it must be remembered, some of this happened when he had not long come to clearer views on the doctrines of grace, and, perhaps, had not seen their full bearing on the way to address sinners. We know that at the time he had not read widely on the subject, nor had much contact with men who had long been addressing sinners with the doctrines of grace in mind. In any case, on a closer look, some of Whitefield's terms are seen to be self-explanatory and proper. For instance, he sometimes used 'our' when, reading back into the context, it is clear he was speaking to believers; sometimes he spoke of 'men' when he meant no more than 'sinners'. What is more, when addressing Indians or slaves, he showed commendable concern to impress upon them that *they* were not excluded from the gospel – it was as much for them as the white man. When, for instance, in his letter to the Allegany Indians, he declared: 'The Lord Jesus died for you, as well as for the white men among you' (Whitefield: *Letters* p174), I think his meaning is perfectly clear.
To conclude this look at Whitefield on a positive note: Christ, he declared, 'was to do something unspeakable for God's people, even "to bring in an everlasting righteousness"... When Christ's righteousness is

here spoken of, we are to understand "Christ's obedience and death"; all that Christ has done, and all that Christ has suffered, for an elect world – for all that will believe on him... Christ's righteousness was intended by the great God to extend to mankind even from eternity... From all the ages of eternity, God had thoughts of you; God intended the Lord Jesus Christ to save your souls and mine... I have loved you with an everlasting love. Hence it is, that the Lord Jesus, when he calls his elect people up to heaven, says: "Come, you blessed of my Father... receive the kingdom prepared for you... from the foundation of the world". All that we receive in time, all the streams that come to our souls, are but so many streams flowing from that inexhaustible fountain – God's electing, God's sovereign, God's distinguishing, God's everlasting love; and therefore the righteousness of Jesus Christ may properly be called an everlasting righteousness because God intended it from everlasting... Since it is brought into the world by Christ, so, in the name, in the strength, and by the assistance of the great God, I bring it now to the pulpit; I now offer this righteousness, this free, this imputed, this everlasting righteousness, to all poor sinners who will accept... it. For God's sake, accept it this night' (Whitefield: *Sermons* pp200,203-204,208).

So much for Whitefield. What about Edwards? What was his position? Clifford, quoting the new Yale edition of Edwards' *Works*, as well as other recent publications of previously unpublished material, and the two volume Banner of Truth reprint of 1974, asserted: 'Edwards is in the company of Calvin, Amyraut, Baxter, Doddridge and others who argue for a dualistic understanding of the atonement'; and, he concluded, without question he was an Amyraldian (Clifford: *Edwards* pp10-22,30-33). As before, I will not enter the lists over Calvin – but is this right? Was Edwards an Amyraldian? I think not. Edwards certainly had 'a dualistic understanding of the atonement', but this does not mean he was a fully-paid-up Amyraldian. As I have shown, a great many Calvinists – mistakenly, I have argued – have taken some sort of a double view of Christ's death – 'sufficient for all, effective for the elect' – but the great majority of them have not been Amyraldians. So with Edwards. And while this is not the place for a full-scale study of the man, let me briefly set out some reasons for my conclusion.

Even though it is far from conclusive, I note that in all his *Works*, Edwards, as far as I am aware, never claimed he was an Amyraldian; nor did he ever cite Amyraut; indeed, I have not even found him using the sufficiency formula.

True, as I have openly recognised, Edwards did hold to sufficiency. See Edwards: *Great* pp111-112; *Wisdom* pp154-156; *Seventeen* p854, for instance. What is more, as Clifford noted, he spoke of a universal aspect of the atonement: 'Christ in some sense may be said to die for all, and to redeem... the whole world by his death'. Even so, this does not make him an Amyraldian. Indeed, let me give a fuller version of this extract: Edwards raised the objection men make to 'the reasonableness and sincerity of the precepts, calls, counsels, warnings and expostulations of the word of God, or with the various methods and means of grace which God uses with sinners to bring them to repentance... and that they [the objectors] infer an inconsistence between the secret and revealed will of God'. Having responded, Edwards then went on: 'From these things it will inevitably follow, that however Christ in some sense may be said to die for all, and to redeem... the whole world by his death, yet there must be something particular in the design of his death, with respect to such as he intended should actually be saved thereby. As appears by what has been now shown, God has the actual salvation or redemption of a certain number in his proper absolute design, and of a certain number only... God pursues a proper design of the salvation of the elect in giving Christ to die, and prosecutes such a design with respect to no other, most strictly speaking; for it is impossible that God should prosecute any other design than only such as he has; he certainly does not, in the highest propriety and strictness of speech, pursue a design that he has not. And, indeed, such a peculiarity and limitation of redemption will as infallibly follow, from the doctrine of God's foreknowledge, as from that of the decree. For it is impossible, in strictness of speech, that God should prosecute a design, or aim at a thing, which he at the same time most perfectly knows will not be accomplished, as that he should use endeavours for that which is beside his decree' (Edwards: *Freedom* p88).

As I have made clear, I dissent from Edwards in this last statement. God does indeed use 'endeavours for that which is beside his decree'; he does, for instance, show his desire to see sinners saved, even though he has not decreed the salvation of all men – see the footnote by Edwards' editor. Getting back to the issue in hand, although Edwards held to a universal aspect of redemption, he said no more here than Owen might have said. Indeed, bearing in mind what I have just observed, in this extract, far from being an Amyraldian, Edwards was close to being a hyper-Calvinist!

Nevertheless, Edwards held to sufficiency. But, as I have noted, this is not enough to make any man an Amyraldian; as I have shown, Owen also held it. So was Edwards an Owenite? After all, Owen could have written: 'Christ... offered a sacrifice that was sufficient to do away all the guilt of the whole world... Christ... laid a foundation for [misery]

---

being utterly abolished with respect to his elect' (Edwards: *Christ* p215). Edwards, again, quoting David Brainerd: Christ 'is said to take away the sin of the world, not because all the world shall actually be redeemed from sin by him, but because (1) he has done and suffered sufficient to answer for the sins of the world, and so to redeem all mankind; (2) he actually does take away the sins of the elect world' (Edwards: *Brainerd* p374). Owen could have made both statements, yet Edwards was certainly no Owenite on the issue in hand, as I will show. My own conclusion is that, similar to Fuller, Edwards was neither an Amyraldian or an Owenite.

What of the evidence Clifford produced to make the case that Edwards was an Amyraldian? The strongest he produced, to my mind, is Edwards' highly commendatory Preface to Bellamy's *True Religion Delineated*, in which he, Bellamy, got as close as maybe to Amyraut without mentioning his name – teaching that by Christ's death, God is reconcilable – reconcilable, please note – to all men, that Christ has provided a conditional salvation for all – on condition that they repent and believe. So close is this to Amyraldianism, Clifford was able to quote G.P.Fisher when he said Bellamy's 'conception resembles Amyraut'. I agree. And Edwards' Preface was no flash in the pan; he sent a copy of Bellamy's book, with one of his own sermons, to John Erskine in Scotland in 1750 (Dwight cxxiii). So... was Edwards an Amyraldian? I am still not persuaded.

Where, I think, Clifford failed to clinch the point, is in being unable to find direct quotations from Edwards to that effect. In Bellamy? Yes, or very close to it. Did Edwards recommend Bellamy? Yes. But in Edwards himself? No. In saying this, I do not detract from the force of Edward's Preface to Bellamy's book, and I cannot account for it – Edwards being nothing if not meticulous – unless he was, at the very least, sympathetic to Bellamy's view.

As for quotations from Edwards himself, in at least one of the extracts Clifford used (see *Great* pp111-112, for instance), Edwards was not adopting Amyraut's stance; rather, he was teaching the all-sufficiency of Christ and his redemption – which, as I have explained, is very different to saying Christ purchased a redemption sufficient for all (although, as I have shown, Edwards did preach this); 'sufficient for all the sins of all who come to Christ' is not the same as 'sufficient for all men'. In another quotation (see the above extract from Edwards: *Christ* p215), as I have noted, Edwards was saying no more than Owen. See also Edwards: *Seventeen* pp929-936,950.

Clifford's strongest extract from Edwards himself is this: 'Christ... was enabled to do and to suffer the whole will of God; and he obtained the whole of the end of his sufferings – a full atonement for the sins of the whole world, and the full salvation of every one of those who were given him in the covenant of redemption, and all that glory to the name of God, which his mediation was designed to accomplish; not one jot or tittle has failed' (Edwards: *Seventeen* p874). This – 'the whole will of God; and he obtained the whole of the end of his sufferings – a full atonement for the sins of the whole world' – Owen would never have said – at least, not without considerable explanation and interpretation. On the other hand, Edwards did not go quite as far as Amyraut. Not quite, I say. What did Edwards mean by 'the whole will... the whole end... a full atonement'? If he was speaking of one aspect of a double decree concerning Christ's death in which he died to purchase a redemption sufficient for all, conditional on faith and repentance, he did not spell it out. And what did Edwards mean by the distinction between 'atonement' and 'salvation'? Was he saying that Christ provided *atonement* sufficient for all, but effectual *salvation* – including the bestowal of faith – only for the elect? And if he was speaking of a sufficient atonement for all, what did he mean by it? The truth is, he may have been saying little, if anything, more than Owen, but without Owen's careful safeguards and nuances. The extract comes, after all, from a sermon, where, surely, one would expect less nuance than in a carefully worked treatise.

And I think we find evidence for what was in Edwards' mind in number 424 of his *Miscellanies*, 'Universal Redemption: Atonement is Sufficient': 'Christ did die for all in this sense, that all by his death have an opportunity of being saved. He had that design in dying that they should have that opportunity by it; for it is a thing that God designed, that all men should have such an opportunity... and they have it by the death of Christ'. And even here, as Clifford admitted, Edwards went on: 'This however is no designing of the atonement but only for the preservation of their being... 1 Tim. 4:10'. Clifford commented: 'Even the brilliant Edwards could not see that what he gave with one hand he took away with the other!' But Edwards was, in my opinion, not giving 'with one hand' as much as Clifford wished. By God's design, argued Edwards, Christ died for all men to warrant the offer of salvation to all men. As I have made clear, I disagree with this. But it still leaves Edwards short of Amyraut.

In other *Miscellanies* (781 & 1226), as Clifford pointed out, Edwards did say: 'Were it not that the sins of men are already fully punished in the sufferings of Christ, all, both angels and men, might justly hate all sinners for their sins. For appearing as they are in themselves, they are indeed infinitely hateful, and could appear no otherwise to any than as they are in themselves, had not another been substituted for them... But now Christ has suffered for the sins of the world, we ought to hate no man, because there is room to hope that Christ has suffered and satisfied for his sins... So that Christ by his sufferings has in a sense made propitiations for men's sins not only with God, but with their fellow creatures; and so by his obedience, he recommends them not only to the favour of God, but of one another'. And: 'If pardon and salvation are designed for the world, it is altogether meet that they should be proclaimed and promised'. But this, once again, in my view, falls short of Amyraldianism. Many questions remain unanswered. What did Edwards mean by 'fully punished'? Was he saying that all the sins of all men are fully punished? What did he mean by 'in a sense'? Was he limiting this to what he called the propitiation of men's sins with respect to their fellow creatures? or did he apply it also to the propitiation of their sins with respect to God? What did he mean by 'men'? Note also 'there is room to hope'; if Christ has fully satisfied the wrath of God for all men, there is no 'hope' about it – it is certain! Edwards, surely, was not saying that Christ has appeased the wrath of God for all men, with a double intention – effectively for the elect, but sufficiently for all on condition that they repent and believe. Rather, in these two *Miscellanies*, similar to the above, was Edwards not saying that, according to God's design, Christ died for all men so that he can warrant us to show love to all men, and offer salvation to them all? Once again, I disagree, but it still is not Amyraldianism.

And while we are talking about the *Miscellanies*, should we in any case place as much weight on these – which take more the form of private jottings than fully worked-out treatises? As Harvey G.Townsend put it: 'The nine notebooks of *Miscellanies*... are, "in effect, a common-place book... As it stands it is a private notebook and must be thought of as a mere record of miscellaneous observations put down from time to time as they occurred to him"' (quoted in Iain Murray: *Edwards* p139). Is it fair to treat Edwards' *Miscellanies* with the same rigour as his finished works? Nor should the passage of time be forgotten, with its inevitable adjustment of his views which must have taken place in the period over which Edwards made these jottings. Above all, why should we expect Edwards to be infallibly consistent?

In his preaching, Edwards would tell sinners: 'Christ suffered enough for the punishment of the sins of the greatest sinner that ever lived... Justice cannot require any more for any man's sins, than those sufferings... which Christ suffered... We may make use of this doctrine to guard those who seek salvation from two opposite extremes – presumption and discouragement... God can bestow mercy upon you without the least prejudice to the honour of his holiness, which you have offended, or to the honour of his majesty, which you have insulted, or of his justice, which you have made your enemy, or of his truth, or of any of his attributes. Let you be what sinner you may, God can, if he pleases, greatly glorify himself in your salvation' (Edwards: *Seventeen* pp851,854). Once again, he was saying God so sufficiently satisfied his justice in the death of his Son, that he can make the free offer to all. Further, without compromising any of his attributes, God can have mercy upon any and every sinner who comes to him through Christ. This is not Amyraldianism.

To sum up: In all this, Edwards does not make it clear to me, at least, that he had come to Amyraut's double-decree explanation of the atonement, with the notion of a conditional redemption for all men. Certainly not in the light of his *Miscellanies* (21), 'Limited Atonement': 'God did not intend to save those, by the death of Christ, that he knew, from all eternity, he should not save by his death. If he intended to save any, it was those he knew would be saved' (extract Clifford sent to me privately on 1st April 2008 in an e-mail). Again, in a sermon: 'These earnest prayers and strong cries of Christ to the Father in his agony, show the greatness of his love to sinners... These strong cries of Jesus Christ were what he offered up to God as a public person, in the capacity of high priest, and in the behalf of those whose priest he was. When he offered up his sacrifice for sinners whom he had loved from eternity, he withal offered up earnest prayers. His strong cries, his tears, and his blood, were all offered up together to God, and they were all offered up for the same end, for the glory of God in the salvation of the elect. They were all offered up for the same persons, *viz.* for his people. For them he shed his blood in that bloody sweat, when it fell down in clotted lumps to the ground. And for them he so earnestly cried to God at the same time. It was that the will of God might be done in the success of his sufferings, in the success of that blood, in the salvation of those for whom that blood was shed, and therefore this strong crying shows his strong love. It shows how greatly he desired the salvation of sinners. He cried to God that he might not sink and fail in that great undertaking, because if he did so, sinners could not be saved, but all must perish' (Edwards: *Seventeen* p875).

I repeat, therefore, my conclusion. Edwards was neither an Amyraldian or an Owenite. Like Fuller, he ended up somewhere in between. In all this, I think he was still mistaken, and is yet another warning to us – he who takes the speculative sword of human logic is liable to cut himself with it.

Finally, since, in the extract I have used in the body of this chapter, Edwards did not base his case on a redemption sufficient for all – of whatever hue the formula might take – it is, I feel, legitimate for me to use him.

[358] Whitefield had 'your' even though he knew that this could only be the case after faith. See the last paragraph of this sermon – which follows below – where he stated: 'Even you may be the children of God, if you believe in Jesus'.

[359] That is, the sand in the hour glass; in other words: 'Your life is just about reached its close'.

[360] Whitefield was not preaching universal redemption; he was simply assuring the slaves that Christ died for sinners, including slaves. See above.

[361] Here I dissent from Whitefield. Why tell them to wait until they got home? Believe now!

[362] Whitefield: *Sermons* pp184-197, emphasis his. See also Whitefield: *Select* pp72-84.

[363] Surely Edwards by this meant nothing more than 'men's salvation', or 'sinners' salvation'. I have explained why I do not think he was saying Christ died savingly for all. The same applies below. Nor was he thinking of sufficiency for all. I acknowledge, as I have indicated, that Edwards did believe Christ's death was sufficient for all (Edwards: *Freedom* p88; *Christ* p215), but I do not think he was taking this line here. He certainly and rightly preached Christ as all-sufficient – see below – but nowhere here did he tell sinners that Christ has provided a redemption sufficient for all, 'for *you*', and that this sufficiency is the basis of, and warrant for, the offer. Moreover, even in the paragraph to which this comment applies, note Edwards' careful distinction between 'our' and 'you'. If he had included all his hearers in the 'salvation' which Christ died 'to procure', surely he would have used 'your' instead of 'our': 'Did *your* salvation lie with such weight...', he would have said. He did not. Note, also, in the following paragraph, Edwards spoke of Christ's death under 'God's wrath *for men's* sins... to procure salvation *for sinners*'.

[364] See above.

[365] Edwards: *History* pp534-535,580-582. See also p619.

[366] Sprague p137; Andrew Bonar p105.

[367] Clifford: *Atonement* pp142-166. I do not pretend that these few notes in this Appendix are the final word on passages which all must acknowledge present difficulties – whatever our system!

[368] Clifford: *Atonement* p135.

[369] See Clifford: *Atonement* pp3-16.

---

[370] But, as I have indicated in the body of the book, not all glossing is bad; indeed, it is, at times, essential. Consider *areskō*, 'to please'. Take: 'We speak, not as *pleasing* men' (1 Thess. 2:4); and 'I... *please* all men in all things' (1 Cor. 10:33). Paul used the same word in these two verses, and, if we do not gloss, we make him guilty of crass contradiction. Similarly, Paul expected us to gloss his rhetorical: 'Do I seek to please men? For if I still pleased men, I would not be a bondservant of Christ' (Gal. 1:10). I will return to 'please'. Take another example: 'They are not all Israel who are of Israel' (Rom. 9:6). To understand the verse, glossing is essential; they are not all *spiritual* Israel who are of the *nation* of Israel. Similarly, compare John 3:16 and 1 John 2:15-16. We well understand the point in everyday English. Without intending the slightest facetiousness, when is a tree not a tree? When it is a *shoe*-tree or a *family*-tree.

[371] Not that all such importing is wrong!

[372] I have done it myself! But it must be carefully nuanced. See my *Battle*; *Infant*. Davenant (of whom both Baxter and Clifford approved so much) gave good advice: When 'no word [on an important topic] occurs in the holy Scriptures', 'it is rash to assert it... In things necessary to be done or known in order to salvation... [if] this is not [explicitly] taught in the Scriptures... it is not to be believed by us' (Davenant p115).

[373] Clifford: *Atonement* pp147-148.

[374] Clifford: *Atonement* pp98-99,142,145.

[375] Gill: *Cause* p100.

[376] See above; my *Offer* pp57-134; *Septimus Sears*.

[377] Clifford: *Atonement* pp144-145.

[378] True, 'sheep' is an 'illustration' (John 10:6 NIV) or 'figure of speech'; and, sure enough, Christ does not use the precise words: 'You do not believe because you are not elect'. But in the context (John 10:1-30), what else can he mean?

[379] Although it is 'importing' another passage, the parallel with John 17:9 cannot be missed: 'I pray for them. I do not pray for the world but for those whom you have given me, for they are yours'. The 'sheep' of John 10 are the 'them', the 'yours', of John 17; they are those 'given' by the Father to Christ (John 10:29; 17:1-26). See also John 6:37,39. Is it far-fetched to place John 10:11,15 & 17:9 alongside each other? 'I am the good shepherd. The good shepherd gives his life for the sheep... I lay down my life for the sheep' and 'I pray for them. I do not pray for the world but for those whom you have given me, for they are yours'. Is it wrong to deduce that Christ prays for the elect and lays down his life for them, but he does not pray for the world and does not lay down his life for them? True, there is Luke 23:34, but however that passage is

reconciled with John 17, the link between John 10 and John 17 is incontrovertible. As for 'importing' John 6 & 17 into John 10, all of them were said by Christ, and all were recorded by John in one book. Surely we are expected to bear in mind chapter 6 when we get to chapter 10, and not forget either when we get to chapter 17. As for reconciling Luke 23:34 and John 17, could it be that in Luke 23:34 Christ prays as a man should under law or gospel (Lev. 19:18; Matt. 5:44), whereas in John 17 he prays as the mediator? that is, in the one he prays as a private individual; in the other, as a public figure? Much as I disagree with Owen's special pleading on Luke 23:34, his comments on *this* aspect of it are valuable (Owen: *Death* in *Works* Vol.10 p196). See below. On John 17:9, Calvin was clear; this prayer of Christ is not to be taken as 'an example' for us to copy in our prayers: 'For Christ does not now pray from the mere impulse of faith and of love towards [all] men, but, entering into the heavenly sanctuary, he places before his eyes the secret judgements of the Father, which are concealed from us, so long as we walk by faith [that is, during our earthly pilgrimage]... Christ [here] prays for the elect only' (Calvin: *Commentaries* Vol.18 Part 1 p173; see also Nicole pp288,301-302). Thomas Manton on John 17:9: 'We must distinguish the prayers of Christ as a holy man, and the prayers of Christ as mediator... He taught us to pray for enemies (Matt. 5:44)' (Manton p138).

Although it is digression, a comment on John 17:21-23 is called for. Whatever interpretation is placed upon these verses, they cannot contradict John 17:9. While I shudder at Calvin's audacious way of expressing himself – John 'inaccurately used' 'to believe' when he ought to have used 'to know' (Calvin: *Commentaries* Vol.18 Part 1 p184) – Christ *was* probably praying that the world would 'believe', 'know' – that is, be convinced – that God had sent him. After all, he did pray 'that the world might know' (John 17:23). See Owen: *Death* in *Works* Vol.10 p197; Manton p369.

[380] Clifford: *Atonement* p145.

[381] Clifford: *Atonement* p146. See my comment above.

[382] Clifford: *Atonement* p148.

[383] 'Came' (AV, NKJV), 'there resulted' (NASB), 'the result was' (NIV), 'the issue was... the issue is' (NEB).

[384] 'Paul does not say that many were constituted "sinful", suggestive of possibility, but that "many were constituted sinners". He does not use an adjective, but a noun. He does not say that because of Adam's disobedience the whole of mankind was made sinful, and therefore liable to sin... He asserts that because of this one disobedience of Adam all were constituted sinners, made sinners, regarded by God as sinners. You

will appreciate the importance of my emphasis at this point, for the second half of this nineteenth verse says that on the other hand in Christ we [the believing elect] have been "made" or "constituted" righteous – and you have to give the word the same force and the same meaning on the two sides... The apostle maintains that because of Adam's one act of disobedience the whole of the human race has been constituted legally as sinners... we are all regarded personally and individually as sinners in the sight of God. That is our judicial standing before God. Because of that one sin of Adam we were all put into the category of sinners... As all that has happened to you in Adam is a fact, realise that all that has happened to you in Christ is also a fact. If the one was certain, realise that the other is equally certain, and more so... That is the apostle's argument' (Lloyd-Jones: *Assurance* pp271-274). I draw attention to Lloyd-Jones' rejection of 'possibility' and 'liability', and his emphasis upon 'certainty' and 'fact'. I also note that the Amyraldian view of the imputation of Adam's sin to the human race differs from mine; see below for references.

[385] But what about faith? Is a sinner not justified by faith? Of course he is (Rom. 3:22-26; 5:1 for instance). *But that is not what Paul is talking about in Rom. 5:18-19.* He is not talking about the individual, and his faith or unbelief. He is talking about the human race and its division into two families under two heads, Adam and Christ. In particular, he is talking about the works of these two heads, and the respective consequences of those works for the entire human race – for all who are 'in Adam', and for all who are 'in Christ'. Now these consequences cannot possibly be provisional. God *decreed* that all 'in Adam' would come under the consequences of Adam's sin, and all 'in Christ' would come under the consequences of Christ's one act of righteousness. These consequences are absolute. That is what God's decree means. Death and condemnation, therefore, came upon 'all in Adam' simply because they were in Adam when he fell, and they were constituted sinners in him as a result of his offence; justification came upon 'all in Christ' simply because they were in Christ, and they were constituted righteous in him as a result of his obedience. I recognise, of course, that a sinner is not *actually* justified until he believes. But that, I repeat, is not what Paul is talking about in Rom. 5:18-19.

[386] Literally, 'as by one offence towards all men to condemnation, so also by one accomplished righteousness towards all men to justification of life'; 'as through one transgression to condemnation to all men, even so through one act of righteousness to justification of life to all men' (NASB margin).

[387] What is more, to suggest that Paul was saying all men are predestined, called, justified and glorified *sufficiently and provisionally*, is, if it were not so serious, risible. A *provisional* predestination? See the body of the book for my remarks on the notion of a *conditional* decree. Throughout the book, I have repeatedly drawn attention to the efficacious-and-particular context of Rom. 8:30.
[388] Paul wrote *hoi polloi*, 'the many', as he did in Rom. 5:15.
[389] Haldane p200, emphasis mine. It is more than 'stronger'. If the 'all' means 'all mankind', then all mankind *are* saved. 'There is no possibility of escaping the conclusion that, if the apostle meant... ['came to all men, resulting in justification'] to be as embracive in its scope as... ['judgement came to all men'], then the whole human race must eventually attain to eternal life. There is no escape from this conclusion by distinguishing between the objective provision and subjective appropriation' (John Murray: *Romans* Vol.1 p202). The notion that all men will be saved, is, of course, contrary to Scripture. There is, therefore, only one conclusion.
[390] The context of Rom. 5:18 could not be more clear; namely, the two heads of the human race, Adam and Christ (Rom. 5:12 on), leading to union and identification with Christ (Rom. 6 and on). For more on union with Christ, see my *Septimus Sears*.
[391] Continuing the earlier extract from Lloyd-Jones, addressing believers he said: 'As all that has happened to you in Adam is a fact, realise that all that has happened to you in Christ is also a fact. If [since] the one was certain, realise that the other is equally certain, and more so, because here it is [that] God's grace comes in and not his wrath and his judgement. That is the apostle's argument. The great truth is that all we are and have comes out of the obedience of this second one. All the benefits of salvation come to us solely and entirely because of the obedience of the Lord Jesus Christ. Our salvation is entirely of him, and from him, and in him. As my being a sinner came entirely from Adam, all my righteousness and my being a Christian comes entirely from the Lord Jesus Christ... This, says Paul, is what has happened to all of us who are in Christ; and it happens to us because of, and on the ground of, his obedience alone... All that was true of you formerly was the result of that one act of Adam. All this is true of you now as a result of the obedience of Christ' (Lloyd-Jones: *Assurance* pp274,276).
John Murray, speaking of believers: 'The same principle of solidarity that appears in our relation to Adam, and by reason of which we are involved in his sin, obtains in our relation to Christ. And just as the relation to Adam means the imputation to us of his disobedience, so the relation to Christ means the imputation to us of his obedience.

Justification means our involvement in the obedience of Christ in terms of the same principle by which we are involved in Adam's sin. Nothing less is demanded by the analogy instituted in [these verses]' (John Murray: *Romans* Vol.1 pp205-206).

[392] In Rom. 5:18, as in 1 Cor. 15:22, 'the "all" of the second clause is therefore restrictive in a way that the "all" in the first clause is not... What the apostle is interested in showing is [that]... all who are condemned, and this includes the whole human race, are condemned because of the one trespass of Adam; all who are justified are justified because of the righteousness of Christ' (John Murray: *Romans* Vol.1 p203).

[393] See also 1 Thess. 4:13-18. At the coming of Christ, 'those who sleep in Jesus', 'the dead in Christ', 'will rise first. Then we who are alive and remain shall be caught up together with them in the clouds to meet the Lord in the air. And thus we shall always be with the Lord'. We? We who are in Christ, of course! In the context (1 Thess. 5:1-11) – there should be no chapter division! – Paul goes on to draw a clear distinction between 'us' in Christ, and the rest, the 'others' (1 Thess. 5:6 AV, NIV), culminating in: 'God did not appoint *us* to wrath, but to obtain salvation through *our* Lord Jesus Christ, who died for *us*, that whether *we* wake or sleep [live or die], *we* should live together with him'. If this does not teach particular redemption for the elect, what does it teach?

[394] That is, in this spiritual sense; they are, of course, raised from the dead to face judgement and condemnation (John 5:29).

[395] Haldane p334.

[396] Hodge: *2 Corinthians* p324, emphasis mine.

[397] Gill: *Commentary* Vol.6 p260, emphasis mine.

[398] Fee noted: 'This... alone fits the context'.

[399] Paul is concerned here only with believers.

[400] For the Greek in this paragraph, see Thayer. Repeating the point Haldane made (see above), as for *zōopoieō*, it 'is never used of the wicked' (Hodge: 2 *Corinthians* p325), further proof that the thrust of the passage is to do with those in Christ, and not all men.

[401] Too weak! Acts 24:15 to my mind *states* it.

[402] Fee pp749-753, emphasis his.

[403] Compare Rom. 3:23-24. Leaving aside discussion about the punctuation (the AV has a semi-colon instead of a comma), consider: 'All have sinned and fall short of the glory of God, being justified freely by his grace through the redemption that is in Christ Jesus' (NKJV); 'all have sinned and fall short of the glory of God, being justified as a gift...' (NASB); 'all have sinned and fall short of the glory of God, and are justified freely by his grace...' (NIV). Does the 'all' mean 'all without

exception'? 'All [without exception] have sinned'; is this what Paul meant? It is a fact, and is in the context (Rom. 3:9,19), but since one of his main themes in Romans is that there is only one way of justification for Jew or Gentile (Rom. 1:14-16; 2:9-11; 3:29-30; 9:24-33; 10:1-21; 11:11-32; 15:8-12; 16:25-27), the apostle may have meant 'all [not only Gentiles, but Jews] have sinned'; or, he may have meant 'all [who believe] have sinned'. But, if we should read it as 'all [without exception] have sinned', what, then, of 'being justified'? Did Paul mean: 'All [without exception] have sinned... [all without exception] being justified'? Certainly not! The meaning is (reading from verse 21): 'But now the righteousness of God apart from the law is revealed... even the righteousness of God, through faith in Jesus Christ, to all and on all who believe. For there is no difference; for all [without exception, both Jew and Gentile] have sinned... [all who believe] being justified freely by his grace'. On balance, however, taking into account Paul's argument here – justification for all believers, all believers without distinction – I prefer: 'But now the righteousness of God apart from the law is revealed... even the righteousness of God, through faith in Jesus Christ, to all and on all who believe. For there is no difference; for all [without exception, both Jew and Gentile, of course, but especially those who believe, even they] have sinned... [all who believe] being justified freely by his grace'. See Murray: *Romans* Vol.1 pp108-116. But whichever it is, some glossing is essential – *and understood.*

[404] Rom. 5:18 must be seen as part of Rom. 5:12 – 7:6, which ought to be read aloud in one sitting. The same goes for 1 Cor. 15:12-58 & Eph. 2:1-10.

[405] And, in particular, I stress once again, this is true even of the elect. But on coming to faith they are no longer in Adam but in Christ. The rest of mankind remain in Adam for ever.

[406] 'The first man [Adam] was of the earth, made of dust; the second man [Christ] is the Lord from heaven. As was the man of dust, so also are those who are made of dust [that is, all men, including the elect]; and as is the heavenly man, so also are those who are heavenly [that is, the believing elect]. And as we [that is, the believing elect] have borne the image of the man of dust, we [that is, the believing elect] shall also bear the image of the heavenly man' (1 Cor. 15:47-49). Nothing merely potential or general for all men here! That which is said of all men, is absolutely true of all men; that which is said of the elect, is absolutely true of the elect. Furthermore, this passage confirms the point I have made repeatedly; namely, Paul's main concern here is with the believing elect. They were in Adam and bore his image. Now they are in Christ and bear his image.

[407] But what about Calvin on Rom. 5:18? '[God] makes this favour common to all, because it is propounded to all, and not because it is in reality extended to all; for though Christ suffered for the sins of the whole world, and is offered through God's benignity indiscriminately to all, yet all do not receive him'. If Calvin's editor was correct to say: 'It appears from this sentence that Calvin held general redemption', then Calvin was mistaken (Calvin: *Commentaries* Vol.19 Part 2 pp211-212). But Calvin may have been saying no more than that Christ is offered to all in the preaching of the gospel, but that all do not receive him. By his ambiguous, 'not... in reality extended to all', he certainly did not mean, 'not *offered* **to** all in the preaching of the gospel' – Calvin was utterly committed to the universal free offer! If he meant, 'not *effective* **for**, though offered **for** all by Christ on the cross', he was an Amyraldian. If he meant, 'not *accomplished* or *offered* **for** all by Christ on the cross, this being shown in that not all receive him when hearing the gospel preached', he was right. His use of 'reality' makes me think Calvin intended the clause in the latter sense. See Calvin: *Commentaries* Vol.20 Part 2 p238, including footnote, which I quoted in the body of the book. I accept, of course, that Calvin stated that 'Christ suffered for the sins of the whole world'. As I have made clear, I have no interest in trying to prove Calvin was right on every point – nor that he was entirely consistent. Like all mortals, in both cases he was not.

[408] In all this, the main issue as far as my book is concerned, let it not be forgotten, is the death of Christ. For whom did Christ die? Note how in all the passages I have cited above (Rom. 5; 1 Cor. 15; Eph. 2), the death of Christ, the shedding of his blood, is never far way – and note Paul's emphasis on its particularity: 'For when *we* were still without strength, in due time Christ died for the ungodly... While *we* were still sinners, Christ died for *us*. Much more then, having now been justified by his blood, *we* shall be saved from wrath through him... When *we* were enemies *we* were reconciled to God through the death of his Son... Christ died for *our* sins according to the Scriptures... In him *we* have redemption through his blood... In Christ Jesus *you* who once were far off have been brought near by the blood of Christ' (Rom. 5:6,8-10; 1 Cor. 15:3; Eph. 1:7; 2:13). Throughout all these passages (Rom. 5, 1 Cor. 15 & Eph. 2), the particularity of Christ's death and resurrection, and the absolute nature of the benefits of both, is undeniable.

[409] I have noted my disagreement with Haldane's view that 'the elect are not described as being, previously to the grace of God applying the atonement, children of wrath even as others'; nor do I see how this fits with: 'True, they were by nature the children of wrath even as others' (Haldane pp351-352). As I have explained, all mankind, including the

elect, are by nature in Adam and under the wrath of God. Indeed, this is central to Paul's argument in these passages. The elect, of course, upon regeneration leading to faith and repentance, are actually in Christ, and have passed from death to life, and are no longer under condemnation.

[410] I let 'nature' stand and will not digress to discuss it here.

[411] Haldane pp134-136,164-165,320,338-339,341-342, emphasis mine; see also pp47-64,196-200,209-210,334-335. As I have already noted, the Amyraldian view of the imputation of Adam's sin to the human race differs from mine; see David Llewellyn Jenkins: *Saumur Redux: Josué de la Place & the Question of Adam's Sin*, Leaping Cat Press, Harleston, 2008. For an overall view of various theories of imputation, see Dabney: *Systematic* pp328-351. For the best statement I know of the position I have set out, see Lloyd-Jones: *Assurance* pp203-225.

[412] Clifford: *Atonement* p151.

[413] Hodge: In 2 Cor. 5:14, 'the word is *apethanon*. It is the same verb, and in the same tense [the aorist]. "If [since] one died, *apethanen*, then all died, *apethanon*". The word must have the same sense in both clauses... "All", literally, "the all", *hoi pantes*, [died]; *i.e.*, the all for whom the one died [died]. His death involved, or secured their death. This was its design and effect, and, therefore, this clause limits the extent of the word "all" in the preceding clause. Christ died for the all who died when he died' (Hodge: *2 Corinthians* pp135-136). While there are nuances, the aorist speaks of something which took place, which took place once, was done and finished. John Murray: 'The tense... points to a definitive act in the past... What the apostle has in view [in Rom. 6:2] is the once-for-all definitive breach with sin which constitutes the identity of the believer' (John Murray: *Romans* Vol.1 p213). Lloyd-Jones: 'It is something that has happened once and for ever; it is a reference to a definite fact that belongs to the past... The apostle [in Rom. 6:2]... is referring to one act, to one event, to something that has happened at one unique point in [the believer's] history' (Lloyd-Jones: *New* pp11-12).

[414] And they will enjoy the fruit of it for ever after the return of Christ. For solid arguments against the hyper-Calvinistic doctrine of 'eternal justification', see Davenant pp112-129. See my *Septimus Sears*.

[415] In addition to what follows on the 'therefore', see the note above on the aorist.

[416] *ara*, 'and so, so then, accordingly' (Thayer).

[417] Indeed, what is a *provisional* death?

[418] I repeat the point I have just made. The elect died with Christ in eternity in God's decree; they died with Christ on the cross; and they die spiritually to sin, law and death when they are united to Christ by faith in

their conversion. As for their death, so for their resurrection. None of it is provisional.

[419] Haldane pp81,197,333, emphasis his.

[420] Contrary to Douty who thought it means all men (saved or not) who have not yet died naturally, 'those who as yet have not descended into the grave... all living people' (Douty pp74,76). In other words, Christ died for all men so that all men, as long as they are physically alive, must live for him. This is clearly wide of the mark, foreign to the context. But Davenant had taken a similar line: 'Unless the death of Christ is understood as a remedy applicable to all, the foundation on which the ministers of the gospel build exhortations of this kind [1 Cor. 6:20, for instance] will always be uncertain, and often false: Always uncertain, because it cannot be known by men who are the elect. Often false, as often indeed as it is exhibited to the non-elect, who by this kind of redemption are not bound to live to Christ, unless it be presupposed that the sacrifice offered by Christ for the redemption of the world was for them' (Davenant p37). Such reasoning is puerile. Let me explore it further.

First of all, exhortations such as: 'You were bought at a price; therefore glorify God in your body and in your spirit, which are God's' (1 Cor. 6:20) – cited by Davenant – are not issued 'to all men', as he claimed. They are issued to believers. Now, of course, as I have observed, no preacher can know for certain if a hearer is truly elect or not – but to suggest that we cannot, therefore, exhort believers because we cannot be absolutely certain who the believers are, is fatuous. Then again, to say that the basis of such exhortations is the death of Christ, provisional, sufficient or applicable to all, is nonsense. Take for example: 'Do not grieve the Holy Spirit of God, by whom you were sealed for the day of redemption' (Eph. 4:30). Is this said to every human being? Is every human being (provisionally) sealed by the Holy Spirit of God for the day of redemption? Of course not. It is said to believers, and believers only. But just because we cannot be absolutely certain that all who hear (or read) us are believers, can we never issue such an exhortation to believers? The suggestion is absurd. We certainly dare not misinterpret and misapply the apostle's words – written to believers – and say he meant all men without exception. As for the passage under consideration (2 Cor. 5:14-15), the idea that Paul was urging unregenerate sinners to live to Christ – is breathtakingly ridiculous. Paul said: 'Those who live should no longer live for themselves, but for him who died for them and rose again'. Who are the 'those who live'? and what about the 'no longer live'? Who are they who should *no longer* live for themselves? Surely those who have been regenerated! And, going on to verse 16, what about the 'from now on'? Paul was speaking about those who had been converted – from now on, they must – they will – live differently to what they did before. They 'no longer' make their judgements 'according to the flesh'; they are 'in Christ', and thus 'a new creation' (2 Cor. 5:16-17). See also Rom. 6:1 – 7:6; 14:7-9; 1 Cor. 6:19-20; Gal. 2:20; 1 Pet. 4:1-2. If, however, it is argued that Paul was thinking historically – now that Christ has died and brought in the new age – and not, as I say, personally, of the conversion of the individual sinner – then are we to suppose that those who lived (and were regenerated) before the death of Christ were not obliged to live 'for him', and could continue to make their judgements as they did before their regeneration? Further comment, surely, is superfluous.

[421] *hina*, 'to the intent that, to the end that, in order that' (Thayer). Not merely, 'is the duty of... are called to [in the sense of urged to]... are obliged to' (Douty pp75-76).

[422] On Clifford's interpretation of the passage, not only do I fail to see the connection between Christ's alleged death for all, and the sanctified life of the regenerate elect, I get the sensation of treading on a step which isn't there. Let me explain. If – if, I say – Christ died for all mankind sufficiently, so that (*hina*) those who live (that is, the regenerated and believing elect in union with Christ – those for whom Christ died effectually) should and will live a godly life – as I have explained, I fail to see the connection, but allowing it to stand for the moment – what is the equivalent 'so that' (*hina*) for the non-elect? Christ, says the Amyraldian, died for the non-elect sufficiently. So what is the *hina* for them? Christ died for all mankind sufficiently 'so that' (*hina*) those who do not live (that is, the unregenerate and unbelieving non-elect, those not in union with Christ, those for whom Christ did not die effectively) should and will... should and will... what? The believing elect should and will live a godly life as an inevitable consequence of the death of Christ for them. What is the equivalent positive 'should and will' for the non-elect? There isn't one. Although I would not build anything on this silence, I repeat the illustration I used. The fact that Paul does not state a positive *hina* for the non-elect – the fact that no such *hina* can be suggested – leaves me with the sensation of treading on the missing step at the bottom of the stairs.

[423] Wesley's comment, of which Clifford approved, is wide of the mark. Christ did not die for all that all *might* be saved. No! He died for all in order that all for whom he died *would* die and be raised.

[424] Just to point out, although it is not relevant to the question in hand, if Clifford was suggesting that water baptism is in view in Rom. 6, I vehemently disagree. See my *Infant*.

[425] Is every man sufficiently or provisionally sitting 'in the heavenly places in Christ Jesus' (Eph. 2:6), provisionally 'glorified' (Rom. 8:30)? And so the questions could go on, and *should* go on!
[426] Clifford: *Atonement* pp152-154.
[427] Calvin was explaining what he meant by God being 'reconciled to the whole world' – God invites all. As, for instance, in: 'If their [Israel's] being cast away is the reconciling of the world' (Rom. 11:15). Without digressing into the historical and prophetical aspects of the chapter, this cannot mean that since Israel has been rejected, the Gentiles have been reconciled in the full sense of the word – that is, because God has turned away from the Israel he has redeemed every last Gentile. This is not Paul's comparison. Rather, because Israel has refused God's offer of mercy, he has now turned from them and offered the gospel to the Gentiles. See the entire section from Rom. 11:11; indeed, from Rom. 9:30. Gill: Paul speaks 'not of... the actual reconciliation of them by [Christ's] sufferings and death, but of the gospel, the word of reconciliation being carried among them upon the Jews' disbelief and contempt of it' (Gill: *Commentary* Vol.6 pp99-100). Poole: 'The rejection of the Jews brought great profit to the Gentiles... *i.e.*, an occasion of preaching the gospel to the Gentiles, by means of which they were reconciled to God. The gospel is "the ministry of reconciliation" (2 Cor. 5:18-20)' (Poole p518). John Murray: '"Reconciliation" is contrasted with "casting away". The latter means rejection from the favour and blessing of God, and reflects therefore on the attitude of God to Israel and the relation he sustains to them. So the accent falls distinctly upon God's attitude and action about that matter. Reconciliation is in contrast, and likewise reflects on the attitude, relation and action of God. The Gentiles are viewed as previously alienated from God and excluded from his favour. By God's action, this alienation was exchanged for reconciliation, and the attitude of disfavour exchanged for favour' (John Murray: *Romans* Vol.2 p81).
[428] Calvin: *Commentaries* Vol.17 Part 2 pp123-126.
[429] Clifford: *Atonement* pp154-155.
[430] Calvin: *Commentaries* Vol.22 Part 2 p173. Interestingly, as Calvin's editor noted, this was the view of Philip Doddridge also.
[431] It will not do, as Douty, to say 'this means that he is the *potential* propitiation only'. Of course, Douty's dilemma is obvious: 'Otherwise the apostle would have been teaching universalism'. Douty glossed 1 John 4:14 in the same way: 'The Father sent the Son as [the provided and potential] Saviour of the world' (Douty p33, emphasis his).
[432] Nor will it do to say the verse is teaching that a sufficient propitiation is *offered* to all. John was speaking about the offering Christ made to his

Father, not the offer made by God through preachers to sinners; the propitiation Christ accomplished, not the pardon held out to sinners in preaching.

[433] See also Luke 2:1; John 12:32; Acts 2:17; 1 John 3:1,13; 4:5-6; Rev. 13:3 as a sample of similar texts. Take John 4:42. The Samaritans believed and confessed: 'We know that this is indeed the Christ, the Saviour of the world'. But it would be ridiculous to read back into this statement all the overtones of a debate about the extent of the atonement, a debate which began to rage at the end of the 16th century. The context makes the Samaritan meaning clear. In the first century, at *that* time, and in *that* place, there was a vigorous Jew/Samaritan dispute over social and religious matters, and this with long historical connections. Salvation belonged to the Jews, not the Samaritans (John 4:9,12,20,22). This is the context of the Samaritan outburst; it was a cry of relief as it dawned on them that *they* were *not* excluded from the saving redemption of the Christ: 'It is not only for the Jews, after all. It is for *us*, too. He is the Saviour of *the world*'. To imagine that they were making a rigorous theological statement about the extent of the atonement, is, as I say, ridiculous. It was nothing more (or less) than a heart-felt expression of joy that they too were included in redemption. As Jesus could say to Zacchaeus: 'Today salvation has come to this house... for the Son of Man has come to seek and to save that which was lost' (Luke 19:9-10), so the Samaritans were in effect saying: 'Today salvation has come to this nation. Indeed, today salvation has come to the world'. But just as only the elect within Zacchaeus' house (those of whom it can be said, 'because he also is a son of Abraham') will be saved, so only the elect among the Samaritans will be saved, and only the elect throughout the world will be saved. And all who will be saved will be saved in and through Christ. In this way, Christ is the Saviour of the world.

[434] Echoes of Christ: 'I do not pray for these [the apostles] alone, but also for those who will believe in me through their word' (John 17:20); in other words, the elect of all ages and nations. As above, Calvin took this view of 1 John 2:2.

[435] Is the context Jewish? If 'the old commandment' of 1 John 2:7 did refer to Sinai – I do not think so myself – see my *Christ is All* – then since the law was given to the Jews and only the Jews, the context would be Jewish. And this would lend weight to the third possibility. See also 1 John 3:4; 5:2-3.

[436] See earlier note on 2 Cor. 5:14-15.

[437] Clifford: *Atonement* pp157-158.

[438] Even on Clifford's terms? According to Amyraldians, Christ died for all men sufficiently – but only for the elect efficaciously – and only the

elect are granted faith. As a consequence, working backwards, all believers must have been elected, and Christ must have died for them efficaciously. Clifford conceded that the man in question is to be viewed as a believer – he must, therefore, be viewed as one of the elect, one for whom Christ died efficaciously.

[439] Once again, we are not dealing with abstract theology here. Paul is deeply concerned – as always – with the pastoral consequences of the gospel. How does what he is saying affect men and women in their daily experience? men and women, that is, who, though believers, stumble, hurt others, get hurt, and so on. He is writing, not for some ivory-towered metaphysician in his study meticulously weighing doctrinal nuances, but for men and women out in the every-day world grappling with practical godliness. All this is infinitely heightened if Clifford was right (see below) and 'destruction' here means 'eternal destruction'.

[440] Was Clifford watering down the idea here? Paul does not speak about a 'danger' as though it is a mere possibility. It is really happening. Some weak brothers are being destroyed. Literally: 'For being destroyed is the weak one' (1 Cor. 8:11). See Fee p387. I will return to the use of the present tense.

[441] See Thayer. Paul used the word in 'destroy the wisdom of the wise' (1 Cor. 1:19), the Israelites 'destroyed by serpents' (1 Cor. 10:9), 'persecuted, but not forsaken; struck down, but not destroyed' (2 Cor. 4:9).

[442] Paul uses a rich variety of words to convey his meaning in Rom. 14 – 15 & 1 Cor. 8. See Thayer: 'weak' (Rom. 14:1-2,21; 1 Cor. 8:9,11-12), *astheneō*, 'to be weak, feeble... to be doubtful about things lawful and unlawful to a Christian'; 'weak' (Rom. 15:1), *asthenēma*, 'infirmity... error arising from weakness of mind'; 'weak' (1 Cor. 8:7,9-10), *asthenēs*, 'weak, infirm, feeble... wanting in decision about things lawful and unlawful'; 'defiled' (1 Cor. 8:7), *molunō*, 'to pollute, stain, contaminate, defile... a conscience reproached (defiled) by sin'; 'stumbling block' (Rom. 14:13; 1 Cor. 8:9), 'with offence' (Rom. 14:20), *proskomma*, 'an obstacle in the way which if one strikes his foot against he necessarily stumbles or falls; that over which the soul stumbles, *i.e.*, by which it is impelled to sin... to furnish one an occasion for sinning... by making no discrimination as to what he eats occasions another to act against his conscience'; 'stumbles' (Rom. 14:21), *proskoptō*, 'to strike against... to be made to stumble by a thing, *i.e.*, to be induced to sin'; 'offended' (Rom. 14:21), 'stumble' (1 Cor. 8:13), *skandalizō*, 'to put a stumbling block or impediment in the way, upon which another may trip and fall... to entice to sin'; 'a cause to fall' (Rom. 14:13), *skandalon*, 'any impediment placed in the way and

causing one to stumble or fall... to put a stumbling block in one's way, *i.e.*, to do that by which another is led to sin'; 'wound' (1 Cor. 8:12), *tuptō*, 'to strike, smite, beat... to wound, disquiet one's conscience'
There is nothing in any of this which remotely approaches eternal damnation. The distress is, in all conscience, serious and sad enough – and I do not for a moment wish to play it down – but it does not amount to the eternal perdition of one for whom Christ died.

[443] I realise I, too, live in this glasshouse, but Clifford's approach here was the same as he criticised in Owen – scholastic. He was linguistically pedantic. He should have taken his own medicine, as supplied by Calvin: 'I am not so minutely precise as to fight furiously for mere words' (Calvin: *Institutes* Vol.1 p112; Clifford: *Atonement* p105. Calvin was here speaking of scholastic terminology). Do we always use words strictly with their fullest meaning? And how about metaphor? If I say: 'I was mortified', does anybody think I died? Does: 'I was petrified', always mean: 'I was turned to stone'? For obvious reasons, neither sentence could mean what it literally says. Not only do *we* sometimes use words in a sense which is not literal, the same goes for Scripture. When Paul told the Philippians: 'I have you in my heart' (Phil. 1:7), or when he calls Onesimus 'my own heart' (Philem. 12), who misunderstands him? See my *Offer* pp82-88 for God himself speaking as a man. Calvin: 'God in a manner makes himself little, that he might accommodate himself to our comprehension' (Calvin: *Commentaries* Vol.22 Part 2 p54).

[444] I admit *krinō* can be to do with 'eternal destruction', but here (Rom. 14:3-4,10,13,22) it is to do with judging in the sense of finding fault, censuring. It is translated 'esteem' in Rom. 14:5, where it sits alongside 'fully convinced in his own mind'. As for *diakrisis*, in Rom. 14:1, it means 'passing judgement on opinions, as to which one is to be preferred as the more correct'. As for *katakrinō*, this can be to do with 'eternal destruction', but here (Rom. 14:23) it means 'to give judgement against, to judge worthy of punishment, to condemn'. Compare John 8:10-11; Rom. 2:1 – where, as in Rom. 14:22-23 & 1 Cor. 11:32, it is distinguished from *krinō*. See Thayer.

[445] Note the 'condemn himself' (Rom. 14:22). If 'condemn' means 'eternally condemn', how can any man eternally condemn *himself*? True, a man can bring condemnation on himself, but only God can consign him to eternal damnation (Matt. 10:28; Luke 12:4-5). See below for the similar point in 1 Cor. 3.

[446] There is a well-attested alternative in the Greek of 1 Cor. 8:11; 'perishes' for 'shall perish'. It should be used. 'He who is weak *is* ruined' (NASB); 'this weak brother, for whom Christ died, *is* destroyed'

(NIV); 'this "knowledge" of yours *is* utter disaster to the weak, the brother for whom Christ died' (NEB). Fee rightly adopted it, and drew the appropriate lesson: 'Note the present tense; already he is experiencing ruin' (Fee p387). But I do not agree with Fee who argued that Paul was here speaking of the 'eternal loss' of salvation when using *apollutai*.

[447] Gill: *Commentary* Vol.6 p202.

[448] As for the Jews and Greeks, Paul's concern is that believers should so act as not to hinder unbelievers hearing the gospel and being saved. See 1 Cor. 9:20-22. This, of course, is a different concern to the one in hand.

[449] Thayer. 'The adjective [in 1 Cor. 10:33] is the negative form of the noun that appears in [1 Cor.] 8:9' (Fee p488).

[450] Fee p489.

[451] As before, Paul's concern for unbelievers here is that they might be saved (1 Cor. 10:33). But as far as the 'pleasing' men goes, Paul had no time for 'buttering them up' (Gal. 1:10; 1 Thess. 2:4), and this tells us a great deal about what he meant by the word. See above on *areskō*. See Fee pp489-490.

[452] Indeed, it always should – unless solid reasons override it, as they sometimes do. See above on Rom. 5:18-19.

[453] In this connection, it does not matter whether 'the temple' is regarded as the individual or the corporate; the individual believer or the church. Taking up a point I made on Rom. 14, no man can eternally destroy a believer (Matt. 10:28; Luke 12:4-5); he may hurt or damage him, but never eternally condemn him. The same goes for the church. Indeed, how can the church be eternally damned?

[454] Fee pp143-144,148; Hodge: *1 Corinthians* p59; Thayer.

[455] Fee p565. As before, I have no wish to take the edge off Paul's words against the offence and hurt in question, but he is not talking about a believer being everlastingly damned.

[456] See Ness pp57-58. So, if 'destruction' here means 'eternal loss', the only way, in the context, this could happen, is if Christ died effectively for the brother who is eternally lost. But this, as the Amyraldian must agree, is impossible. No! The 'destruction' here is not 'eternal loss'.

[457] As above, I do not wish to minimise the thoughtless or wilful offence of the believer in question. But I am talking about emphasis. In these passages, the believer has *caused* the offence and its consequences. If this is eternal destruction, Paul here lays the *cause* of that eternal destruction at the feet of the offending believer. But all the time, according to Clifford, God has not elected the one who perishes, Christ has not died for him effectively, and that unbeliever has wilfully refused

to come to Christ! Clifford's argument, it seems to me, has no connection with the emphasis made by Paul in these passages.

[458] Thayer. 'For a long time their judgement has not been idle, and their destruction does not slumber' (2 Pet. 2:3) proves it, as does the entire context. Peter was speaking about 'the day of judgement' (2 Pet. 2:9), and the consequent 'they... will utterly perish' (2 Pet. 2:12).

[459] Clifford: *Atonement* pp158-161.

[460] Yet, staggeringly, Davenant: 'To all men, after this mystery of the death of Christ has been opened to them, that may be truly said which is contained in 1 Cor. 6:20: "You were bought at a price"'. Davenant linked it with 2 Cor. 5:15 (see above) (Davenant p37). What a glaring misapplication, to all men, of a verse written to believers concerning the elect. See earlier note.

[461] Note also, those who were 'afterward destroyed' upon leaving Egypt were Israelites, part of 'the people' of God (Jude 5); that is, in name – they were regarded as such until proved otherwise. See also Heb. 3:7 – 4:7, especially 3:16. Haldane, citing Phil. 3:2,18-19; Tit. 1:10; Jude 4, and quoting Moses: 'Do you thus requite the Lord, O foolish people, and unwise? Is not he your Father which has bought you?' (Deut. 32:6), said of the men of 2 Pet. 2:1: 'The natural alienation of their heart broke out, they denied him, and showed that they did not know him, *although they said* he was their God (John 8:54-55)' (Haldane pp280-281, emphasis mine). Many followers of Christ were called disciples, or believers, or were said to have believed on him, even though they eventually proved they did not belong to him (John 2:23-25; 6:2,26,60-66; 8:30-59). Some who call Christ, 'Lord, Lord', will be told by him that he never knew them (Matt. 7:21-23). Some who 'honour' Christ 'with their lips' have 'their heart far from' him (Matt. 15:8). Simon (the sorcerer), though he 'believed... and... was baptised', proved his heart was 'not right in the sight of God', that he was 'poisoned by bitterness and bound by iniquity' (Acts 8:9-23). All these, however, before being unmasked, would have looked like true believers, and have been treated as such by others.

[462] Note also the use of 'deny' in some of these passages – the same word as in 2 Pet. 2:1.

[463] See Ness pp58-59. Note how Peter introduced his chapter (2 Pet. 2:1).

[464] 'Pretend' is to 'claim or assert falsely so as to deceive' (*Concise*). They use 'deceptive words' (2 Pet. 2:3). Deceptive? Peter said they used *plastois* (plastic) words; 'words which are artfully formed for the purpose of deceiving' (Calvin: *Commentaries* Vol.22 Part 2 p395), 'speeches craftily moulded' (Lillie p444). Compare 'smooth words and flattering speech' (Rom. 16:18), 'persuasive words' with 'an appearance of wisdom' (Col. 2:4,23).

---

[465] If this interpretation is thought to be forced, it is, at least, the view which Calvin took of those spoken about in Heb. 10:29-31. 'God cannot govern the church without purifying it, and without restoring to order the confusion that may be in it. Therefore this governing ought justly to be dreaded by hypocrites, who will then be punished for usurping a place among the faithful, and for perfidiously using the sacred name of God, when the master of the family undertakes himself the care of setting in order his own house. It is in this sense that God is said to arise to judge his people; that is, when he separates the truly godly from hypocrites'. As Calvin's editor, a couple of pages earlier, had noted: 'He who professes the Christian faith, professes to believe in the atoning sacrifice of Christ'. On 2 Pet. 2:2, Calvin's editor: 'They denied Christ as their sovereign... though they may have professed to believe in him as a Saviour' (Calvin: *Commentaries* Vol.22 Part 1 pp248,250; Part 2 p393; see Nicole pp296-297).

[466] See Thayer; Lloyd-Jones: *Final* pp286-288.

[467] Others have come to the same conclusion, but done so by an examination of 'Lord' and 'bought' (Owen: *Death* in *Works* Vol.10 pp362-364; Gill: *Cause* p61; *Commentary* Vol.6 p860; Lloyd-Jones: *Final* pp288-291). Despite this heavy-weight opinion, I still prefer what I have set out.